Thomas Merton
and the
Noonday Demon

Thomas Merton
and the
Noonday Demon

The Camaldoli Correspondence

Donald Grayston

Foreword by Douglas E. Christie

 CASCADE *Books* · Eugene, Oregon

THOMAS MERTON AND THE NOONDAY DEMON
The Camaldoli Correspondence

Copyright © 2015 Donald Grayston. All rights reserved. Except for brief quotations in critical publications or reviews, no part of this book may be reproduced in any manner without prior written permission from the publisher. Write: Permissions, Wipf and Stock Publishers, 199 W. 8th Ave., Suite 3, Eugene, OR 97401.

Cascade Books
An Imprint of Wipf and Stock Publishers
199 W. 8th Ave., Suite 3
Eugene, OR 97401

www.wipfandstock.com

ISBN 13: 978-1-4982-0937-3

Cataloging-in-Publication data:

Grayston, Donald.

    Thomas Merton and the noonday demon : the Camaldoli correspondence / Donald Grayston ; foreword by Douglas E. Christie.

    xxii + 298 p. ; 23 cm. —Includes bibliographical references and index.

    ISBN 13: 978-1-4982-0937-3

    1. Merton, Thomas, 1915–1968. 2. Abbey of Our Lady of Gethsemani (Trappist, Ky.). 3. Eremo di Camaldoli. 4. Monastero di Camaldoli. 5. Acedia. 6. Monastic and religious life. I. Christie, Douglas E. II. Title.

BX4705.M542 G7 2015

Manufactured in the U.S.A.   05/14/2015

For my beautiful children—
Megan, Rebekah, and Jonathan—
from their imperfect father

Contents

Permissions | ix
Foreword by Douglas E. Christie | xi
Preface | xv
Acknowledgments | xix
Abbreviations | xxi

Introduction: The Roses at the Hermitage | 1

1   The Noonday Demon: *acedia* | 12

2   Thomas Merton: *non finis quaerendi* | 33

   The Camaldoli Correspondence | 55

3   The Greater *acedia*: What the Letters Tell Us | 170

4   *Acedia* and the Will of God | 204

5   The End of the Dream of Camaldoli | 218

6   After the Dream | 236

7   Solitude and Love | 255

Bibliography | 281
Index of Subjects and Names | 289

Permissions

The following permissions are gratefully acknowledged.

Unpublished letters and notes of Thomas Merton are used with permission of The Merton Legacy Trust and the Thomas Merton Center at Bellarmine University. Previously unpublished letters by Thomas Merton, Copyright © 2015 by The Trustees of the Merton Legacy Trust.

Unpublished letters of Abbot James Fox are used with permission of Abbot Elias Dietz on behalf of the Abbey of Our Lady of Gethsemani. Extracts from *The Sign of Jonas*, p. 226 [265 words] and 228 [80 words, for a total of 345 words]. Used with permission of Abbot Elias Dietz on behalf of the Abbey of Our Lady of Gethsemani.

Unpublished letters of Dom Anselmo Giabbani and the anonymous description of the Italian Camaldolese houses are used with permission of Dom Alessandro Barban, prior general of Camaldoli.

An unpublished letter of Dom Pablo Maria, O.Cart. (Thomas Verner Moore) is used with permission of the Carthusian Foundation, Arlington, Vermont.

Unpublished letters of Archbishop Giovanni Battista Montini (Pope Paul VI) are used with permission of the Archivio Storico Diocesano di Milano.

Letter "To Dom Gabriel Sortais" October 18, 1955 from *The School of Charity: Letters of Thomas Merton on Religious Renewal and Spiritual Direction*, by Thomas Merton, edited by Brother Patrick Hart. Copyright © 1990 by the Merton Legacy Trust. Reprinted by permission of Farrar, Straus and Giroux, LLC.

Excerpts from *Survival or Prophecy? The Letters of Thomas Merton and Jean Leclercq*, edited by Brother Patrick Hart. Letters by Thomas Merton copyright © 2002 by the Abbey of Gethsemani. Reprinted by permission of Farrar, Straus and Giroux, LLC.

Excerpts from *Witness to Freedom*, by Thomas Merton, edited by William H. Shannon. Copyright © 1994 by the Merton Legacy Trust. Reprinted by permission of Farrar, Straus and Giroux, LLC.

Quotes from pp. 35, 126, 380, 457, 459 [319 words] from *Entering the Silence: Becoming a Monk and Writer*, vol. 2 of *The Journals of Thomas Merton*, edited by Jonathan Montaldo. Copyright © 1995 by The Merton Legacy Trust. Reprinted by permission of HarperCollins Publishers.

Seventeen quotes [pp. 17–359: 1941 words] from *A Search for Solitude: Pursuing the Monk's True Life*, vol. 3 of *The Journals of Thomas Merton*, edited by Lawrence S. Cunningham. Copyright © 1996 by The Merton Legacy Trust. Reprinted by permission of HarperCollins Publishers.

Quotes from pp. 46–7, 73, 79–80, 158–9, 288–9 [684 words] from *Turning Toward the World: The Pivotal Years*, vol. 4 of *The Journals of Thomas Merton*, edited by Victor A. Kramer. Copyright © 1996 by The Merton Legacy Trust. Reprinted by permission of HarperCollins Publishers.

Quotes from pp. 68, 224, 278, 282, 291 [385 words] from *Dancing in the Water of Life: Seeking Peace in the Hermitage*, vol. 5 of *The Journals of Thomas Merton*, edited by Robert E. Daggy. Copyright © 1997 by The Merton Legacy Trust. Reprinted by permission of HarperCollins Publishers.

The hymn "Yield Not to Temptation," quoted in chapter 1, is in the public domain, and is reprinted from *The Book of Common Praise*, copyright 1938 by the Anglican Church of Canada, and published by The Anglican Book Centre.

LETTER 32, from Cardinal Arcadio Larraona, CMF, to Thomas Merton, is reprinted with the permission of Father Jose-Félix Valderrábano, CMF, Secretary General of the Claretian Congregation.

Foreword

A long-neglected cache of letters is unearthed in an ancient Italian monastery. They are copied and with the consent of the monastery made available to us by an intrepid soul who understands their value. He turns them into a book that promises to offer new insight into a renowned spiritual writer—the very book you have before you.

It is a strange tale, and an intriguing one. And if it sounds like a story more suited to a tabloid newspaper than the pages of the book, you would not be far wrong. It has all the elements of a potboiler: some of the letters were written secretly, sometimes in code. They involve a not entirely transparent effort to manipulate and possibly deceive certain persons in order to achieve a particular end. It feels like a plot, or to use language common in old Jimmy Cagney movies, a caper. And in a sense it is. Which is part of the charm of the letters and the story they tell. Still, to characterize the story in this way hardly does justice to its complexity and depth. Neither does it adequately express why these letters and the story they tell matter, or might matter to us. Which, I believe, they do.

The story Donald Grayston tells in this book does indeed arise from his discovery of said cache of letters. The author? Thomas Merton, who was at the time of their writing in the mid-1950s living as a Trappist monk (and well-known spiritual writer) at the Abbey of Gethsemani, in Kentucky. He had come to a kind of impasse in his monastic vocation and thought it would be best for him to leave Gethsemani, ideally for a monastic community where solitude was taken more seriously. Thus his correspondence with the superior of the Monastery of Camaldoli in Italy. And yes, it had to be conducted in secret, with code words used for delicate matters having to do with Merton's possible "transfer" ("say the roses are in bloom" if the way looks clear, Merton says to the Italian superior)—lest his abbot at Gethsemani discover what he was planning and put an end to Merton's hopes for a transfer.

Much of this is humorous, both in the intended and unintended senses. It is indeed hard not to smile (or wince) when reading parts of this correspondence. The intrigue, the evasions, the secrets. The only thing missing is invisible ink. Still, for Merton, the stakes were high. He did, after all, feel as though he had reached the end of something in himself and was no longer certain he would be able to continue his monastic vocation at Gethsemani. He was pinning all his hopes on a transfer to Camaldoli. Perhaps he was justified in being cautious, secretive, even devious in the way he conducted this correspondence. He was in turmoil and he was seeking a way forward, a way out.

All of this matters to our understanding of the correspondence. But it is not all that matters. That, it seems to me, is the insight these letters provide about a moment in Thomas Merton's life that would determine so much of what was to follow. A moment of truth, as we sometimes say. For the letters reveal, not always in a way that places Merton in a favorable light, what it feels like to grapple with the kind of fear, anxiety, and uncertainty that can sometimes undo a person. A moment of crisis in which it no longer feels possible to imagine a future. When life has lost its savor. When the struggle you are engaged in to understand and come to terms with yourself is no casual matter but will determine how you will live from this point forward. It is in this sense that the letters matter, or might matter—not only to our understanding of the life and writings of Thomas Merton but also, potentially, to our understanding of ourselves.

For the crisis Merton experienced, while utterly particular to him and rooted in the particular circumstances of his life, also has a more universal resonance. It was after all a crisis of meaning, in which his very capacity to live his life with feeling and hope and purpose had come into question. Sensitive readers will perhaps ask themselves whether Thomas Merton was at times suffering from depression. Certainly this is possible. And it might help us account for something of what we encounter during this period in Merton's life. Still, this term, at least in our own time, has become so maddeningly fluid and opaque that it is good to exercise caution in making quick judgments about its use in relation to any given person's experience. The author of this book exercises such caution. But he actually does more than this. In drawing on the ancient Christian monastic idea of *acedia*, he offers another way of thinking about the kind of crisis of meaning Merton experienced, a way of thinking about this phenomenon that can perhaps serve as a complement and even a corrective to our predilection for oversimplifying such experience and locating any number of different struggles under the general rubric of depression.

However we understand the crisis Merton was undergoing during this time, the letters serve as an important window into his experience and help us feel the texture and complexity and difficulty of his struggle. In particular, they offer us an opportunity to think carefully about the sources and meaning of this moment of impasse, about how he sought to resolve it, and about all that eventually emerged from it. He never did leave Gethsemani: instead, he stayed and (mostly) thrived. How and why this happened is at the heart of the story this book tells. And, given the important contributions Merton was to make over the next fifteen years or so to peacemaking, interreligious dialogue, nonviolence, and social and cultural criticism, all arising out of his contemplative vocation, we are entitled, I think, to view this experience as having been a critical turning point in his life. And to ask how and why he managed to navigate these treacherous waters.

In this and other senses, then, these letters can be seen (to paraphrase Lévi-Strauss) as good "to think with." With their sharp focus on an acute moment of crisis in Thomas Merton's monastic journey, they provide us with a window into a larger world of concerns and help us see them with new eyes. If Merton's struggle was focused somewhat narrowly on his own monastic vocation (understood at the time in terms of where he would live), we can sense in the letters other questions emerging that have a larger, more encompassing focus.

For example, the question of how to discern "the will of God" in his life, a critical concern in almost all great spiritual writing in the Christian tradition, but too often misconstrued as blind submission or an abdication of personal needs and desires. Merton's struggle revealed (to him and to us) how complex and difficult and demanding such questions can be; and how challenging it can be (to use Ignatius of Loyola's language) to discern the authentic ground of our own desires. This is in no small measure what Merton was seeking to do, even if he sometimes inadvertently undermined the process by giving in to his fears and anxieties, or by seeking to exert control over a situation that required detachment and openness. And if he does not always come off as wholly admirable in his response to these events, he nevertheless continues seeking this ground, as honestly and wholeheartedly as he can. This in itself is instructive and can help us read Merton's more mature writing with greater perspective and balance, knowing that his more assured statements about spiritual life and practice arose out of his own crucible of doubt and struggle.

Let me conclude by saying a word about the author of this book. Donald Grayston is not only an authority on Thomas Merton, having read and taught and written on him for more than forty years. He is also someone who takes very seriously the contemplative vision of life that Merton struggled to articulate over a lifetime. Not in the sense of living as a monk: his contemplative life has unfolded amidst marriage and fatherhood; in the daily delights (and grind) of priesthood in a parish; as a leader of pilgrimages; as a person deeply committed to the struggle for peace and justice between Israelis and Palestinians; as a spiritual director and teacher of the art of spiritual direction; as a lover of Shakespeare and of the tango. There is an infectious joy that readers of this book will feel, a sense of intimate connection (though not an uncritical one) between the author and his subject, a deep feeling about the importance of asking questions to which there are no easy answers, a sense that contemplative thought and practice (Merton's as well as ours) *matters*. That our beautiful, fractured world needs us to take this seriously. And that thinking carefully through the questions raised in this book might help us rekindle our own commitments to living out such a vision with integrity and authenticity.

That is, as they say, a tall order. But neither the author of this book nor its principal subject was ever one to shy away from a challenge. The story told in these pages transpired well over fifty years ago, during a time that is so far in the past that many of us can hardly imagine it any longer. And the deeply monastic character of this story may also feel distant from us, far removed from the lives most of us live. But somehow this story and all that it expresses about what it might mean to live with openness, honesty, and freedom also feels close to us, familiar. These are still our questions. And this monastic figure from the past century who grappled with and struggled to overcome a debilitating restlessness and listlessness that sometimes threatened his monastic vocation and his very sense of well-being? He still speaks to us, and he can still teach us and accompany us along the way.

Douglas E. Christie, PhD
Professor of Theological Studies, Loyola Marymount University, Los Angeles

Preface

How did Thomas Merton become Thomas Merton? Starting out from any one of his earlier major life moments—wealthy orphan boy, big man on campus, fervent Roman Catholic convert, new and obedient monk—we find ourselves asking how at the end of his life he had moved from where he was at any one of those moments to becoming a transcultural and transreligious spiritual teacher read by millions. This book takes another such starting point: his attempt in the mid-fifties of the last century to move from one monastery to another, from a Gethsemani that had become, in his view, noisy beyond bearing, to a Camaldoli that he idealized as a place of eremitical peace. The ultimate irony, as I relate in chapter 6: the Camaldoli of that time, bucolic and peaceful outwardly, was inwardly riven by a pre-Vatican II culture war; whereas Gethsemani, which he had tried so hard to leave, became, when he was given his hermitage there in 1965, his place to recover Eden, to take up residence in the new Jerusalem.

As you read through the letters, or the chapters that frame them, and acquaint yourself with the details of Merton's life as a member of a traditional Roman Catholic monastic community of its time, you may be inclined to wonder how important this all is, or if it is important at all. In our world of so many pressing needs, in which the corporal works of mercy—feeding the hungry, healing the sick, housing the homeless, and bringing an end to war (cf. Mic 6:8, Isa 2:4 and 58:7)—make insistent claims upon our awareness and compassion, what is my justification for giving so much space to what from some perspectives may seem trivial? Why do we need to know so much about the struggles Merton had so long ago with his abbot, Dom James, or with his own scrupulous conscience?

My response to this goes back to the first sentence of this preface—how did Thomas Merton *become* Thomas Merton? This book, then, relates a story of *becoming*. I believe there is great value, indeed the possibility of real illumination, in seeing how someone such as Merton undertook this journey of becoming, or, as W. B. Yeats says, how he went from being "the unfinished man and his pain" to being "the finished man among his enemies" ("A Dialogue of Self and Soul"). His journals and his letters lay this journey out for us in raw and marvelous detail. In reading them we see how the *pacte autobiographique* that Merton makes and remakes over the years with his readers shifts from a strongly didactic or proclamatory one in *The Seven Storey Mountain* to one of dialogue, vulnerability, and intimacy in his journals, and to one of self-revelation in his letters. After reading Merton in depth, it is only one short step for us, as reader and writer in intimate dialogue with him, to ask ourselves where we are on our *own* journeys of spirit and flesh, how we arrived where we now are, and where from here we see ourselves going.

Two advance readers of the book have been of great help to me in identifying two particular dynamics that may for some readers interfere with their assent to the book's basic argument. The first of these has to do with Merton's relationship with Dom James. An early biography of Merton cast Dom James as the abbatial ogre, with Merton as the subject of his abuse. Later and more realistic treatments of the relationship have tried to counter this approach with a rehabilitation of Dom James as someone faced with the considerable challenge of guiding the life and work of a brilliant and volatile personality, a monk like no other monk in the history of Christianity—a man committed to the monastic ideal who finds himself falling in love; a man with an intense focus on interior life who becomes a public intellectual; a committed Christian who finds himself criticized by certain other Christians for his engagement with practitioners of other religious traditions. This first reader, in sum, told me that I was too easy on Dom James and too hard on Merton, that I over-empathized with Dom James in his twenty-years-long challenge of being Merton's abbot, and that I was too critical of Merton's impulsiveness and volatility. I can only leave it to the reader to decide to what extent this early reader was right or not. I am trusting that any critical comments I make about Merton will be read in the purview of my essential view of him as the outstanding Christian spiritual writer of the twentieth century; and I am looking forward to Roger Lipsey's forthcoming book on Merton and Dom James, which will certainly give a fuller picture than I have been able to provide in this study.

The second advance reader took issue with the orientation of the book, with what kind of book it was to be. Was it to be a solid piece of scholarship, or, conversely, did it run the risk of being a work of excessive empathy, a work in which I might be perceived as claiming a closeness with Merton which I don't possess, never having met him in the flesh, and so being limited, as all others now interested in him, to what I can learn or intuit about

Preface

him from his writings and the recollections of those who did know him personally? It was clear that this good friend was favoring the first approach and raising a serious question about the second. Alas, or perhaps not alas, I have found myself helpless (a favorite term of Gandhi's when he found himself unable—or unwilling!—to change his mind about something) not to do both. Yes, Merton is regularly and appropriately the subject of serious scholarship, and he deserves all the care and discernment we can give to him in that regard. At the same time, in his inimitable and, to some, irresistible way, he invites his readers to sit beside him, to come to know him in a personal way. Many readers (not all, to be sure) regularly testify to this, and add to it the mysterious intuition that not only do they know him, but that *he knows them*—from whatever realm of spirit he now inhabits. There is no agreed-upon explanation of how this happens, but it happens all the time.

Another wondering: should I use as many longish quotations as I have? I know that there needs to be a sense of proportion between the text as such and the quotations that, one hopes, adorn rather than dominate the text. I concluded that I should, because I wanted the voices of the *dramatis personae* to be clearly heard: Merton's voice, Dom James's voice, and the voices of the other correspondents. Merton himself is my model here: in "Day of a Stranger" he speaks of the "voices" he heard in his hermitage: "the dry disconcerting voice of Nicanor Parra," "the golden sounds of John of Salisbury," and the feminine voices of Angela of Foligno, Teresa of Avila, Julian of Norwich, and Raïssa Maritain. I will leave it to my readers to choose the adjectives that speak most clearly to them of the particular tonalities of the voices of Merton and his confrères.

With these caveats, provisos, justifications, and special pleadings, I release this book from my computer and, through the good offices of the publisher, place it in your hands. I invite you to read it both with critical intelligence and with a tender heart for this great, vulnerable, and brilliant man.

Donald Grayston
Vancouver, British Columbia
October 21, 2014

Acknowledgments

I am happy to acknowledge the many forms of generous assistance I have received in the writing of this book. I first of all acknowledge Merton's monastic brothers—John Eudes Bamberger, OCSO, James Conner, OCSO, Alfred McCartney, OCSO, Elias Dietz, OCSO, and Joseph Steinke—the latter no longer a member of the OCSO, but someone who when he was a member played an important role in Merton's attempt to go to Camaldoli, as LETTER 19 testifies. Each of them has been of very specific assistance to me in understanding Merton's lived monastic experience.

I next express my gratitude to the professional staff of the Thomas Merton Center at Bellarmine University, in Louisville—Paul Pearson and Mark Meade. Paul and Mark have been enormously helpful in responding to the many picky-picky questions I have asked them. Their expertise is astonishing, and I am grateful for it. Very special thanks also to Anne McCormick for her strong support, and to Anne and her colleagues in the Merton Legacy Trust, for their guidance through the thickets of copyright. And to my colleagues in the Thomas Merton Society of Canada and in the International Thomas Merton Society, again my sincere thanks for collegial encouragement of many kinds over the years of our time together in search of Merton in all his complexity, inconsistency, and authenticity—what a trip! I thank in particular David Belcastro and Douglas E. Christie for their illuminating intuitions about Merton's journey, and Patrick F. O'Connell for the inspiration of his magisterial scholarship. Again in particular I thank those who responded to specific enquiries and whom I have named at the end of the Bibliography.

Then the translators: chief of these, Larissa Fielding (LDSF), who also, in effect, acted as my research assistant in matters Italian. Her help in contacting the Milan Archdiocesan Archives was particularly helpful. And to the other translators: Tiziana De Angelis (TDA) and Anna Terrana (AT), for further help with Italian; Philippe Barois, Suzanne Barois, and Jean-Claude

Bazinet for help with French; Monica Escudero (ME) for help with Spanish; Douglas E. Williams (DEW) and David Mirhady for help with Latin; David Mirhady again for his help with the Greek roots of *acedia*; and finally David Mivasair for the Hebrew of Ps 90:6. Their help was invaluable. Thanks also to Dave Chang for inviting me one spring evening to a sit at Mountain Rain, the Zen community to which he belongs, and for his tracking down of the Zen reference to *acedia* which so fortuitously arose during my visit—sincere thanks to all.

Very special thanks also to Thomas Matus for his elucidation of the Camaldolese tradition on the basis of his decades of living the Camaldolese life; the book is much the stronger for his contributions. And again to Douglas E. Christie for his wise and kind words in the Foreword, graciously written at a time when his plate would have been already very full without one more writing assignment with a deadline!

I further acknowledge with thanks the research grant I received from the Faculty of Arts and Social Sciences at Simon Fraser University here in Vancouver, where I spent fifteen happy years teaching, and to Dean John Craig and the other staff of the Faculty who made it possible for me to spend two weeks in the summer of 2013 in Louisville, working in the Archives of the Thomas Merton Center.

The most practical help I received, help very much needed, came from my computing consultant, Adrian Buckley. Adrian: in the most literal sense, couldn't have done it without you! Many thanks to you, and be assured that I will need you again.

And last but certainly not least, I thank the unknown acquisitions staff person of the Dunbar Library in Vancouver who, in preparation for its opening, purchased on the library's behalf a book with an unusual binding, a kind of burlap, which was what drew my attention to it on the shelf when I was browsing there on the library's opening day in 1954: *Seeds of Contemplation*, by someone of whom I had never heard: Thomas Merton. Her choice was doubtless unintentional in regard to my noticing the book, but no less providential for all that.

Abbreviations

References to works other than those with abbreviations as below will be found in the footnotes. Initial references to the works named below will be footnoted, with succeeding references included in the text. For full publishing information for these works, see the Bibliography.

CFT	*The Courage for Truth* (Letters 4)
DWL	*Dancing in the Water of Life* (Journals 5)
ES	*Entering the Silence* (Journals 2)
HGL	*The Hidden Ground of Love* (Letters 1)
IMT 1	*Cassian and the Fathers*
IMT 2	*Pre-Benedictine Monasticism*
IMT 3	*An Introduction to Christian Mysticism*
IMT 4	*The Rule of Saint Benedict*
IMT 5	*Monastic Observances*
IMT 6	*The Life of the Vows*
LTL	*Learning to Love* (Journals 6)
NAA	*Nazarena: An American Anchoress*
NMI	*No Man Is an Island*
OSM	*The Other Side of the Mountain* (Journals 7)
SCH	*The School of Charity* (Letters 3)
SFS	*A Search for Solitude* (Journals 3)
SJ	*The Sign of Jonas*
SSM	*The Seven Storey Mountain*
ST	*Summa Theologica*
TTW	*Turning Toward the World* (Journals 4)
WF	*Witness to Freedom* (Letters 5)

Introduction: The Roses at the Hermitage

Thomas Merton: monk, writer, cloistered hermit and public intellectual, prophet and poet, social critic and Zen calligrapher, marginal man and trickster, solitary and lover, a man of flesh and blood. A wealthy orphan with a fractured childhood, then a carousing university student, he found in his twenties the faith and meaning that led him into a lifelong monastic commitment; by the end of his life he had grown into a transcultural, transreligious spiritual teacher. Spiritual director *in absentia* to thousands if not millions, myself included, and the outstanding Christian spiritual writer of his century, he is the man of whom Tenzin Gyatso, His Holiness the Dalai Lama, speaks when he says, as he regularly does, that he never understood Christianity until he met Thomas Merton. Or, as he most recently has said, "His death was a great loss. If Father Thomas Merton were still alive, I am sure we would have been comrades working closely together to further the dialogue between religious traditions and to help bring real peace to our world."[1]

It's summer 1952. Thomas Merton has been a monk at the Trappist abbey of Gethsemani in Kentucky since 1941, almost eleven years. He is thirty-seven years of age. His great desire is for a life of silence and solitude in which without impediment he could seek God and his own soul. It isn't happening, and he is restless. The abbot is building factories, for cheese and fruitcake: he wants to set the abbey on a firm financial base, and when the royalties for Merton's bestseller, *The Seven Storey Mountain*, begin to arrive in the spring of 1949, this is a big help. Along with the factories, however, come tractors

---

1. An encomium in Henry and Montaldo, *We Are Already One*, 358.

and jackhammers and air compressors, and the noise is driving Merton crazy. This is not, he tells himself, what he had signed up for in 1941, when Gethsemani was a quiet, bucolic place. He is a very large personality in a small institution; some of his friends are telling him that he has outgrown the abbey, that it is time for him to go somewhere else.

In August, Arcadio Larraona, secretary of the Vatican's congregation dealing with members of religious communities, visited Gethsemani. Merton conversed with him in Spanish, in which he was fluent, and their conversations gave him a strong sense of the universality of the Roman Catholic Church. The Church, after all, was bigger than the abbey of Gethsemani, something he had always known; but Larraona's visit brought that wider world vividly into Merton's cloistered environment—and a door opened.

On September 11, he wrote to Dom Anselmo Giabbani, prior of the ancient monastery of Camaldoli, in Italy, and prior general of the Camaldolese Order. He told Giabbani that he wanted to join Camaldoli's community of hermits, the *eremo*. Giabbani responded promptly and positively: there would be a place for Merton at Camaldoli if he decided to come (and was able to come). Both those letters have been lost; but the first extant letter in what I am calling the Camaldoli Correspondence reveals how serious Merton was about this, how intensely he felt he was in the wrong place, and how deeply he desired the life of solitude that he believed would never be his at Gethsemani. His letters to Camaldoli launched him on a track that continued through his journey of the next sixteen years, in which, already a well-known author, he became a public intellectual, a social critic who looked through the lens of contemplation at the urgent social issues that concern us still—racism, nuclear weapons, the environment.

In the years covered by the Camaldoli Correspondence he was tormenting himself with many questions. Was he seeking this change for the right reasons? Was he being honest with himself about his motivations? Could he be sure that it was the will of God that he leave Gethsemani? (His abbot was very sure that it was the will of God that he *not* leave.) These deeply monastic questions were utterly personal to Merton at this time. They also have a more universal character, as they point us to the process, often very mysterious, by which we *come to know* (that is, not know-all-at-once) what is right for us; in Christian spiritualty this process is called discernment. It is in this sense that Merton's very personal questions may open new perspectives for us on our own questions. How in fact do any of us respond at moments of confusion or impasse? What do we do when the salt of our job or our marriage has lost its savor? Where is the solid ground in our lives, and where the sinking sand? How can we live with authenticity, with integrity? Do we—do I—still know who God is, or did I ever know?

Introduction: The Roses at the Hermitage

Merton's questions reached fever pitch in the three letters he wrote on April 25, 1955. The letters he received in response in August and September of that year told him that his request for an authorized transfer to Camaldoli had been denied. Camaldoli as the focus of his hopes faded, but the restlessness continued. Perhaps there is no one of whom St. Augustine's aphorism "You have made us for yourself, and our hearts are restless till they rest in you" was more true than Thomas Merton. His restlessness sprang up again two years later, with Merton asking himself all the same questions in a second attempt to leave Gethsemani, this time to go to an experimental Benedictine community at Cuernavaca, near Mexico City. This too was not to be realized. But in 1965, still, amazingly, a monk of Gethsemani, and still sparring with his abbot, he was authorized to become a hermit on the abbey grounds. For the last three years of his life he had as much solitude and silence in his hermitage as he needed. Ironically, it was while living as a hermit that he fell in love, and so experienced the challenge of how to bring together his love for M—Margie—with his life of solitude. The relationship ended, as it had to; but out of it he learned that the deepest meaning of solitude was love.

In our present time, a time even more fractured than Merton's, I believe we need deliberately to make the acquaintance of women and men who inspire, challenge, sometimes irritate, astonish, and encourage us. We need to encourage *ourselves* by standing back from the superficiality of so much of the media, indeed so much of the culture, and by spending reflective time with the great ones, as we understand them—people who can awaken in us our own capacity for deep humanity. Thomas Merton, I have no hesitation in saying, is one such person. One prime example of his humanistic thinking and modeling is found when Merton brings together perspectives from psychoanalysis, Sufi mysticism, and Christian spirituality in his description of what he calls the "finally integrated" person.[2] The concept of final integration comes from a book that strongly engaged Merton—*Final Integration in the Adult Personality*, by Iranian psychoanalyst Reza Arasteh.[3] Merton didn't apply the concept directly to himself, but many of his readers are ready to make that connection. Such a person "apprehends his life fully and wholly from an inner ground that is at once more universal than the empirical

---

2. Merton, "Final Integration," 219–31.
3. See on this Shannon, *Silent Lamp*, 287–88.

ego and yet entirely his own."[4] (We will revisit this concept in chapter 2.) Characterized by "transcultural maturity,"[5] the finally integrated person is one who can help us, in a culturally shrinking world, in our need to stretch and develop our intentional capacity for encounter with persons different from ourselves without "othering" them into stereotyped categories, often simply for the sake of convenience in our busy lives. When Merton wrote an article about Thich Nhat Hanh the day after meeting him, for example, he didn't title it "Thich Nhat Hanh: Exemplary Buddhist"; he called it "Nhat Hanh is my Brother."[6] Our historical moment calls us to renew and live out a primal sense of our shared humanity, which Merton alluded to when, in an informal talk in Calcutta (now Kolkata) shortly before his death in 1968, he said, "We are already one."[7] This is one of Merton's great gifts, and indeed a mandate for our own spiritual growth: that he invites us to go ever deeper into our own humanity and thereby equip ourselves for transcultural, transreligious and thereby deeply human exchange. At the same time, by his own example he calls us to self-acceptance, something that he himself only painfully achieved. And lest this challenge discourage us, it is good to remember that he also invites us "to forget ourselves on purpose, cast our awful solemnity to the winds and join in the general dance."[8]

Merton, of course, was also a flawed human being. There are many comments in the Camaldoli letters that testify to his fretfulness, anxiety, and vulnerability, and to the smallness of attitude that often characterized the institutional context in which he had freely chosen to live. They give us the backstory to the many intriguing, sometimes oblique references in his journals to the Camaldolese, the Carthusians, and Latin America. As you read through them, you will encounter some very unattractive moments in Merton's life; there is a sense of rawness and confusion in many of the letters, as Merton opens his heart and soul to his correspondents. Yet within and beneath the manifest level of his struggles with himself and with the authorities of his Trappist-Cistercian order are to be found the larger issues that Merton explored and with which he struggled throughout his monastic career, issues that concern us all: personal integrity; the value of silence and solitude in a hyperconnected time; the search in that solitude for the True Self; the recognition that in finding the True Self, we are finding God, in whose image according to Jewish and Christian tradition we are made (cf.

---

4. Merton, "Final Integration," 225.
5. Ibid.
6. Merton, *Thomas Merton on Peace*, 262–63.
7. "Thomas Merton's View of Monasticism," in Merton, *Asian Journal*, 308.
8. Merton, *New Seeds of Contemplation*, 297.

Gen 1:26); and, not least, the question of love. By naming the questions and concerns that I observe as active in the life of Thomas Merton, I offer an intuition and hope for myself: that the universal can become personal in my own life; indeed, that if I will listen to Merton, open my eyes, recognize it and live from it, I will see that this has already happened, on the level of love.

Camaldoli is the name of a *frazione*, a tiny hamlet, in the *comune* or municipality of Poppi, a few miles/kilometers due north of Arezzo, in Tuscany.[9] It is also the name of the monastic community established there in 1012 by St. Romuald (951–c. 1027), a nobleman of Ravenna; Camaldoli celebrated its millennium in 2012.[10] It was here, according to legend, that, already himself a monk, he was met by a nobleman called Maldolus, who after describing to Romuald a vision he had had of monks in white habits ascending a ladder to heaven, offered him a field for a monastic settlement. The gift of the field was readily accepted by Romuald, who built there the hermitage in the place afterwards known as *Campus Maldoli*, "the field of Maldolus"—Camaldoli. In the same year he received from Maldolus a villa at the foot of the mountains, where he established a monastery. Thus from the beginning Romuald's foundation was composed of two coordinate cohorts, monks and hermits, and so it continues to this day.[11] There is very little else in the hamlet, tranquil and secure in its setting in the Appennine hills, and embraced on all sides by the forests of the Casentino. A stream of traffic, it is true, moves relatively quietly along the road between the façade of the monastery and the large fountain that faces it, erected in the fifteenth century in celebration of another ancient name of the place, Fontebona. A busier road runs past the entrance to the *eremo*, the hermit village, some three miles/seven kilometers up the hill from the monastery. But to the casual visitor or observer, this does not diminish the general peacefulness of the place.

Such a casual visitor to Camaldoli was I in the summer of 2008. I had not come on retreat in a formal sense. I was simply wanting some down time after an intense ten days of teaching in a study program on Thomas Merton in Rome sponsored by the Thomas Merton Society of Canada.[12] I settled into my room, identified by the plate above the door as being under the patronage and protection of St. Pachomius, founder of cenobitic (i.e.,

---

9. Frigerio, *Camaldoli*, 63.
10. See Appendix I, San Gregorio section, note 6.
11. monasterodicamaldoli.it.
12. merton.ca.

communal) monasticism, and prepared to enjoy with his encouragement and oversight a time of prayer and rest.

As I recall, it was two days after my arrival that the guestmaster, realizing from my telling him what I had been doing before my arrival that I was interested in Thomas Merton, asked me if I would care to see the contents of "a file of old letters" from and to Merton, kept for more than fifty years in the monastery's archives, and, to my knowledge, untouched since they were filed there. Of course I did so care—and soon held in my hands a file of letters from the 1950s that testified to Merton's attempt to transfer his monastic stability from the abbey of Gethsemani, in Kentucky, where he had lived since 1941, to the Camaldolese branch of the Order of St. Benedict, indeed to the very monastery in which I was a guest.

It was a great moment for me to come so close through these letters to the agonies and ecstasies of someone whom I had been studying for more than thirty years (now more than forty). There were two particular prizes among the letters. One was Merton's letter of May 3, 1955, to Anselmo Giabbani, the prior (LETTER 20), in which, in what I am calling variant (a), we find a handwritten postscript as follows.

> Dom James [Merton's abbot] will be back in a few days. If you write me, don't say anything about this matter [his hopes for a transfer], even in Italian. But if you want to tell me that you have taken steps to obtain the *transitus* [the official permission for a transfer], tell me something like "We have planted the roses at the hermitage." And if you have obtained the *transitus*, tell me that "The roses are *in bloom* at the hermitage."

Here we encounter Merton as trickster. Yet he saw this deception as necessary if Dom James, who in those days, as did all abbots, read all the mail coming in and going out, except for letters marked "conscience matter," was not to discover the extent of his attempt to leave Gethsemani. As we shall see, Merton's conscience soon got the better of him, and the matter came out into the open between himself and Dom James.

The second particular prize was the *eight-page, handwritten* letter to Merton from Giovanni Battista Montini, then archbishop of Milan, later Pope Paul VI (LETTER 27). The letter is pastoral and empathetic, but it is also very clear in giving Merton the archbishop's considered view, that his place of sanctification is Gethsemani, not Camaldoli. That someone with as demanding a position as archbishop of Milan would give time to write a personal, pastoral and handwritten letter of this length and thoughtfulness to someone he had never met remains to me remarkable.

Introduction: The Roses at the Hermitage

From the discovery of this file of letters, then, only some of which were held in the archives of the Thomas Merton Center at Bellarmine University (TMC), in Louisville, Kentucky, the major repository of Mertoniana, has come this present study. To the letters in the file, I have added the others held in the TMC, and others in the Merton Dossier of the archives of the archdiocese of Milan, so that what I am calling the Camaldoli Correspondence now consists of thirty-six letters, seven of which are not extant. Reading these letters, you will encounter Merton himself, who of the twenty-nine extant letters wrote seventeen, and was the recipient of six others. The remaining six were written *about* Merton, by James Fox, his abbot; Anselm (Joseph) Steinke, in 1955 prior of Gethsemani; Archbishop Montini; and Anselmo Giabbani, prior of Camaldoli and prior-general of the Camaldolese order. It was a letter of September 1952 to Giabbani, no longer extant, that initiated the correspondence, and a last letter to him from Merton that concluded it in March 1956. A complete listing of the letters, and brief biographies of their authors and recipients, you will find at the beginning of this central section of the book. (I have added to the heading of these brief biographies the words *Dramatis Personae*, because it seems to me that a fascinating play could be written on the basis of the struggles and interchanges that the letters offer.) Following the letters you will find the text of two appendices related to them; a note on the languages in which the letters and the appendices are written; a note on Merton's fluency in the languages represented in the letters and appendices; and a note on orthography.

And what do the letters tell us? I go into this question in detail in chapter 3. To speak generally here, they tell us about a critical time in Merton's life, a time when he was very much afflicted, in my view, by the monastic malady that the ancient monastic writers called *acedia*, and that I am using as an interpretive paradigm for Merton's experience. They saw this as the work of the noonday demon to which Ps 90:6 in the Latin Vulgate of St. Jerome refers (Ps 91:6 in contemporary English versions), and about which I write in chapter 1. The monks and hermits of that ancient time—St. Anthony the Great, St. Benedict, and others—exteriorized and personified their spiritual difficulties and challenges as demons to which they attributed metaphysical reality. At the same time they recognized the close connection between their interior fears and terrors and the demons so conceived. We still speak of people wrestling with their demons. Merton, as did his monastic ancestors, essentially understood them as interior, as parts of himself, with no need to exteriorize or personify them. In chapter 1 we will also encounter the work of Kathleen Norris, who asserts that she finds it likely "that much of the restless boredom, frantic escapism, commitment phobia, and enervating despair that plagues us today is the ancient demon of *acedia* in modern dress."[13] So it is a paradigm that can illuminate our contemporary experience, cultural and personal, as well as that of monks and hermits ancient and modern. For Merton it was a time when he worked out some crucial matters for himself, which would manifest themselves in the years following in mature living and writing.

I see this particular demon—if in using this word we can suspend our postmodern disbelief and attempt to enter the thought-world of the fourth-century monastic theorist Evagrius Ponticus, whose teaching was very much alive for Merton—as having visited Merton on three particular occasions. The first such occasion was the mysterious period, beginning after his ordination in 1949 (a post-ordination sag being a not uncommon phenomenon) and ending in December 1950, about which he writes in *The Sign of Jonas*; this I call the time of the preliminary *acedia*, and I deal with it in chapter 2. This period[14] I see as critical for Merton's spiritual and theological development, a time after which his perspectives expanded from the narrow focus on life in the monastery that had marked the years since his arrival there in 1941. I see this time as revealing the first identifiable appearance of the noonday demon, and a time that manifestly presages its later visitations (cf. Luke 4:13). The second visitation, what I am calling the *greater acedia*, coincides with the time of writing of the Camaldoli Correspondence, 1952 to 1956, a three-and-a-half-year period, with its first and last letters to Giabbani (LETTERS 1 and 36) acting as brackets to that period. The third visitation, the *lesser acedia*, which I describe in chapter 6, begins in the year after the end of the second, and concerns Merton's attempts to find a way of moving to some place in Latin America, the Caribbean, or the American west, eventually settling on Cuernavaca, in Mexico, a period ending in 1960.

Merton's vulnerability to *acedia* may be likened to the way a virus operates in the body. It is there all the time, and when the immune system is diminished, it flares up and wreaks its specific havoc. We see it rising in the post-ordination period, the summer and autumn of 1949, falling at the end of 1950. Recognizing after a few months that Merton has to a large extent recovered, Dom James appoints him as Master of Scholastics, that is, the officer of the monastery responsible for the theological education of

---

13. Norris, *Acedia and Me*, 3. Basset, *The Noonday Devil*, is a pop spirituality/pop psych book that deals with some of what Norris mentions here in the context of the challenges of midlife. He makes no mention of *acedia*.

14. The third phase (1949–50) of his time at Gethemani, the time of his "critical sickness," or breakdown. See SJ, 226.

those among the younger monks who were studying for the priesthood; and this responsibility for others keeps the virus under some control. But it rises again and breaks out in September 1952 with the writing of the first letter to Camaldoli. It remains active until September 1955, when the letter from Cardinal Larraona, secretary of the Congregation for Religious in Rome, provides a definitive denial of his hopes for a transfer, and when he is shocked by the realization that Dom James and the abbot general are ready to authorize his entry into the hermit life so long as he becomes "a hermit one hundred per cent."[15] Instantly realizing that he is not ready for this, he offers himself to Dom James and to the community as novice master. Again there is a time of respite; but by 1957 the virus is again active, and remains active until the letter of December 1959 from Cardinals Valeri and Larraona communicating their official unwillingness to authorize a transfer. I would argue that it remains relatively inactive for the rest of his life, meaning that I do not see his time with M, his late-life partner in love, something completely unexpected although to some extent foreshadowed, as related to *acedia*. Evagrius would simply have called it *epithymia*, lust, his name for one of *acedia*'s fellow-demons; but as I say in the last chapter, it cannot be so simply accounted for.

As I have noted, the correspondence spans some three and a half years. It is significant, I believe, that thirty-three of the thirty-six letters were written between March 10, 1953, and July 17, 1956, dates that mark the beginning and end of a three-and-a-half-year gap in Merton's journal of the time.[16] I would posit in this regard that during this gap, much of the energy that Merton typically invested in his journal writing was redirected to his transfer project and to his correspondence, of which the Camaldoli-related letters represent only one layer. Another such layer consists of the letters he wrote to his friends, soliciting support for his hopes—Jean Leclercq, monk of Clervaux, in Luxembourg, notable among them.[17] Another layer, an intra-Trappist one, includes his many letters to his own abbot, and to the abbot general, Dom Gabriel Sortais,[18] their letters to each other, and their replies to him not included in the Camaldoli Correspondence. It will be clear that all the writers and recipients of the letters other than Merton have

15. Letter of Dom James Fox to Dom Gabriel Sortais, October 18, 1955 (TMC).

16. *A Search for Solitude* (SFS) covers July 1952 to March 1953, and from July 1956 to May 1960, with the notable three-and-a-half-year gap in the middle.

17. Merton and Leclercq, *Survival or Prophecy?*

18. Oury, *Dom Gabriel Sortais*. It is noteworthy, given the very large number of letters that passed between Merton and Sortais, that there is not a single reference to Merton in the book. It is also interesting to note that Merton and Dom James wrote each other frequently, even though they lived in the same monastic house.

a strong and direct, and to a large extent institutional interest in the working out of his vocational struggle, not that this excludes personal and pastoral concern on their part. The letters also give us a benchmark, a beginning point from which to trace the spiritual growth of their author/recipient/subject from the restless and unhappy man that he was at the time of their writing to the far more peaceful and self-accepting person that he was at the end of his life. His order, the Trappist reform of the Cistercian tradition, began in France in the seventeenth century; and there is very little in the letters, with a few exceptions (notably LETTERS 15 and 18), that could not have been written in that century. The ecclesiastical relations of that time, in the matrix of which, culturally and spiritually, Merton was to some extent living, are vividly represented, for example, in the letters' flowery and (to the contemporary mind) overly submissive, even subservient, complimentary closings. He had a lot of work to do to become the autonomous man of the wise heart to which one of his favorite mystics, Julian of Norwich, pointed him, and to become such a man in the contemporary and future-oriented way in which he did so. My own take on this is that when he died in 1968, he was operating, so to speak, from about 2050. It will take us some time to catch up with him.

I give an account in chapter 1 of the concept of *acedia*, from its first extant treatment, by Evagrius Ponticus in the fourth century, through some of the high points of the Western humanist tradition to contemporary times, and the work of Andrew Solomon and Kathleen Norris. In chapter 2 I offer, not a full biographical treatment, but rather a biographical framework for Merton's life, with particular attention to the critical time in 1949–50 that I have called the time of the preliminary *acedia*. Then comes the Camaldoli Correspondence itself. In chapters 3 and 4 I set out my close reading of the letters, what I read in them about Merton's soul journey of those years. Chapter 5 is concerned with what I think of as the fading, indeed the ending, of Merton's long-cherished dream of Camaldoli. In chapter 6 I attempt to weave together the threads of enquiry that I have followed in the previous chapters, as well as exploring the challenges of the hermitage years. It will not be until chapter 6 that we will be able to have a sense of the entire trajectory of Merton's journey of solitude from the way he conceived it when he was writing to Camaldoli to how he understood it in the hermitage years, especially after his time with Margie. I note here that in quoting from Merton, I have not changed his sometimes hypermasculine style into something more inclusive. If everyone writing about Merton tinkered with his style, we would end up with a variety of emendations rather than hearing him speak from his own time to ours. I am certain that had he lived into our time, he would have understood why inclusive language is important and written accordingly.

James Finley was a novice under Merton, and is now himself a noted spiritual teacher, author, and retreat leader. I close this introduction with what he says about the most foundational aspect of Merton's "wise and trustworthy guidance." It is located, he says, in

> Merton's emphasis on the importance of grounding our search for God in our customary experience of ourselves as human beings. The ring of authenticity that resonates in Merton's writings flows, in part at least, from the honesty with which he shares with us his own struggles and breakthroughs in the day by day realities in which he searched for and found God in his life. His down to earth honesty lets us know he is like us and in doing so lets us know we are like him.[19]

Yes, we are like him and he is like us: not that we are comparing ourselves to him, but the likeness is there in the foundational, creational reality that we are all human beings. In this age of so many forms of dehumanization, few things, I would hold, are more important to affirm than this, our common humanity.

---

19. Finley, "Turning to Thomas Merton as our Guide in Contemplative Living" (in press).

I

The Noonday Demon: *acedia*

The noonday demon: we meet it first in the Hebrew Bible, in Ps 90:6, as it is numbered in the Vulgate of St. Jerome (91:6 in the King James and subsequent English translations). The Hebrew reads *mi-ketev yashud tsohorayim*: "from destruction that despoils at midday."[1] Then in the third century before the common era, the Hebrew Bible was translated into Alexandrian Greek, a translation called the Septuagint ("the work of the seventy" translators). There the verse reads, *apo pragmatos diaporeuomenou en skotei apo symptwmatos kai daimoniou mesembrinou*: [you need not fear] "the pestilence that walks in darkness, nor the destruction that wastes at noonday." The Vulgate's reference to the noonday demon, the *daemonium meridianum*, comes from Jerome's translation of the Septuagint into Latin, in which he has personified the word *daimonion*. There we find these words: *Non timebis . . . ab incursu et daemonio meridiano* ("You will not fear . . . because of assault [or invasion, incursion] and the noonday demon"). The element of demonic personification holds firm in the Douay translation of 1609, where the Latin is translated literally—"the noonday devil"—but in the King James Version of 1611, the translation follows the Hebrew: "the destruction that wasteth at noonday"; and this is echoed in the most

---

1. From Rabbi David Mivasair: "*Mi-* is a preposition, meaning 'from.' *Ketev* means 'destruction.' *Yashud* is a verb, meaning 'destroying, plundering, despoiling.' It is related to the Hebrew word *sheid*, meaning 'a demon.' *Tsohorayim* means 'noon' or 'midday.' I understand this phrase, the second half of verse 6, to be parallel to the first half, and to say something like 'from destruction that plunders during midday,' or 'from ruin that runs at noon.' It has nothing to do with demons other than speaking of destruction as a force with power analogous to demonic power and agency." My thanks to Rabbi Mivasair for his assistance with the Hebrew text (e-mail message to author, July 1, 2014).

commonly used contemporary translation, the New Revised Standard Version, as "the destruction that wastes at noonday." Particularly through the influence of the Vulgate, however, "the noonday demon" has come down to us through the Desert Fathers and Mothers, the Christian hermits of Egypt, Syria, and Palestine in the fourth and later centuries, who found it had strong resonance with their ascetical experience.

When we come to Evagrius Ponticus and later writers, we will encounter the noonday demon as specifically responsible, so to speak, for *acedia*, the production of which in the lives and hearts of human beings in general and monks and hermits in particular is its accepted task. The term has a Greek antecedent, *akedia*, from *kedos*, meaning grief or anxiety; and with the alpha-privative negating the root word, *a-kedia* means a lack of concern or anxiety, a kind of listlessness or disconnection.[2] We can stretch these meanings to connect with what the word comes to mean in the Latin tradition; but it would be simpler to say that the word as it moves from Greek into Latin takes on a different tone and acquires different shades of meaning. The one related term in English that I would encourage my readers to set aside is *sloth*, the name by which it is commonly known in the received lists of the seven deadly sins. I say this because in contemporary English, sloth immediately connotes laziness, which, as we will see when we reflect on the place of *acedia* in the life of Thomas Merton, is as far as possible from describing Merton's situation. I find support for this in John Eudes Bamberger's translation of Evagrius' ascetical treatise, *The Praktikos*.[3] There he gives English translations for the names of the other deadly sins, but retains the Latin for *acedia*; for, as he says, it "is such a complex reality and the term has such a technical significance [for Evagrius] that it seems best always to retain it without translation."[4] Kathleen Norris supports this view in a quotation from Andrew Crislip: "The very persistence of the term 'acedia' betrays the fact that none of the modern or medieval glosses adequately conveys the semantic range of the monastic term."[5]

Evagrius Ponticus (345–99) was born in Pontus, now northern Turkey, into a family of Greek ethnicity. After his student days, he was ordained a lector by St. Basil the Great, and may have considered a monastic vocation at that time. But he went instead to Constantinople, attracted by its

---

2. My thanks to Prof. David Mirhady for his assistance with the Greek origins of *acedia* (e-mail messages to author, June 8 and 9, 2014).

3. John Eudes Bamberger was a close associate of Merton's at Gethsemani. See the section on Zilboorg in chapter 2.

4. Evagrius, *Praktikos*, 24, note 40.

5. Quoted in Norris, *Acedia and Me*, 2–3.

stimulating intellectual life. There he fell in love with a married woman, an experience that resulted in his decision to move to Jerusalem. Once more he fell into worldly ways, but after an experience of conversion, went to the desert of Nitria, in Egypt, where he joined a group of hermits, living there until his death. He was the first, as John Eudes Bamberger tells us, "to write extensively on the spirituality of the desert and the first to reduce to a system a monastic ascetic and mystical theology which included many elements of desert wisdom,"[6] the system that we find in *The Praktikos*. Although it is believed he did not join St. Basil's community because of its socially oriented activities, once in the desert his view shifted to an appreciation of a psychology of a practical and experiential kind, as *The Praktikos* demonstrates.

And why were the monks in the desert at all? Because they were resisting the co-opting of the Church by the newly "Christian" empire, and the luxurious lives to which many bishops and other clerics had quickly become accustomed. By going to the desert, a fearful place where, they believed, demons lived, they went to be closer to Christ himself, who had gone to the desert to be tempted by Satan, over whom the gospel tells us he was victorious (Matt 4:1–11), notably through his use of scripture in refuting Satan's temptations. A belief in demons, differently understood at different times, had been part of Greek culture since the time of Plato. Their existence was an accepted aspect of human experience, and was confirmed for the monks by their presence in the ministry of Jesus as recorded in the New Testament. Once in the desert, the monks found that as external distractions diminished, interior distractions, the work of the demons, increased, "and they began to study their thoughts as they arose, noting which were life-giving and which destructive"[7]—that is, which ones came from the demons (the passionate thoughts, the *logismoi*[8]) and which ones from God. They were learning how to "discern the spirits" (1 Cor 12:10; 1 John 4:1).

Evagrius' demonology was central to his theology and his proto-psychology. He describes angels as made of fire, human beings as made of earth, and the demons as made of ice-cold air.[9] Here is what he says about them:

> We must take care to recognize the different types of demons and note the special times of their activity . . . so that when these various evil thoughts set their own proper forces to work we are

---

6. Evagrius, *Praktikos*, xli–xlii.
7. Norris, *Acedia and Me*, 88.
8. Evagrius, *Praktikos*, lxviii.
9. Ibid., lxxvi.

The Noonday Demon: *acedia*

in a position to address effective words against them, that is to say, those words which correctly characterize the one present.[10]

Of all the demons, although anger is the fiercest,[11] it is the demon of *acedia* that causes the most trouble,[12] because whereas each of the other demons is found in only a part of the soul, the noonday demon "is accustomed to embrace the entire soul."[13] Here then is Evagrius' advice about how to respond to its attacks:

> The time of temptation is not the time to leave one's cell. . . . Rather, stand there firmly and be patient. Bravely take all that the demon brings upon you, but above all face up to the demon of *acedia* who [note the personification] is the most grievous of all and on this account [if defeated] will effect the greatest purification of soul.[14]

To "stay in one's cell," that is, to hold your ground against the demon as well as to remain physically in the cell, is primary, because it offers the monk the opportunity to read, watch (i.e., keep vigil), and pray.[15] In this enterprise, what the monks called meditation was critical:

> Meditation was not, as the world has come to imply today, an interior reflection on the meaning of certain words. It was first and foremost the utterance, or exclamation of words, which were gradually digested and interiorized. Meditation on Scripture was an oral phenomenon.[16]

The utterance of scripture had something of a talismanic function, with a kind of "brute power" attributed to it.[17] The classic such utterance, which survives in contemporary monastic offices (as also in Anglican liturgy), came from Ps 70:1: "O God, make speed to save us. / O Lord, make haste to help us." The Psalms, anything from the gospels, and the very name of Jesus formed the staples of the monastic armory. In their use of scripture, the monks and hermits were identifying themselves with Christ's own use of scripture to confound Satan, to which they added the power of his name.

10. Ibid., 8.
11. Ibid., 18.
12. Ibid., 22 n. 36.
13. Ibid., 26.
14. Ibid., 24.
15. Ibid., 20.
16. Burton-Christie, *Word in the Desert*, 123.
17. Ibid., 124.

Evagrius numbers the capital sins, or passions, as eight, and names them as follows: gluttony, impurity (lust), avarice, sadness (in later times folded into *acedia*), anger, *acedia*, vainglory (i.e., boasting or vanity) and pride; he describes them in chapters 6 through 14 of *The Praktikos*, each chapter consisting of one paragraph. Here then is chapter 12, on the demon of *acedia*, the noonday demon, so named because its attack is so often experienced at midday,[18] to which we may add, in Merton's case, midlife (a point also made by Kathleen Norris[19]), sometimes called by C. G. Jung "the noon of life," the moment when there is still time to make a fundamental change in one's life in the expectation of a good number of years to live out that change:

> The demon of *acedia*—also called the noonday demon—is the one that causes the most serious trouble of all. He presses his attack upon the monk about the fourth hour [10:00 a.m.] and besieges the soul until the eighth hour [2:00 p.m.].[20] First of all he makes it seem that the sun barely moves, if at all, and that the day is fifty hours long. Then he constrains the monk to look constantly out the windows, to walk outside the cell, to gaze carefully at the sun to determine how far it stands from the ninth hour [3:00 p.m., dinnertime], to look now this way and now that to see if perhaps [one of the brethren might appear from his cell]. Then too he instills in the heart of the monk a hatred for the place, a hatred for his very life itself, a hatred for manual labor. He leads him to reflect that charity has departed from among the brethren, that there is no one to give encouragement. Should there be someone at this period who happens to offend him in some way or other, this too the demon uses to contribute further to his hatred. This demon drives him along to desire other sites where he can more easily procure life's necessities, more readily find work and make a real success of himself. He goes on to suggest that, after all, it is not the place that is the basis of pleasing the Lord. God is to be adored everywhere. He joins to these reflections the memory of his dear ones and of his former way of life. He depicts life stretching out for a long period of time, and brings before the mind's eye the toil of the

---

18. Evagrius, *Praktikos*, 26 n. 43.

19. Norris, *Acedia and Me*, 200. See also Carfagna, *Contemplation and Midlife Crisis*, 144–46, where she presents Merton's love relationship as the context of his midlife crisis, whereas it seems to me that his failed attempt to go to Camaldoli, with its many indications of *acedia*, provides a more likely context.

20. Noonday, of course, the time of the apex of the demon's power, occurs exactly in the middle of this four-hour period.

ascetic struggle and, as the saying has it, leaves no leaf unturned to induce the monk to forsake his cell and drop out of the fight. No other demon follows close upon the heels of this one (when he is defeated) but only a state of deep peace and expressible joy arise out of this struggle.[21]

As we shall see later, a good number of the descriptors in this chapter resonate with the internal struggles Merton experienced in his attempts to move to Camaldoli, and later to Latin America.

It was John Cassian (360–435) who transmitted the ascetical theology of Evagrius to the Latin West, although because of accusations of heresy against Evagrius that were beginning to circulate at the time Cassian was writing, he doesn't acknowledge him as the prime source of his work in the *Institutes*, in which he describes what he has learned about monasticism in the Egyptian desert, including his own take on the capital vices, *acedia* chief among them.[22] Cassian was born in Scythia Minor and was bilingual in Greek and Latin. With his friend Germanus, he traveled to Bethlehem, where they lived in a hermitage for three years. From there they went to Egypt, where they met Evagrius. As a result of a theological controversy over the materiality or immateriality of God, they moved to Constantinople. He was not long afterward sent by the patriarch to Rome, where he was invited to found a monastery in Marseilles. He did so, and lived there until his death. Through the influence of his writings on St. Benedict, he has exercised enormous influence on Western monasticism. It is in Book 10 of the *Institutes* that we find his consideration of *acedia*, in which his indebtedness to Evagrius is obvious.

> Our sixth struggle [he has previously dealt with five other capital vices] is [with] what the Greeks call *akedia,* which we can refer to as a wearied or anxious heart. It is akin to sadness and is the peculiar lot of solitaries and a particularly dangerous and frequent foe of those dwelling in the desert. It disturbs the monk especially around the sixth hour [12:00 noon], rushing in upon him like a kind of fever at just this time and inflicting upon the enfeebled soul the most burning heat of its attacks at regular and set intervals. Some of the elders declare that this is the noonday demon that is mentioned in the ninetieth psalm.[23]

---

21. Evagrius, *Praktikos*, 18–19.
22. Cassian, *Institutes*, 219.
23. Ibid.

By identifying the effects of *acedia* with "a wearied or anxious heart," he builds on the meaning of the original Greek term. His reference to "the most burning heat of its attacks" is surely based on the fact that the heat of the desert is at its height at noon, a time of day when a monk, particularly a young one, would be likely to question his decision to embrace the monastic state ("Whose idea was this?" in our contemporary demotic). The need to endure "the burden and heat of the day" (Matt 20:12 KJV) at its height was of course not restricted to monks; but it was much more likely that a monk would question his chosen vocation at this time than that his neighbors, Egyptian peasants, linked by their labor and age-old custom to the land and thereby their lot, would do so. Cassian continues,

> Once [*acedia*] has seized possession of a wretched mind it makes a person horrified at where he is, disgusted with his cell, and also disdainful and contemptuous of the brothers who live with him . . . , as being careless and unspiritual. . . . He groans quite frequently that spending such a long time there is of no profit to him and that he will possess no spiritual fruit for as long as he is attached to that group of people. . . . He makes a great deal of far-off and distant monasteries, describing such places as more suited to progress and more conducive to salvation, and also depicting the fellowship of the brothers there as pleasant and of an utterly spiritual cast. . . . Thereupon he says that he cannot be saved if he remains in that place.[24]

Any reader of Merton's diaries for the years 1952 to 1960 will immediately recognize the ways in which this psycho-spiritual phenomenon appeared in Merton's life. Lawrence S. Cunningham, while he was editing *A Search for Solitude*, Merton's journal for precisely those years, tells us that he stumbled upon these very passages just quoted from Cassian.

> Describing the temptation to *accedia* [*sic*], Cassian (borrowing rather freely from Evagrius . . .) sets out the symptoms of monastic *accedia* (boredom; listlessness) with almost clinical exactitude. The monk begins to feel a "horror of the place where he is" and "disgust with his cell." The same monk begins to "complain that he is making no progress" . . . Finally, he "sings the praises of monasteries located in other places" and concludes that "he cannot get any better as long as he stays in his present place" (*Institutes* 10.2). Ironically, I first read those words while sitting one evening on the porch of Merton's hermitage in Kentucky as the sun slowly went down on a lazy June evening. I

24. Ibid.

> wrote Cassian's words in my journal with the notation: "an exact description of TM in 1959." One must agree that these ancient monastic writers were shrewd students of human psychology and exact observers of human frailty. They seem to intuit that it was not the harshness of the monastic life but its regularity, its sameness, its boundedness, that could enervate a person. In that sameness one could fancy other places, other settings, other people who would add vigor and freshness to the routines of the ordinary monastic round. (SFS, xviii)

I had decided to use *acedia* as a hermeneutic before reading Cunningham's comments, but I am glad to have his confirmation that it was indeed what the ancient writers framed as *acedia* that Merton was struggling with, a hermeneutic that will help us understand what was going on for Merton in those midlife years.

It is to Gregory the Great (540–604, pope from 590) that we owe the revised list of the deadly sins, reduced from eight to seven by folding sadness into *acedia*,[25] vainglory into pride, and adding envy; and it this revised list that Dominican friar and theologian St. Thomas Aquinas (1225–74) used in the *Summa Theologica*.[26] In section 35 of the second part of the second volume of the ST, Aquinas discusses *acedia*, which his translators have rendered, unhelpfully to the contemporary ear, "sloth." In that section he asks and responds to four questions. After considering objections and replying to them in each case, he comes to the following conclusions (my summary):

(1) Is sloth a sin? Yes, sloth is a sin, because it is forbidden in scripture (cf. Sir 6:26).

(2) Is it a special vice? Yes, sloth is a special (i.e., distinct) vice, because Pope Gregory distinguishes it from the other vices.

(3) Is it a mortal sin? Sloth can be both a venial and a mortal sin: venial if it is indulged in the struggle between flesh and spirit, mortal if temptation is yielded to, and becomes sin.

(4) Is it a capital vice? Yes, sloth is a capital vice, that is, one which gives rise to other vices, prompting those who suffer with it to do many things on account of it.

St. Thomas, as we know, has had a massive intellectual impact on Christian philosophy and theology, beginning with his own time and

---

25. Evagrius does make some connections between *acedia* and sadness: *Praktikos*, 17.

26. Thomas Aquinas, *Summa Theologica*, II.ii.35.1–4.

continuing well into our own time, not least through his taxonomy of the deadly sins.[27] We see this influence very soon after St. Thomas' own time in the great *Commedia* of Dante Alighieri (1265–1321), so named by himself, with the honorific *Divina* added by Boccaccio some years later. It is in the *Purgatorio*, the central volume of the *Divine Comedy*, that Dante in three places reflects on *acedia* (IV.13–17, XVII.82–87, XIX.49–51). In Canto IV, he recounts his meeting with his old friend Belacqua, another Florentine, who died sometime between 1299 and 1302, close to the time when Dante began writing, and whom Dante had chided in his lifetime for his indolence. "He shows himself more indolent / than if sloth had been his very sister," says Dante. For "sloth" he uses the word *pigrizia*, "laziness" (IV.111), rather than *accidia*, the Italian form of *acedia*; however, he does use *accidia* later in the poem (XVIII.132) as a term equivalent to *pigrizia*. Belacqua is in ante-purgatory, as he testifies of himself:

> I must wait outside [purgatory] as long as in my lifetime
> the heavens wheeled around me
> while I put off my sighs of penance to the end,
> unless I'm helped by prayers that rise
> from a heart that lives in grace. (IV.13–17)

Dante editor Robert Hollander comments, "His way of phrasing the possibility makes us tend to agree with him that he will do the full term of his sentence, since it seems unlikely that any of *his* friends would seem to be possessed of 'a heart that lives in grace.'"[28]

In Canto XVII, the middle canto of the middle volume of the *Comedy*, and thereby the keystone canto of the whole work, there is a brief exchange between Dante and Virgil just as they reach the fourth terrace of Mount Purgatory. Dante, then:

> Sweet father, tell me, what is the offense
> made clean here in this circle that we've reached?
> If our feet must rest, do not arrest your words.

And Virgil:

> . . . A love of good that falls short
> of its duty is restored here in this place.

---

27. Merton, at Columbia, was strongly impacted by his reading of Thomist philosopher Etienne Gilson's *The Spirit of Medieval Philosophy*, especially by the concept of *aseitas*, which he encountered in that book; that is, the notion that God exists (a word that can be challenged) *a se*, i.e., by Godself, and not contingently, requiring no cause (SSM, 171–75).

28. Dante, *Purgatorio*, 85.

Here the slackened oar is pulled with greater force. (XVII.82–87)

The offense of "the slackened oar," of course, is *acedia*, with which, halfway up the mountain, Dante's treatment of the deadly sins comes to its central moment. Below this terrace are found the vices that begin in the love of what is wrongful; the ones above, beginning with *acedia*, result from insufficient or improper desire to attain the good. Hollander brings St. Thomas (ST I.lxiii.2) into the discussion by referring to his understanding of *acedia* as "a kind of spiritual torpor accompanied by (or even causing) physical weariness."[29] Thus to listlessness, restlessness, and anxiety, we may now add torpor and weariness as dimensions of this central and capital vice.

Geoffrey Chaucer (1343–1400) holds a position in the birth of literature in English similar to the position held by Dante as the father of Italian literature. *The Canterbury Tales* is his best-known work; and it is there, in the Parson's Tale, that we find his discussion of *acedia*, or *accidie*, to use the Middle English spelling.[30] Unlike most of the tales, the Parson's Tale is in prose rather than poetry, and in fact it is not a tale but a sermon on the seven deadly sins. After prefatory statements about penitence and confession, the Parson deals in turn with each of the sins. Following the Thomistic and Dantean order, he relates how pride, envy, and anger precede *accidie*, and how avarice, gluttony, and lust follow it (the last-named with its charming Latin and Middle English equivalents, *luxuria* and *lecherie*). Each sin is dealt with in two sections: the first a general description, the second providing the *remedium contra peccatum* ("remedy for sin"), the remedy against each particular sin in its order. *Accidie*, says the Parson, will make us *hevy, thoghtful and wraw* ("sad, anxious and angry"); envy and anger produce bitterness in the heart, and this bitterness is the mother of *accidie*. The person so afflicted *dooth alle thing with anoy, and with wrawnesse, slaknesse, and excusacioun, and with ydelnesse, and unlust* ("does everything with annoyance, and with anger, slackness, and self-excusing, and with idleness and disinclination").[31] However, there are, as he tells us, remedies. The chief of these is *fortitudo*, the cardinal virtue of strength, magnanimity, and courage, which will enable sinners to resist the demon of *accidie by wit and by resoun and by discrecioun* ("by knowledge and by reason and by discretion"), which

---

29. Ibid., 358. Merton took the title of his autobiography from the seven storeys of Mount Purgatory, each one representing one of the seven deadly sins, of all of which Merton believed himself guilty. *The Divine Comedy* also provided the substructure for Merton's only published novel, *My Argument with the Gestapo*, as Patrick O'Connell explains in "Merton's Earlier *Commedia*."

30. Chaucer, *Complete Works*, 228–65.

31. Ibid., 249.

will strengthen them with *sikernesse* ("assurance") and with *constaunce, that is, stablenesse of corage* ("constancy, that is, stability of courage"). With *fortitudo* must be joined the theological virtues of faith and hope; and with their exercise will sinners find the demon departing from them.[32] As with Evagrius and Cassian, the Parson recommends energetic resistance in the spirit of Jesus in the wilderness or the letter of James: "resist the devil, and he will flee from you" (4:7).

Chronologically, while acknowledging that it is a long leap from Chaucer to Merton, this is where we would look at what Merton himself says about *acedia* in his lectures to the novices when he was novice master between 1955 and 1965. By way of preparation to read what Merton has to say, however, it seems more useful to me, first, to review two later works of related interest, and then to conclude this chapter by returning to what Merton himself has earlier said about *acedia*. The first of these is the widely acclaimed *The Noonday Demon: An Atlas of Depression*, by Andrew Solomon (b. 1963). Solomon tells us that he chose his title "because it describes so exactly what one experiences in depression."[33] Is then *acedia* depression? And was Merton depressed? My answer to the first question is no, that depression is a clinical condition (mental and/or biochemical), whereas *acedia* is a spiritual or perhaps attitudinal condition; and, moreover, that a hermeneutic of *acedia* fits Merton's experience far more exactly than does a diagnosis of clinical depression. My answer to the second question, aided by John Eudes Bamberger, is also no. Bamberger, longtime abbot of the Trappist abbey of the Genesee, in northern New York, is also a psychiatrist. For some time while Merton was master of novices, Bamberger worked with him in regard to their mental health. Having embarked on this exploration of *acedia*, I asked him for clarification on this point, and received this reply:

> Merton was certainly NOT suffering from depression, to judge from his enthusiastic style in teaching us in 1950 [the year that Bamberger arrived at Gethsemani], nor did such a condition outwardly interfere with his formation efforts from 1952–55 [more accurately, 1951–55] when he was Master of Juniors [or

---

32. Ibid., 251. Andrew Solomon has a very bleak view of the Parson's Tale; see *Noonday Demon*, 293–94.

33. I note here an error in transcription in Solomon's *Noonday Demon*, p. 293, where he quotes Ps 90:6 as *ab incrusus* instead of *ab incursu*. A second correction: for *conobia*, note to p. 292 on p. 478, read *cenobia* or *coenobia*. Having offered these tiny corrections, I feel it only fair to acknowledge that Solomon's book, now translated into twenty-four languages, received the 2001 National Book Award, was a finalist for the 2002 Pulitzer Prize, and was included in the *New York Times* list of the one hundred best books of the decade.

Scholastics]. However, I had come across him unexpectedly around 1954 in the woods, when I got the impression that he looked rather sad and preoccupied before he noticed me. He quickly then changed his demeanor and greeted me [in] his usual outgoing friendly way. So at that time he may well have been struggling with some depressive tendencies, but kept them strictly controlled; so they could not have been very serious. Otherwise he gave the impression of being full of energy, kept a ready sense of humor and had a good appetite. Loss of appetite, by the way, commonly accompanies depression. Nor did he show weight loss, another indication, though not invariable. Later, in connection with [his] operation for a cervical disk and the events surrounding his hospital stay [in March 1966], I'd say he had some depressive tendencies that were in part a cause of some of the behavior he displayed at that time.[34]

Bamberger's reference to 1954 suggests to me that Merton may have been struggling, as he says, with the hopes he had (active between 1952 and 1955) of leaving Gethsemani and transferring to Camaldoli, which we will relate in the next chapter. The "events surrounding his hospital stay" in March 1966 refers to the relationship that developed after Merton's operation between himself and M—Margie Smith, the young nurse who cared for him in his immediate postoperative time, a relationship that we will explore in chapter 7.

Back then to Solomon. Even if we do not equate *acedia* with depression, what Solomon has to say about the connection between them is very illuminating. Christianity, he says flatly, "was highly disadvantageous for depressives."[35] Over the centuries after Evagrius and Cassian, St. Augustine was more influential than anyone else through his declaration that what separated human beings from the animals was the gift of reason (we note his influence on Chaucer's reference to reason in the Parson's Tale), and that in consequence, a loss of reason was a mark of divine disfavor. In the monastic subculture out of which and for which Evagrius was writing, on the other hand, all the monks knew that all the other monks were struggling with the same demons with which they were struggling, of which the demon of *acedia* was chief. So there was little likelihood that a particular monk would be singled out or shunned for this reason, as non-monastics were in the post-Augustinian period. In later centuries, and notably in the Renaissance, the term *melancholia* was used to refer to what we now call depression and, given an Augustinian interpretation, was understood as meaning

34. E-mail message to author, January 31, 2013.
35. Solomon, *Noonday Demon*, 292.

that "the melancholic's despair suggested that he was not suffused with joy at the certain knowledge of God's divine love and mercy."[36] Non-monastic Christians of the time, as with Evagrius, would often ascribe melancholia to the possession of a soul by a demon; but because they were not part of a monastic subculture in which a struggle with the demons was an accepted feature, they could, if their demons were not exorcised, be shunned by their Christian neighbors. By the time of the Inquisition, which began with the Dominicans in the thirteenth century, some depressives could even be fined or imprisoned for their malady.

Solomon notes that the word *acedia* seems to have been almost as widely used then as is *depression* today, sharing as it does many of the same symptoms, although the latter is a clinical condition, a disease of the mind and body, whereas the second is an affliction of the soul, an attitudinal rather than a mental disorder—and if not resisted, then (according to the mediaeval writers) a sin. Monks and hermits, as Evagrius teaches, were vulnerable to *acedia* for what today we might call occupational or social reasons: the sameness of the daily routine; the social limitations of living in a controlled environment with the same group of people; and, in the deserts where monasticism originated, the heat and the starkness of the landscape. Kathleen Norris and others would assert that it can also be generated by a perfectionist or absolutist attitude on the part of the sufferer, arising out of the desire to be one with the will of God in all ways. It is from these understandings, according to Solomon, that "the stigma still attached to depression today has grown."[37] The process of the secularization of our understanding of the psyche, particularly through the work of Freud, Solomon asserts, moved society away from a dependence on religious categories in regard to depression, but without shedding the stigma of imperfection (if not sinfulness) and shame that was the legacy of the mediaeval church.

Kathleen Norris (b. 1947) is well known as a lay advocate of the relevance of monastic values to contemporary life. In her *Acedia and Me: A Marriage, Monks, and a Writer's Life*, she offers a very personal exploration of *acedia*, particularly in relation to depression. In integrating her study of *acedia* with the stories of her marriage and her life as a writer, she gives us a kind of case study of *acedia* in the life of someone who, though not a monastic, finds inspiration in contemporary monasticism. She has read all the writers we have considered so far—Evagrius, Cassian, Dante, Aquinas, Chaucer, and Solomon—as well as Merton himself, and integrated their

---

36. Ibid.
37. Ibid., 294.

thinking into her own understanding. Here is how she frames the *acedia*-depression connection:

> While we may find it convenient to regard [*acedia*] as a more primitive word for what we now term depression, the truth is much more complex. Having experienced both conditions, I think it likely that much of the restless boredom, frantic escapism, commitment phobia, and enervating despair that plagues us today is the ancient demon of acedia in modern dress. The boundaries between depression and acedia are notoriously fluid; at the risk of oversimplifying, I would suggest that while depression is an illness treatable by counseling and medication, acedia is a vice that is best countered by spiritual practice and the discipline of prayer.[38]

This of course is precisely what Evagrius recommended in the fourth century. Norris is particularly articulate in her framing of *acedia* as "the noonday demon":

> The desert monks termed acedia "the noonday demon" because the temptation usually struck during the heat of the day, when the monk was hungry and fatigued and susceptible to the suggestion that his commitment to a life of prayer was not worth the effort.... It is risky business to train oneself ... to embrace a daily routine that mirrors eternity in its changelessness.... Under these circumstances acedia's assault is not merely an occupational hazard—it is a given. It is also an interfaith phenomenon. When I asked two Zen Buddhist monks how they defined the boredom that is endemic to monastic life, one replied that as her community was founded by an Anglican, they called it acedia.[39]

It is clear to Norris that *acedia* is a sin if one yields to its temptations, less in a moralistic understanding of sin as a sinful *act* or as a breaking of the law of God than in the contemporary understanding, set forth by Paul Tillich and others, of *sin as separation*—but even so, a sinful state of soul for which those so affected are responsible before God. To the extent that the monks were affected by the demons, they were separated from their true or deep

---

38. Norris, *Acedia and Me*, 3.

39. Ibid., 5–6. The Anglican in the Norris quotation above was Houn Jiyu-Kennett (1924–96), born Peggy Teresa Nancy Kennett, a British roshi most famous for having been the first woman sanctioned by the Soto School of Japan to teach in the West. Having wished to become a priest in the Church of England, she was unable at that time to be ordained because of her gender, and so turned to Buddhism. My thanks to Dave Chang for this information.

selves, from their monastic brothers, and from God. Depression, on the other hand, is not a sin; and this recognition provides another way by which *acedia* and depression may be distinguished. As Norris says, by "treating acedia as a sin, I am not suggesting that people bear responsibility for being overwhelmed by the medical condition diagnosed as depression, which is not a moral failing, but an illness."[40]

Beyond sin or spiritual vice, her taxonomy of *acedia* offers us many perspectives. Susceptibility to *acedia* may be related to a superfluity of zeal,[41] or a compulsive productivity.[42] It can manifest itself as "weariness, despair, ennui, boredom, restlessness, impasse, futility."[43] It is revealing to her that "acedia is a given of monastic life, whereas depression is not,"[44] and that "depression generally has an identifiable and external cause that acedia lacks."[45] She goes ahead to the last writer we shall consider in this chapter, Merton himself, to affirm his intuition that *acedia* is far more insidious than depression, as Merton frames it: it is "the sadness, the disgust with life, which comes from a much deeper source—our inability to get along *with ourselves*."[46] This is virtually Merton's opening statement in his treatment of *acedia* in the lectures he gave to novices on the subject.[47]

These lectures have now been edited by Patrick F. O'Connell, the dean of contemporary Merton scholars, and published in his magisterial edition of *Cassian and the Fathers: Initiation into the Monastic Tradition*. Merton became novice master in October 1955, after the previous novice master was elected abbot of Genesee. As O'Connell comments, there was "an element of unexpectedness and perhaps even risk"[48] in Merton's offer, given his recurring desire to transfer to another order, in which he would, he hoped, find greater solitude than was available to him at Gethsemani. Dom James was ready to accept his offer, on one condition: "I would not want you to be teaching the novices to become Camaldolese or hermits."[49] Merton agreed with this condition, and "pledged to represent fairly and fully the authentic

40. Norris, *Acedia and Me*, 34.
41. Ibid., 96.
42. Ibid., 160.
43. Ibid., 231.
44. Ibid., 143.
45. Ibid., 147.
46. Ibid., 148.
47. Merton, *Cassian and the Fathers* (hereafter IMT 1), 183.
48. IMT 1, xv.
49. Letter of Dom James to Dom Gabriel, October 18, 1955 (TMC).

Cistercian tradition, not an idiosyncratic personal vision"[50] in which preferential treatment would have been given the eremitical life over life in community.

It is clear from the lectures that he kept this promise. They convey his "deep love for and commitment to monastic tradition";[51] however, monastic tradition as understood in its classic formulations by Cassian and the Fathers, and not necessarily as practiced in the Gethsemani of his time. As with Evagrius, the orientation of the lectures was practical rather than academic, focusing on spiritual formation rather than historical information,[52] although Merton also gave the novices abundant historical context. O'Connell finds it initially surprising that Merton in his notes gives more attention to "the less lofty, more pedestrian *Institutes*" (of Cassian) than to his "masterpiece of the contemplative life, the *Conferences*."[53] But he finds this explicable in view of Merton's audience, the novices—newcomers to monastic life with a prime need for training of a practical kind.

To read the lectures at this remove shows us Merton "functioning as an integral and important member of his monastic community"[54]—important, indeed, given that the novice master is the second most important member of the community after the abbot, insofar as to his stewardship, in a very real sense, is entrusted the future of the monastery. The lectures cast substantial light on Merton's exercise of this stewardship, as teacher, novice master, and, not least, monk himself, for certainly the novices saw him as a model of monastic life and commitment. Merton, faithful to his pledge to Dom James, refrained in the lectures from any references that might have alerted the novices to his own struggles with stability. Discussing the signs of *acedia*, for example, he points out to the novices that one of its symptoms, identified centuries earlier by Cassian,[55] is the desire to transfer to other monasteries: "imagining the perfections and advantages of other communities, seeing the drawbacks and deficiencies of our own vocation."[56] O'Connell rightly calls this a "startling assertion (given Merton's own repeated efforts to do just that)"[57]—efforts which he did not share with the novices. Another such irony may be seen in his straightforward affirmation that the will of God is

50. Ibid.
51. IMT 1, xvi.
52. Ibid., xviii–xix.
53. Ibid., xxii.
54. Ibid., xxiii.
55. Cassian, *Institutes*, 219.
56. IMT 1, 189.
57. Ibid., xxxix.

mediated to the monk through the superior understood as the representative of Christ in the monastery, as St. Benedict states in the second chapter of his *Rule*. When we reflect in chapters 3 and 4 on what the Camaldoli correspondence tells us, we will find frequent and strong differences of opinion between Merton and Dom James on just what the will of God is and whether it may be simply said that whatever a superior decides is in accordance with the will of God. Again O'Connell frames this discerningly:

> Considering Merton's own struggles with his own superior, Dom James, one might be inclined to treat such statements as suitable instruction for the novices but not reflective of Merton's own attitudes. . . . But such a reading would be reductivist and overly simplistic. While Merton continued to chafe against what he sometimes saw as arbitrary exercise of authority, and cautioned against a kind of blind obedience that abdicated any role [for himself] in the process of discerning God's will, he was clearly aware of the dangers of self-will, . . . and of the role of obedience in the development of necessary self-discipline.[58]

Having reaffirmed St. Benedict's understanding of obedience, Merton goes on to say that the monk who insists on "running his own life . . . is left to do so by God, and as a result leads a life that is a sterile and laborious succession of projects and anxieties,"[59] a view that Dom James from time to time held of Merton, and that Merton would have been hard-pressed to deny, given his frequent excoriation of himself for this very tendency. Is he then being disingenuous or hypocritical in saying what he says to the novices? No, says O'Connell: he is "preaching to himself as well as to [them],"[60] that is, he is remaining faithful to the pledge he made to Dom James, and even perhaps hoping that the day will come when he himself can practice more fully what he is preaching.

A final and very valuable comment from O'Connell about the value of the conference notes. Most readers of Merton come to him through a reading of his explicitly autobiographical writings, the SSM or one of the journals; O'Connell sees the conference notes as providing a "salutary check against 'over-privileging' the journals."[61] The journals express Merton's immediate feelings, impressions, and judgments; and we are mistaken if we believe that they show us Merton in his authentic fullness. Indeed, an assertion in a journal can frequently be found to have been turned on its head within

58. Ibid., xliii.
59. Ibid., 120.
60. Ibid., xliv.
61. Ibid., xlvi.

The Noonday Demon: *acedia*

a page or two. Thus to the journals the conference notes, as O'Connell says, provide a valuable corrective. "The dialectical relationship between Merton's private and more public statements, including those made to his novice classes, allows for and makes possible a more complex and thus a richer picture of his monastic identity and so of his personal identity."[62]

I have given as much space as I have to contextualize Merton's conference notes because I see it as necessary preparation for encountering what he has to say to the novices about *acedia*. He follows Evagrius' paradigm, meaning that he gives separate treatment[63] to *lype* or *tristitia*, "sadness" in Evagrius, chapter 10,[64] which Gregory the Great integrated with *acedia* in what became the standard list of the deadly sins. He begins his treatment of *acedia* with a comment that Kathleen Norris,[65] as already noted, finds particularly illuminating:

> *Tristitia* seems to be a sadness caused by adversity and trial in social life. [It] comes from lack of peace *with others*. *Acedia* is rather the sadness, the disgust with life, which comes from a much deeper source—our inability to get along with ourselves, our disunion with God.[66]

There was even a special term for a man afflicted with *acedia*: he is an *acediosus*;[67] a female monastic similarly afflicted is an *acediosa*. Merton quotes Cassian[68] as distinguishing two kinds of *acediosi/ae*: those who yield to torpor and sleep, and those who are driven to instability and wandering—surely a category in which Merton might have recognized himself. He follows this with his most substantial description of *acedia*:

> It is a weariness of life itself, . . . a disgust with *everything* which modern psychology might in most cases trace to a kind of neurotic depression. It certainly implies discouragement . . . combined with restlessness and indecision. Acedia is in fact one of the great spiritual diseases of our time. In a sense it is a disease of the best minds. The intellectual elite is faced with despair because it sees the utter hollowness of the world that man has made for himself and sees no hope for an improvement. . . .

---

62. Ibid., xlvi.
63. Ibid., 178–83.
64. Evagrius, *Praktikos*, 17.
65. Norris, *Acedia and Me*, 148.
66. IMT 1, 183.
67. Ibid., 184.
68. Ibid.

> Acedia is the disease which afflicts the whole world, especially the unbelieving world. A Christian knows how to face the disastrous conditions of the world today with sobriety, compassion, without false and shallow exuberance, but with [the] theological [virtue of] hope. In order to do so he must resist the temptation to acedia which has infiltrated even into the heart of man's spirit and of his intellectual life (viz. existentialism).[69]

This is a passage that cries out for deconstruction or exposition. The first point here that requires comment is his linking of *acedia* with depression. His wording is ambiguous. Is he equating acedia with depression? If so, he would find Solomon and Norris disagreeing with him. Or is he saying that modern psychology, not for the most part being aware of *acedia*, will misdiagnose *acedia* as depression? With Norris, he sees *acedia* as culture-wide, even if not so identified. When he speaks of *acedia* being "a disease of the best minds" and an affliction of the "intellectual elite," it is very hard to believe that Merton is not thinking, consciously or otherwise, of himself. In his ponderings about going to Latin America, he regularly refers to his hope that he could have there a ministry to such intellectuals, believers and nonbelievers. Of course, he has been exercising such a ministry for years already, through his correspondence; and it is arguable whether his assertion that *acedia* "especially" afflicts nonbelievers would be sustained by a reading of this correspondence. Again his assertion that Christians know how to deal with the discouragements of contemporary culture is too sweeping. Some Christians do, and he is one who has tried to do so; many do not, or have tried and given up. Finally, it is interesting to note his comment on existentialism. Was he thinking of Sartre and *Nausée*? If so, he might be able to make his case. But he himself was at this time moving steadily in the direction of an existentialist stance. Certainly his admiration for Camus, to whose writings he gave sustained attention in seven of his essays in the 1960s, belies this comment,[70] and I am certain that he would not have stood by it in later years. Later he mentions the noonday demon: ". . . it was the worst around Sext[71] when the hermit was hot, bored and hungry, worn out and disgusted with life and yearning for a bite of food. Here acedia is purely and simply a passion. To feel this is no sin, if we do not consent."[72] This accords with Evagrius' view that all the passions, *acedia* included, arise and take root in us with greater or lesser strength at various moments in our

---

69. Ibid., 185–86.
70. Burton, *More Than Silence*, 103.
71. He means the time of the office of Sext at Gethsemani, currently 12:15 p.m.
72. IMT 1, 187.

lives as we offer them opportunity. *Acedia*, then, is not *by its mere presence* a sin.

This last point—that temptation is not sin, but that only consent, *yielding to the temptation*, constitutes sin—took me back to my childhood and to a children's hymn that we often sang, which I now find offers in its first stanza a compact summary of Evagrian thinking on the spiritual challenge of the desert, and which I cannot resist including in this solemn consideration of monastic spirituality:

> Yield not to temptation, for *yielding* is sin;
> Each victory will help you some other to win;
> Fight manfully onward; dark passions [the *logismoi*!] subdue;
> Look ever to Jesus—He will carry you through.[73]

I find it delightful to think of myself and the other children of that time unwittingly belting out Evagrian sentiments. But alas, this experience has been taken away from contemporary children, because the mainstream churches (at least in Canada) have deleted this hymn from their hymnals, probably as not upbeat enough in our feel-good age.

Merton concludes his teaching on *acedia* with reflections on Cassian's reference to Paul's admonition in 1 Thess 4:11-12: "Let it be your ambition to keep calm and look after your own business, and to work with your hands, as we ordered you, so that you may command the respect of those outside your own number." Here is Merton's exegesis:

> *To be decent and reserved in relations with outsiders*—not thrusting oneself upon them, seeking novelties and flattery—note this temptation of monks. It is so easy to seek out occasions to be with seculars and to hear the news of the world, while being admired and praised by them—taking to oneself all the credit that belongs to the whole monastery.[74]

I find awkward his use of the word "seculars," indicating a dismissive othering of non-monastics, dwellers in "the world" that monks had left behind. It is a distinction that, along with his comment on existentialism, I am convinced would have embarrassed him at a later time, when it had become very clear to him that leaving the world behind when coming into the monastery was an illusion, that monks brought with them their own secularity, their own experience of living at their particular historical moment in a particular society. As for seeking contact with those beyond the monastery,

---

73. Palmer, "Yield Not to Temptation"; italics mine. Palmer was an American Congregationalist minister; the hymn dates from 1868.

74. IMT 1, 190.

this became one of his primary activities, as he sought to connect with intellectuals (and others) in the wider world. I don't see Merton taking to himself "all the credit that belongs to the whole monastery"; but I am aware that there were some of his brothers who *felt* that this is what he was doing. Gethsemani in the present time is careful in its self-presentation to make it clear, without belaboring the point, that there is more to the monastery and its life and history than Thomas Merton, something with which, one trusts, he would have entirely agreed.

As O'Connell points out,[75] there are no direct personal references in the lecture notes. In his discussion of *acedia*, Merton at no point acknowledges that he may have struggled with it. Nor, interestingly, is there a single reference to *acedia* in the indices of his seven journals, nor in the index of the SSM, although I did find one use of the term in his journal of August 10, 1965, when he was preparing to move into the hermitage full time:

> No concentration is required, only *being present*. And also working seriously at all that is to be done—the care of the garden of paradise! By reading, meditation, study, psalmody, manual work, including some fasting, etc. Above all the work of *hope*, not the stupid, relaxed, self-pity of *acedia*. (DWL, 278)[76]

However, as already noted, many aspects of *acedia*, named by the authors whose works we have consulted for this chapter, are easily identifiable in Merton. These we will revisit in chapters 3 and 4 when we explore what I am calling the greater *acedia*, his attempt to move to the ancient monastery of Camaldoli.

---

75. Ibid., xxxix.
76. The editor added the term "sloth" after *acedia*.

2

Thomas Merton: *non finis quaerendi*

Thomas Merton is a writer, to use the language of the Enneagram, who engages the reader head, heart, and gut. Further to the point, he is a human being who was engaged in his own life, head, heart, and gut. He was not a philosopher, nor an abstract or analytic thinker; nor would he have claimed to be a theologian, at least in the systematic sense. Because he regularly dealt with theological matters, he more than once found himself criticized because he did not bring system to what he wrote. But Evagrius would have recognized him as a theologian, because he was a man of prayer, and this for Evagrius was what made a person a theologian. He wasn't in any major sense a novelist, although he did publish one novel, *My Argument with the Gestapo*, and he did write some early novels that he had no luck in getting published. He was certainly a poet, but he did not confine his poetry to those short pieces of very condensed writing that we call poems. His prose, confounding our neat categories, is full of poetry, not only in the sense of those chunks of it that jump out at us as found poems, but in his ability to combine an image with a phrase in a way that activates both sides of our brains. As well as being a poet, he was a gifted essayist, as demonstrated by the recent publication of *Thomas Merton: Selected Essays*.[1] Above all, he was a diarist and a correspondent, one of the great diarists and letter writers of his century, inspired to publish edited versions of his diaries by reading the

---

1 I have cited six of these essays, each from its original volume of publication with the exception of "Notes for a Philosophy of Solitude," *Selected Essays*, 65–85. The others are "From Pilgrimage to Crusade," "Rain and the Rhinoceros," "Day of a Stranger," "The Spiritual Father in the Desert Tradition," and "Final Integration: Toward a 'Monastic Therapy.'"

diaries of Rainer Maria Rilke.[2] His letters under various headings, as with this study, or to particular individuals, continue to be published by scholars and editors. The complete journals have been published in seven volumes, and condensed into one—*The Intimate Merton*. He had mined them while they remained private to himself for what he would include in his autobiography, *The Seven Story Mountain*, and in his edited journals, notably *The Sign of Jonas*, *Conjectures of a Guilty Bystander*, and *A Vow of Conversation*.

Published journals are in fact a particular form of autobiography; I regularly point out to people that the SSM is simply the first volume of his autobiography, not by itself his autobiography *tout entier*. The published journals can then be understood as further installments of his larger autobiographical corpus. Beyond this, as has often been said, everything he wrote had an autobiographical dimension, whether on the surface it so presented itself or not. *New Seeds of Contemplation*, for example, which presents itself not as autobiography, but as an *encheiridion*, or handbook of the inner life, fell open for me when I realized that almost everything he said in that book in the third person could be transposed into the first person singular, when it would then speak to us directly about its author.[3]

And because his writing is so strongly autobiographical, it is personal. It is not simply that from time to time he addresses the reader directly in his writing, but that it possesses qualities of vulnerability, openness, and invitation that bring the reader close to the writer in a very special way. Read Merton long enough—and it may not take very long—and he becomes your personal friend; and so it is as with writings received from a friend, even letters from a friend, that you find you are reading him. He is a seeker, writing for other seekers, as he indicates in the Latin tag with which he ends *The Seven Storey Mountain*: *sit finis libri, non finis quaerendi*—"it's the end of the book, not the end of the seeking." I'm inclined to tweak that a little, and translate it as "it's the end of *this* book: the seeking continues." It's not that he has not found anything; it is simply that he affirms that there is always more to be found.

Finally, he is a spiritual writer; but *spiritual* is a slippery word, and it must be understood in what senses he is a spiritual writer. In the first sense, he is a spiritual theologian, because he deals with spiritual practice and the interior life. In a second sense, he is a "spiritual" writer, because he appeals to many beyond his own Christian community, especially those who describe themselves as "spiritual but not religious." Third, he is a holistic spiritual writer, who understands that spirituality has as much to do

---

2. Mott, *Seven Mountains*, 257.
3. See Grayston, *Development of a Spiritual Theologian*, chapter 2.

with politics and sex as it does with religion (the three topics we used to be told to avoid in polite conversation). Spiritual and physical are not opposing terms; a healthy spirituality includes the physical realities of human life, including the natural order and its other-than-human species. His spirituality is not "spiritualized," that is, restricted to matters identifiably religious or otherworldly. He points to this in "Day of a Stranger": "The spiritual life is something that people worry about when they are so busy with something else they think they ought to be spiritual. Spiritual life is guilt."[4] He might have made this clearer by italicizing the word *spiritual* in these sentences, but his meaning is clear. He has no respect for a bloodless spirituality, one that is less than inclusive of what the Spirit includes, namely, the entire cosmos. Thomas Berry makes the same point when he refuses to use the natural/supernatural dichotomy: there is only one universe, one life, one reality, with of course its inner and outer dimensions.

THE EARLY YEARS

Thomas Merton was born on January 31, 1915, in the enchanting little French town of Prades, a name it shares with five other towns in France. But his is the Prades in the department of Pyrénées-Orientales, in the Roussillon region, and in the Catalan-speaking part of France, something that Merton picked up on when the SSM was translated into Catalan.[5] If you take the milk-run train that runs west out of the coastal city of Perpignan, after forty-five minutes or so it will let you off on the platform which is perhaps half a mile/one kilometer from the center of town. His parents, Owen Merton and Ruth Jenkins Merton, both artists, had come to Prades, half an hour north of the Spanish border, because they had been told that the light for painting there was exceptional, which it is. Here is what he says about his birth in Prades in the opening paragraph of the SSM, a *locus classicus* in the Merton corpus. In brief compass, it is biographical, astrological, psychological, biblical, historical, theological and, not least, geographical.

---

4. Merton, "Day of a Stranger," 217.

5. In a letter to the publisher of the Catalan translation of the SSM, Merton wrote, "You should know that I consider myself, in a sense, a Catalan since I was born in France in the area still known as 'Catalane.' . . . I need no more compensation than to feel through this more united spiritually with a noble and ancient culture and to think that some pious souls may pray for me in the old churches and cathedrals of Catalonia" (*"Honorable Reader,"* 33). The name of the region in French is in fact *Catalogne*, and in Catalan, *Catalunya*: 'Catalane' is the feminine form of the adjective, Catalan.

> On the last day of January 1915, under the sign of the Water Bearer, in a year of a great war, and down in the shadow of some French mountains on the borders of Spain, I came into the world. Free by nature, in the image of God, I was nevertheless the prisoner of my own violence and my own selfishness, in the image of the world into which I was born. That world was the picture of Hell, full of men like myself, loving God and yet hating Him; born to love Him, living instead in fear and hopeless self-contradictory hungers. (SSM, 3)

The Water Bearer—Aquarius, yes; but I have always read this as an oblique pointer to his baptism in 1938 at Corpus Christi Church in Manhattan, an event of profound significance for him (SSM, 216–25). A great war? Indeed, then and for many years afterwards it was called *the* Great War. His view of the infant he was has more of course to do with the young adult he became than with the innocent child born to Owen and Ruth. His doctrine of man, to use an antique phrase, his Christian anthropology, harks back to St. Augustine, and Augustine's formulation of the doctrine of original sin which dominated Christian thinking until well into the twentieth century. It is a sad, even savage view, at this remove, to apply to the newborn infant that he was, or any other child.

Owen was a New Zealander, and thereby a British subject, which gave Merton his official nationality until he became an American citizen in 1951. Ruth was an American, of a family originally from Ohio that had moved to New York. He was born in the house on *Rue du 4ième septembre* (September 4th Street), on which the visitor may now see a plaque that reads, *Ici est né Thomas Merton, écrivain américain* (American writer Thomas Merton was born here). He and his parents lived there for the first eighteen months of his life, then fled the havoc of war-torn Europe for the peace of Long Island, where Ruth's parents lived. There they settled in the community of Flushing, where in 1918 Merton's younger brother, John Paul, was born. His father's religious background was Anglican and carried with it a certain dimension of religious feeling, but with no particular relationship to the community of faith. His mother's background was nondenominationally Protestant, although by the time the Mertons arrived on Long Island, her parents had affiliated with Zion Episcopal Church, in Douglaston; she had also spent some time with the Quakers. Merton had been baptized at Prades, according to the rites of the Church of England (there was a chaplaincy based in nearby Villefranche), but he says, acerbically and melodramatically, "I don't think there was much power, in the waters of the baptism I got in Prades, to ... loose me from the devils that hung like vampires on my soul" (SSM, 5). He was given no particular religious instruction until his father's mother, visiting from New Zealand, taught him the Lord's Prayer, when he was five years old (SSM, 9).

In 1921, when he was six, his mother died; and his account of this in the SSM (14–16) is very moving. He tells us that his father gave him a note from his mother—this was in the days when children didn't visit in hospitals—telling him that she was about to die: "And a tremendous weight of sadness and depression settled on me. It was not the grief of a child . . . [but] had something of the heavy perplexity and gloom of adult grief" (SSM, 14). For the four years following his mother's death, he accompanied his father on painting trips, John Paul being left with the grandparents. Some would call this kind of childhood "unsettled," but Merton describes it as natural, free, and pleasant (SSM, 19), although it involved its own costs, as he later recognized. By 1925 his father had made enough money from painting to return to France; and Tom, then aged ten, went with him. They settled in the charming medieval town of St-Antonin, in the department of Midi-Pyrénées, in the old province of Rouergue, living first in a hotel, and then in an apartment near the center of town. When not painting, Owen Merton spent his time there in building a house for himself and Tom now called the Villa Diane, and located on a quiet street in St-Antonin now called *Chemin Thomas Merton* (Thomas Merton Lane). After a couple of years he was sent to a Protestant boarding school in the nearby city of Montauban, the *Lycée Ingres*, which he hated, and where he was very lonely. Even so, he did well academically. In his first year at the *lycée* he won the English prize—no surprise there; and in the second year, besting all his French fellow students, the French prize. I take this moment to say that Merton's French origin continued to mean a lot to him over the years. He spoke French at native-speaker level, read many French writers, and acted as interpreter at the abbey of Gethsemani for visiting French speakers. He was proud of his French connection, and thereby of his "European sensibilities" (LETTER 33), for which he sometimes stated a preference when comparing them with his American identity. As a Four on the Enneagram, it was one of the factors that made him special in a monastery in rural Kentucky.

In 1929, Tom and his father moved again, this time to England: Owen didn't finish building the house in St-Antonin, and he and Tom never lived there. In England Tom was sent first to Ripley Court, a preparatory school, and then to Oakham, an old "public" school, as the British say—meaning by that what North Americans would mean by private school—a good school of something less than the first rank. He continued there the habit of active reading that had begun as he sat with his father when he was working on the house in St-Antonin, adding Blake, Hopkins, Lawrence, and even Joyce to the list of his favorite authors. Only two years later, his father died of a brain tumor (SSM, 81–85), and Merton, now aged sixteen, was entrusted to his godfather, Tom Bennett, a Harley Street specialist, who looked after his financial interests and facilitated his application to Cambridge University. This was not a good time for Merton; and when his godfather discovered that he had lost his scholarship because of bad grades, and had made one of the household staff in his college residence pregnant, he washed his hands of Merton and sent him packing to the United States and to the care of his grandparents. This was a decisive moment for him; from then on he would live and work in the United States.

COLUMBIA AND FAITH

Living with his grandparents, of whom he was very fond, he went to Columbia University, from which in 1938 he graduated with a BA. He found a mentor there, Mark van Doren, and, significant for his writing career, discovered that he had an enormous capacity for work. The friends he made there—van Doren, Dan Walsh, Bob Lax, Ed Rice, and others—he kept throughout his life. He also made friends with Mahanambrata Brahmachari, the Hindu monk who encouraged him to read St. Augustine's *Confessions* and *The Imitation of Christ* (SSM, 191–98).[6] He lived hard and fast, and brought himself to the edge of a breakdown, which he forestalled by becoming a Roman Catholic. At the same time as he was living hard and fast, he was also reading Gilson, St. John of the Cross, St. Ignatius, and Gerard Manley Hopkins: a corpus of reading that moved him toward membership in the Roman Catholic Church. He was conditionally baptized—conditionally, in case his baptism at Prades had not been valid, something about which many Roman Catholics in that time would have had doubts—on November 16, 1938, at the age of twenty-three (SSM, 216–25). It can be understood not simply as an act of faith, or as a response to his sense of God's call, but also as his way of finding security for himself in a very insecure world, one that less than a year later would find itself engulfed in the second Great War, World War II.

The three years after his baptism were pivotal and transitional. He started an MA on Blake at Columbia and then began to teach English—first at the City College of New York, then at St. Bonaventure College (now University), near Olean, New York. He was also experiencing an increasing desire to live out the meaning of his baptism in a fuller way. This letter of the period to his Columbia friend Ed Rice describes his sense of living a not-yet-fulfilled life.

6. Cf. Harford, *Merton and Friends*, 19–21; Buchanan, "Search for Brahmachari," 11–13.

> I am not physically tired, just filled with a deep, vague, undefined sense of spiritual distress, as if I had a deep wound running inside me and it had to be stanched.... The wound is only another aspect of the fact that we are exiles on this earth. The sense of exile bleeds inside me like a hemorrhage. Always the same wound, whether a sense of sin or of holiness, or of one's own insufficiency....[7]

In a first attempt to stanch the wound, he approached the Franciscans (SSM, 265–66) and was accepted as a member of their next cohort of novices. But he had not told them about his misadventures at Cambridge or his high life at Columbia, and later, in the interest of full disclosure, decided to share these parts of his life with his interviewer, Father Edmund. The revelations were too much for Father Edmund, and he told Merton that he would not be going to the novitiate (SSM, 288–96). There was also a canonical impediment; anyone entering a religious order needed to have been a Roman Catholic for at least two years, and Merton had been baptized less than two years before, a fact that perhaps only came out at this second interview. He was miserable, and concluded in his characteristic all-or-nothing way that this meant that he had no vocation to the religious life. However, in Holy Week of 1941, at the suggestion of his teacher and friend, Dan Walsh, he went on retreat to the flagship Trappist abbey of the United States: Gethsemani, in Kentucky. Here he describes the impact made on him by his first visit to the place that would be his home for twenty-seven years:

> This is the center of America. I had wondered what was holding the country together, what has been keeping the universe from cracking in pieces and falling apart. It is places like this monastery.... This is the only real city in America.... It is an axle around which the whole country blindly turns and knows nothing about it.[8]

Beyond the hyperbole, the message is clear: he has found the hospital where his bleeding can be stanched, and the place where his own personal universe, which before his baptism had been on the point of cracking in pieces and falling apart, could be reconnected to its *axis mundi*, its spiritual center. Returning to St. Bonaventure, he went through a process of discernment involving not only the appeal of Gethsemani but also his interest in the Baroness Catherine de Hueck's Friendship House in Harlem, and his need to deal, in the run-up to the entry of the United States into the war, with the

---

7. Rice, *Man in the Sycamore Tree*, 48.
8. Merton, *Secular Journal*, 167.

selective service administration. It was December 10, 1941, three days after Pearl Harbor, and having received a deferment from the draft board, that he entered Gethsemani, intending thereafter to live life in community with the Cistercians of the Strict Observance, as Brother and then Father Louis, his monastic name.

GETHSEMANI

The abbey of Gethsemani, then under the fatherly direction of Abbot Frederic Dunne, was to become the permanent home that he had never had. It was for him, he then believed, the "one good place,"[9] a place for a fresh start. According to his close associate and sometime confessor and physician, John Eudes Bamberger, for Merton Gethsemani was the context in which he would recognize and work through all the crises of identity and vocation with which his gifts and his desires challenged him: "The Abbey of Gethsemani was the place where he achieved his identity as a man, a monk, a priest, a man of God, a poet and a prophet. For he was all of these, and he grew into them and developed in them in this one place."[10] His life there falls into six identifiable major phases:

> (1) 1941–44: his novitiate—a time of prayer, manual labor, and initiation into the monastic tradition, as well as some writing and translating;
>
> (2) 1944–49: a time of assigned reading, writing, and translation, of his life profession as a monk and his ordination to the priesthood;
>
> (3) 1949–50: the critical time of "sickness" that I shall explore later in this chapter as a possible precursor to his two major periods of *acedia*;
>
> (4) 1951–55: his work of teaching and spiritual direction as Master of Scholastics;
>
> (5) 1955–65: his work of teaching and spiritual direction as Master of Novices—first the choir novices only, later the brother novices as well, after the integration of the two novitiates; and
>
> (6) 1965–68: the final years—the time in the hermitage, his relationship with M, and the journey to Asia.

---

9. Allchin, "Importance of One Good Place," 93.
10. Bamberger, "Homily," 226.

Within this whole stretch of years, it is the third period, the period of "sickness," that stands out, in my view, as critically important. It was a time of tremendous strain and inner upheaval that seems to have been precipitated by two factors in particular. The first of these was occasioned when Merton reached the last of the institutional goals prescribed for him by his membership in a Cistercian community of the forties, ordination to the priesthood, on May 26, 1949, Ascension Day. So what was to follow? All he could see ahead, having made a vow of stability, was monastic life at Gethsemani year following year—life lived within a featureless horizon. This thought takes me to Shelley's great poem "Ozymandias," which ends with these lines: "boundless and bare / The lone and level sands stretch far away." Those boundless and bare sands are the lone and level sands of the Egyptian desert of Evagrius and the other hermits, which in their sameness and featurelessness, as Evagrius intimates, invite the arrival of the demon. Merton was aware of this dynamic, as he indicates in "A Life Free from Care," the address he gave to the novices on the day he entered the hermitage in 1965: "A life that has nothing but a straight line towards the grave . . . is a life of care. . . . But you go into solitude to cast your care upon the Lord."[11] The second factor was the writing of *The Seven Storey Mountain*, published in 1948. This, I conjecture, effected in him a profound *kenosis*, a deep psychic self-emptying. He had poured his entire life into the book: what now was left? Only the daunting and elusive challenge of becoming a saint, which his good friend Robert Lax had some years earlier told him ought to be his goal (SSM, 237–38). He affirms this in *The Sign of Jonas*, linking his becoming a saint with his writerly vocation:

> If I am to be a saint—and there is nothing else that I can think of desiring to be—it seems that I must get there by writing books in a Trappist monastery. If I am to be a saint, I have not only to be a monk, which is what all monks must do to become saints, but I must also put down on paper what I have become. It may sound simple, but it is not an easy vocation. (SJ, 228)[12]

These two factors came together symbolically on the day of his ordination, when his publisher, Robert Giroux, presented him with the 200,000th copy of his autobiography, bound in morocco.[13] Here is how Merton describes what was happening to him in this critical period after his ordination:

11. Merton, "Life Free from Care," 220; cf. 1 Pet 5:7.
12. There is general consensus among readers of Merton that the likelihood of Merton being canonized in the formal sense is slim in the extreme.
13. This copy of the SSM is preserved in the archives of the Thomas Merton Center. In a number of citations, the figure is erroneously given as one hundred thousand; see, for example, Shannon, *Silent Lamp*, 140.

> When the summer of my ordination ended, I found myself face to face with a mystery that was beginning to manifest itself in the depths of my soul and to move me with terror. Do not ask me what it was. I might apologize for it and call it "suffering." The word is not adequate because it suggests physical pain. That is not at all what I mean. It is true that something had begun to affect my health; but whatever happened to my health was only, it seems to me, an effect of this unthinkable thing that had developed in the depths of my being. And again: I have no way of explaining what it was. (SJ, 226)

And then, with the freedom from consistency that any careful reader of Merton soon comes to recognize, and having asserted his inability to explain what is happening to him, he immediately sets about explaining it:

> It was a sort of slow, submarine earthquake which produced strange commotions on the visible, psychological surface of my life. I was summoned to battle with joy and with fear, knowing in every case that the sense of battle was misleading, that my apparent antagonist was only an illusion, and that the whole commotion was simply the effect of something that had already erupted, without my knowing it, in the hidden volcano. (SJ, 226)[14]

A volcano: a mountain with fire in it, a fire that in these months was consuming something of the unfinished emotional business that Merton had accumulated in his psyche. It also had physical ramifications, long stretches of influenza, and even inability to write. Henri Nouwen sees this time in Merton's life, a time of spiritual darkness and confusion that was also a time of physical debility, as both "a period of terrible anxiety and uncertainty" and a "purification which prepared him for a new task," teaching and caring for the scholastics, and later, for the novices. Nouwen borrows the motif used for the title of the journal in which Merton recounts these experiences: "God called Jonas [Jonah] to go to the people, but Jonas fled to solitude until God let him be brought back ... to where his real calling lay."[15] It was a time in which isolation, the false self of solitude, contended with the true solitude in Merton's heart and mind. In entering into the true solitude, and realizing in depth the existential loneliness of every human being, he came to know that he had "entered into a *solitude that is really shared by everyone*. Even though he may be physically alone, the solitary remains united to others and

---

14. His phrase "my apparent antagonist" suggests the personified activity of a demon of some kind.

15. Nouwen, *Pray to Live*, 45–46.

lives in profound solidarity with them. . . . He realizes that he is one with them in the peril and anguish of their common solitude."[16] A handwritten note to Dom James, written in the middle of this period (June 1950, TMC), testifies to the depth and darkness of this time:

> Things are pretty dark. I feel as if I had a hole burnt out of my heart. My soul is empty. . . . I am less troubled when Jesus gives me solitude and silence. The hole in my heart doesn't upset me so much when I can sit still. The Liturgy fills me with trouble and fear unless I just take it negatively in blind faith, knowing Jesus is acting on me with His love through it all. . . . Please pray for me and bless me.

And yet, as Merton reflects elsewhere in *Jonas*, "there is a return from solitude" (SJ, 261).[17] The solitary does not wall himself up in a solipsistic aloneness, but having found in the true solitude compassion both for himself and for others, he returns to the human community. So sickness had taken him into solitude, and solitude had returned him to health. For, as he says,

> in the depth of this abysmal testing and disintegration of my spirit, in December 1950, I suddenly discovered new moral resources, a spring of new life, a peace and happiness that I had never known before and which subsisted in the face of nameless, interior terror. . . . As time went on, the peace grew and the terror vanished. It was the peace that was real, and the terror that was an illusion. (SJ, 226)[18]

So was this a time of depression? The abrupt way in which it came to an end in December 1950 might suggest that. John Eudes Bamberger says that he never knew Merton to be depressed; but this time of difficulty began before Bamberger arrived at Gethemani. Was it then some kind of breakdown? Merton does use that word in his journal entry of October 22, 1952, a month after his first letter to Camaldoli: "Since my retreat I have been having another one of those nervous breakdowns. The same old familiar business . . . since the old days in 1936, when I thought I was going to crack up on the Long Island Railroad, and the more recent one since ordination. And now this" (SFS, 20). Or is it better understood as a precursor to the major attacks of *acedia* that he experienced in relation to Camaldoli and Latin America? What signs would Evagrius and his spiritual descendants have noticed in

---

16. Merton, *Disputed Questions*, 146–47.

17. A comment of particular interest when we recognize that it was written in the early part of this difficult period.

18. "[N]ameless, interior terror"—another reference to the "antagonist."

Merton's own account of what was happening? I have already mentioned the apparent featurelessness of the future that stretched out before him with no identifiable goals ahead except that of being a saint. Cassian would have remarked on his wearied or anxious heart. Solomon would have noted Merton's listlessness and wondered about the limitations placed on his psyche by the prospect of living for the rest of his life in a controlled environment with the same group of people. Norris would have identified his tendency to ennui and impasse. Evagrius again would probably have identified Merton's "apparent antagonist" as without doubt the very demon of *acedia*, an illusion, to be sure, when brought up against the reality of Christ, but very real otherwise; and he would have commended Merton for engaging in spiritual warfare, especially with fear, which his condition demanded. It seems that although Merton's struggle of 1949–50 did not last as long as the two later attacks, and though it did not involve the many others whom Merton pulled into his struggle at those times, it provides us with sufficient evidence to consider it as recognizably akin to those later struggles.

MASTER OF SCHOLASTICS, MASTER OF NOVICES

At the abbot's request, Merton had started giving occasional lectures to the novices in November 1949. In mid-1951, observing that Merton was once again in good mental and moral shape, Dom James asked him to take on the newly created position of Master of Scholastics, an office that he held until 1955. We can see a certain turning toward the world in this time of return from solitude, first of all in Merton's needing to pay attention to the needs of the scholastics, leaving him much less time to obsess over his own difficulties; and then as time went on, an even larger turning, in his new interest in and concern for the world which he had mistakenly thought he had left in 1941. The great moment of realization in this regard was the Louisville epiphany of March 18, 1958, during his time as Master of Novices:

> In Louisville, at the corner of Fourth and Walnut [now Muhammad Ali], in the center of the shopping district, I was suddenly overwhelmed with the realization that I loved all those people, that they were mine and I theirs.... It was like waking from a dream of separateness, of spurious self-isolation in a special world, the world of renunciation and supposed holiness.... This sense of liberation from an illusory difference was such a relief and such a joy to me that I almost laughed out loud. And I suppose my happiness could have taken form in the words: "Thank

God, thank God that I *am* like other men, that I am only a man among others." To think that for sixteen or seventeen years I have been taking seriously this pure illusion that is implicit in so much of our monastic thinking.[19]

Everyone who reads Merton pauses over these words; and everyone who writes at any length about Merton will refer to them. This is the moment when Merton turns 180 degrees, so to speak, from a focus on the monastery to a focus on the world *as seen from the monastery*. He saw in this moment that he had been thinking for years that the monastery was a world of its own, a world of renunciation, separateness, and "supposed" holiness. There is some truth in this; but as he vividly realizes, to make it the whole truth is to enter into illusion. Under this illusion, monks are one species of being, the rest of us another species. Now he realizes that *to be a human being is primary, to be a monk secondary* to so foundational a reality. To be a monk is to be someone "special," he had thought, and not to be a monk is to be "ordinary." Now he realizes that the most special thing one can be is to know oneself as and so to be—ordinary.

Merton completed his term as Master of Scholastics in 1955, the same year in which he was so vigorously attempting to leave Gethsemani for Camaldoli, as we will read in chapters 3 and 4, and in the letters. In the fall of 1955, the dream of Camaldoli gone, he became Master of Novices, holding that office until 1965. His work as Master of Novices had a profound effect on him, compelling him to focus not only on his own solitude but also on the solitude of others, and on his attitude to the monastery and its abbot. In 1963 he says this:

> The work is hard, though I am doing more than I probably should, in my concern to be well prepared. But also realize the limitations of anything short of prayer and abandonment, as preparation. . . . Hence in everything I have come to feel more than ever my need for grace. . . . Never has this been so clear to me.
>
> . . . In consequence my attitude toward the monastery changes. They [the novices] have need of me and I have need of them. . . . It is an existential situation which God has willed for me, and it is part of His Providence. . . . I must simply obey God, and this reaches out into everything. . . .
>
> In this new condition my attitude toward the abbot is changing. Of course it is obvious that my complaints and discontent have been absurd. . . . He is what he is, and he means well, and in

---

19. Merton, *Conjectures*, 156–57. Cf. the original of this in SFS, 181–82.

fact does well. He is the superior destined for me in God's Providence, and it is absurd for me to complain. No harm will ever come to me through him—it *cannot*. How could I have thought otherwise? (TTW, 288–89)

Earlier he had testified to the impact his work was having on him when in the preface to *New Seeds of Contemplation* (1962), his major revision of *Seeds of Contemplation* (1949),[20] he says that its writing

> has been no less solitary than the first: but the author's solitude has been modified by contact with other solitudes; with the loneliness, the simplicity, the perplexity of novices and scholastics of his monastic community; with the loneliness of people outside any monastery; with the loneliness of people outside the Church.[21]

His years as novice master (1955–65) overlap the years of his attempt (1957–60) to go to Latin America, which we will discuss in chapter 6. Somehow he managed to do his work to the satisfaction both of the novices and of the abbot, and simultaneously to put a lot of energy into attempts to leave Gethsemani and the work in the novitiate, as well as continuing with his writing. He both loved the novices and wanted to be somewhere else.

ZILBOORG[22]

Early in his tenure as Master of Novices, Merton became interested in psychoanalysis. He read widely in the field, and in 1956 wrote a draft for an essay, "Neurosis in the Monastic Life," which he sent out to various friends for their feedback.[23] One copy went via Naomi Burton, his longtime literary agent, to Gregory Zilboorg, a New York analyst of wide reputation.[24] Zilboorg was unimpressed with the essay, which he regarded as amateurish, but even so wanted to meet Merton. An opportunity arose when Dom James, who was having his own anxieties about Merton and about the novices who were leaving Gethsemani for psychological reasons, learned that Zilboorg

---

20. *Seeds of Contemplation* was first published in March 1949; a revised edition was published in December of the same year. See Grayston, *Development of a Spiritual Theologian*, 64–113.

21. Merton, *New Seeds*, x.

22. Gregory Zilboorg (1890–1959), psychiatrist and historian of psychiatry.

23. Merton, "The Neurotic Personality in the Monastic Life," 3–19. Cf. Mott, *Seven Mountains*, 290.

24. Mott, *Seven Mountains*, 290–99; Shannon, *Silent Lamp*, 172.

had been booked to speak at a two-week workshop on psychiatry and the religious life, in July 1956, at St. John's University in Collegeville, Minnesota. This was also the location of a Benedictine abbey, where Merton and John Eudes Bamberger, who accompanied him, could be housed, and where they would be able to join the Benedictines in their offering of daily prayer. Dom James was to join them for the second week of the workshop. Merton made notes on the lectures, and in their first personal conversation,[25] Zilboorg told Merton, in sum, that he was a neurotic and a narcissist and that his desire for the hermit life was pathological. Merton, it would seem from his account, was entirely ready to believe anything negative about himself, especially when it came from an authoritative if not authoritarian personality such as Zilboorg; he had already, in fact, in a letter to Naomi Burton (March 3, 1956), spoken of his "own neurosis [as] so old and so well entrenched."[26] In a later letter to Naomi, written while he was at the workshop, he says that he sees Zilboorg as "the first one who has really shown conclusively that he knows exactly what is cooking."[27] This comment of Zilboorg—"You and Fr. Eudes can very easily become a pair of semi-psychotic quacks" (SFS, 59)—faithfully represents the tone of Zilboorg's dressing-down of Merton. In a second conversation with Merton, at which Dom James was present, Zilboorg repeated his critique of Merton: "You want a hermitage in Times Square with a large sign over it saying 'HERMIT.'"[28] This reduced Merton to tears of rage and embarrassment. It was entirely unprofessional on Zilboorg's part, as Glenn Crider makes clear in his "Editor's Note" prefatory to David Belcastro's article "Praying the Questions: Merton of Times Square, Last of the Urban Hermits."[29] So far from Zilboorg's comments being any kind of professional analysis of Merton, Crider says that their meeting at St. John's "likely amounts to little more than a clash between two high-profile figures who were unwilling or unable to dialogue about their vastly different worldviews."[30] Michael Mott calls this second conversation "the most damaging ten minutes [for him] since [Merton] had left the world for the monastery."[31] David Belcastro's 2007 article offers a brilliant riff on Zilboorg's comment, wondering what might have happened if Zilboorg, instead of accusing Merton of various pathologies, had simply said, "Ah, I

25. There is a full account of this in SFS, 55–60.
26. Merton, WF, 131.
27. Mott, *Seven Mountains*, 296.
28. Ibid., 297.
29. Belcastro, "Praying the Questions," 123–24.
30. Crider, "Editor's Note," 124.
31. Mott, *Seven Mountains*, 297.

see you as a hermit in Times Square. What an odd image, Merton. What are you to make of it?"[32] Belcastro then goes on to bring together the urban, and indeed urbane, side of Merton with his eremitical side, placing Merton in the tradition of Clement of Alexandria, also an urban hermit.

Dom James, however, found the whole experience illuminating, as he relates to Dom Gabriel Sortais, the abbot general (September 4, 1956, TMC). Somewhat simplistically, he says that "Father Louis definitely has some very serious neurosis. In fact, that is the explanation for all his occasional upsets and crises he has been going through the last several years, and pulling the rest of us along with him." "The rest of us," yes—Dom James himself chief among those so pulled. Zilboorg he describes as "wonderful," and at first he was inclined to agree to Zilboorg's suggestion that Merton go to him in New York for a five-day-a-week analysis for three months, which, Zilboorg told Dom James, and which Dom James relayed to Dom Gabriel, would be all the time he would need to "make a new man out of him," or, more ominously, "make him or break him":

> The Doctor told me that Father Louis is a very difficult case because of his terrific mind. . . . He had Father crying from the tremendous punch behind his penetrating remarks. . . . "You would probably want a hermitage in the midst of the *Place de l'Etoile* [in Paris] with neon signs announcing the fact to all the world. Here sits Father Louis the hermit."

It is to smile, as the French would say, to run across this variant reading of the location of Merton's imagined urban hermitage. Was it there because Zilboorg actually said it or because Dom James thought it would help Dom Gabriel understand what Zilboorg was saying? Merton's journal makes no reference to Times Square; Mott does mention Times Square, but without a source reference; Shannon follows Mott in referring to Times Square, as does David Belcastro in his article; and Dom James, in a letter written two years later to Riccardo Lombardi, SJ, does cite Zilboorg as having said Times Square (August 4, 1958, TMC). Our estimation of Merton will not of course hang on where his never-to-exist urban hermitage was to be located; but the two locations together, New York and Paris, neatly represent both the American and European dimensions of his identity, to which he will later refer (LETTER 33).

It is beyond my comprehension, given Zilboorg's public excoriation of Merton, that they stayed in touch, but they did. They corresponded, and Zilboorg came to see Merton at the end of December at Gethsemani.

---

32. Belcastro, "Praying the Questions," 129.

Zilboorg's plan that Merton should spend time with him in New York was finally vetoed by Dom James. But the encounter did have two positive outcomes. Merton, on behalf of the novices, and on his own behalf, made contact with a psychiatrist in Louisville, James Wygal, whom Zilboorg had recommended and with whom Merton became good friends; and John Eudes, already a physician, was commissioned by Dom James to qualify as a psychiatrist for the benefit of the abbey, particularly the novices.

The question of Merton's relationship with Zilboorg, and the relevance of Zilboorg's assessment of Merton, came up again around the time of the refusal of Merton's request for exclaustration to go to Mexico. Merton told Dom Gregorio Lemercier, prior of the monastery in Cuernavaca to which he hoped to go, in a letter of December 17, 1959 (TMC) that John Eudes believed that Dom James had told his colleagues in Rome at the time of his visit there in November 1959 what Zilboorg had said about Merton's desire for eremitical solitude: namely, that it was pathological. Later, however, as he told French theologian Jean Daniélou in a letter of April 21, 1960, he had received a letter from Cardinal Larraona, secretary of the Sacred Congregation for Religious, in which he assured Merton that the Zilboorg incident had not come up in the discussion in the Sacred Congregation about Merton's 1959 request for an indult. "So there my suspicions overshot the mark. Meanwhile I have consulted the psychiatrist in Louisville[33] who tells me that I am not neurotic and that my problem here in the monastery is quite a natural reaction to the situation" (HGL, 134–35).

Reading this I am conscious once again of an uncomfortable feeling that Merton, in his insecurity, even with a tendency to self-laceration, is once again accepting as gospel whatever he has heard in his last conversation with someone to whom he grants some kind of authority. Zilboorg tells him he's neurotic, and he accepts this; later James Wygal tells him he is not neurotic, and he accepts this. It will be some time yet before Merton comes into full possession of his own soul.

CAMALDOLI AND AFTER

In chapter 3 we trace the narrative that the letters offer us for the years from 1952 to 1956, his attempt to go to Camaldoli. Chapters 4 and 5 will offer some exegesis and exposition on the letters of the Camaldoli Correspondence. In chapter 6 we will follow him as he tries once again to leave Gethsemani, this time seeking a place in Latin America. This brings us through the refusal of his request for an indult to move there, to the end of 1959 and

33. James Wygal.

the beginning of 1960. After that, he had about eight and a half years left: the first five and a half devoted to his work as Master of Novices, the last three in the hermitage. They were years of vital creativity. It was in those years that he wrote the passionate letters published so many years later as the *Cold War Letters*.[34] He also published *New Seeds of Contemplation*, his thoroughgoing, Zen-influenced revision of *Seeds*, and a dozen other books.[35] It was also the time that he fell in love, with M, the nurse he met in the hospital in Louisville in March 1966. That very significant relationship we will consider in chapter 7, in which we will follow his struggle to remain faithful to his longtime vocation to solitude and at the same time to understand and honor what he had found with M. After that tumultuous time, only two years remained to him in the hermitage, which, much as he loved it, he was finding less and less conducive to real solitude. So when his new abbot, Dom Flavian Burns, elected in January 1968, permitted him to accept an invitation from Jean Leclercq to go to a monastic conference in Thailand in December, he began to prepare for that trip by searching out possibilities, with the abbot's encouragement, for a new location for his hermitage in California and Alaska, and even to consider the possibility of finding it on another continent. Having accepted this invitation, Merton then arranged an itinerary by which he could visit a number of Asian monasteries and religious centers, and meet religious practitioners of many faiths, notably the Dalai Lama and Chadral Rinpoche. As he left for Asia, he said this: "I am going home, to the home where I have never been in this body."[36] And so it was in Asia, many thousands of miles from Gethsemani, yet still in a monastic setting, and thereby still "at home," that Thomas Merton died accidentally on December 10, 1968, twenty-seven years to the day from the date on which he had entered Gethsemani and there begun his monastic journey.[37]

FINAL INTEGRATION

By way of a "big picture" look at the life and importance of Thomas Merton, let me refer to a review essay that he wrote in 1968 on the book by Iranian psychiatrist Reza Arasteh that I mentioned in the Introduction, *Final Integration in the Adult Personality*. Merton particularly liked the book because

34. Merton, *Cold War Letters*, published forty-five years after they were written.
35. Burton, *Merton Vade Mecum*, 43–133.
36. Merton, *Asian Journal*, 5.
37. Ibid., 344–47, for the letter written to Dom Flavian by some of Merton's fellow attendees at the conference.

it integrated the goals of psychotherapy with a reference to Sufi mystical attainment, the Sufis being the mystical cohort within Islam. By including the word *monastic* in the title of his article ("Final Integration: Toward a 'Monastic Therapy'"), he was pointing toward what he thought should be the result of the vow of *conversio morum* (literally, "conversion of morals or mores," that is, of ongoing transformation) taken at solemn profession, one he had taken himself: the journey to the true self, liberation, transformation, rebirth, "the final and complete maturing of the human psyche on a transcultural level."[38] Speaking out of his experience as novice master, he asserted that people were "called to the monastic life so that they [might] grow and be transformed, 'reborn' to a new and more complete identity, and to a more profoundly fruitful existence in peace, in wisdom, in creativity, in love."[39] In his experience, however, the institutional monasticism of which he was a part was often less than conducive to this kind of growth. Some novices, discovering this, would leave to look for other contexts in which it might be possible. Others, "the mildly neurotic," would stay and adjust themselves to the institution, "nestling fearfully in the protection of the monastery,"[40] hoping that further and painful growth would not be demanded of them. What then, he wanted to know, would be that "final integration" to which psychoanayst, Sufi practitioner, and Christian monk could all commit themselves? He answers his own question with a description of the finally integrated "man":

> Final integration is a state of transcultural maturity far beyond mere social adjustment, which always implies partiality and compromise. The man who is "fully born" has an entirely "inner experience of life." He apprehends his life fully and wholly from an inner ground that is at once more universal than the empirical ego and yet entirely his own. He is in a certain sense "cosmic" and "universal man." He has attained a deeper, fuller identity than that of his limited ego-self which is only a fragment of his being. He is in a certain sense identified with everybody; or in the familiar language of the New Testament . . . he is "all things to all men."[41] He is able to experience their joys and sufferings as his own, without however becoming dominated by them. He has attained to a deep inner freedom—the Freedom of the Spirit we read of in the New Testament.[42]

38. Merton, "Final Integration," 222.
39. Ibid., 221–22.
40. Ibid., 224.
41. Cf. 1 Cor 9:22.
42. Ibid., 225; cf. John 3:1–12.

There are many resonances in this passage with what we will read in chapter 6 about Merton's understanding of solitude: the inner ground, the journey beyond the ego-self to the true self, the identification with all people, the freedom of the spirit. I wonder, as the reader may already have done, to what extent, when Merton wrote those words, he was aware that he was describing himself, or, more modestly, describing his own spiritual *telos*. With the last sentence, he is pointing us toward a much older reference to rebirth, the conversation between Jesus and Jewish elder Nicodemus, in which Jesus says to him, "You must be born from above. The wind blows where it chooses, and you hear the sound of it, but you do not know where it comes from or where it goes. So it is with everyone who is born of the Spirit" (John 3:7–8). Perhaps this emphasis in Merton is why so many conservative evangelical Christians give major credit to him for nudging them toward faith, toward their becoming "born-again" Christians.[43]

Even so, he asserted that this experience was not limited to Christians. Applying to others the passage I have just applied to Merton himself, he found a fascinating transcultural and transreligious parallel in Arasteh's description of what Sufis call *fana* and *baqa*. *Fana* is annihilation or spiritual disintegration; *baqa* is reintegration and new life on a totally different level. The passage from *fana* to *baqa* is one that involves a terrifying interior solitude and an "existential moratorium," a crisis and an anguish beyond analysis or intellectualization. In sum, it is an experience of disintegration, existential moratorium and reintegration on a higher, indeed, universal level: and here of course I think of Merton's "breakdown" and recovery described earlier in this chapter. According to Merton, the risen ones in every tradition can recognize each other (cf. his visit with Thich Nhat Hanh or Chadral Rinpoche), because the finally integrated person, while retaining all that is best in his or her own culture, can become a transcultural person, "able to bring perspective, liberty and spontaneity into the lives of others."[44] In philosopher Ken Wilber's intriguing expression, he or she is able to "include and transcend." In his conclusion to *Silent Lamp*, his biography of Merton, William H. Shannon also discusses Merton's review of Arasteh, and then asks whether Merton did achieve final integration as he has described it, concluding that it would be presumptuous of him (and if for him, dean as he then was of Merton scholars, then certainly for the rest of us) to try to answer the question in any definitive way. But he does say that "final integration was the direction in which Merton was always moving in the

---

43. Cf. Lovelace, *Dynamics of Spiritual Life*, 17.
44. Merton, "Final Integration," 226.

real journey of life that is interior and [in] 'an ever greater surrender to the creative action of love and grace in our hearts.'"⁴⁵

In more specifically Christian language, in a book of some seven years earlier, Merton speaks more personally about this "creative action of love and grace":

> If I allow the Holy Spirit to work in me, if I allow Christ to use my heart in order to love my brother with it, I will soon find that Christ loving in me and through me has brought to light Christ in my brother.... This, then, is the mystery of Christ manifesting Himself in the love which no longer regards my brother as an object or a thing, which no longer treats him merely as a friend or associate, but sees in him the same Lord who is the life of my own soul.⁴⁶

If we put these two passages together, taking them as lenses through which we can refract a holistic image of Merton, we see him as a Christian who has become a transcultural and transreligious spiritual teacher. Along with Thich Nhat Hanh, the Dalai Lama, and Leonard Cohen, each so different from the others, he has burst the bonds of cultural and religious constraint and become a spiritual teacher honored both by the religious and the non-religious.⁴⁷ He is prophet and poet, monk and writer, marginal man and trickster, cloistered hermit and public intellectual, solitary and lover, teacher and disciple.

2015: the centenary of Merton's birth. The occasion has generated many ideas for books, papers, exhibitions, workshops, and so on; and my colleagues who work in the Merton industry will like me have toiled on some aspect of the great man's significance for the edification of others. Their experience, I trust, will parallel my own, which is that in keeping company with Thomas Merton and his friends, we find ourselves members of a community of hope, faith, insight, and challenge.⁴⁸

---

45. Shannon, *Silent Lamp*, 288.

46. Merton, *Disputed Questions*, 126.

47. For my view that Leonard Cohen belongs in this august cohort, see my "'Monastic in His [Own] Way': Thomas Merton and Leonard Cohen," 3–9.

48. The commemorative volume produced for the Merton centenary gathers together some one hundred testimonials from members of this virtual community: Henry and Montaldo, *We Are Already One: Thomas Merton's Message of Hope*.

For myself, I acknowledge that at some point in this journey, Merton shifted from being simply the object of academic study to being my spiritual director *in absentia*. I realized that I had taken his major concerns—contemplation, war and peace, and the engagement in transforming depth with the world's great religious traditions—as together comprising a paradigm for my walk as a Christian, for my pastoral and academic work, and for my understanding of our world in this time of "the great turning" (Joanna Macy's term). My sense of him is that when he died in 1968, he was operating from about 2050. We still have a long way to go to catch up with him.

I give the second last word here to Ed Rice: "Merton was part of the great Catholic tradition and yet seemed not to be confined by it.... Thomas Merton never left us. The journey goes on."[49] And I give the last word in this chapter to Merton himself, the phrase mentioned earlier that he put at the end of *The Seven Storey Mountain*: *sit finis libri, non finis quaerendi* ("the book is finished, the seeking goes on")—for him and for all of us.

---

49. Quoted in Harford, *Merton and Friends*, 217.

The Camaldoli Correspondence

CAMALDOLI BEFORE THE LETTERS

Merton first became aware of Camaldoli in Lent 1941. He was planning to spend Holy Week at Gethsemani, and by way of preparation looked up the Trappists in the *Catholic Encyclopedia*. Here is his recollection of this in the SSM. "I found out that the Trappists were Cistercians, and then, in looking up Cistercians, I also came across the Carthusians, and a great big picture of the hermitages of the Camaldolese" (316). This simple statement is followed in the SSM by three pages of rhapsodic prose, of the variety commonly called purple. The Carthusians and the Camaldolese, says Merton,

> were free from the burden of the flesh's tyranny . . . were poor, had nothing, and therefore they were free and possessed everything. . . . Everything about them was simple and primitive and poor. . . . [They had] concealed themselves in the Secret of [Christ's] Face. . . . [These] hidden men had come so close to God in their hiddenness that they no longer saw anyone but Him (316–17).

William Shannon, who sets out in *Silent Lamp* (147–52) a full chronology of Merton's Carthusian temptations, brings the matter to a more sober level: "It is a marvelous, paradisal description of a monastic ideal, but hardly a description of actual monastic life lived by monks made of flesh and blood."[1] The rhapsody in the SSM concludes with this dramatic statement:

> I had to slam the book shut on the picture of Camaldoli and the bearded hermits standing in the stone street of cells, and I went out of the library [at St. Bonaventure], trying to stamp out the

1. Shannon, *Silent Lamp*, 147.

> embers that had broken into flame, there, for an instant, within me. (318)

Stamp out the embers, yes, because at this point he could not bring himself to believe that he could have a vocation even to the priesthood, let alone the privilege of the eremitical life of the Camaldolese and the Carthusians.

In these early years, it was the Carthusians rather than the Camaldolese who captured his imagination. His attraction to them continued, at different levels of temptation, from 1941 to 1955. Had not the war prevented his entering a European charterhouse (there were none in the United States until 1951), he would, as he admitted to his novice master on one occasion, have chosen the Carthusians over the Trappists. As he quotes himself saying to his novice master, "I have always liked the Carthusians. In fact if I had had a chance I would have entered the Charterhouse rather than coming here [to Gethsemani]. But the war made that impossible" (SSM, 383)—to which the novice master, in the best tradition of Trappist founder Armand-Jean de Rancé, replied that among the Carthusians Merton would not have found the emphasis on penance that characterized Trappist life (SSM, 384). What he says about the Carthusians and the war also applies to the Camaldolese, because until 1958 there were no Camaldolese houses in the United States. This Carthusian attraction came and went, flaring up notably when he learned in 1947 that Thomas Verner Moore, for many years a Benedictine, and conductor of a retreat for the Gethsemani community in 1945, had become a Carthusian, as Dom Pablo Maria, in the Charterhouse of Miraflores, in Spain. "The dog!" says Merton. "When I went to him with my [vocational] problem [at the retreat], he told me, 'Oh no, you don't want to be a Carthusian'" (ES, 98). Later, as LETTERS 15 and 18 indicate, Moore gave Merton a more sympathetic response. However, as *The Sign of Jonas* narrates, and as Merton says in a letter of April 14, 1954, to Dom Gabriel, it was while writing that book that he "could see for [himself] that [he] was not made to be a Carthusian" (SJ, 74).

This is not to say that his attraction during these years to the life of *solitude* was any less strong; and Dom James, understanding this, and also adamantly opposed to his transferring to the Carthusians or the Camaldolese, perceptively and pastorally gave him a number of opportunities within the common life of Gethsemani to find something of the solitude that he sought. Simultaneously with his Carthusian flare-ups, however, came regular moments of attraction to the tradition of Camaldoli. This, then, from January 7, 1947:

> We had a wild Epiphany [January 6]. First, the devils were trying to mess me up yesterday afternoon. I could not pray at first, and

then a lot of highly suspicious "graces" came along. I had a series of big, spurious lights about becoming a Camaldolese hermit. Finally I went to confession and got straightened out. (ES, 35)

A more realistic comment about the Camaldolese than the rhapsody in his autobiography appears in his journal entry of October 19, 1947. Most of the SSM was written before 1947, but it was not published until 1948; and yet Merton was not moved to temper its rhapsodic character with the realism expressed in this journal entry:

> One thing about the eremitic life, it is hard. St. Peter Damian is always talking about conversion from the free and easy life of monasteries to the "narrow way" [cf. Matt 7:14] of the hermitage.... And then I think of how easy things are for me, the soft straw mattress, nice warm clothes, cooking done for you.... Anyway I am pretty sure I could never lead the life the first Camaldolese led, fasting four or five times a week on bread and water and reciting two psalters a day ... and going barefoot all winter in the Appennines! (ES, 126).

The first Camaldolese: but perhaps, although he doesn't say so, we can infer that he would have considered the life of the contemporary Camaldolese quite bearable, once they came inside, of course, from standing out in the snow in the stone street of the cells. In December 1949, by contrast, comes this statement of peaceful acceptance of his life at Gethsemani, where by now he has made life vows and been ordained to the priesthood:

> I am happy—perfectly happy to be a Cistercian—not a Carmelite or Carthusian or Camaldolese, but a Cistercian—and sit in the top of a barn with more beautiful stove pipes and strawberry boxes and lovelier old junk than a Carthusian ever saw....
> (ES, 380)

But the eremitical itch continued; and he continued to scratch it, revealing it, beginning in 1950, to his friend Jean Leclercq. Leclercq agrees with Merton that where the cenobitic life is real, it will generate eremitical vocations:

> The solution for such vocations is nearly always to move to an eremus [a hermit community], a charterhouse, or the eremi of the Camaldoli [sic: not the English plural], that I know for sure.... I can quite understand that your Abbot would like you to find a solution within the Cistercian life.[2]

---

2. Merton and Leclercq, *Survival or Prophecy?*, 18.

And so it finally proved, when in 1965 Merton was authorized by Dom James to live as a hermit in the little house originally built for ecumenical conversations, which he christened St. Mary of Carmel, surely on the understanding that the original Palestinian Carmelites were hermits, and not friars, as they later became.

The last sixteen months before he wrote his first letter to Camaldoli, in September 1952, saw two notable moments in Merton's journey. The first of these was his ready acceptance of the May 1951 decision of Dom Louis de Gonzague le Pennuen, abbot of Melleray, in France, and father immediate and visitor of Gethsemani, that he should relinquish his time in the woods by himself, granted to him two years earlier by Dom James. It is characteristic of Merton, and testimony to Dom James' characterization of him, surprising to many, as the most obedient monk in the monastery, that when he was presented with an authoritative decision rather than simply a negative opinion, which is how he understood many of Dom James' responses to his requests, he accepted it wholeheartedly—as with the two refusals of his requests to the Sacred Congregation for Religious, in 1955 for a *transitus* to Camaldoli, and in 1959 for an indult of exclaustration that would have permitted him to go to Cuernavaca. Here is his reflection on this decision of Dom Louis:

> I was surprised how little it cost me to accept Dom Louis' decision—almost nothing at all.... Only twenty-four hours later did I realize the implications of this easy acceptance. I was sitting in the refectory . . . when I was suddenly overwhelmed with the conviction that, if I had given up the woods so easily, it must be because I love God. (ES, 457)

Manifestly this is a deeper response to the decision than looking for a silver lining in a dark cloud. Dom James, in a letter of February 5, 1952 (TMC), reported Merton's "easy acceptance" to Dom Louis, who replied on February 10 that Merton had made a good impression on him during his visit of the previous May, notably through his respect for the directives of his superiors.

The second major shift in Merton's life at Gethsemani came when Dom James, in June 1951, only a month after Dom Louis' visitation and decision, appointed Merton as Master of Scholastics. Again seeking the deeper meaning of a decision, Merton says this: "now I know that the reason why I had to resist the temptation to become a Carthusian was in order to learn how to help all the other ones who would be one way or another tempted to leave the monastery" (ES, 459). Yes, a Carthusian, or, we may add, a Camaldolese. This conviction, however, had worn very thin by August 1952, the month before Merton wrote LETTER 1, when he wrote, in a handwritten note (TMC) to Dom James after a day of recollection, that he was convinced, as he says,

> that I must seriously turn my face toward the solitude God desires for me, whatever it may be. I am not made for the active life and it does me no good. I must give myself to God and follow him into the desert [cf. Matt 4:1–11]—even if it be only interior. I believe he wants me to be a kind of pioneer of solitude and silence in our Order, if it be at all possible. . . . I know you will support and guide me in my desire to seek any way that can bring me closer to God.

Indeed, Dom James did support and guide him, although not always in the ways he most fervently desired; and indeed, Merton did become "a kind of pioneer of solitude and silence" in his Cistercian order. How that began to happen over the next three and a half years is what the letters set before us, and to the reading of those letters we now turn.

CHRONOLOGY OF THE LETTERS AND APPENDICES

The Letters

LETTER 1 / Merton to Giabbani, September 11, 1952—*not extant*

LETTER 2 / Giabbani to Merton, September 1952—*not extant*

LETTER 3 / Merton to Giabbani, December 25, 1952
    I write to you this time in French . . .

LETTER 4 / Giabbani to Merton, Easter 1953—*not extant*

LETTER 5 / Merton to Giabbani, May 4, 1953
    It was a pleasure for me to receive your letter just after Easter . . .

LETTER 6 / Giabbani to Merton, September–October 1953—*not extant*

LETTER 7 / Merton to Giabbani, November 6, 1953
    I am embarrassed when I consider how much time has passed . . .

LETTER 8 / Giabbani to Merton, January 21, 1954
    I enclose the information requested about our houses . . .

LETTER 9 / Merton to Giabbani, December 20, 1954
    You have perhaps asked yourself if I have forgotten you . . .

LETTER 10 / Merton to Giabbani, January 10, 1955
    I have just finished the text I spoke to you about.

LETTER 11 / Giabbani to Merton, January 24, 1955
    I read your two letters with pleasure . . .

LETTER 12 / Merton to Giabbani, February 9, 1955
    I am sending you under separate cover . . .

LETTER 13 / Giabbani to Merton, April 10, 1955
    In these past days I have prayed for you again . . .

LETTER 14 / Giabbani to Merton, April–May 1955—*not extant*

LETTER 15 / Merton to Moore, April 25, 1955
    When our former Fr Alberic went to Sky Farm . . .

LETTER 16 / Merton to Montini, April 25, 1955
    It is some time since I have had the honor . . .

LETTER 17 / Merton to Giabbani, around April 25, 1955—*not extant*

LETTER 18 / Moore to Merton, April 29, 1955
    I received your letter yesterday a little before Vespers . . .

LETTER 19 / Steinke to Giabbani, May 3, 1955
   Not knowing at all the usages of your holy Order . . .

LETTER 20 / Merton to Giabbani, May 3, 1955
   St Romuald and St Peter Damian are here . . .

LETTER 21 / Merton to Giabbani, May 6, 1955 . . .

LETTER 22 / Merton to Giabbani, May 10, 1955
   Thanks with all my heart for your fine letter from Stapehill . . .

LETTER 23 / Fox to Montini, May 16, 1955
   This is the first letter I have ever written to you . . .

LETTER 24 / Merton to Giabbani, May 17, 1955
   Here is another letter. Forgive me.

LETTER 25 / Giabbani to Merton, May 17–28, 1955—*not extant*

LETTER 26 / Merton to Giabbani, May 28, 1955
   Thank you for your letter . . .

LETTER 27 / Montini to Merton, August 20, 1955
   I am writing to you after so much delay . . .

LETTER 28 / Montini to Fox, August 20, 1955
   Taking advantage of a moment's quiet today . . .

LETTER 29 / Montini to Giabbani, August 21, 1955
   I find it my duty to inform you that Father Merton wrote to me . . .

LETTER 30 / Merton to Larraona, August 24, 1955
   Although I know that you are the busiest man in the Roman Curia . . .

LETTER 31 / Giabbani to Montini, August 24, 1955
   Your letter, written with your usual goodness of spirit . . .

LETTER 32 / Larraona to Merton, September 26, 1955
   I was not in Rome when Your Reverence's letter of August 24 arrived . . .

LETTER 33 / Merton to Montini, October 1, 1955
   Your Excellency's long and wise letter . . .

LETTER 34 / Merton to Sortais, October 18, 1955
   I thank you for your good letter from Citeaux.

LETTER 35 / Fox to Montini, October 20, 1955
   We have just returned from our General Chapter in Europe.

LETTER 36 / Merton to Giabbani, March 24, 1956
   Once again I have obtained permission to write a word to you . . .

The Appendices

Appendix 1

Brief descriptions of the Camaldolese houses of Montegiove, Fonte Avellana, San Gregorio al Celio, and Montecorona; sent with the letter of January 24, 1954, from Giabbani to Merton.

Appendix 2

Certificate of authentification of relics of St. Romuald and St. Peter Damian, dated March 13, 1955, from Giabbani to Merton.

THE WRITERS AND RECIPIENTS OF THE LETTERS / *DRAMATIS PERSONAE*

Thomas Merton, OCSO (1915–68)

James Fox, OCSO (1896–1987)

James Fox arrived at Gethsemani in 1927, having previously been a Passionist priest. Elected abbot in 1948, and with a strong business orientation, he discovered that the abbey's finances were not healthy. For the sake of the finances, he commissioned factories to produce cheese and bourbon-laced fruitcake (a fudge factory came some years later). He also mechanized the agricultural work of the abbey—all changes that Merton found very hard to take because of the noise. It is arguable that *contra* Merton's frequent complaints, Dom James was, as many have said, Merton's best friend. His term as abbot ended in 1968, after which he, as Merton, became a hermit on the abbey grounds.

Anselmo Giabbani, OSBCam (1908–2004)

It was to Anselmo Giabbani that Merton wrote in September 1952 when he began his quest to leave Gethsemani for another monastery with a stronger tradition of solitude. Giabbani entered the Order of Camaldoli in 1924, becoming procurator general of the Order in 1945, and from 1951 to 1963 prior of Camaldoli itself, and thereby prior general of the Order. He was a major influence in the renewal of the Order, responsible for the revision of its Constitutions, for starting its journal, *Vita Monastica*, and for initiating an American foundation. In 1957 he visited the United States, and is primarily responsible for founding Immaculate Heart Hermitage in Big Sur, California. For forty years he was the confessor and spiritual director of Sister Nazarena, an American-born recluse who lived with the Camaldolese sisters of Sant' Antonio in Rome.

Arcadio Larraona y Saralegui, CMF (1887–1973)

Born in Navarra, in Spain, Arcadio Larraona entered the Congregation of the Missionary Sons of the Immaculate Heart of Mary, the Claretians, at the age of twelve. Ordained to the priesthood in 1911, he studied in Rome, where he later taught Roman law. In 1929, he began to work with the Sacred Congregation of Religious, of which he became Secretary in 1949, becoming Prefect in 1962. In 1961, John XXIII named him cardinal.

Giovanni Battista Montini (1897–1978)

Born in Lombardy, he was ordained in 1920, later earning a doctorate in Canon Law. In 1922 he began his work in the Vatican's Secretariat of State, where from 1944 to 1954 he was, with Domenico Tardini, co-Secretary of State. In 1954 he was appointed archbishop of Milan by Pius XII, and cardinal in 1958 by John XXIII. Elected pope in 1963, he took the name of Paul VI. He was responsible for many reforms and the encouragement of ecumenical and interfaith relations. Most controversial was his promulgation of the encyclical *Humanae Vitae*, in 1968, in which he announced that he would not accept the recommendation of the commission he had appointed that contraception be accepted in the Roman Catholic Church. He was beatified by Pope Francis on October 19, 2014.

Pablo Maria, OCart / Thomas Verner Moore (1877–1969)

Born in Louisville, Kentucky, Thomas Verner Moore was ordained to the priesthood in 1901, as a member of the Paulist order. He later studied medicine and became a psychiatrist. In 1923, looking for a more monastic identity, he became a Benedictine. He founded St. Anselm's Abbey in Washington DC, and taught at The Catholic University of America. Retiring from CUA in 1947, he entered the Carthusian order at Miraflores, in Spain, under the name of Pablo Maria. The first American Carthusian, he founded the first American charterhouse in 1951, in Vermont. For reasons of health, he returned to Miraflores in 1961, living there until his death.

Gabriel Sortais OCSO (1902–63)

Born in Bellevue, near Versailles, André Sortais entered the Trappist-Cistercian abbey of Bellefontaine in 1924, being elected abbot in 1935. He volunteered as a chaplain during World War II, returning to Bellefontaine in 1941, after the defeat of France. Elected abbot general of the Cistercian Order in 1951, he held the office until his death in 1963.

Anselm (Joseph) Steinke (1925–20??)

Anselm Steinke (after leaving the Trappists he was again known by his birthname, Joseph) was prior of Gethsemani and only thirty years old at the time of the writing of LETTER 19, very young to have been given the position of prior. Two months later, he was sent by Gethsemani to a new foundation, New Clairvaux, in Vina, California, as founding superior. When at its first abbatial election he was not elected abbot, he left the Trappists and became a diocesan priest. In 1963 he left the active priesthood as a result of his disagreement with the Vatican's position on birth control. Later he taught philosophy at Ohlone College in Fremont, California. A registered letter sent in 2014 to his last known address was returned, marked "unclaimed"; but since he is not listed in the Social Security Death Index, it may be that he is in a care facility.

THE LANGUAGES OF THE LETTERS AND APPENDICES

Five languages are represented in the letters and documents of the correspondence: Italian, French, English, Spanish, and Latin. Of the thirty-six letters, seven are not extant. Six of these, all in Italian, were written from Giabbani to Merton; one, in French, from Merton to Giabbani. Of the twenty-nine extant letters, eight were in Italian. Three of these went from Giabbani to Merton; three from Montini to Merton, Fox, and Giabbani, respectively; one from Giabbani to Montini; and one from Larraona to Merton. Appendix 1, the account of the Camaldolese houses, was also written in Italian. Of the letters in French, all were written by Merton: eleven were addressed to Giabbani, and one each to Larraona and Sortais. Merton and

Moore of course corresponded in English. Both Merton and Fox wrote two letters to Montini in English, and Merton one to Giabbani. Steinke wrote one letter, in English, which is extant only in Italian and has been translated back into English. Spanish appears in only one letter, that of Cardinal Larraona to Merton (LETTER 32), in three proverbial sayings; and Latin in Appendix 2, the certificate of authentication of the relics of St. Romuald and St. Peter Damian, and in a number of Latin phrases in the letters.

How fluent, then, was Merton in the languages of the correspondence? For a sense of this, I turn to Virginia Bear's marvelous article on Merton's linguistic capacities.[3] In that article, she rates Merton's facility in a number of languages according to the ILR scale—the Interagency Language Roundtable, developed by the United States Foreign Service Institute. Using this scale, and without of course being able to test Merton directly, she rates his proficiency in Italian as 3–4, that is, somewhere between professional working proficiency and full professional proficiency. His education in Italian began at Oakham School with his purchase of *Hugo's Italian Self-Taught*, from which he worked on a few verbs in the waiting room of the hospital where his father lay gravely ill.[4] At Cambridge, he studied Dante—"the one great benefit I got out of Cambridge"[5]—and one of the moments when I have felt closest to Thomas Merton was when I held in my hands at the Merton Center in Louisville the edition of Dante that he had used at Cambridge. So we may take it that his Italian was entirely adequate for a letter to Giabbani. Even so, and after having received Giabbani's reply, also in Italian, he wrote in French, in which he had more facility than in Italian (with the exception of LETTER 5, written in English). Virginia Bear rates his French as at level 5 (native or bilingual proficiency).[6] Born in France, he spoke French with the accent of Toulouse; studied French in school from the age of ten; and in his second year at the Lycée Ingres in Montauban won the annual French prize, winning out over all his French-born fellow students. In later years he interpreted for French-speaking monastics who visited Gethsemani, and "routinely corrected the printer's proofs of the French translations of his works."[7] Bear makes the interesting point that although his handwritten letters in French included all the diacritical marks, his typewritten letters

---

3. Bear, "Woodshed Full of French Angels," 136–54.

4. SSM, 90, quoted in ibid., 145.

5. SSM, 135, quoted in Bear, "Woodshed Full of French Angels," 146. Later Merton reports reading Dante's *Paradiso*, in the original Italian, while recovering from an appendectomy: SSM, 303.

6. Bear, "Woodshed Full of French Angels," 149.

7. Ibid., 150.

rarely exhibit them—omitted by reason of the speed with which he wrote, the fact that none of his assisting typists knew French very well, and also by the lack of a properly equipped typewriter.[8] He continued to the end of his life as an interpreter for French speakers, notably at the conference in Thailand at which he died.[9] She rates Merton's proficiency in Spanish as between levels 4 and 5, full professional proficiency and native or bilingual proficiency, second only to his fluency in French.[10] He began his study of Spanish at Columbia and put it to good use during his visit to Cuba in 1940. His appreciation of Spanish was an idealized one that parallels his idealization of Cuba as an integrally "Catholic" culture very unlike the religiously heterogeneous United States; here is what he says about it in *The Seven Storey Mountain*:

> After Latin, it seems to me there is no language so fitted for prayer and talk about God as Spanish: for it is a language at once strong and supple.... It has some of the intellectuality of French but not the coldness that intellectuality gets in French: and it never overflows into the feminine melodies of Italian. Spanish is never a weak language, never sloppy, even on the lips of a woman. (SSM, 306)

Bear somewhat protectively relegates the offensive last seven words of this sentence to a footnote in her article.[11] It was one of the statements in the SSM that if pointed out to him in later years would have certainly elicited an expression of regret. He used his Spanish with Spanish-speaking novices and interpreted for Spanish-speaking visitors. When Cardinal Larraona (see LETTERS 30 and 32) came to Gethsemani, he preached in Italian, and Merton interpreted for him; but when they had private conversations, they spoke Spanish (SFS, 10–11). Some of his translations of Latin American poets have in fact become standard textbook translations.

Latin, of course, is the language of Heaven, as Merton suggests in his comment about Spanish; although I have heard the same claim made for Welsh, which would also have appealed to Merton.[12] Bear gives him a 5 in Latin, native or bilingual fluency. He took part daily in the Latin liturgy at

---

8. Ibid., 151.

9. Ibid.

10. Ibid., 147.

11. Ibid., 148. Its offensiveness evokes his comment about "the sensual dreams of the Sufis," in the first edition of *Seeds of Contemplation*, 87, which he excised in later editions.

12. "It is the Welsh in me that counts: that is what does the strange things and writes the books, and drives me into the woods." Merton, *Conjectures*, 200.

Gethsemani from 1941, when he entered, to 1966, when the abbey switched to the vernacular, a change that did not please him.[13] It was when he was a child at school in England that he began to study Latin, and he tutored in Latin when he was at Columbia. He made a number of translations from Latin into English, notably his translation of *The Solitary Life: A Letter of Guigo 5th Prior of the Grande Chartreuse*. In the correspondence, only Appendix 2, the certificate of authentication of the relics of St. Romuald and St. Peter Damian, is entirely in Latin; Merton, in addition, regularly uses Latin phrases in the letters.

I am happy to take Virginia Bear's conclusion about Merton's linguistic facility as my own: ". . . though his adult life was ultimately spent within the confines of a monastery, Merton's life journey, facilitated by his multilingual abilities, was paradoxically most far-reaching when he stayed in one place."[14] Which, as we read through the letters, we will find was what most of his correspondents were trying to tell him he ought to do.

ORTHOGRAPHY AND THE NOTES

Merton's use of capitalization, punctuation, and italicization is inconsistent. Sometimes he will write "Superiors," other times "superiors." Sometimes he italicizes words not in English (mostly Latin), other times he doesn't. I have left these words as he wrote them. Everything in italics is Merton's, unless I have marked an italicization with "italics mine." I have corrected simple typos, but have marked the occurrence of unusual or misplaced words with [*sic*].

Some of the information in the notes is repeated elsewhere in the book. However, at the risk of repetition, I have included it there so that readers will not have to search the book for specific information about a person or situation mentioned in the letters.

---

13. Bear, "Woodshed Full of French Angels," 152.
14. Ibid., 154.

LETTER 1 / *Merton to Giabbani*

This first letter in the series is not extant. It was written, in Italian,[1] on September 11, 1952, as evidenced by Merton's statement in his journal entry of September 13: "First letter was to Camaldoli and I didn't feel so great about it" (SFS, 15).[2] It would have contained statements of Merton's interest in the hermit life, of his hopes for greater solitude; and it may also have directly asked Anselmo Giabbani if he could be accepted at Camaldoli in the *eremo*, the village of hermits associated with the cenobitic community there.

1. See LETTER 3, note 1.
2. The other two letters he wrote at the same time were to Dom Humphrey Pawsey, superior of the very new Carthusian foundation in Vermont, and to Dom Jean-Baptiste Porion, prior general of the Carthusians in Rome.

Letter 2 / *Giabbani to Merton*

This second letter in the series is also not extant. It was written, certainly in Italian, sometime in September 1952—Merton refers to it in Letter 3 as "your good letter of September." He received it on October 10, as again he records in his journal:

> Today, I got a letter from Dom Anselmo Gabbiani,[1] Prior of the Sacro Eremo, at Camaldoli. It was the best yet.[2] Very simply, said I could come if I wished and start right out as a hermit—everything about it seemed just as it should be....[3]

This was exactly what Merton wanted to hear. "Its contents," says Merton in Letter 3, "brought me joy and peace"[4]—and encouraged him to continue the correspondence in the face of strong opposition to the project from his abbot, Dom James Fox.

---

1. For Gabbiani, read Giabbani.

2. Here he refers to the replies he had earlier received from the two Carthusians (Letter 1, note 2). Dom Humphrey "told me to come to Vermont and talk it over." "Dom Porion said it would be difficult to be received into a Charterhouse, but that he would put in a good word to the General [i.e., the Cistercian abbot general], if I wished. He strongly recommended [my] going to *Camaldoli* in preference to the Chartreuse [the Carthusian motherhouse, in France], but strongest of all was his recommendation to stay where I am and abandon myself completely into the hands of God" (SFS, 19).

3. Ibid.

4. Although in his journal he also says that, given the abbot's opposition, he remained "both certain and uncertain" (ibid., 20).

Letter 3 / Merton to Giabbani: handwritten, in French, trans. DG; original at Camaldoli.

OUR LADY OF GETHSEMANI
Trappist-Cistercian Abbey
TRAPPIST, KENTUCKY

Christmas Day, 1952

Right Reverend and dear Father,

I write to you this time in French,[1] because I do not know whether you read French or English more easily. I do not dare write to you again in Italian, because I would make too many mistakes. Forgive me for having taken so long to reply to your good letter of September.[2] I confess to you that its contents brought me joy and peace. If I had the power to follow the leadings of my heart, I would want to join you soon at Arezzo [the city nearest to Camaldoli]. I am convinced that your life would suit me perfectly, especially if it matches [what is said in] the beautiful pages of your book *L'Eremo*,[3] of which I have just read the section on the eremitical life with the greatest attention. Yes, a truly contemplative life is lived there, totally consecrated to God, without the "monastic vanity" which suffocates souls in the cenobitic life, in which one must submit oneself, at whatever cost, to a kind of liturgical autocracy which, I admit, suits the majority of monks very well, but which cuts off the spiritual breath of those souls whom God calls to simplicity and solitude. O my father, I have an immense need for that silence, for that *quies*[4] in which the soul rests, unmoving, in the obscurity of an immense and simple activity which is God himself, communicated to the soul by the ineffable light of the Word and in the embrace of the Holy Spirit. I am worn out by the intense activism of the life of a writer, of a spiritual director, of a cenobite subjected to the demands of a timetable full of movement and activity which is more or less external.[5]

    1. His first letter to Giabbani was in Italian.
    2. LETTER 2, not extant.
    3. Giabbani, *L'eremo: Vita e spiritualità eremitica nel monastero camaldolese primitivo*.
    4. A prayerful and nonverbal resting in God.
    5. Cf. Merton's comment in the SSM, 389: "it seems to me that our monasteries

It is true that my superiors here have made many concessions to me. There is a little hermitage in the woods[6] to which I have permission to retreat for several hours each day, while remaining a cenobite and subjecting myself to the very heavy responsibility of supervising our forty students in theology and philosophy.[7] I admit to you that this apostolate has its consolations, but it uses up all my spiritual energies. I am *not made* for this. Overwork has made me sick, and my spiritual directors advise me to look for a life which is truly contemplative and solitary. Of course my superiors are opposed to this. Truly, I would like to be able to submit myself entirely to their decisions, but with all the good will in the world I am unable to do so. It is always there, a call to the true solitude which makes me lift my eyes to the *interiora deserti* ["the inner realities of the desert"]. This call is becoming stronger and stronger. I must reckon with the fact that it is unlikely that I will be able to stay here unless I receive permission to live completely as a hermit—which is again very unlikely

Only one thing worries me. Father Paul Philippe, OP,[8] in Rome, has advised me not to leave America. But I would be ready to leave this country if I believed that I could find a real hermitage somewhere else. Again this question: [should I try to live] the hermit life in an order or, rather, completely independently? It seems to me that this last choice would take more strength than I have. I would be safer in a truly monastic context, living under a rule.

Right Reverend Father, I hope that I am completely clear on this point. I am seeking a truly solitary life because of my *misery* and my *poverty*. I especially need to be alone because the apostolic life *is too much for my strength*, and the active life of the cenobium deprives me of a real interior life.

If I need solitude, it's because I need to *be nothing*, to disappear, to be completely obscure and forgotten—*tamquam purgamenta huius mundi*

---

produce very few pure contemplatives. The life is too active. There is too much movement, too much to do. That is especially true of Gethsemani."

6. This was a former tool shed that Merton was permitted to use from time to time. He christened it "St Anne's." See Mott, *Seven Mountains*, 274, 311; SFS, 29–30, 32–34, 36.

7. He refers here to his work as Master of Scholastics from 1951 to 1955. Cf. Anselm Steinke's comments on this in LETTER 19.

8. French Dominican priest, whom Merton had met when he visited Gethsemani; he was later made an archbishop and secretary of the Vatican's Congregation for Religious. See Merton, WF, 221–23, 225, 228, 229, 279, 307.

["like the rubbish of the world."][9] I am fearfully ashamed of the stupid public image which is attached to the name of Thomas Merton![10]

Will you send me your constitutions so that I may acquaint myself with your life as it presently is? I will write to you again about the possibility of an American foundation. I believe it is *necessary*. We need you.

Pray for me, dear Father. I have prayed for you and for all your solitaries this morning at my three masses.[11]

Your very unworthy little brother in Our Lord and Our Lady,

[Signed] F. M.[12] Louis

---

9. 1 Cor 4:13 (Vulgate and NRSV).

10. Cf. Merton's comment in the SSM, 412: "my double, my shadow, my enemy, Thomas Merton, the old man of the sea. . . . If he suggests books about the Order, his suggestions are heard. If he thinks up poems to be printed and published, his thoughts are listened to. There seems to be no reason why he should not write for magazines."

11. The traditional three masses (midnight, dawn, and morning) of Christmas, the day on which he is writing.

12. For *Frater* ("Brother") and *Maria,* which he had taken as part of his monastic name in honor of the Virgin Mary, as did all Trappist monks.

Letter 4 / Giabbani to Merton

Again, this letter is not extant. We know that it was written, again presumably in Italian, around Easter 1953: in LETTER 5, Merton says that it was "a pleasure for me to receive your letter just after Easter..." In it, again according to LETTER 5, Giabbani asked Merton to send him "a word concerning the prospects of a Camaldolese foundation in the U.S."

LETTER 5 / *Merton to Giabbani: typewritten, in English; original at Camaldoli.*

OUR LADY OF GETHSEMANI
Trappist-Cistercian Abbey
TRAPPIST, KENTUCKY
May 4, 1953

Rt Rev Dom Anselmo Giabbani, OSB.[1]
Prior of Camaldoli.

Dear Father in Christ:

It was a pleasure for me to receive your letter just after Easter,[2] reminding me of my promise to send you a word concerning the prospects of a Camaldolese foundation in the U.S.[3] I am writing this in English still ignorant whether you prefer me to write in English or French.[4]

I have not yet received the copy of your constitutions, but perhaps on the general knowledge I have of the Camaldolese life I can make the following remarks.

1) Much depends on what would be your source of revenue. It would be quite easy for a monastery of contemplatives to support itself here with a big retreat house, or several retreat houses which could be largely staffed by family brothers or secular employees and would not interfere too much with the peace of the hermits—as at Camaldoli the retreat house could be far distant from the hermitages.[5] You could also easily support yourself with parishes, provided that did not interfere too much with the peace of the

---

1. For "Order of St. Benedict," of which the Camaldolese form a branch.

2. LETTER 4, not extant.

3. This came to be in 1958, when Immaculate Heart Hermitage, also called New Camaldoli, was established in California.

4. This is the only letter Merton wrote to Giabbani in English. There is no written evidence that Giabbani ever answered the question directly, unless he attached a note to the missive (LETTER 6) he sent to Merton sometime between the writing of this letter and November, when Merton wrote to him again (LETTER 7). In any case, all the rest of Merton's letters to Giabbani were written in French.

5. At Camaldoli, the very large retreat house, or *foresteria*, is part of the monastery, opening on the main street of the very small village of Camaldoli itself. The *eremo*, or hermits' village, higher in the mountains, is at some distance from the monastery—three to seven kilometers, depending on the route taken.

eremo. No doubt you have a way of handling the problem of parishes. But in this country parish work is far more intense and absorbing than it is in Italy, I believe. And there is much more effort wasted in sheer useless noise—to raise money. I would suggest that if any begging were undertaken here it should be done with great discretion, not that it would not be easy to get quick results by American publicity methods, handled cleverly. But these are most inadvisable in the case of a contemplative Order. What is at stake is not the existence of a particular monastery but the purity of the contemplative ideal. There is a fervent minority in America seeking the very purest ideal of the contemplative life in all its simplicity and poverty—the true simplicity and humility of St Benedict, which is actually so incompatible with the spirit of secular life in America. The purity of this ideal can be stained by the slightest faux pas which would take us into the mire of materialism which is present everywhere, and I believe that if Camaldoli comes here, you should do so determined not to abandon the most perfect simplicity of ancient monasticism and to protect yourself against many unsuspected invasions by the noise and bustling business spirit[6] of America. For this, I assume that the best thing would be to have one or two very big benefactors who would launch the whole foundation.

2) One of the dangers you might have to guard against would be a too rapid expansion, assuming that you got off to a good start. It would be well to plan only *one* eremo and choose vocations with extreme care, being very difficult in selecting them. It would not be advisable to take men directly from the monastic Orders of America into the eremo without a novitiate, with the sole exception of the Trappists, for we do have a true monastic cenobitic life. The Benedictines here are not at all the same as in Europe and they do not have a real monastic life, except in a few new foundations which are planning to return more closely to the simplicity of the primitive observance.[7] I don't think you would have much difficulty in obtaining vocations. You do not need large numbers, especially in the hermitage, and the popularity of the contemplative life here is now at its height.

3) As to a book by Thomas Merton—I have neither the time nor the material to write a full-length volume on the Camaldolese ideal but it is possible that I might obtain permission to produce a short booklet. My suggestion is that the burden of your message should be presented in pictures. If you can provide a hundred good photographs of Camaldolese life against

---

6. I.e., like Gethsemani under Dom James.

7. Such as Mount Savior, in Elmira, New York, or Christ in the Desert, at Abiquiu, New Mexico.

the beautiful background of your mountain forest,[8] all that will be needed from me will be about fifty pages of text. I do not say I have received permission to do such a work, and it would have to wait a while in any case. But perhaps I could obtain this permission.[9] Meanwhile I would be grateful to receive any books that clarify your life and spirituality, in addition to L'Eremo which I already have and admire. I need especially to have a clear idea of the daily life as it is led today. I have your *Annales*, and therefore all the sources of your tradition, together with St Peter Damian[10] in Migne.[11]

4) A good friend of our monastery, Mrs Clare Booth [sic] Luce, has just been appointed American Ambassador to Italy.[12] I think she might possibly be able to help you and I have mentioned your cause to her. However we must be discrete [sic] in approaching her, as she is in a difficult position. Catholics in public life in the U.S. are always under attack from the Protestant majority, accused of being interested in using their political power to further Catholic aims. Her intercession would have to be prudent and unofficial. She could probably do nothing for you directly with the government in Washington, but she could nevertheless be of great service.

You see, dear Father, that I am striving to help you in some small way. I do so because of the deep love in my heart for the solitary life and the contemplative ideal. I am convinced that the Church in America needs Camaldoli, needs the eremitical life. I am sure that the good American nun-recluse of whom you speak will agree with me and will keep praying for this

---

8. The Casentino National Forest, of which the Camaldolese were stewards from the eleventh century until the government of the new Italian state took over all forest administration in the nineteenth century, when Italy based its new national forest code on Camaldoli's long experience of stewardship.

9. This project finally took form in the publication of *The Silent Life*, a general work on monastic life; section on the Camaldolese, 144–71. The process by which the book came to be is described in a number of the letters.

10. Giabbani later sent Merton a relic of the saint (see LETTER 20 and Appendix II).

11. Merton is referring here to the *Patrologia Latina*, an enormous anthology of the writings of the Latin Fathers, edited by J.-P. Migne and published in the nineteenth century in France.

12. Clare Boothe Luce (1903–87) was a playwright, editor, journalist, socialite, and member of the U.S. House of Representatives from Connecticut. In 1935, in a second marriage, she married Henry R. Luce, publisher of *Life* and *Time* magazines. Her daughter from the first marriage, Ann Brokaw, was killed in an automobile accident in 1944; and it was this that ultimately led her to join the Roman Catholic Church, and brought her into touch with Merton. Her appointment as ambassador to Italy became official on the very day Merton was writing to Giabbani, May 4, 1953; she continued in the position until April 1957. Letter 17 in *Cold War Letters*, 42–44, is addressed to her.

intention.[13] It surely will succeed. I will help you as much as I can, with my many other duties. My first duty remains to my own monastery and to the scholastics whose spiritual director I am, but I need not tell you how deeply my heart is engaged in the project of a Camaldolese foundation in America, even though I may have no visible hope of ever having anything much to do with it when it is made.

In conclusion, the best thing I can tell you is to repeat that the eremitical life should come to this country with all the simplicity and humility and poverty and austerity St Benedict would desire. Jesus, Our Lord, will certainly provide for our material needs if we seek first the Kingdom of Heaven. The purpose of the solitary life is, it seems to me, the pure glory of our Risen Savior—it is orientated to Him, not to men. The function of the contemplative is not first of all a "temoignage" ["act of witness"][14] in the eyes of men. The contemplative confesses Christ before His Father in Heaven, and only afterwards before men. Hence there is no need of wide or great publicity. A discrete [sic] and dignified and deep presentation of the

[*The rest of the letter is typed vertically in the left-hand margin of the page.*]

eremitical ideal, and a visible example of that ideal lived out in all simplicity, without any anxiety to attract the notice of the crowd: this is the thing we really need. A hidden life that is really hidden cannot, in the end, be hidden. It inevitably shines out before men.[15] But a hidden life that seeks to attract attention by publicity is doomed in advance to the condemnation of everyone retaining a grain of logic. Publicity and rapid expansion, together with the injudicious acceptance of unfit subjects, are the great dangers of the contemplative life in America today. I beg your blessing and your prayers, dear Father, and promise to remember Camaldoli frequently at Holy Mass.

[Signed] F M Louis Merton

---

13. Sister Nazarena of Jesus, born Julia Crotta in Connecticut, in 1907, who lived as a recluse in the church of Sant'Antonio on the Aventine Hill in Rome from 1945 until her death in 1990. Her story is told in Emanuela Ghini, *Oltre Ogni Limite*, and in Thomas Matus, *Nazarena*. Giabbani, who was her spiritual director, must have referred to her in either LETTER 2 or LETTER 4, neither of which is extant.

14. In this letter, the French word lacks the acute accent on the first *e* that it normally carries.

15. Cf. Matt 5:16.

Letter 6 / *Giabbani to Merton*

This was a missive sent from Giabbani to Merton, as evidenced in Letter 7. It consisted of photos of Camaldoli, requested by Merton in Letter 5, a book about St Romuald, and a covering letter, no longer extant.

This letter, which Merton would have received in September or early October 1953, is mentioned in a letter in the archives of the Merton Center that he wrote to his abbot, Dom James Fox, on October 9, 1953: "I got a letter from Camaldoli when you were away but still haven't had time to write them . . ." He did reply in Letter 7.

LETTER 7 / *Merton to Giabbani; typewritten, in French, trans. DG; original at Camaldoli.*

OUR LADY OF GETHSEMANI
Trappist-Cistercian Abbey
TRAPPIST, KENTUCKY
November 6, 1953

Right Reverend and dear Father:

I am embarrassed when I consider how much time has passed since I received your beautiful photos of Camaldoli.¹ I have taken a long time to thank you, but I do that now wholeheartedly, both for the photos and for the book about St Romuald. I think that I have what I need to begin a little work on Camaldoli. But I must give you the satisfaction of knowing that I have already written something. It's a dozen pages which have been finished and sent yesterday to Dom Jean Leclercq, of Clervaux,² as a preface for the French edition of his book on Blessed Paul Giustiniani.³ In that piece I talk about Camaldoli and the eremitical ideal. Of course, it's for France. Even so, let us hope that I will be able to publish the same piece somewhere else in English.⁴

But here is the difficulty. I had thought first of all to take advantage of your photos and some background information in order to write a magazine article. One of my friends has just started a new Catholic magazine, a very attractive one, called *Jubilee*.⁵ I am very often obliged to *turn down* the often very urgent requests from people who solicit articles from my pen. Consequently if something of mine should appear in a magazine, a number of people will be offended. In consequence, I have stopped writing magazine articles, in principle.⁶ Now I have just had to refuse an abbot of our

1. See LETTER 6.

2. Merton's longtime friend (1911–93), who invited him to the conference in Thailand at which he accidentally died. Their letters have been collected in *Survival or Prophecy?*

3. Leclercq, *Seul avec Dieu*; Merton's preface, 7–18.

4. Leclercq, *Alone with God*; Merton's preface, xiii–xxvii.

5. On *Jubilee*, see Harford, *Merton and Friends*. Ed Rice is the friend to whom Merton refers here.

6. This comment can only be called hilarious, disingenuous, or self-deluding. Similar statements appear on many occasions in Merton's letters; Merton continued to write articles to the end of his life.

order who was asking for an article for a project of his. Our Father Abbot has told me that if I publish this new article on Camaldoli right away, this other person will be offended. So I must wait a while before I will be able to write a little book about you. While I am waiting, I am going to write to my friend, the editor of *Jubilee*, to tell him that he ought to publish an article on Camaldoli as soon as possible. We'll see what he says.

Our Father Abbot spoke to me for a long time about Camaldoli, about its enchanting solitary ambiance. He was really captivated by it.[7] But for all that, he is not encouraging me to become a Camaldolese. I'm not expecting anything at all from him, because he is convinced that God in his goodness wants me here. *Fiat* ["Let it be," or "May it be so"]. It's only by an effort of will and by faith and by love, and not by any attraction or inclination that I am staying in the cenobitic life. I hope that this sacrifice will be acceptable, and that I will be able to expiate my sins by making it. Without doubt I am unworthy to be a solitary. But in any case, I am hanging on to my preference for the solitary ideal. I could not do otherwise without losing my connection to the divine grace which desires me to be a hermit in my heart and a cenobite with my body—and to God's will. My confessor tells me that if God really wants me to be a hermit, he himself will remove all the obstacles. I continue therefore to pray to God with filial abandonment so that his Holy Will may be done in me.

I am without doubt late for the issue of your bulletin on St Bernard.[8] Nevertheless, if you would like to print a long article which is already in the process of being published in the *Collectanea* of our Order, I will send it to you: it's a study on "Action and Contemplation in St Bernard."[9] Naturally, if you wish to publish my few pages on Paul Giustiniani, I think that Dom Leclercq would permit that. You only have to ask him for them. Later I will send you a few notes on the solitary life—meditations in the genre of "Semi di contemplazione."[10] In spite of it all, our Father Abbot has given me a bit of solitude. I even have a sort of hermitage dedicated to St Anne.[11] It is quieter than the monastery, and I have the privilege of spending part of the day

---

7. Merton's abbot, James Fox, visited Camaldoli and Frascati in the fall of 1953 in the course of his attendance at the General Chapter of the Trappists, in order to ask Giabbani to discourage Merton's idea of transferring to Camaldoli (Ghini, *Oltre Ogni Limite*, 252). He mentions this visit in a letter of November 26, 1953 (TMC) to Dom Gabriel Sortais. Cf. Mott, *Seven Mountains*, 271. Mott speaks there of "the Camaldoli," meaning either "Camaldoli" or "the Camaldolese."

8. In commemoration of the eight hundredth anniversary of his death in 1153.

9. *Collectanea* is the international Cistercian French-language journal.

10. Merton here uses the title of the Italian translation of his *Seeds of Contemplation*.

11. See LETTER 3, note 6.

there, which is *a lot* for a Cistercian! There I am able to pray and to meditate a little under the gaze of God and to sound something of the depths of his infinite mercy. As a result of this, you will obtain some of the fruit of this solitude.

Now to return to the problem of our little book. Here is the information I would like to have.

1) I would like to know the location of your other monasteries, for example, Fano, Fonte Avellana, etc.[12] Is this last house your house of studies?

2) Some biographical notes about your modern-day hermits—especially about the confessor of Pius X.[13]

3) Some information about the retreats that people make at Camaldoli or at San Gregorio in Rome.

4) How many different Camaldolese congregations exist at the moment? Where are their houses? What distinguishes each one from the others? And what about Camaldolese nuns?

Doubtless I could find all that in print somewhere. Just tell me where I can find it or send it to me if you have it available.

Finally, I come back to the idea of your American foundation. I am convinced that this country only needs your *eremo*—or that especially. Perhaps if some Americans on their own start to live as hermits they could affiliate afterwards with your Order. I don't know, however, how practical that is. But that way it would be easy enough to have a foothold in this country. I would willingly undertake this experiment if it comes to pass that I receive permission to do it, which is close to impossible.

I commend myself once again to your prayers and to those of your hermits. Bless me, dear and right reverend father, and ask Our Lord to guide me in his own way to himself. I assure you again of my entire devotion and of my most sincerely religious sentiments[14] in Our Lord and Our Lady.

[Signed] F. M. Louis OCSO[15]

In Merton's handwriting, below the signature, are found these words:
We are on retreat November 13–21. Remember us during [*an illegible phrase follows*].

12. See Appendix 1.

13. Girolamo Bianchi, the Italian recluse at Camaldoli.

14. This translates, awkwardly in English, a classic French complimentary closing: *mes sentiments les plus sincèrement religieux*.

15. The letters stand for *Ordo Cisterciensis Strictioris Observantiae*, "Order of the Cistercians of the Strict [literally, 'stricter'] Observance" (i.e., stricter than the other Cistercians)—the official name of the Trappists.

LETTER 8 / *Giabbani to Merton; typewritten, in Italian, trans. LDSF; original at the Thomas Merton Center. As all letters from Giabbani to Merton, this letter is written on the Camaldoli letterhead, with the prior's coat of arms in the top left-hand corner of the page.*

THE PRIOR GENERAL
OF THE CAMALDOLESE HERMIT MONKS OSB
The Holy Hermitage of Camaldoli
Arezzo [Italy]
January 21, 1954

Dearest Father Louis,

I enclose the information requested about our houses,[1] and I hope also to see, when you believe it is opportune, the booklet about the Camaldolese.

I wrote to Dom Leclercq[2] to obtain the article. He promised it to me, and perhaps he will send it to me; but he prefers to publish it first in French.

Did you receive the last number of our bulletin dedicated entirely to St Bernard?[3] It is meant to be a tribute to the great Father [of the Church] and to the Cistercians.

Your eremitical vocation is very interesting, even if you never come to the *eremo*. You demonstrate, however, the growing need of cenobitic spirituality, which as it develops wants to flow over into solitude. Did you know that between the Belgian and French Benedictines there is a real cenobitic crisis, in the Camaldolese sense? The abbots and the bishops are opposed to a change in the *status quo*; but the crisis remains. During this Marian year,[4] our new Constitutions, in which the passage of professed monks without a further novitiate to our Camaldolese *eremo* is affirmed, will be approved, and I would like to hope, therefore, to have [from this change] some true vocations to solitude [for Camaldoli]. What do you think of this? On the other hand, I believe that monasticism without eremitical solitude cannot and will not be complete.

1. See Appendix I.
2. See LETTER 7, notes 2, 3, and 4.
3. See LETTER 7, note 8.
4. The centenary of the promulgation of the dogma of the Immaculate Conception of the Virgin Mary by Pius IX, in 1854.

I continue to hope to be able to open an *eremo* in America, when the Lord wills; and your counsels, even if they are not at present concrete, will always be valuable to us.

The four recluses—the French one, the Belgian one, the Italian one,[5] and . . . the little American one[6]—are praying for you; and all of us send our good wishes that you increase in holiness and always do the Lord's will.

I bless you with all fraternal affection.

Your very devoted in Jesus and Mary,
Dom Anselmo, Cam.[7]

---

5. Name of the French recluse not known; Jérome Bradfer (Belgian), Girolamo Bianchi (Italian).

6. Sister Nazarena; see LETTER 5, note 13.

7. "Cam." for "Camaldolese." Sometimes written OSBCam. for the Order of St. Benedict, Camaldolese congregation.

LETTER 9 / *Merton to Giabbani; typewritten, in French, trans. DG; original at Camaldoli.*

OUR LADY OF GETHSEMANI
TRAPPIST, KENTUCKY
December 20, 1954

To [the Right Reverend—crossed out] Father Dom Anselmo Giabbani

Camaldoli

[Right Reverend—crossed out] My dear Father:

You have perhaps asked yourself if I have forgotten you, and if I have let go of my suggestion that I write something for you. No. I often think of you and of Camaldoli, and my heart often travels to your solitary and silent refuge hidden in the heart of the Appennines. And I also think about the book project. But I must tell you frankly that chances are a little slim that I might write a book about Camaldoli. My superiors seem to think that such a book from my pen would perhaps give a wrong impression to certain people, especially members of our order. Thus: I have no choice but to submit in this regard. But it seems to me that even so I can do something for you. If it were simply a question of a book on *the monastic spirit* with an emphasis more or less strong on *solitude*, perhaps that would accomplish what you want.

At the moment, the Benedictines of La Pierre-Qui-Vire,[1] in France, are going to produce a beautiful album of photographs evocative of the monastic spirit—not only Benedictine, but Cistercian, Carthusian, and so on. I have written quite a long piece[2] for this album. So now I suggest that I offer this text to you as well, to be published in Italian. I could even add to this some pages on the hermit life and on Camaldoli in particular. Then on your end, you could replace the photographs of the French monks with photographs of Camaldolese monks. Finally, you will see.[3] But this is a conditional

---

1. A Benedictine monastery in the French *département* of Yonne, in the Morvan region of France. The name ("the rock that turns") comes from a natural feature, a rock on top of another rock that at one time could be moved by simple human effort. Today the rock has been fixed in place and is surmounted with a statue of the Virgin Mary.

2. Merton, "In silentio" ["In the silence"], in *Silence dans le ciel*, 12–18, and 57–59; in the American edition: *Silence in Heaven*, 17–30.

3. In the original "*Enfin, vous verrez*"—a curious comment.

promise. I will have to ask the monks of La Pierre-Qui-Vire to authorize it. I don't think they will raise any objection.

I very much regret that my Italian publisher did not want to leave the translation of *Bread in the Wilderness*[4] in the hands of one of your hermits. Apparently he had already promised the work to another translator. And I well know that an author does not have much to say to a publisher in a distant country. They pay no attention. But in regard to the text abovementioned, that is really something which could be translated by and for your own people.[5]

Are you still thinking about your project of a foundation in America? It seems to me that it's an important idea, and that you shouldn't give it up. But God does things in his own good time, without doubt. I think the simplest thing would be first of all to send someone here in order to see what it's all about. You need to know the country. Why in fact don't you come yourself? I could give you all my ideas in person.[6] And I have a lot of ideas on this subject.

In the meantime, if you still want something for your Camaldoli publication, I have given to the same monks at La Pierre-Qui-Vire two parts of a new book which will perhaps please you—one about solitude, the other about recollection.[7] I am giving you the Italian rights for these pieces, but I would ask you to ask La Pierre-Qui-Vire for the English text that I have sent to them; I don't have another copy at the moment.[8] But when I have the proofs I will certainly be able to send you other copies of much better quality. Or in fact you could produce your own version from the French translation.

---

4. In the event, the Italian edition was not published until three years later, in 1957.

5. This didn't happen.

6. Merton says "will give" (*donnerai*) rather than "could give" (*donnerais*), but idiomatically I prefer this translation; it may simply be that Merton unintentionally left off the *s* at the end of *donnerais*. Giabbani did visit the United States in 1957 but did not see Merton on that visit.

7. "Nel deserto" ["In the desert"], published by Camaldoli in its own journal, *Vita Monastica*; see Burton, *More Than Silence*, 143. *Vita Monastica* is named there as *Camaldoli*, the earlier name of the journal. For a complete bibliographical account of this article and related pieces by Merton, see Shannon, "Reflections on 'Notes for a Philosophy of Solitude,'" 83–99.

"Raccoglimento" ["Recollection"], *More than Silence*, 154; *Vita Monastica* is again named there as *Camaldoli*.

8. The English original of "Nel deserto" has been lost; "Raccoglimento" was published in English in *No Man Is an Island*, 217–29.

So write to the Reverend Father Dom Claude Jean Nesmy, at La Pierre-Qui-Vire, near St-Leger-Vauban, France (Yonne), and he will send you these texts. He might even let you have some of his photographs of monastic life for an eventual Italian edition of the album I told you about—it's called *Silence in Heaven*.[9] So ask him. From my end, I will write him a word about this.

In the meantime, I leave you at one with the Lord who is soon going to come to live among us where we live in exile,[10] far from our heavenly homeland.[11] I wish for you all the best graces [from God]. I pray every day at Holy Mass for you and for your hermits and recluses. Do not forget me, and ask the good Lord to listen intently to the deepest desire of my heart. You know what this desire is. In the end, it is always necessary to abide not in our own desires, but in the Holy Will of God. *Fiat voluntas Patris* ["May the will of the Father be done"].

I ask you to bless me, Right Reverend Father, and to accept this expression of my most devout sentiments in Our Lord and Our Lady.

[Signed] F. M. Louis Merton

On the copy of this letter in the Camaldoli archive, Dom Giabbani has added a note in his own handwriting: Scr a D Nesmy il 7.2.55 ("wrote to Dom Nesmy on February 7, 1955").

---

9. See note 2.
10. A theme that runs all through Merton's writings; cf. SSM, 350, 352.
11. Cf. Heb 11:13–16.

Letter 10 / Merton to Giabbani: typewritten, in French, trans. DG; original at Camaldoli.

OUR LADY OF GETHSEMANI
TRAPPIST, KENTUCKY
January 10, 1955
Feast of St Paul the Hermit

Dear [Right Reverend—crossed out] Father,

I have just finished the text I spoke to you about.[1] Indeed, I have added a long chapter on Camaldoli to our little book on the monastic life.[2] I am going to have a typist copy the text and I will send it to you right away. In the meantime, I can tell you that Father Dom Claude Nesmy, of La Pierre-Qui-Vire, tells me that he would be very happy to let you have the Italian rights for the text and the photographs. I told him that doubtless you would want to add to add a few good photos of Camaldoli. I suggest to you, Right Reverend Father, to take[3] twenty or so first-class photographs that you could include in the Italian edition of the book. But we would also like them for the American edition. The postcards that you sent me are beautiful, but only some of them are capable of reproduction in a book. It's always necessary to have original photos, real snapshots and not lithographs or heliographs.[4] Dom Nesmy will also be very happy to send you the two articles[5] I mentioned to you for your bulletin.

I wonder, Right Reverend Father, if it would be possible for me to have a small relic of St Romuald.[6] Truly, I think that it would help me a lot in my spiritual life, and in my desire for union with God. And especially, Right Reverend Father, I commend to you again the spiritual problem which touches me ever more intensely and which you know about. Perhaps the moment has arrived to restart the efforts of two years ago. I hope that we

---

1. See LETTER 9, note 2.

2. See the reference to "a special chapter on Camaldoli" in LETTER 12.

3. I have translated Merton's word, *faire*, as "take" rather than "make," as more idiomatic in English.

4. Prints made by the light of the sun on photosensitive paper. But see also Merton's comment about heliogravure in LETTER 12.

5. See LETTER 9, note 7.

6. Giabbani did send Merton some relics; see LETTER 20 and Appendix II.

will be able to accomplish them this time with more success. But in any case, bless me, and pray for me. And let us leave everything in the hands of God, who wants us to be holy! [I will write again] very soon.

I ask you to accept, dear and Right Reverend Father, this expression of all my devotion in Our Lord and Our Lady.

[Signed] F M Louis Merton

Letter 11 / Giabbani to Merton; typewritten, in Italian, trans. LDSF; original at the Thomas Merton Center.

THE PRIOR GENERAL
OF THE CAMALDOLESE HERMIT MONKS OSB
The Holy Hermitage of Camaldoli
Arezzo [Italy]
January 24, 1955

Reverend and dear brother Louis,

I read your two letters[1] with pleasure and I await your article about Camaldoli. I will send you the photographs which I commissioned from a fine photographer who is waiting for the sun[2] and a beautiful day, so that they may be really beautiful. So, I'm still occupied with the photographs. I will also happily send you a relic of St Romuald and another of Saint Peter Damian. Is that all right?[3]

As to the founding of our *eremo* in America, I continue to be in favor of that if you and another well-known American[4] will help me. After your booklet on Camaldoli [is published], we'll see what the response is from the Americans—and are you convinced that we will have vocations? In the next couple of months the new Statutes of our congregation will be approved, which will permit a lot of freedom to adapt, so that we will be able to study together what type of hermit community (with or without apostolic responsibilities) corresponds more closely to the needs and aspirations of the American spirit (in other words, to the Holy Spirit who [of course] works in American souls); then we will decide what to do. But, if you suggest it, I could come to America[5] next September to acquaint myself with the concrete possibilities.

---

1. LETTERS 9 and 10.
2. See LETTER 10, note 3.
3. Merton had asked only for a relic of St. Romuald; the relic of St. Peter Damian was a bonus. See LETTER 20 and Appendix II.
4. Presumably Clare Boothe Luce.
5. He didn't come then, but did come two years later, in 1957, when, interestingly, he did not visit Merton.

I can count on the support of the Holy See, especially that of Monsignor Montini, who is now archbishop of Milan,[6] who has read some of your letters to me, and was very interested in your solitary vocation.

I will write to Dom Nesmy and we'll come to an agreement on the Italian edition of your book. Thank you for everything.

In the unity of prayer and with brotherly affection in Christ Jesus,

Dom A. Giabbani
Greetings [also] to your Father Abbot.

---

6. This is the first reference in the correspondence to Montini, who will play a very significant role toward the end of this correspondence (see LETTERS 16, 23, 27, 28, 29, 31, 33, and 35). He had a strong connection with Camaldoli, having led theological study conferences there for laypeople for eighteen years (1936–54). He was formally installed as archbishop of Milan on January 6, 1955, just a short time before Giabbani wrote this letter.

LETTER 12 / *Merton to Giabbani; typewritten, in French, trans. DG; original at Camaldoli.*

OUR LADY OF GETHSEMANI
TRAPPIST, KENTUCKY
February 9, 1955

Dear and Right Reverend Father:

I am sending you under separate cover and by regular mail the entire text of the little book of "Silence in Heaven" (*Silence dans le ciel*).[1] This text includes not only the pages that I sent in December to La Pierre-Qui-Vire, but also a special chapter on Camaldoli which will appear in the American edition as well as in yours. I take it that you are in contact with Dom Claude Jean Nesmy. I am waiting with the greatest pleasure for the photographs of Camaldoli for our American edition.

I don't want to get mixed up in the technical problems of your Italian edition; but Dom Nesmy is having a problem that we can help him solve. He is going to reprint his excellent photos in heliogravure for *les Editions Braun de Mulhouse*. He asked me if my American publisher would be able at the same time to have these images printed for our edition by the same company. This would be a good business decision and would at the same time help Dom Nesmy to retain the size he wants for his edition. Otherwise, the cost of the work would require some cutbacks. I think that you could also do well to co-operate with him by having your photos printed at the same time by this publishing house. But I leave to you the task of talking with Dom Nesmy on this subject.

I was very happy to receive your letter, Right Reverend Father. I will write you at greater length about the project of your American foundation. In the meantime, I think it would be better to wait until the book comes out at the end of this year. Pray for me; I will attempt to make some contacts which could help you. This project interests me in the highest degree. I believe it is necessary for America. Apart from the Carthusians,[2] who move very slowly, we do not have a fully contemplative and solitary form of life in the United States. But the Church very much needs it. The Cistercians don't fill this need. The Cistercian life is something very different. Although clois-

---

1. See LETTER 9, note 2.
2. There is still (in 2014) only one Carthusian foundation in the United States.

tered, it is, rather, active and liturgical. The Camaldolese would not in any way hinder the growth of the Cistercians. There will be vocations, yes, but it will be necessary to exercise a lot of discernment and to wait very patiently. The *numbers* will not be lacking, but for *quality* it will be necessary to wait a while. It will also be necessary to test those with nervous temperaments very carefully, even though they may be full of good will. There will be questions [of vocation] which will require no inconsiderable discretion. But there are souls in America who need a truly contemplative life, who have an immense thirst for a life which is available practically nowhere. So I think that Camaldoli ought to focus on the hermit life and leave aside the cenobitic life almost completely.[3] As far as an apostolate goes, it would only be a question of operating a retreat house, which would certainly be a very big success. But it would also be necessary to maintain its contemplative character. It will be necessary above all to approach the highest level of the clergy and the laity, and to offer them a place of retreat which is silent and poor, and not a kind of spiritual gymnasium with a lot of talks and exercises—that will be a temptation to which it would be easy to succumb!

I had the great joy and consolation of singing the community mass on February 7, the feast of St Romuald.[4] I thought of you then, and of all your wonderful hermits and recluses. I love you all. I pray for Camaldoli every day at mass, praying that the Holy Spirit may sustain its fervor and its contemplative love of solitude and silence. Without doubt, that will demand both strength and sensitivity. But that is what we need in the world today. We have no lack of writers, of great speakers, or of missionaries. But what we need is hermits, men engulfed in the poverty and silence of God himself (because God made himself in this world very poor for our sake!). And we especially need to love the solitude of the heart in which we can suffer in silence before God, the Only One Who[5] can understand this. Although I am not able to become a real solitary, I continue to become one in my heart. I have again asked for formal permission to transfer to a more solitary order, but this permission has been flatly refused by my Father Abbot. I am not without hope about this, but I will have to wait for God's timing. In the

---

3. Merton here disregards the foundational Camaldolese tradition of combining the eremitical and cenobitic forms of monastic life in one community, as expressed in their traditional emblem, which shows two doves drinking from one cup. Nor does the reference a few lines later to "hermits and recluses" take into account the monks of Camaldoli, who historically have formed the greater part of the bipartite community. On the other hand, Giabbani had himself referred to the foundation of a "hermit community" in LETTER 11.

4. Now June 19.

5. Capitalization Merton's.

internal forum,⁶ there is no longer any question on my part. I must seek, so far as possible, both solitude and the desert. But before anything, I must seek the will of God. I cannot go forward apart from obedience; and in the external forum,⁷ there is the categorical "no" from God's representative. *Usquequo?* ["Until?" or "To what point in time?" or "How long?"]

I am very happy to know that Monsignor Montini is interested in these matters. I want to write him a brief word to congratulate him on his elevation to the see of Milan. Perhaps he could offer us some suggestions. I would like to help you as much as possible. Do you know that in our order's calendar we commemorate a Cistercian monk who was ordered by the Holy See to transfer to Camaldoli to help them carry out some reform?⁸ You are doubtless acquainted with him. Could such a situation not repeat itself?

I hope that you will enjoy reading the short manuscript which I am sending you and that it will help your foundation and expansion projects. I am very happy to be thus able, in a modest way, to show devotion to so noble and beautiful a cause—for Our Lord seeks with all of his Sacred Heart those souls who truly wish to follow him into the wilderness.

You are very kind, Right Reverend Father, to send me relics of both St Romuald and St Peter Damian. I am waiting for them with the greatest joy. These two great saints will help me mightily in my crossing of the Red Sea in order to seek God in the wilderness.

Forgive me, Right Reverend Father. I am speaking to you about silence, and here I have written you a long letter.

I bid you farewell, devotedly in Christ, and I ask you humbly to bless me and to continue to pray for me, because I definitely feel the effect of the prayers of Camaldoli. In any case, they bring me closer to God. Thank you.

[Signed] F M Louis Merton

---

6. That is, in regard to the spiritual good of the individual as determined by the individual's conscience.

7. That is, the public good of the Church and its members, as decided by "God's representative[s]," in Merton's case, his abbot.

8. The traditional Cistercian menology, or annotated calendar of saints, no longer in regular use, contains this entry: "September 4. At the monastery of San Salvatore di Settimo, in Tuscany, was honored the memory of the Venerable David, a monk of this monastery, who became a prior or superior of the Camaldolese. Pope Boniface VIII gave him, eminent for many virtues and a great lover of the desert, to the Camaldolese, who asked for him, that he might support and promote their Institute. This he did in a holy and praiseworthy manner." I am indebted to Father Elias Dietz, abbot of Gethsemani, and fourth successor to Dom James, for this citation (e-mail message to author, December 7, 2009).

LETTER 13 / *Giabbani to Merton; typewritten, in Italian, trans. LDSF; original at the Thomas Merton Center.*

THE PRIOR GENERAL
OF THE CAMALDOLESE HERMIT MONKS OSB
The Holy Hermitage of Camaldoli
Arezzo [Italy]
Easter Day [April 10], 1955[1]

Dear Father,

In these past days I have prayed for you again, in thanksgiving for the manuscript of the booklet that you sent me and for the good publisher who is translating it into Italian. We will put out a beautiful edition, not unworthy of the name of Merton, and I hope you will be happy with it. First, however, I will wait for the French edition so that I can at least make it match! I will keep you informed in any way possible, about everything. I had several photos sent to you and also some relics of St Romuald and St Peter Damian; I hope you received it all. I'm also hoping for some photographs to document the Camaldolese life, and I'm taking them from a film,[2] because subjecting hermits to the lens is not a simple task, and rightly so! Therefore, I will send you some better photos.

In a couple of days, I will speak to Montini about the future foundation in America. Think about it, and, if you can, send me some notes, or at least some sketches under the patronage of St Romuald, as if everything depended on you. Perhaps—forgive me for this—you are a bit too enthusiastic about the hermit lifestyle because you don't have the experience of living as a hermit, but I would like to be mistaken; and, in any case, it is necessary always to start with enthusiasm: there is always time to give up [later]! But we have to make a foundation: I'm certain that it is the will of the Lord, and that you will have all your powers ready to help and direct us. We entrust everything to the Madonna, *Mater contemplantium* ["Mother of contemplatives"].

---

1. The date is handwritten, but does not include month and day. The copy in the Thomas Merton Center archives bears the date of April 2, but April 10 was the date of Easter in 1955.

2. A semiprofessional documentary made about the Camaldolese house of Fonte Avellana (Thomas Matus, OSBCam, personal conversation, December 10, 2008).

Happy Easter, dear Father Louis, with all fraternal affection. Greetings also to your Father Abbot.

Affectionately in Christ Jesus,

[Signed] D[om] Anselmo

Letter 14 / Giabbani to Merton

This is the "fine letter from Stapehill" mentioned in Letter 22, presumably written in Italian, and sent sometime in April or May 1955. *Not extant.*

Letter 15 / Merton to Moore; typewritten, in English; original, if extant, in the archives of the Charterhouse of the Transfiguration, Arlington, Vermont.

April 25, 1955

Dear Dom Pablo Maria:

When our former Fr Alberic[1] went to Sky Farm[2] I asked him to speak to you about a personal matter of my own and write to me giving your answer. I believe he probably did this, and that the answer somehow failed to reach me.[3] Now, with the permission of our Father Prior[4] who is in charge of the monastery during the two weeks' absence of Father Abbot, I am approaching you directly. I also wrote to Sky Farm two years ago under another Prior about this same matter, but the answer again did not reach me until it was too late to be of any value. However, Father Prior who is now in the saddle for two weeks is directing me more or less[5] in this same matter and assures me that he will see that I receive your reply, if it comes under his jurisdiction (that is to say if it arrives within the next two weeks).

Father, I believe you are fairly well acquainted with the situation. For more than ten years I have been desiring ardently to lead a more solitary and contemplative life than is possible here at Gethsemani. I will try as simply as possible to give you the outline of the present status of this question.

1. Dom James, our Father Abbot, has always in principle recognized that my tendencies to greater solitude are God's will for me, but he has always tended to settle them by compromises and special permissions here at

---

1. Later Denys Brackley, OCart.

2. The first home of the American Carthusians, in Whitingham, Vermont.

3. An oblique reference to the possibility that Dom James didn't pass on Dom Pablo Maria's letter to Merton.

4. Anselm Steinke; see LETTER 19.

5. Here Merton claims too much. In his letter of May 17, 1955 (TMC) to Dom Gabriel, Dom James, having heard from Merton that Father Anselm was his spiritual director, asked Merton's permission to speak to Father Anselm on that point—"because personally I did not believe that Father Prior was [his] director. Father Louis gave me his permission and I asked Father Anselm. He was very disturbed that Father Louis was calling him one of his directors. He absolutely denied it and went to see Father Louis about it. Indeed Father Louis spent quite a bit of time with Father Anselm in my absence, but that is a different thing from being one's [spiritual] director."

Gethsemani. Our Abbot General recognizes frankly that I am not exactly well placed as a Cistercian, that I have a "mentality" of my own which is God's will for me. But he thinks it would be futile for me to go anywhere else, as he thinks I would not be perfectly adapted anywhere in any religious Order. He does not think, by the way, that I am seriously unadapted to the religious life or to the monastic life.

2. In January, with the departure of Fr Alberic for Sky Farm, I felt that the time had come for me to get busy on this question again. (I had opened it in Sept. 1952 with the advice of a director who thought I really did not belong in the cenobitic life and should go to the solitary life.[1] At that time, I did not face the issue squarely enough. I too easily let myself be put off by the difficult and delicate situation created by urging something that my Superior definitely does not desire in the external forum.) This time I consulted a wise director in Louisville, a Passionist[2] who knows both the Trappists and the Carthusians. He told me he thought the reasonable way to settle this difficulty was to ask permission to try out the solitary life somewhere, and see if that would solve my problem. As far as I was concerned, I felt that this definitively settled the question for me in the internal forum, for with his blessing I decided that even if the permission were refused I would *act as if* I had a vow to go to a more solitary order. Since that time I have had no doubt that this is God's will for me in the internal forum. The idea of asking this permission, and my other dispositions, were confirmed by the advice of our present Father Prior. Father Abbot however simply refused me permission to come to Sky Farm and talk the matter over, alleging that it was simply an "illusion of my nature."

My confessor at Gethsemani is a man who does not seem to me to understand this question or to appreciate the problem involved.[3] I have never considered him my director although I occasionally mentioned the affair to him. He never approved of it, his principle being that since I have a solemn vow of stability here it is not licit for me even to consider a change. He however says that I can leave the matter to the judgement of my Superiors in the external forum. I have ceased consulting him about the question, as the Passionist in Louisville told me it was much wiser to leave him out of it. I have no real director here.

---

1. Father Bellarmine (September 13, 1952; SFS, 15).

2. Father Vincent Mary Oberhauser, CP (d. 1979), a member of the Louisville Passionist community (e-mail from Joseph Mitchell, CP, November 2, 2009); mentioned in a letter of May 17, 1955 (TMC), from Dom James to Dom Gabriel.

3. Father Andrew, also mentioned in the letter of May 17, 1955 (see note 7).

3. In the meantime I have been in contact with the Camaldolese, both at Arezzo and Frascati. Dom Porion, your Procurator General, advised me that I would probably do better at Camaldoli than with the Carthusians. I have made known my desires to Camaldoli and the Prior there is very ready to accept me, eager in fact to do so. He is also eager to make an American foundation. I have in fact already done something to that end by writing—and this was highly approved by the Secretary of the S[acred] Congregation for Religious. The Prior of Camaldoli tells me that Archbishop Montini (a good friend of theirs) is "very interested" in my solitary vocation.

4. We have just had, at Gethsemani, a regular visitation in which the Visitor suppressed some of the concessions given to me and others by Dom James in the matter of solitude.[4] The whole tenor of the Visitation report was that "there is a dangerous eremitical spirit creeping into this monastery" which must be stopped at once. The chief aim of the Visitor was to guarantee that this "hermit mentality" would disappear from the house altogether. I assured him that one of the best ways of bringing this about was to see that I myself should disappear from the monastery, but he said that was not necessary. He agrees, incidentally, that my own mentality will always be what it is, and he only asks that I do not preach too much solitude to my brethren here.

5. At this same time, a French doctor friend of mine[5] happened along for a visit, and as soon as he had some inkling of my vocation problem he told me at once that he felt it was most advisable for me to leave this monastery and go to another kind of life in which I would not be caught in such complete ambivalence.

6. I had for a long time been thinking of taking a formal vow to leave and go to the solitary life. The other day at Mass, the thought came to me very strongly at the offertory and, believing it to be the will of God, I made the vow at the moment of my Communion. I felt that I had done something

---

4. Merton describes this "suppression" of his special permissions by the visitor, Dom Louis de Gonzague le Pennuen, in a letter of April 27, 1955, to Jean Leclercq (*Survival or Prophecy?*, 59). The word sounds harsh in English, but he derives it from Dom Louis' usage of the French *supprimer*, which simply means "to stop."

5. Dr. Philip Law, a psychiatrist friend of Merton's, from Chicago, thought Merton should leave Gethsemani and "start something new." In his journal Merton writes that he "explained to him the Camaldolese set up and he said that sounded fine. Offered to help in any way he could" (September 25, 1952, SFS, 17). On December 29, Merton quotes him again as saying that Merton shouldn't wait three years, as he was thinking of doing, but that he should leave immediately (SFS, 27). Then in the letter to Jean Leclercq mentioned in note 9, Merton says that he has "a friend who is willing to pay [his] steamer fare" to Italy. However, Dr. Law was not to my knowledge French, and this comment comes three years after Merton's conversations with Law; so the doctor friend must be someone else.

God wanted me to do. I have mentioned the fact of having made this vow to Fr Prior, with the understanding that [if] he objects to it, I will consider it a mistake. He is thinking it over. For my part, I feel that it is what I ought to have done.

There is the situation, Father. When Dom James returns, the thing is going to be rather difficult to handle. He will not face it directly. He will beat around the bush and try to put the whole thing off with some kind of an evasion. He will definitely not grant a permission to go to try things out at Camaldoli (incidentally this French doctor offers to pay my fare to Italy).[6] The Abbot General will also try to stall the thing again. In short, every effort will be made to see that I do not leave the Cistercian Order. I am here without much advice or support, and rather diffident about putting up a strong front because I do not know when I may simply do "my own will" and "defy" God's representatives. Usually, when it comes to a showdown, I become timid and reticent because I am afraid of getting mad.

I am asking you, Father, the following questions:

1) Do you think it is really the will of God for me to leave the Cistercians and seek a solitary life in some other order?

2) If so, what would be a practical way of urging my claims?

3) What about this vow? For one thing, it should convince people that I mean business (for indeed I do).

4) Is there any simple and effective thing that can be done from the other end—e.g., by Archbishop Montini, or, since Fr Larraona[7] is friendly to me, perhaps I should approach him directly? The fact remains that without the support of my Superiors I will get nowhere.

Father, I apologize for this long letter but you can certainly help me with a prompt reply and I will value your judgment and ...[8]

---

6. See note 5.

7. Merton describes the warm and substantial connection he made with Larraona on the occasion of his visit to Gethsemani in August 1952, when Merton translated for him from Italian and conversed with him in Spanish (SFS, 10).

8. The text of the letter ends here.

LETTER 16 / *Merton to Montini; typewritten, in English; original in the Merton Dossier in the Montini Archive in the Milan Archdiocesan Archives.*

jhs[1]
OUR LADY OF GETHSEMANI
TRAPPIST, KENTUCKY
April 25, 1955

Most Reverend and Dear Archbishop Montini:

It is some time since I have had the honor of communicating with your Excellency but I nevertheless remember you in my prayers and so you are often in my thoughts. On this occasion, I am happy to be sending you a copy of our[2] latest book, *No Man is an Island*, as a token of my veneration and esteem. Your Excellency will also be interested to hear that I recently completed a short book on the monastic life with emphasis on the Camaldolese *eremo*.[3] Perhaps Dom Giabbani has already spoken to you of this. He tells me, in fact, that your Excellency is interested in the question of my vocation to solitude.[4]

This information makes me happy and gives me courage to support the trials which, evidently, must be undergone by one who attempts to pass from the cenobitic life in one Order to the eremitical life in another. For ten years[5] I have been through this conflict and now by the grace of God it seems that things are reaching the point of maturity at which perhaps action will at last be taken. Your Excellency's interest in this matter makes me bold enough to tell you what is going on at present, in the hope that perhaps you might be able to offer me valuable help.

Your Excellency is aware that Dom Giabbani wishes to make an American foundation. You also know that he is eager to have me help him. It is

---

1. The initials for the Latin phrase *In hoc signo [vinces]*: "by this sign [you will conquer]," the sign here being the cross.

2. The "monastic we": Merton is being coy. Of course he means "my."

3. Perhaps he means *The Silent Life*, but this was not published until 1957.

4. See LETTER 11, note 6.

5. This would take his eremitical hopes back to 1945. However, the first written evidence is in the second volume of his journals, *Entering the Silence*, dated December 24, 1946.

logical that if I am to pass some day to the Eremo of Camaldoli, this is the time to do it. You know that Dom Giabbani is glad to receive me if I come, and has already welcomed my petition. I also have a friend who is ready and eager to pay my passage to Italy.[6] Unfortunately my Superiors still oppose this transitus. For my own part, I have made a vow to embrace a more solitary and contemplative life (without abandoning the work of writing which I believe to be the manifest will of God). I am firmly determined never to renounce this desire for solitude and to do everything within my power to follow what I believe to be the voice of God.

If it were possible for me to convince my Superiors of the real desirability of my change to Camaldoli, matters would be much simpler. A strong word of approval or encouragement from someone like your Excellency would be of very great assistance, if such a thing can properly be asked. I also wonder whether it would be advisable to take some initiative in Rome. In these matters I am inexperienced and if I have said anything out of place, I hope your Excellency will understand. In any case, I am sure that if our Father Abbot[7] here did not have to take the whole responsibility for the decision on himself, and if there were chances of someone in a high position viewing my case with positive favor, he would much more easily assent to my leaving for Camaldoli. I believe the only reason why he really refuses is that he does not want to be criticized and blamed.[8] My Superiors all seem to recognize that I am more of a hermit than a cenobite.

I close with all the sentiments of deepest esteem and grateful veneration for your Excellency, begging your blessing I kiss your hand and remain, in Christ, Your Excellency's most devoted servant[9]

f. m. Louis Merton

---

6. See LETTER 15, note 5.

7. Merton refers directly here to his abbot, Dom James, rather than the evasive "my Superiors."

8. A serious misreading. Dom James saw Merton as a very valuable member of the community; within six months he had been named novice master, the officer of the monastery responsible in a sense for its future. He also had a concern for Merton's stability and believed he was acting in Merton's best interests by preventing him from leaving Gethsemani. Most commentators would support this view.

9. These concluding terms of respect, which sound as if they could have come from the sixteenth or seventeenth century and which strike the contemporary ear as exaggerated or obsequious, were not uncommon in this period in communications from the lower to the upper levels of the hierarchy of the Roman Catholic Church.

Letter 17 / *Merton to Giabbani*

A letter written about April 25, presumably in French; see note 3 in Letter 22. *Not extant.* In it, as we learn from a letter of Dom James to Dom Gabriel (May 17, TMC), Merton had again asked Giabbani to negotiate a *transitus* to Camaldoli for him.

LETTER 18 / *Moore to Merton; handwritten, in English; the original is at the Thomas Merton Center.*

Carthusian Foundation in America, Inc.
Whitingham, Vermont
Telephone Jacksonville 40
April 29, 1955

My dear Father Louis:

I received your letter yesterday a little before Vespers and recommended you to God during the service. I did the same at Matins and Lauds of the day at our midnight office; and in our *missa sicca*[1] afterwards, I recommended your problems to God. This morning, having a free intention left for April, I said mass for you.

And so now I will tell you my opinion, but with *no claim whatever to being supernaturally illuminated.* I have merely done my best to be helpful. Your long persistent desire for solitary contemplative life may well be a grace that God has bestowed upon you. The fact that the Prior of the Camaldolese is willing to accept you is a further sign that God may be calling you. The fact too that he hopes to make an American foundation seems to me to point in the same direction. Your going would no longer be a mere personal matter with yourself, but the means of opening solitary contemplative life to many in our country. This possibility *should not be laid aside without investigation and perhaps trial.* It seems to me that further light on your solitary contemplative vocation is not to be expected until you make an actual trial.

How can that actual trial be made [?] An incident in my own career may be suggestive. When I was in the First World War,[2] I received a furlough to England and made a retreat at Downside Abbey[3] and decided to enter and was accepted. When I returned and had made known my intentions to the Superior General of the Paulists,[4] it was suggested that I have an interview

---

1 *Missa sicca*—literally "dry mass," traditionally prayed by the Carthusian choir monk alone, in his cell, without vestments, generally attached to the end of the offices of Prime or Terce of the Office of the Blessed Virgin. Today its use is optional.

2. Following the entry of the United States into World War I, Moore enlisted in the army as a captain in the medical corps; see Neenan, *Thomas Verner Moore*, 105–12.

3. An abbey of the English Benedictine Congregation at Stratton-on-the-Fosse, Somerset, England.

4. The order to which he at that time belonged. In a note in the left-hand margin

with the then Archbishop Hayes[5] (later Cardinal). In the course of the interview he remarked that the new canon law was designed to discourage such transfers to religious orders. I wrote to Abbot Butler[6] and he at once wrote to his *Procurator in Curia* and *my transitus came from Rome almost by return mail.* A peculiar circumstance blocked my going there, 1919; and only in 1923 was it possible for me to become a Benedictine and then Fort Augustus[7] opened its doors to a group of Americans. The Carthusians had refused me about 1915. I was never disappointed in Benedictine life. My Carthusian vocation was personal and I regard my Carthusian vocation as envisaged by St. Benedict when he spoke of some who after long probation in the monastery would go forth from the ranks of the brethren to the single-handed combat of the desert. I think this applies to you. You will not be false to Cistercian life when you answer God's call to the wilderness.

Now the practical way for you to get to the Camaldolese is to get in touch at once with the Prior of Camaldoli and ask him to explain your situation to Archbishop Montini and have him or someone [else] send your transitus to your Abbot with a request for an answer. He could do that very easily and promptly, but Rome might, otherwise, never act without the full consent and recommendation of your Abbot. But if Rome knows the actual situation on good authority you may expect prompt action. So send at once to the Prior of Camaldoli a letter from the Prior of Gethsemani and if possible from the Passionist in Louisville.

May I suggest that you think of locating [the proposed Camaldolese foundation] in California somewhere between the Coast Range and the Pacific.[8] In this region it is never cold and never hot. You could have little wooden hermitages cheaply constructed and a cheap [sic] central church in a hilly region far from busy centers. Since you would never have snow you could build your hermitages well apart, each hidden from every other, with a good footpath from each to the church. In the rainy season on rainy nights you could have one of our modern, light waterproofs (with a hood) reaching almost to the ground. A five or ten minute walk to the church would be easy and be more than repaid by the greater solitude.

---

of the letter, Moore wrote, "The Archbishop of New York was then the canonical superior of the Paulists."

5. Archbishop Patrick Joseph Hayes (1867–1938), fifth Roman Catholic archbishop of New York, 1919–38; cardinal from 1924.

6. Cuthbert Butler, OSB (1858–1934), abbot of Downside, 1906–22.

7. Properly St Benedict's Abbey, Fort Augustus, Inverness-shire, in Scotland; now closed.

8. The Camaldolese foundation was made in precisely this region, at Big Sur.

I shall follow you with my prayers. You have not suffered in vain.
Faithfully yours in St. Benedict,
[Father—stroked out] Fr. Pablo Maria Moore

Letter 19 / Anselm Steinke[1] to Anselmo Giabbani: the original in English, not extant; portions of it in Italian are included in Emmanuela Ghini, Oltre Ogni Limite: Nazarena monaca reclusa 1945–90 *(Casale Monferrato, Italy: Piemme, 1993).*

I was unable to contact Joseph Steinke, as the copyright holder, to obtain permission to publish his letter, and am therefore summarizing it here rather than reproducing it as translated by Larissa Fielding from the abbreviated form in which it is found in the Ghini book. Ghini calls the letter a "penetrating depiction of the Trappist writer,"[2] commenting further, "The irony [in the letter] is amiable and imbued with brotherly charity. But the portrait that the young prior delineates of Merton reveals a great depth, real love, and prudent tact in his attitude toward a monk who, for all his talent, was exposed to risks, [and] could take false steps. . . ."[3]

The letter was written to Anselmo Giabbani on May 3, 1955, a day that Steinke identifies as the feast of the Invention of the Holy Cross, that is, the reputed finding in Jerusalem by the Empress Helena, mother of the Emperor Constantine, of the remains of the cross on which Jesus was crucified. The observance was dropped from the Roman Catholic calendar in 1960, probably because of its legendary character.

He tells Giabbani that he is writing on behalf of Merton's aspiration to the solitary life, and that he desires to assist him, as a monastic brother, in his discernment of the will of God in regard to his vocation. He acknowledges his relative incapacity—young, ordained only two years, not a scholar, and with limited experience in offering spiritual direction. He tells Giabbani that he was a student of Merton's for four years, during which time he was able to observe him "casually." He describes him as a poet and a

---

1 Anselm Steinke (after leaving the Trappists, again known by his birthname, Joseph) was born in 1925 (see the biographical note in the introduction to the letters) and was thus only thirty years old at the time of the writing of this letter—very young to have been given the position of prior of Gethsemani. Given that he was a former student of Merton's, it is arguable that this letter was written not entirely of his own free will.

2. Ghini, *Oltre Ogni Limite*, 260.

3. Ibid., 263–64 n. 4.

man of genius, with strong and impetuous emotions and an extraordinarily active mind. He notes Merton's tendency to wax enthusiastic about many things, revealing, in Steinke's view, that he needs more maturity and mental discipline. This tendency of Merton's moves him to think that in his desire to be a solitary he is indeed responding to God's will, because it has been a constant with him for more than ten years. He is unable to say definitively whether this truly is Merton's vocation, but believes that "at this point in his life" he should be given the opportunity to test his vocation to solitude. He takes seriously the opposition to this prospect of Dom James, who is after all the ultimate superior of the abbey, the one through whom in the monastic tradition God speaks to the monks.

He asserts that if Merton were to go to Camaldoli, it should be on condition that he return to a Cistercian house, not necessarily Gethsemani, if it were to be discerned that Camaldolese life was not for him. He calls this an opportune stipulation, given Merton's tendency to instability and, in light of this, his need for a superior to guide him. He acknowledges that in Dom James' absence he has allowed Merton to write to the Carthusian Dom Pablo Maria, Thomas Verner Moore, and to consult him about his vocation; and he states his awareness that Moore has written back in support of Merton's desire to test his vocation to solitude. He admits that at first he agreed with Moore, but then began to question his position on the grounds that Moore was not acquainted with life at Gethsemani, nor did he know Merton personally.[4]

He then says that he supports Merton's desire to test his solitary vocation, saying that he will "pray intensely" for him, in case after a time at Camaldoli, Merton might begin to look for other opportunities to live monastic life elsewhere, which Steinke would take as a sign of Merton's resistance to monastic discipline. Recognizing that the process of obtaining a *transitus* is a slow one, he posits that Merton would not leave Gethsemani for about a year. He is happy about this because he believes that Merton's students could suffer if Merton left in the middle of their formation period, stating his conviction that Merton's presence with them was at this time indispensable, something with which he is aware that Merton disagrees.[5]

He ends by telling Giabbani that he has written to him against his will, because he knows it will cause suffering for the abbot when he finds out about it. Even so, he has done so because deep in his soul he feels he is acting in accord with God's will, and ends with the assurance of his prayers.

---

4. See LETTERS 15 and 18.

5. Cf. Merton's comment in LETTER 20, in which he states his hope that he might arrive at Camaldoli not a year or more later, but only a month later (note 28).

Letter 20 / Thomas Merton to Anselmo Giabbani; typewritten, in French, trans. DG; Italian quotation from Cardinal Larraona, LDSF.

There are three carbon copies of this letter: (a) one with a typed postscript about the "roses" (see the end of the letter); (b) one sent later, without the postscript, but bearing a note in Merton's handwriting asking Giabbani if he had received the letter of which this was a copy; and (c) one lacking both the postscript and the note, but bearing, again in Merton's handwriting, the notation, in English, "To Dom Giabbani." The originals of variants (a) and (b) are at Camaldoli; variant (c) is at the Thomas Merton Center.

jhs

OUR LADY OF GETHSEMANI
TRAPPIST, KENTUCKY
May 3, 1955

Right Reverend and dear Father:

St Romuald and St Peter Damian are here,[1] not only to console me but to put themselves seriously to work and to [help me] come to a decision about my vocation. A thousand thanks—it's magnificent.

So, my Right Reverend Father, the decisive moment has arrived. It seems that this is really the moment willed by God[2] for my *transitus* to Camaldoli. The indications are clear. I mustn't miss the moment. The opportunity may not come again for a long time. I have just received a letter from a Carthusian father, the first American Carthusian,[3] who tells me that I need to follow my vocation as a solitary, that it is necessary to obtain the *transitus*, and that it must be obtained by *your* Procurator General, and not by ours. Then, he says, if the *transitus* arrives from Rome, sent by Monsignor Montini or by some other person well regarded[4] at the Holy See, and if our Father Abbot is asked to make a favorable response, perhaps things will move ahead well. But doubtless there is no hope for this *transitus*. Dom

---

1. He means by this the relics described in Appendix II.
2. On Merton and Dom James' understanding of the will of God, see chapter 4.
3. Thomas Verner Moore/Dom Pablo Maria, OCart. Letter 18, from Moore, was written only four days before Merton wrote this letter to Giabbani.
4. In the original, *bien pensée*, inserted in Merton's handwriting.

James is opposed to it. It will be clear to you that Dom James is away from the monastery, for two weeks, and I am writing to you with the permission of the Father Prior,[5] who is directing me,[6] and who is encouraging me to seek solitude at Camaldoli. *So this letter comes to ask you, formally, to take steps as soon as possible to obtain my transitus to Camaldoli.* That is to say, to obtain it if you are really willing to receive me. I know that I am not worthy of such a vocation, but I believe that God is calling me to it, and I am leaving everything in order to respond to his call. I want to give myself totally to him in the solitary life. I want to offer myself to help create an eremitical foundation in the United States, and to open for others the road to the holy desert. It seems to me that this is very important for the Church in America. I know that my work at Gethsemani is finished,[7] and I nonetheless believe that my superiors[8] want to keep me here for reasons which are doubtless sincere, but which are motivated by impulses and considerations on human and natural levels.[9]

In sum, here is the situation in which I find myself; and the Holy See will have to understand this situation exactly—otherwise it could make a mistake.

(1) In the internal forum, my very strong pull to the solitary life, which has been with me for the last ten years, and which cannot be resisted, has been accepted by the directors whom I have consulted as an indication of the will of God. They tell me that I need to have experience of the solitary life. My Father Abbot, moreover, has always acknowledged that this pull toward solitude is from God, and he has been willing to arrange things for me, by means of special permissions, here at Gethsemani.[10] Even the Abbot

---

5. Anselm Steinke; see LETTER 19.

6. Cf. his contradictory comments in LETTER 15, both that Father Anselm is directing him "more or less, and that "I have no real director here."

7. An ironic statement, given that his major piece of monastic responsibility, as Master of Novices (1955–65), lay immediately ahead of him.

8. A misleading term, in that although the abbot was opposed, the prior was supportive. Merton here is fudging the reality that the abbot alone would make all the important decisions, including the decision to keep Merton at Gethsemani or to release him to a trial of the hermit life at Camaldoli.

9. Which I conjecture might include, understandably, given the abbot's fiduciary responsibility, the desire to keep the royalties from Merton's many books coming to Gethsemani. This remains conjectural, because there is to my knowledge no statement in writing that would support it.

10. Such as permitting him to use the tool shed, which Merton christened "St Anne's," on a limited basis; see LETTER 3, note 6.

General of the order[11] is ready to admit that I am not quite a Cistercian, that I am not fully adapted to the Trappist life. He[12] has accepted a vow that I made never to become an abbot, and he says that I wasn't cut out for that, that I was never a complete Cistercian. He adds that I am not the kind of person who can wear "off the rack" clothes in the spiritual life. Nor does he believe that I must become a hermit, and he is pressing me to stay in the order, even though he says that I am not well suited to it.

(2) In January, a Passionist spiritual director[13] told me to ask for permission to go to Camaldoli. The Father Prior was in agreement with this, and he asked the Father Abbot, who absolutely refused the request, with no explanation. Dom James has always done everything possible to block and hinder my attempts to transfer to Camaldoli, and he will not even permit me to consult with a Carthusian.[14] He intercepts any letters which arrive from a Charterhouse,[15] even the ones marked "conscience matter."[16] Thus he is not letting me decide this question of conscience in a completely free way. But I do have to state that Dom James has told me officially that he is not keeping me here because he needs me in a monastery position.[17] He has acknowledged that he would be able to get along without me. I am therefore in no way necessary to this Trappist community.

11. See introduction, note 18.

12. The vow was made not to the abbot general, but privately to Merton's own abbot, on October 8, 1952, and "accepted" by the abbot general; see Mott, *Seven Mountains*, 283.

13. See LETTER 15, note 7.

14. Manifestly this didn't stop Merton from doing so; cf. note 4.

15. I.e., a Carthusian monastery.

16. Letters containing matter that would normally be considered confidential both by the writer and the intended recipient. On Dom James' return from his time away, and in conversation with Merton, he flatly denied this: ". . . he thought certain people had written him letters he did not receive, even letters marked 'res conscientiae.' But such never happened. He only suspected that such letters had been received here. He mentioned that a certain Dom Humphrey [Pawsey], who had been the Superior of the Carthusians in Vermont with Doctor Moore, had written him a letter. . . . But that absolutely never happened. Last January one of the students [Fr Alberic] . . . decided he wanted to try the Carthusians. . . . [Merton] told the student . . . to tell Doctor Moore all about his (Father Louis') desires for a life either with the Carthusians or with the Camaldolese. Then this student was to write back the opinion of Dom Moore, marked 'res conscientiae,' so I would not be able to open it. Father Louis never received that letter because none ever came" (letter of May 17 to Dom Gabriel Sortais, TMC).

17. The following October, after he had concluded that he had no chance of receiving a *transitus* and that the abbot general was challenging him, if he wanted to be a hermit, to be a hermit "one hundred percent," Merton made himself available to be novice master (letter of October 18, 1955, TMC, Dom James to Dom Gabriel).

(3) Not only am I not needed here, but my presence tends to upset the community. The regular visitation which has just been completed focused on "the hermit mentality" which some say is in the process of sliding into[18] this community of cenobites. I spoke to the Visitor[19] and told him about my wish to go to Camaldoli; he didn't say yes or no. So I can say that he wasn't opposed to the idea, but he didn't want to try to convince Dom James that I ought to leave. The Visitor said that he wasn't expecting any change whatsoever in my "mentality" or in my spirit. Clearly then, I must continue to move in the direction of the eremitical life—but not at Gethsemani!

(4) After the visitation, I *made a vow* to move forward to a more solitary and contemplative life, and this vow has given me a lot of peace. Even if our efforts don't come to fruition, I will always have made this vow, and I will hang on to it.

(5) The Carthusian father, Dom Verner Moore, said to me: "The fact that Camaldoli hopes to make an American foundation makes me think more and more that your desire for solitude is the will of God. This being so, your leaving [Gethsemani] would no longer be a purely personal thing, but a means of making the contemplative and solitary life accessible to many vocations in our country. We must not let this possibility go sideways without going into it more deeply . . ." etc.[20] On the subject of the foundation, the Most Reverend Father [Arcadio Maria] Larraona [Saralegui][21] said to me: "*Ho vivo piacere che con cuore aperto e generoso cerchi d'aiutare les diverse forme di vita contemplativa nel loro immenso paese. E una santa e bella missione che il Signore Le affide*" ["I am greatly pleased that with an open and generous heart you are seeking to promote the different forms of the contemplative life in your vast country. It is a holy and beautiful mission that the Lord is entrusting to you"].[22]

---

18. *Se glisser*—what snakes do: the "hermit mentality" was regarded by some in the community as a kind of serpent in Eden (cf. Gen 3).

19. Dom Louis de Gonzague le Pennuen, abbot of Melleray, in France, and father immediate of Gethsemani; i.e., the abbot of the monastery from which Gethsemani was founded, the official charged with the office of visitor, and thereby with the duty of regular visitation of Gethsemani to assure himself and Gethsemani that it was faithfully living according to Trappist-Cistercian tradition.

20. Merton here is quoting, but not *verbatim*, from Moore's letter of April 29 to him (LETTER 18). Although Moore is supportive of Merton's desire for the solitary life, Merton here, in saying "we," is exaggerating the degree of his support.

21. Cf. LETTER 15, note 12.

22. Merton cites this from Larraona's first letter to him, dated March 2, 1955 (TMC).

(6) Finally, a few days after I received the relics of St Romuald and St Peter Damian, a friend of mine suddenly and spontaneously offered to pay the cost of my travel by liner to Camaldoli.[23] This friend, who is a doctor,[24] said to me: "Your life here at Gethsemani is on its way to becoming completely sterile." He believes that I would not be able to keep writing creatively in this atmosphere to which I am not at all suited. So if I stay here, my work as a writer will gradually wither away.[25]

(7) But even with all these very clear reasons for leaving, I know that Dom James will oppose my leaving with every means that he has at his disposal, overt and covert. However, if the *transitus* comes from Rome, and if he sees that the Roman Curia fully understands the situation and *wants* my transfer, in support of an American Camaldolese foundation, etc., he will yield without a lot of difficulty.

I enclose a letter from the Father Prior of Gethsemani.[26]

Thus I am waiting with the greatest hope for the arrival of the *transitus*, which will be obtained for us by your Procurator and sent by Monsignor Montini or someone else. I keep on praying, and especially I am praying for you and for all the dear Fathers, recluses, hermits and cenobites, without forgetting the good sisters and women recluses. I have very much felt the influence of their prayers. Now I know for certain that this project is going to go ahead.

How happy I would be if in June I could celebrate with you the Solemnity of St Romuald, and even that of St Benedict![27]

I assure you, dear and Right Reverend Father, of the fullness of my deepest gratitude and of all my devotion. My greatest joy will be to join your little white[28] band in solitude. *Deus vult* ["God wills it"].[29]

Your devoted son in Our Lord and Our Lady,

[Signed] F. M. Louis Merton.

---

23. I.e., to an Italian port; Camaldoli is inland.

24. Cf. Letter 15, note 5.

25. But cf. Letter 3, in which he speaks of being worn out by the work of writing.

26. Letter 19.

27. June 19 and June 11, respectively, only a few weeks later than the date of this letter—a mark of Merton's tendency to let his hopes outweigh the realities of his situation.

28. The Camaldolese wear white habits.

29. An unhappy choice of words, given that it was the war cry of the First Crusade (1096).

Then, in variant (a), there follows this postscript, not so identified:

Dom James will be back in a few days. If you write me, don't say anything about this matter, even in Italian. But if you want to tell me that you have taken steps to obtain the *transitus*, tell me something like "We have planted the roses at the hermitage." And if you have obtained the *transitus*, tell me that "The roses are *in bloom* at the hermitage."[30]

On the first page of variant (b), which lacks the postscript, is found this note in Merton's handwriting:

I think that the best thing is for me to send you this copy of my letter of [May] 3, in case you didn't receive it.

And on the first page of variant (c), which lacks both the postscript and the handwritten note, is found, again in Merton's handwriting, the notation

To Dom Giabbani

---

30. This subterfuge was necessary if the letter did not come marked "conscience matter" and was read by Dom James. Merton finally told him about his request to Camaldoli for a *transitus* after his return in mid-May 1955 from an absence of three weeks (letter of Dom James to Dom Gabriel, May 17, 1955, TMC). See also LETTER 24.

LETTER 21 / Merton to Giabbani; handwritten, in French, trans. DG; original at Camaldoli.

+[1]
OUR LADY OF GETHSEMANI
Trappist-Cistercian Abbey
TRAPPIST, KENTUCKY
May 6, 1955

Right Reverend and dear Father,

Have you sent the photographs of Camaldoli to La Pierre-Qui-Vire for the French edition of our book? I was happy to receive the ones you sent us here; they are very beautiful. I would also like to have them for the French edition. Can you ask the photographer—Marioni—to find in his archive #743 the following negatives: numbers 428, 317, 403, 439, 422, 312; and make proofs of them for La Pierre-Qui-Vire? I will send the photographs that I have here to my publisher in New York. I hope that the Italian translation of the book is going well, and that you are pleased with it.

I especially hope that you received my important letter of the third of this month, which is to say, of last Tuesday.[2] It was sent by our Father Prior along with one of his own letters—it concerns my *transitus* to Camaldoli—that I am asking you to agree to obtain through the good offices of Monsignor Montini or some other highly placed person. I am going to send you a letter from a Passionist confessor which is also favorable to this.[3] Altogether, I have more than five spiritual directors who are encouraging me to seek the solitary life in a definite way, and there is only my superior who is opposed to it. I find this question important not only for myself—it's a *question of principle*. It concerns the rights of the Holy Spirit in the souls of monks: can someone move from the cenobitic life to the eremitical life, yes or no? According to Trappists, every vocation to a solitary life, any movement for a Trappist to the eremitical life, is an illusion. On the contrary, it is necessary to fight against this error. If you haven't received this letter tell me immediately, please. If you have received it, I am sure that you will know how to use the best methods for obtaining the necessary permission for me

---

1. The sign of the cross, used as a devotional heading to a letter.
2. LETTER 20.
3. Not extant.

to move to Italy in order to test [my vocation to] the Camaldolese life, and I think that my abbot will accept that document once the Holy See sends it to him. I pray constantly for this favor from God.

At this point I have some new suggestions for a Camaldolese foundation in America.

1) Manifestly, cenobites will be part of this foundation. I think that the cenobium will also be a retreat house for laypeople. The cenobites will look after it. But in any case I believe that the hermitage will be the most important part [of the foundation], even if there were only two or three hermits. For the Church in America, the *witness of the eremitical life*, the search for God alone in perfect silence and solitude, is especially necessary. I do think it is necessary to maintain the Camaldolese ideal in a complete sense, but without doubt with a lot of flexibility. To set up a Camaldolese foundation here without hermits would be a very serious error. We need to present to the United States the real face of Camaldoli—hermits first of all, and cenobites as well.

2) We perhaps ought to envisage two Camaldolese foundations, each one with both a cenobium and an *eremo*, one in the mountains of the eastern United States, the other in the mountains of the West. California would be an ideal place for the Camaldolese.[4]

3) Without too much difficulty we can find some generous benefactors who will help establish the foundation. It will be much easier to establish a Camaldolese foundation than a Trappist one.

4) The Camaldolese foundation, especially the cenobium, ought to radiate interior life and contemplative spirituality through sermons and conferences[5] as at Camaldoli, that is to say, all of them good.

I therefore continue to pray in the most fervent way for this foundation, and especially that the Lord will deign to give me an intimate share in this, in one of the first foundations of an American *eremo*! Everything is in God's hands. I am anxiously awaiting a reply from you that will tell me that you did receive my letter of May 3 and that steps are going to be taken at the court of Rome. I thank you in advance.

Bless me, Right Reverend and dear Father, and ask the Holy Virgin to bring me safely into port.

[Signed] F M Louis.

---

4. Camaldoli did in fact make two foundations, but both in the West, in California—the first, New Camaldoli, near Big Sur, a hermitage with no attached cenobium, the second an urban house of studies, in Berkeley.

5. By "conferences," he means spiritual addresses or presentations.

P.S. The publisher has decided not to publish the entire text of *Silence in Heaven* with the collection of photos; but the complete text will appear as a separate book with two or three photos only. I think that that will also work better for the Italian edition.

LETTER 22 / *Merton to Giabbani; typewritten, in French, trans. DG; original at Camaldoli. The copy of this* LETTER *at the Thomas Merton Center has no* LETTER*head address, but is a carbon copy on plain paper.*

jhs
May 10, 1955

Right Reverend and dear Father,
Thanks with all my heart for your fine letter from Stapehill;[1] I await the other letter which you promise me. I am writing you in case you will not yet have had time to write that other, because on April 25 a decision was made.

    I want as quickly as possible to let you know what is happening. But first I do thank you for the good advice you give me in your letter. I am in full agreement with it. If I am seeking a more solitary life, it is indeed in order to be more alone and more silent with God. I have no desire whatever to write a new *Sign of Jonas*[2] in order to defend myself against the voices of those who have something to say about my leaving. I no longer desire to display to the public the small amount of intimate life that I have with God. There is hardly enough of that for myself; so why would I invite everybody else to enter into that life in order to see my spiritual poverty? If I do come to Camaldoli, we will talk about this question again. I think my Superiors would like me to write something about the solitary life, especially because Camaldoli would like to make a foundation in America. But I assure you, Right Reverend Father, that I will make every effort to avoid everything which is worldly, everything which smacks of publicity. I have seen enough of that, I am already too mixed up in it, and I am sick of it. God doesn't need it. If however I do become a solitary, and it is necessary to write, I will try to convince my Superiors that God's cause will be served in a unique way by writings which are austere, simple and monastic; by meditations, by short books on prayer, on Holy Scripture, and on the monastic life, and not big treatises or autobiographies. But as I say, we will talk about this again.

    1. LETTER 14. Stapehill Abbey is near Wimborne, in the West Country county of Dorset, in England, and was at that time home to a community of Trappistine nuns. The "other letter" from Giabbani to which Merton refers, LETTER 25, is also not extant.
    2. Merton had only managed to have *Jonas* published over the objections of the Trappist censors through the intervention of Jacques Maritain.

In sum, as a writer, I see more and more that my first duty is to become more and more a man of God. I've even been told that this is one of the reasons why I should leave Gethsemani. If I want to transfer to another Order, it is not in order to write more, but to write less and pray more.

So that is why I am writing to you, Right Reverend Father. I must warn you about what I believed myself obligated to do.

At the same time that I was writing to you, about April 25,[3] I also wrote to a Carthusian, Dom Verner Moore, who is, so to speak, the founder of the American Charterhouse. I had tried a number of times to consult him, but Dom James has always refused me permission to do so, saying, without explanation, that "it's not the will of God." I must also tell you that, two years ago, when I did have permission to write to and receive letters from the Vermont Charterhouse, instead of giving me a reply which came marked *res conscientiae* ["conscience matter"],[4] he kept the letter for several weeks after having opened it, and didn't give it to me until it was too late for me to do what the letter was telling me to do: I had been invited to make a retreat at the Charterhouse in order to come to a decision. Now in this letter,[5] Dom Verner Moore told me flatly that he thought that there was no way I could decide on my vocation without going to a solitary order to experience the life. He told me that it was necessary for me to do this, and knowing that Dom James (who was away: the Father Prior permitted me to read this letter) would forbid this, told me that the best thing would be to ask for a *transitus*. He told me to ask for the *transitus* via the good offices of Camaldoli. The Father Prior (Anselm),[6] who is my spiritual director, was in agreement, and I wrote to Camaldoli so that you could begin to do whatever is necessary for me to have a *transitus*.

I told you, Right Reverend Father, in the other letter[7] that I believed that it was the will of God for me to test my vocation to the solitary life. I did not say that it was absolutely the will of God for me to be a solitary. But the spiritual direction which I received from this Carthusian father and from our Father Prior, along with two other very objective and impartial directors, prompts me to believe that God wills this effort on my part.

You will perhaps say to me that I have acted precipitately. I would have preferred to move more slowly, to follow the regular procedures. But the circumstances render this morally impossible. Dom James doesn't look at

---

3. LETTER 17; not extant.
4. See LETTER 20, note 17.
5. Not the letter of two years previous, but the letter of April 29 (LETTER 18).
6. Steinke; see LETTER 19 and LETTER 15, note 5.
7. LETTER 17.

these things directly. If I should run it by him, he will close his eyes and say, "It's not the will of God." You said in your letter that one cannot tell what the will of God is without a careful self-examination. But this is precisely what Dom James is doing. You can tell him about the problem.

But he is occupied by the foundations,[8] by administration, etc., etc. (which is fine: I don't criticize him for that); but while the telephone rings five or six times, and while he is answering those calls, he is "thinking" about the question; and after a few minutes he says,[9] "It's not the will of God."

Given what my spiritual directors tell me, and given my personal conviction, I see that there is no way to work through this issue at Gethsemani, and that in order to see clearly it is necessary for me to place myself in the environment of a solitary Order. That's what I want to do, and it is for that reason that I have had to take the steps which I have been advised to take by a real man of God.[10]

I believe that you really understand me, that you will take the side of my conscience in order to protect my right to decide this issue freely, in the light of God, and not in the midst of the racket[11] and the moral pressure which exists here. Someone will pay for my trip, it won't cost the monastery anything, and as I said,[12] I can use a make-believe excuse[13] to take a trip without anyone knowing the reason for it. They could even let it be believed at Gethsemani that I had gone to the [new] foundation in California.[14] But I confess to you that I don't like these evasions, and I am not ingenious enough to make them up. I will leave all that to others.

To conclude: I ask you to believe, Right Reverend and dear Father, that I have full confidence in your sense of justice and paternal love for one of your sons who certainly has a problem—one which appears large and

---

8. Overflowing with monks at this time, Gethsemani was establishing a number of new monasteries, an enterprise for which Dom James was chiefly responsible.

9. Merton here typed *de* ("of") instead of *dit* ("says").

10. Given that Merton had been collecting support from at least four spiritual directors, it is not clear here to which of these he is referring, although most probably he means Thomas Verner Moore. However, it *is* clear that he is insulting Dom James, by inferring that he is *not* "a real man of God," at least in the same sense or to the same degree.

11. Probably a reference to the noise made by the factories that Dom James had had built at Gethsemani. See TTW, entry of October 19, 1961 (170–71)—an indication that six years later, the noise had not abated.

12. In fact, he hasn't previously said this in an extant letter to Giabbani.

13. The French is *un prétexte spécieux*, "a specious excuse."

14. New Clairvaux, at Vina, California, established in July 1955, two months after Merton wrote this letter.

important to him, since it concerns my life and my very vocation.[15] Yes, I know that I could be under an illusion, but so long as I stay in the situation in which I find myself, I will not come out from under it. But since I have received very positive advice from more than four very objective and prudent spiritual directors, I am not too afraid that I would be making a mistake in going to see what the solitary life would be like for me. It's just a question of testing it. In my heart, I am persuaded that such a testing would be successful, if I were permitted to undertake it. But I can't prove that in advance. I ask you simply, humbly, with all the simplicity of your own son, to support me in relation to Dom James, and to give me some positive encouragement which will help my Father Abbot to let go of his prejudices and those actions of his which have at least the appearance of injustice as well as being imprudent and uncharitable. (I readily admit that Dom James doesn't think so. He believes that he has the right to deal with these questions in a way which[16] would appear to other people to be ill-considered and arbitrary.) The Holy Virgin will not let us stray from the straight path. We love her and we have confidence in her Immaculate Heart. You have placed me in her hands, and I am very happy to be there. I ask you to bless me, and to forgive me for any way in which I may have offended you in what I have done, but as I have told you, I have persisted in my belief before God that I have been doing what he wanted of me, and I believe this more strongly as the days go by. I remain affectionately and devotedly yours in Our Lord and Our Lady.

The copy is not signed.

---

15. The inconsistent use of pronouns here is Merton's own.

16. In Merton's view; others believed, contrary to Merton's inference, that Dom James was protecting Merton from his own restlessness, his *acedia*.

LETTER 23 / *Fox to Montini, typewritten, in English; original in the Merton Dossier in the Montini Archive in the Milan Archdiocesan Archives.*

[The Most Reverend Giovanni Battista Montini
Archbishop of Milan]
May 16, 1955

Your Excellency:

This is the first letter I have ever written to you, Your Excellency, but we have received many letters signed by you, when you were the Substitute Secretary of State for our Holy Father.[1] They were acknowledgements of Mass intentions, which we try to send regularly, about one thousand every month, to our Holy Father.

We are writing to you in regard to our good Father Louis, who is known to the world as Thomas Merton. Some of his books have been sent to you. Good Father Louis, as you know, is really a genius in writing books. He is very dynamic and bubbling over with energy, and has a very expansive imagination. He is writing you a letter[2] concerning his vocational difficulties. I thought that it would be to the purpose for me to write also, so you would have as complete a picture as possible.

Father Louis came to Gethsemani in 1941, some fourteen years ago. He made his solemn vows eight years ago, and was ordained here six years ago. He has been troubled by vocational difficulties for the last several years. For a while he thought he should join the Carthusians. More recently he has changed his desires and wishes to join the Camaldolese. In all this matter, we keep before us that the question is, what is God's Will? Not what is Father Louis' Will, or what is my will, or anybody else's will.

God does not send a telegram; we have to form our judgment by various external and interior indices that we can perceive. My thoughts fall into two divisions. First, the thoughts about Father Louis in himself; secondly, in regard to Father Louis and his relations with others.

Father Louis in himself, as we said, he is very dynamic, more extrovert than introvert. He spends most of his free time in reading and writing books.

---

1. Pius XII, pope 1939–58.
2. He had already written this letter (LETTER 16, April 25, 1955).

I provided a small cabin for him within our enclosure, in some woods, principally in order that he might be able to pray and to be alone with God. He uses most of that time for typewriting his manuscripts.

"The Following of Christ"[3] says, "Inspirations come from God, but not all inspirations come from God." Father Louis gives great importance to the fact that he has had the urges and inclinations and desires for a more solitary life for many years, and they still persist.

If you will allow me to be personal, I myself had terrific inclinations and attractions and urging to leave Gethsemani for the Carthusians. These have persisted, not for ten years, as with Father Louis, but for some twenty years. And yet I know that it is not God's Will for me to follow those urges, even though they remain very vivid in my soul.

It becomes more and more clear to me that what God wants is the immolation of my desires and wills to His spoken Will, no matter how I feel about it.

In my heart, Your Excellency, I think that if God had followed your desires and inclinations, you would never have accepted to become the Archbishop of Milan; but you immolated your inclinations and ideals to God's Sovereign Will.

Good Father Louis was not born in a Catholic family, but came into the Church when he was some twenty-three or twenty-four years old.[4] He is inclined to give much weight to subjective feelings.

Anyone who resists God's Will cannot have peace with himself, or with companions. This is the fault, not of our companions, or the externals of our life. The fault is in our interior; namely, a lack of submission, keeping up the effort, no doubt unconsciously and without any positive deliberate effort, to make God conform to our will, rather than for us to conform to His Will.

As regards his relations with others, Father Louis does not realize that he is a public figure in our community and in the great world outside, both Catholic and non-Catholic.

In our community, he is the Master of the Students, of whom he has had at various times some forty under his charge. He is very well liked by every one of the students. They look upon him as an oracle of spirituality and lean heavily upon him for their guidance in the spiritual life. If he ever were to leave here, it would be a source of great scandal to our young professed

---

3. Perhaps a reference to *The Following of Christ*, by Johannes Tauler (c. 1300–1361).

4. He refers here to Merton's conditional baptism on November 16, 1938, when he was twenty-three; see SSM, 221–25.

and would betray them into the spirit of instability and change. I can hardly picture what the results of his change from here would be.

Concerning his relations with the outside world, both Catholic and non-Catholic, good Father Louis does not realize that he is a public figure of tremendous importance.

In my travels, I hear comments on how much confidence priests and religious place in Father Louis and in his writings. Here again there would be tremendous scandal to know that he was really quite restless and unsure of himself after having spent fourteen years in one monastery.

His influence as a writer would be destroyed in a marked degree, as indeed some of his friends have written to him when he broached the question of changing orders.[5] They would not distinguish between a higher Order and a lower Order, so to speak; they would just know that he was unstable.

For example, a certain Father Barnabas Mary [Ahern], C.P., of Chicago[6] wrote to me about Father Louis when he had asked him about changing Orders. Father Barnabas is a very wonderful religious and is a recognized theologian. He wrote that if Father should leave his present Order, it would cause tremendous scandal among the American reading public, both Catholic and non-Catholic.

Father Barnabas wrote Father Louis directly, as follows:

> Father, in St. Thomas' treatment of change (II-II, Q 189, art. 8),[7] he points out one feature that renders it 'not commendable'—the danger of scandal. If a change will needlessly upset a number of people, then the law of charity forbids us to put this stumbling block in their way. You have no idea of the upset a radical change on your part would cause:
>
> 1—It would be an encouragement to all people in religious life who are 'itching' for change.
>
> 2—It would cut vocations to your Trappist way of life, since your change would be a frank confession that you have not found there the prospect you have held out to others.

---

5. Whereas, of course, other friends communicated to him their views to the contrary.

6. Passionist priest and noted biblical scholar (1915–95). The letter is held in the archives of the Thomas Merton Center.

7. A reference to the *Summa Theologica* of St. Thomas Aquinas.

3—It will lessen the influence you have exerted and the good you can do. Many will say, 'I told you so!' and will point to your change as proof that your writing has not come from conviction but from emotion.

4—It will make many good religious uneasy in their way of life. Most nuns and many male religious do not reason; and so they will conclude, 'If Thomas Merton could not find union with God at Gethsemani, how can I expect to find it in my way of life.'

5—'Practical people' will make capital of this in decrying contemplation; and, once more, in many quarters, contemplation will again become suspect. Superiors will ban Thomas Merton[8] the way they have banned St. John of the Cross and St. Teresa: 'They all put too many crazy ideas in people's heads.'

In other words, Father, so much of the value of your previous and future writing depends on your stability and perseverance in the life you have chosen. In a previous generation people could make changes without causing commotion—as did St. Romuald and St. Bruno;[9] but not so in our age. Today we look upon change as an indication that one is living emotionally rather than by faith. As one of our old Masters put it, 'We must be able to find Jesus in the here and now—even on the corner of State and Madison; or we are not men of Faith. We would be looking for feeling rather than for fact.'

So, Father, I think that God's will rivets you to Gethsemani, as He was riveted to His Cross. Let others do what they want and what they think God's Spirit prompts them to. You have the external manifestation of His Will which closes the issue for you. That Will of His is manifest in the very Providence that has used your writings to do good. If you change you shall tear from your written works the seal of Him who never changes. Father, I do not think that under any condition you can leave Gethsemani, any more than a Bishop can leave his diocese; you are wedded to it until death—for better or worse.

One other example, Your Excellency, is that our Most Reverend Abbot General Gabriel Sortais wrote me that recently he met in Rome the Bishop

---

8. I.e., his writings.
9. The founders, respectively, of the Camaldolese and the Carthusians.

of Copenhagen, Denmark. They were talking together, and the Bishop of Copenhagen said that he had heard that Father Louis was thinking of transferring from the monastery, and he added, "That would be a very grave scandal." The Bishop was thinking of his Denmark Diocese, of course, where there are very few Catholics, and where he is trying to popularize Father Louis' books.

Father Louis thinks that I do not give his case sufficient consideration. Just this very day we have talked for over an hour and a quarter together, and it is not the first time. I did tell him I wanted more time to consider it all, but at the present moment it seemed [sic] to me there was more of nature than of grace, more of self-seeking than of seeking God.

Your Excellency, before God I say to you, and I am ready to meet this decision at the Last Judgment, that I cannot see the finger of God in Father Louis' desire to change. I am in no way afraid of taking the entire responsibility for this decision on myself. I do not fear any criticism in any way.

Having been through the whole experience myself—maybe that is why God permitted it—in order that I might more easily see into similar trials of others—it is very clear to me that whereas God may truly draw us to a life of greater silence and solitude with Himself alone, these attractions need not require a change of externals, but a change in our interior.

All the monks of Gethsemani have a special and affectionate remembrance for you, Your Excellency, and for all your needs, personal and official, material and spiritual, temporal and eternal, in the daily round of our Trappist Cistercian life,

> All for Jesus—thru Mary—with a smile,
> Fr. M. James, O.C.S.O.
> Abbot

> His Excellency,
> The Most Reverend Giovanni B. Montini
> Pallazzo Archiepiscopale[10]
> Milano, ITALIA

---

10. For *Pallazzo*, read *Palazzo*; for *Archiepiscopale*, read *Arcivescovale*.

LETTER 24 / *Merton to Giabbani; typewritten, in French, trans. DG; original at Camaldoli.*

Gethsemani
May 17, 1955
jhs

Right Reverend and dear Father:

Here is yet another letter. Forgive me. Clearly this issue interests me greatly. I am trying too hard, too zealously, to assert my reasoning. In any case, I have the feeling that I am not in a normal situation, that unlike other religious, I don't have the good fortune to be able to decide this question about transferring to another order in a simple enough way. That is the whole question.

Dom James came back on Sunday. I laid everything in front of him, both in writing and conversation. He was very hurt to think that I had asked for a *transitus* without consulting him. But I had consulted him in January and I came to the conclusion then that nothing could be worked out with him. Even so, I think that the fact of my having asked for a *transitus* produced a helpful reaction, because for the first time we really considered the issue in detail, and for the first time Dom James gave me his reasons why I should remain at Gethsemani.

I told him that *five* spiritual directors had advised me to go to Camaldoli to test my vocation to the solitary life. (I had told you about four, I think.[1] But I have also consulted a Jesuit theologian, one of the best moral

---

1. In his letter of May 6, LETTER 21, he had said that he had consulted "more than five"; in his letter of May 10, LETTER 22, he says "more than four." So far he has mentioned Thomas Verner Moore, Anselm Steinke, and Father Vincent, the Passionist (LETTER 15, note 14). To these we may now add this Jesuit, not here named, but named elsewhere as "Father Ford, a great friend of Father Raymond" (letter of Dom James to Dom Gabriel Sortais, May 17, 1955, TMC). This would not have been Father Barry Ford, a diocesan priest and not a Jesuit, pastor of Corpus Christi Church in New York, to whom Merton first spoke about becoming a Roman Catholic (SSM 215–16, 218, 340). The fifth is another monk of Gethsemani, Father Timothy, also named in Dom James' letter of May 17. When we combine these five "spiritual directors" with Merton's statement in LETTER 15 that he has *no* real director, it is irresistible to place beside these statements the conversation of Jesus with the woman at the well: "Jesus said to her, 'Go, call your husband' . . . The woman answered him, 'I have no husband.' Jesus said to her, 'You are right in saying "I have no husband," for you have had five husbands, and the one you have now is not your husband'" (John 4:16–18).

theologians in the U.S. He was more than astonished by the ways in which Dom James has been trying to keep me away from any contact with the Carthusians of Sky Farm, to prevent me from consulting spiritual directors outside the monastery, and so on.)

Dom James replied that spiritual direction from these men was worthless; that he, the abbot, was *the only one* who could make a decision which would really be God's decision. He spoke of that in a way which included both the internal forum and the external forum at the same time. He said that it was a "natural"[2] spirit which had led me to consult these spiritual directors, and that I would have listened to my superior and to a confessor from here who is in agreement with Dom James if I had been led by a "supernatural" spirit in this matter.

He went on to say that from the moment that one makes a solemn vow of stability, it is impossible [for that person] to receive permission to go elsewhere: not that the *transitus* would be impossible to obtain, but that it was such a great evil that it should never be requested.[3]

His strongest reason is that people would be scandalized if I change orders. But all the same, I think that he very much exaggerates this possibility of scandal. The Jesuit theologian told me flatly: "You're not that important!" Dom James forgets the possibility *of edification*.... It could do some good, even here at Gethsemani. Manifestly Dom James is thinking of the reputation of his house.[4] But after all, the reputation of Gethsemani doesn't depend on me. And if it is true that I ought to leave, then I must leave even if the reputation of the house should suffer a little. God would see to it that this small loss was compensated.

I am writing to you again because I more and more believe that this issue will eventually fall into your hands. Dom James will not accept the *transitus*, and the Congregation[5] will perhaps ask for your opinion. Furthermore, I am convinced that you are in a better position to make a fair and objective decision. I am sorry to say that I no longer have confidence in Dom James' assessment of this issue because I have seen him *judge in a precisely opposite way* in the entirely comparable cases of religious who want to leave another order in order to come to Gethsemani. If I were a Benedictine who wanted to come to Gethsemani, then my spiritual directors would be

---

2. I.e., not supernatural or spiritual.

3. Here Dom James contradicts chapter 1 of *The Rule of St. Benedict*, which speaks of anchorites or hermits, who have "spent much time in the monastery testing themselves ... for the single combat of the hermit," 47.

4. I.e., the monastery.

5. The Congregation for Religious at the Vatican.

angels of good counsel, my motives purely supernatural, my abbot a tyrant who would try to get in God's way, and so on.

It's very possible that my human nature may be mixed up in my attempts, but even so, I am convinced that justice and divine grace and the normal practice of the Church should require on my behalf the right and the opportunity *to go to see* if the life of this other order suits me, instead of being treated like a madman who is trying to escape from his asylum.

In speaking to Father Prior, Dom James expressed his unhappiness that Father Prior had permitted me to write to a Carthusian and to consult a Jesuit.[6] On Sunday I asked Dom James if I had his permission to consult one of these spiritual directors by means of a sealed letter marked *res conscientiae*, and he told me that he did not believe that permissions of that kind were given in our Order!

Right Reverend Father, you can see the problem. Dom James, because he has a "feeling" or an "intuition" that I am acting "out of natural motives," is determined, cost what it may, to block every attempt on my part to test this vocational issue. I believe that in doing that, in the present situation, he is doing violence to my conscience. Of course, if he succeeds, I will accept everything without complaint, but I believe, though I may be mistaken, that I have the right to acquaint our Abbot General with the facts of the situation.

Because these very fine spiritual directors, these objective guides, these holy men, who are impartial and solid, have told me that *it is necessary* to ask for a *transitus* so that I can test my vocation elsewhere, I have done so. I beg you to let me undertake this testing. I beg you not to leave me totally at the mercy of the "suppositions" and "feelings" of Dom James, who is energetically "supposing" that once I am out of Gethsemani, I will walk the entire world[7] living it up (that's what he said to Father Prior). I know that *nemo est judex in propria causa* ["No one is judge in his own trial"], but even so I have the impression that Dom James *knows* me without *understanding* me.

I beg you also, Right Reverend Father, to guarantee to me the possibility of consulting a spiritual director from time to time—three or four times a year—by means of a sealed letter.[8] I ask that not only because of Dom James, but especially because of his secretary, who is more autocratic

---

6. Joseph Steinke's memory of this is that Dom James "threw a fit" (personal conversation, September 15, 2009).

7. Surely a reference, conscious or unconscious, to Job 1:7, in which Satan tells God that this is what he has been doing.

8. A curious comment, because had he gone to Camaldoli he would have had a spiritual director there.

than any superior whatsoever, who sticks his nose into everything, and even gives orders to Father Prior during Dom James' absence.[9]

Again a long letter. Pardon, Right Reverend Father. I hope that it's finished. I place myself now, and once again, into the hands of God. I [will] accept very willingly however this will be settled by the Church. If I have not been humble enough, forgive me, bless me, pray for me. I am the most devoted of your sons, and perhaps the most miserable (sometimes). I remain fully united with you in Jesus and Mary.

This copy of the letter is not signed.

---

9. Brother Alfred McCartney, secretary to Dom James from October 1948 to January 1957 (e-mail message to author from Brother Alfred, November 21, 2009).

Letter 25 / Giabbani to Merton

A letter, presumably in Italian, written between May 17 and 28, 1955, referred to in Letter 26—*not extant.*

LETTER 26 / *Merton to Giabbani; typewritten, in French, trans. DG; original at Camaldoli. There is another copy of this* LETTER *in the file at the Thomas Merton Center, unsigned.*

jhs
Gethsemani
Trappist Ky.
May 28, 1955

Right Reverend and dear Father:

Thank you for your letter,[1] which assures me that everything is going well with the translation, etc. I must however warn you that the article "In the Wilderness of God"[2] will perhaps make a rather amusing impression in the *Bolletino*[3] if you don't add a note such as the following: "This article deals particularly with the individual eremitical life outside the religious state. Thus it is aimed at the very special insecurity which is part of pure eremitism. But what is said here can be applied, with certain reservations, to all solitary life, for every solitary is a poor brother of God,[4] poor because he has nothing except God alone, and therefore infinitely rich in his very poverty." You can edit that as you wish. Thank you.

I have just written you a little letter of introduction to Mrs Luce,[5] and I am enclosing it for you. I think you can find a benefactor in America without too much difficulty. I am thinking a lot about a possible location. Of course, there's no rush. Right now I am not in a very good position to be thinking about locations because I don't know the mountain country of the West, which without doubt would be the most solitary location.

I spoke to Dom James about the whole question of the *transitus*. He opposes it frankly and completely, and he wants to find a solution for the question here,[6] so as not to have recourse to the *transitus*. But since I have

1. Presumably LETTER 25.

2. Published in Italian, in *Vita Monastica*, as "Nel deserto": see also LETTER 9, note 7.

3. I.e., the "bulletin" of Camaldoli, *Vita Monastica*.

4. Cf. the last page of the SSM, 423, where he speaks of "the Cistercian abbey of the poor men who labor in Gethsemani."

5. See LETTER 5, note 12. The letter of introduction is not extant.

6. Which he finally did, when he permitted Merton to use the building previously

made a vow and since I have asked for the *transitus*, I really think that the will of God for me is always to move in the direction of the most perfect solitude. Dom James insists that I will create a very great scandal, which will injure souls.

That's his strongest reason for setting himself against the *transitus*. I have asked him to leave the final judgment on this question in the hands of the Sacred Congregation, and doubtless Monsignor Montini would be able to shed some light on it. Our Right Reverend Father Dom Gabriel Sortais told me that, while opposing changes in the Order in principle, he would be willing to let me leave for Camaldoli if it really was the will of God, and he is leaving the responsibility for a decision to my conscience instead.[7] I pray always, and truly believe that the will of God for me is becoming more and more clear. If I had the power to do what I believe I ought to do, I would leave for Italy tomorrow. But I don't know if Dom James will end up keeping me here anyway, since the *transitus* depends in part on the abbot *a quo*.[8] Let us keep on praying that the will of God be done. Tomorrow is the day of Pentecost, and I will redouble my prayers for the light and strength of the Holy Spirit for all those who have the power to make decisions, and most of all for myself. I thank God for having given me Superiors with much good will and with a truly supernatural spirit, and I am very sorry for having made them suffer because of my desire to leave the Cistercian Order, but even so I believe that God has called me here for a spiritual formation which will prepare me for a more solitary life.[9]

I truly believe that the powerful prayers of the hermits of Camaldoli[10] are exerting a major influence in my favor. I thank them for this, and I hope that they will continue to pray for me, for I am a man without virtue, one who does not deserve such a calling from God. Bless me, Right Reverend

---

used for ecumenical discussions as his hermitage (1965–68). See Mott, *Seven Mountains*, Part Six, "Mount Olivet."

7. Instead of Dom James making the decision. But in 1959, he colluded with Dom James in having the Congregation for Religious refuse Merton the indult he had requested, which would have given him a three-year leave from Gethsemani.

8. Dom James also uses the term in his letter to Dom Gabriel Sortais of May 17 (TMC), insisting that "for a *transitus* to become effective it must have the permission of the superior 'a quo.'" Abbot Elias Dietz writes, "When a monk transfers from one community (or institute) to another, formal consent is needed from the superiors of the respective communities: the abbot he is leaving (*a quo*, literally, 'from whom') and the abbot he is going to (*ad quem*, literally, 'to whom')." E-mail message to author, July 7, 2014.

9. As affirmed by St. Benedict in the first chapter of the *Rule*.

10. Again he neglects to mention the cenobitic members of the Camaldoli community.

and dear Father, and receive herewith the assurance of my most devoted regards in Our Lord and Our Lady.

[Signed] fr M. Louis

LETTER 27 / *Montini to Merton; handwritten, in Italian; original at the Thomas Merton Center; original translator unknown, translation checked by LDSF. As* LETTERS *28 and 29, it is written on official letterhead, which in the upper left-hand corner shows the coat of arms of the archdiocese of Milan, under which appears, in Italian, Montini's title:* L'Arcivescovo di Milano (The Archbishop of Milan).

Camaldoli di Gussago[1]
Brescia, Italy
Feast of St Bernard
August 20, 1955

Dear and Reverend Father Merton,

I am writing to you after so much delay, I know, and about one of your questions which would have deserved an immediate reply. I can imagine your wonder and impatience at this silence of mine. Please forgive me.

But your letter was a source of much thought to me, so that my thoughts have held me for a long time in a state of perplexity; the search for a greater good is always something that deserves much consideration, [and] when such a seeking becomes manifest in the souls we come across, a feeling of respect invades our spirit. Usually it is the indication of the operative presence of God in the soul; and there is no need to disregard and impede this mysterious action. Now, the soul of Father Merton inspired me with particular reverence and fear; I also have read some of your writings with much interest and have blessed the Lord who has made you capable of leading our world to some salutary meditations. To this reverent fear was added my daily work which is never enough, even on a small scale, to satisfy the cares of a diocese like Milan; [thus] the necessary occupations of my ministry have prevented hitherto my complying with that duty to you. I repeat: please forgive me.

But today I write. St Bernard brings before me the Monastery of Our Lady of Gethsemani with so vivid an impression that I hope he will give to my reply some light emanating from him. And, moreover, I am at an old Camaldolese monastery, which for many years has stood abandoned by

---

1. A Camaldolese house, the site of a former *eremo*, as he says later in the letter, where he was staying at the time of writing.

its monks, so that it has lost the characteristic look of the hermitage. The cells of the monks have disappeared, as has every indication of a cloister. But there remains a little church of pure and severe lines, a few humble dwellings surrounding it. A little villa, further off, shelters the owner, who is the old and venerable bishop of Mantua, now in retirement. But the natural surroundings of this ancient place of prayer and of silence are tranquil and serene. The bare hills bear upon their sides the ancient hermitage, and in front of them stretches in placid immensity the beautiful Paduan plain, overlooking a vision of the world, where human life hums with the modern intensity of its traffic, of its fatigue, of its ambitions; and from here one contemplates in silence, with a higher abandon that appears to discover in the open spaces and the heights a wisdom capable of judging, of giving to things their true value, and of feeling oneself the closer to God the further one is from human beings and their affairs. I say this because I wanted to be closer to your spirit, which knows the language of silence and is still interrogating its mysterious fascination.

Reverend Father Giabbani had with much reserve hinted to me of the idea which had blossomed in your soul of leaving Gethsemani and coming to the Camaldolese house of Arezzo, in search of a silence and a solitude which should be still deeper, still fuller of the Divine Word. Your letter shows me that this idea has not faded. You ask me for advice and I hesitate to give it. I am favorably inclined to the Camaldolese monks and follow with interest the efforts they are making to give back to their religious family a consistency which time, adversity, [and] the diversity of internal opinions have caused them to lose. They are outlining more sharply their spiritual features, their constitutions, their function in the Church of God, the numbers [they need]. The effort is a noble one but it is not finished. It will, I hope, succeed in giving Italy an example of contemplative life which at present is almost lacking in it. Contemplative life, organized in the classical form of western monasticism, has not yet acquired in Italy a full expression since Napoleon,[2] and since the political unification of the nation.[3] A renewal, a very generous one, is to be observed in some Benedictine monasteries, but it is still suffering under a great number of material difficulties and from a scarcity of vocations. Neither the attraction nor the influence of these centers of contemplative life could be said to be notable in Italy at present.

For these first considerations I would not care to encourage your transfer from a house where religious life is flourishing and blessed to another

---

2. I.e., since Napoleon's invasion of northern Italy in the early years of the nineteenth century, at which time many monasteries were closed. See Appendix I.

3. In 1861.

which could scarcely offer you what you desire, in spite of the goodness of the people around you.

But there are other considerations which make my opinion hesitate still more as to how opportune your transfer might be. I am looking at your position from afar off and from outside, and I see that it now through the grace of God causes many spirits to look to Gethsemani. If this position were to change, many souls would receive a terrible shock. This judgment is not purely utilitarian. It ends up in recognizing that the Lord has given Father Merton a capacity for good, a mission to fulfill, a service to render, which a change of place would ruin. The Lord, I think, has tied up your liberty by giving to your present religious life a fecundity which no longer belongs to you alone; it belongs to souls, it belongs to the Church. On this point you must admit that your superiors, and also your far-off spiritual friends, such as myself, have a judgment which is clearer than your own.

But all this is still outside your intimate spiritual problem, on which you are the first, and, in the end, the only one to feel and to judge, and on which you must speak to and want God alone, and he alone must guide you. On this essential aspect of your problem I must hold my peace. I know too little to speak or to advise. Let it however be permitted me still to submit two suggestions for your consideration. The first is elementary, and you know it well: to trust yourself to the advice of him who wishes you well and who is your superior; put your soul under the influence of a[4] spiritual director and under that of your abbot. The humility of this procedure is agreeable to God's way of life.

The other is one which considers the dissatisfaction which often accompanies souls desirous of perfection as to the means employed for achieving it. I say only that this dissatisfaction cannot be the sole criterion for the practical governance of one's own life, especially when it has already settled on a state which already favors perfection. You must also remember that perfection does not consist in the circumstances which favor it, but rather in the charity of the soul seeking it; and that the search at a given moment does not turn on the modification of the external conditions of life, but on the interior conditions of spiritual feeling and orientation. Usually no one enjoys the achievement of conditions agreeable with their own plans and dreams. Providential circumstances change the practical program of our life; and in the end it is necessary to love and serve that form of life which the providential vicissitudes of our pilgrimage impose on us, and to

---

4. I take this to mean that he was advising Merton to confine himself to working with a single spiritual director, rather than the four or five whom he had been consulting.

leave desires for change which separate the heart from the present moral reality and transplant it to a kingdom of fantasy.

All this tells you that—unless a better counsel should prevail—it seems to me that your place of sanctification is the one where you now are. There you can have solitude, silence, peace and fervor, and from there you can give to so many souls that which God has given to you: the interior dwelling with him.

I shall pray for you. Please recommend me to the Lord. In Christ,[5]

+[6] G. B. Montini
Archbishop

---

5. For "Christ" (as in LETTER 29), he uses the chi-rho symbol (XP), the first two letters of the word in Greek.

6. Roman Catholic (and many Anglican) bishops preface their signatures with the sign of the cross. He uses here the Italian abbreviation for "archbishop," *Arciv.* (for *Arcivescovo*).

LETTER 28 / *Montini to Fox; handwritten, in Italian; original at the Thomas Merton Center; original translator unknown; translation checked by LDSF.*

No place of writing is stated, but given that it is written on the same day and on the same letterhead as Letter 27, it may be presumed that it too was written from Gussago.

August 20, 1955

Right Reverend Father Abbot,

Taking advantage of a moment's quiet today, I have written to Father Louis. I also[1] think he would do well to stay at Gethsemani, tranquilly, and engaged in his work.

It would be requisite to favor his desire for silence and solitude, not to oblige him [to take part in] excessively absorbing relations with the community, nor to incite him to write too much and on a fixed schedule.

I thank you for your confidence and trust which your esteemed and long letter shows to me. I will repay the spiritual commemoration tomorrow, Sunday, in Milan Cathedral, at the sung mass.

Yours in Christ,

+ G. B. Montini
Archiep.[2]

---

1. Dom James had written to the archbishop ("your esteemed and long letter") on May 16, stating his view that Merton should not transfer to Camaldoli; see LETTER 23. Later, Giabbani (LETTER 31), writing to Montini, made the same point.

2. Here he uses the Latin abbreviation for archbishop, *Archiep.* (for *Archiepiscopus*).

LETTER 29 / *Montini to Giabbani; handwritten, in Italian, trans. LDSF; original at Camaldoli.*

August 21, 1955

Right Reverend Father,

I find it my duty to inform you that Father Merton wrote to me telling me about his need for silence and his vague idea of becoming a Camaldolese, just as you had told me confidentially.

After thinking about this for a long time, and after obtaining some information about this,[1] I believed it best to express to him my counsel that he not leave the monastery where he is. I think, in fact, that the uneasiness that he demonstrates wouldn't calm down with this type of change; rather it could get worse. All the good that he is doing would then be compromised, without any benefit for Camaldoli.

I've thought a lot about its future in recent days, praying, remembering and imagining. I spent several days at the Camaldolese house at Gussago,[2] near Brescia, in the place where there used to be an *eremo* of the sons of St Romuald. Now there is nothing left but a small church with fifteenth-century features and a few modest buildings; but also an enchanting peacefulness, and an amazing panorama.

With a devoted remembrance of you,

Yours in [Christ,][3]
+ G. B. Montini

---

1. From Dom James' letter of May 16 (LETTER 23).
2. Indicating that he has now returned to Milan.
3. Again he uses the chi-rho symbol (cf. LETTER 27, note 5). Here it is followed by an illegible word.

LETTER 30 / *Merton to Larraona, typewritten, in French, trans. DG; the original, if extant, would be in the archives of the Sacred Congregation for Religious in Rome.*

To the Most Reverend Father Arcadio Larraona,
S.C. for Religious
August 24, 1955

Most Reverend and dear Father:

Although I know that you are the busiest man in the Roman curia, I address this long letter to you because I believe that you can help me come out of an impasse. It concerns an important matter. And I have no other recourse than yourself.

For ten years, as you know, I have had a very active desire for the solitary life. This desire has been encouraged by my spiritual directors, and even my Superiors have tried to respond to it by special adaptations of the Cistercian life. I have now come to believe that these adaptations are not helping. The last regular Visitor to Gethsemani even found that it was not acceptable[1] to give too much encouragement to the solitary spirit in the community, recognizing at the same time the theoretical possibility of letting a Cistercian live as a hermit in the shadow of his abbey. It seems to me that this would be a very difficult thing to do well, and that it would upset the community.

In 1952—two months after your visit[2]—I was able to write to Camaldoli and Dom Giabbani declared himself ready to receive me as a hermit at Arezzo if I were able to obtain permission to come there. My Superior refused me his permission to go to Camaldoli to make this test [of my vocation]. He also refused me permission to visit the Carthusians in Vermont (USA) in order to speak with them about this attraction and to seek some direction.

In 1955, in January, I consulted a Passionist director, who knows me and who knows Gethsemani, and he told me that I ought to ask again for

---

1. The French original says *il ne fallait pas*, "it was not necessary," but the context requires a freer translation. Given Merton's fluency in Spanish, it is curious that he writes to Larraona in French.

2. Larraona visited Gethsemani August 23–24, 1952; see SFS, 10–11. Merton wrote Camaldoli about three weeks after Larraona's visit, not two months.

permission to test my call to the solitary life. This advice was approved by the Father Prior of Gethsemani. Once again, the Father Abbot refused permission, and did not even permit me to write to another director.

In 1955, in April, the Father Prior gave me permission to write about this to a Carthusian director, Dom Verner Moore. I explained the situation to him, letting him know about my desire to transfer to the Camaldolese, and to ask his opinion. He immediately advised me to ask for a *transitus*, in the following way: to write to Dom Giabbani at Camaldoli, and to ask him to do whatever needed to be done to obtain the *transitus*. With the approval of the Father Prior, I did that in May. I know that Dom Giabbani received my letter, but I have heard nothing since [from him]. The Father Prior, who was only Superior in the absence of the abbot, was not able to give me permission to go to Camaldoli. The Father Abbot was very annoyed with the Father Prior because he had permitted me to consult a Carthusian about this matter of conscience. The Father Abbot does not give me the freedom to write letters of conscience about this, nor even [to write] open letters. He wants to keep me at Gethsemani at any cost.

So there is my situation. I have asked for a *transitus* to Camaldoli, through the good offices of the Camaldolese themselves. In this process, I have [consulted] five spiritual directors, including two Trappists, all of whom have encouraged me to become a Camaldolese hermit. My Father Abbot refuses me permission to go to Camaldoli, or even to correspond on the subject with my spiritual directors outside the monastery. He refused me permission to write to one of them, and simultaneously to Dom Giabbani, when I wanted, for peace of soul, to know right now what to do. I am waiting.

But in waiting, he has permitted me to receive a letter from Dom Jean Leclercq, OSB (Clervaux), who advised me to go instead to the Camaldolese of Frascati, who are more solitary and more austere.[3] They also said that they would willingly receive me in their *eremo*, if I was able to come there. The reason that Dom Leclercq gave me in favor of Frascati is that, according to him, Camaldoli would try "in a particular way to exploit me as a celebrity," whereas at Frascati I could remain incognito.

So there is my current problem. I would like to write to Camaldoli, to know if they would really want to promise me a truly solitary life if I could come to them, and also to know what is happening with the *transitus*. But I am refused permission to do this. At any cost, I would like to be able to take a trip, incognito, to visit both Frascati and Camaldoli, and to see what kind of life they lead there. I am also refused this permission.

3. Than their brethren at Camaldoli.

If Dom Giabbani has requested a *transitus* for me, you will certainly know something about it. I have wanted to write this [letter] to you in order to ask you to reply to the following questions:

1) Unless I obtain permission to live as a hermit here at Gethsemani, something which is decidedly improbable and uncertain, in order to follow the attraction which my spiritual directors tell me comes from God, I will need to obtain permission to test my vocation to Camaldolese life. I have even made a vow to seek permission to undertake this testing. It seems to me that my Father Abbot is acting in an unfair and unreasonable way toward me in refusing me this permission. I am therefore asking the Sacred Congregation for permission to attempt this. If this permission is only given in the form of a *transitus*, I [hereby] renew the request for a *transitus* for myself which has already been made by the Camaldolese (?). Or is there another means of obtaining this permission?

2) My Father Abbot gives me *one reason only* for preventing my departure: that it would injure the reputation of Gethsemani. He has no need of me as a functionary in the community, because, in fact, after this year, I am resigning as Father Master of the Scholastics. He has no need of me as a writer, because he has said to me, "If you want solitude, don't write anything else." This in fact is fair enough. But my spiritual directors are all in agreement in telling me that this reason isn't good enough, because there is a question of a real call from God in my soul to live the solitary life. All the more so, since the Frascati community is ready to receive me completely incognito and as my leaving of Gethsemani would be unadvertised, am I not right in standing up for the call of God against the material and opportunistic interests of the Father Abbot?

3) In such a situation, it seems to me that I ought even so to be able to write to Dom Giabbani and to those who have really wanted to help me find my way forward in this matter. Forgive me if I am making a serious error, but is it possible to ask you to forward the attached page to Dom Giabbani? If that cannot be done, destroy it, please.

I told you in another letter about the possibility of a foundation from Camaldoli in the United States. I believe that if I were able to go to Camaldoli, I could give a lot of help to this foundation, but here I am no longer able to do anything. Knowing my attraction to the Camaldolese life, my Father Abbot is preventing me from doing anything whatsoever to assist this foundation.

My Most Reverend Father, I am not speaking to you about Gethsemani. It's a good monastery, which exercises a very large influence for the good of souls. Also, the question of my vocation doesn't depend on this monastery, because, according to my spiritual directors, it concerns an attraction to the solitary life, which can only be verified by a testing of that life. At Gethsemani, however, we are undergoing a worrying evolution. Among us there is a spirit which is more and more superficial, external, technological, noisy, commercial. We are beginning to lose the respect of the clergy and of those who know how to appreciate the truly simple and hidden life of the monastery. I am not criticizing this monastery, but it makes me heartsick to think that I am being refused the satisfaction of a genuine desire for solitary life in order for my person to be used as a "façade" for this house where I live somewhat as an outsider who simply doesn't belong. I am not really at home here, Most Reverend Father, and my conscience obliges me to try to withdraw to a solitary life which is *authentically* contemplative. I know that one finds human imperfections everywhere. I know that even at Camaldoli everything isn't perfect. But the fact of living as a hermit, in complete solitude for the greater part of the time, is for me a spiritual necessity. I beg you, help me fulfill this necessity.

As I wait, Most Reverend Father, I ask you to believe that I am your very devoted son in Our Lord and Our Lady. Once again, forgive me for bothering you with this long letter. I thank you for your charity and your patience. I ask you to bless me.

[*There is no signature on the carbon copy.*]

P.S. If I stay here, I will write nothing more. My Superiors have decided that it was necessary to have at least that [degree of] solitude here. I am obeying very willingly, but this *is not at all the solution to the problem!*

If I go to Camaldoli, I would naturally do what they told me to do about this. My feeling is that it would be better that I stay hidden there and that I write very few things. I could all the same assist in the making of the American foundation, which is a *necessity* for this country. I could give a lot of help to this project if I go to the Camaldolese, but if I stay here, nothing more will happen.

In writing all this to you, Most Reverend Father, I know that the Sacred Congregation will give me the Church's answer and God's answer.

LETTER 31 / *Giabbani to Montini; handwritten, in Italian, trans. LDSF and AT; original in the Merton Dossier in the Montini Archive in the Milan Archdiocesan Archives.*

[Coat of arms]
The P[rior] General of the Camaldolese
Camaldoli
August 24, 1955

Most Reverend Excellency,

Your letter, written with your usual goodness of spirit toward us, encourages me to explain briefly what is happening in regard to Father Merton.

On the 24th of June, I came to Milan hoping to meet Your Excellency, and to give you the letters from Father Merton and from those of his spiritual advisors who are in favor of his transfer to Camaldoli. I had earlier spoken to Father Lazzaro,[1] and we had agreed to forestall Father Merton's coming to Italy.

Now he is insisting, and I think he is committed to leave his monastery, no matter the cost. In my opinion, therefore, [this is a moment when] an eremitical Camaldolese foundation could be established in America,[2] and when we could ask the Abbot of Gethsemani to give Father Merton leave, for a period of time, to help me with this foundation.

Perhaps in this way many desirable aims could be realized. What does Your Excellency think? In regard to Camaldoli, Your Excellency knows my torment and the daily struggle I've had since I was sixteen years old.[3] It's a shame, though, that the authority we have always looked up to with so much

---

1. Archbishop Lazzaro da Arbonne, OFMCap, a Capuchin friar, a consultant for the Sacred Congregation for Religious, and the apostolic visitor charged by the Vatican with the oversight of the Camaldolese monks and hermits during the 1950s.

2. Immaculate Heart Hermitage was established in Big Sur, California, in 1958, without any involvement from Merton.

3. From the time of his clothing as a Camaldolese novice at age sixteen (1924), Anselmo Giabbani felt strongly that many external observances of the hermits, dating from the Middle Ages, together with the prohibition of theological studies, other than those minimally sufficient for ordination, were psychologically damaging for young men and impeded their spiritual growth and their understanding of God's word (Thomas Matus, OSBCam, e-mail message to author, June 11, 2014).

trust was not able to give us clear direction,[4] nor has yet corrected the rules that the same authority has recognized as wrong after approving them.

Now we are waiting for the new Constitutions;[5] and I'm trusting that the Lord will provide for those who have trusted [Him] since our childhood *in simplicitate cordis* ["in simplicity of heart," or "with a simple heart"].

Excellency, if I could speak with Your Excellency, I would be very happy. But will it be possible? Trusting that I will be able to meet with Your Excellency some time in the future, I once again express my grateful and affectionate devotion.

Devotedly in C[hrist] J[esus],

A. Giabbani

P.S. In the next few days, I will be speaking to a group of Ambrosians[6] who have asked me insistently [to do this]. I trust I may count on your blessing, may I not?

---

4. Thomas Matus suggests that this probably refers to Giabbani's predecessors in office as prior general of the Camaldolese, to which office he was elected in 1951. Deeply convinced of the rightness of his intended reforms, Giabbani sometimes acted in the authoritarian manner common in the Church of his time, before the Second Vatican Council. The "clear direction" he himself gave was sometimes obscured by the harshness of his manner (e-mail message to author, June 11, 2014). I would also conjecture, given the phrase "the rules that the same authority has recognized as wrong after approving them," that this could also refer to the Sacred Congregation for Religious.

5. Confirmed by the Vatican in 1957 (Thomas Matus, e-mail message to author, July 26, 2014).

6. The faithful of the archdiocese of Milan, so named as spiritual descendants of St. Ambrose, first bishop of Milan (340–97), and heirs of an ancient liturgical tradition, the Ambrosian rite, still in use in Milan and other parishes of the diocese as an alternative to the Roman rite, as well as in parts of Switzerland (Thomas Matus, e-mail message to author, June 11, 2014).

LETTER 32 / *Larraona to Merton; handwritten, in Italian, with some sentences in Spanish; original in the Merton Center Archives; Italian translated by LDSF, TDA, and AT; Spanish by ME.*

Father Arcadio Larraona C.M.F.[1]
Secretariat of the Sacred Congregation for Religious
Palace of the Sacred Congregations
Piazza San Callisto
Rome, Italy
Private and Confidential
September 26, 1955

Reverend and dear Father,

I was not in Rome when Your Reverence's letter of August 24 arrived, and so my reply has been delayed.

I knew about your crises[2] not only from your books but also from news [I had received] from Camaldoli. After having thought and prayed about this, here is the response I can now give you in terms of the different dimensions which your situation presents.

1) It is clear that as Your Reverence has no other desire but to know the will of God, I feel in consequence the holy duty in all loyalty to help you fulfill this desire, whatever it may be.

2) Starting with the external aspects of the issue, with the hypothesis [you offer] about the will of the Lord, I believe that right now it would not be advisable [for you] to go to Camaldoli, because there are many question marks about the direction of that congregation—a direction which will be serenely but seriously studied shortly—and because, also, irrespective of what transpires, the internal conditions [at Camaldoli] could expose you to painful disappointments.

3) In its orientation, the congregation of Monte Corona (Frascati) is more settled. Even there [however], you might have serious disappointments. The old sayings of St John of the Cross are so true: *Si santo has de ser,*

---

1. The initials of the congregation of the Claretians, to which Larraona belonged, founded by St. Anthony Mary Claret in 1849, in Spain. They stand for *Congregatio Missionariorum Filiorum [Immaculati Cordis Beatae Mariae Virginis]*—Congregation of the Missionary Sons [of the Immaculate Heart of the Blessed Virgin Mary].

2. This seems very strong in English, but is not too strong as a translation of the Italian *crisi*.

los frailes te han de hacer ["If you are going to be a saint, the friars will make one out of you"]; and the other [saying], *Hombres dejé, hombres encontré* ["I left men, I found men"].³

4) On a first impression, the Carthusians might be better [for you]. Last year I visited the Grande Chartreuse, and to some extent at least, I know its situation.

5) Coming to the root of your personal situation, naturally I could not be your spiritual director, quite apart from other reasons which are also clear, the most important of them all being that I don't know Your Reverence's conscience. Given this, however, it seems to me right and proper, as regards an actual testing of your vocation, to make some observations to help you reflect and see *in Domino* ["in the Lord"] [the truth of this saying]: "It is discreet and urgent to wait"—not so? Your Reverence knows Spanish and will understand our saying: *no por mucho madrugar amanece mas temprano* ["No matter how early you get up, dawn will not come any sooner"].

a) As regards the personal aspect, I praise your thirst and hunger for solitude. I still remember the striking motto at the Grande Chartreuse: *O beata solitudo, O sola beatitudo!* ["O blessed solitude, O solitary blessedness!"]. I don't know why, but now as I am thinking of Your Reverence, there comes to mind a profound saying of St Teresa and two points from our first Fathers: St Teresa used to say, "Recollection is not [just] recollection, but the love of and thirst for recollection." And our Holy Founder, St Anthony Mary Claret (I don't know if you are acquainted with him), who [himself] had a strange [kind of] Carthusian vocation, used to say of himself, "I never find myself more recollected than when I am surrounded by thousands of people crowding around me." And one of our co-founders, the Servant of God⁴ Father Giacomo Clotet, a very busy man, did not lose the sense of the presence of God for some years, not even for a single moment. Forgive me this indiscreet digression; let me now continue as before.

b) Besides, I would not be sincere if I did not make you observe, first, that in assessing your vocation, you cannot overestimate nor must you underestimate the not unimportant effects that you must have had on the Trappist order and on Gethsemani. It would be a little like disowning your own books. Consider then, dear Father, that it is probable that [such a] crisis in your Trappist order would upset everyone a little, involuntarily on your part without a doubt. Its origins, its ideals, its practices, etc., have at least found a [strong] resonance in your books. Don't you think the question deserves a second thought?

3. The term *friars* refers to the members of the Carmelite order, to which St. John of the Cross belonged.

4. The first-level designation given to a candidate for sainthood.

And second, that your books have had enormous positive effects, and your taking of this step could cause disconcerting reactions on the part of many good and sincere souls. And this is all I want to tell you.

I have tried to be, as is my duty, calm and sincere [in responding to you]. I neither desire nor seek anything other than the adorable will of God. I commend myself to your prayers and I profess myself, in the Sacred Congregation [of Religious], most devotedly yours.

[Signed] Father A. Larraona, C.M.F.

LETTER 33 / *Merton to Montini; typewritten, in English; original in the Merton Dossier of the Montini Archive in the Milan Archdiocesan Archives.*

Gethsemani
Trappist, Ky.
Oct. 1, 1955

Your Excellency and Dear Archbishop Montini—

Your Excellency's long and wise letter,[1] written with such charity and such understanding, was to me not only a very pleasant surprise but even a great grace, and I do not know how to thank you adequately for it.

You were answering the short and rather cryptic statement[2] of a problem which I had made before the full unfolding of that problem last spring. Even then it is quite probable that yours is really the final solution. Since the matter is now being discussed fully by my Superiors in Europe, and while I wait to hear some news of their decision,[3] I feel it would be an act of filial gratitude and respect to your Excellency to give you, as briefly as I can, an outline of the whole situation.

This May, after long consideration, and with the advice of a wise Carthusian[4] who knew me since preaching a retreat here, and with the advice of a Passionist[5] who knew me and who had been here, and also with the advice of the Fr. Prior of Gethsemani[6] and of my confessor,[7] I had decided to apply through Dom Giabbani for a transitus. That idea emanated from the Carthusian Father, Dom Verner Moore,[8] and our Fr Prior said I should follow it through. Naturally Father Abbot was displeased.

1. LETTER 27.
2. LETTER 16.
3. The decision was that if Merton wanted to try the hermit life, he should try it "one hundred percent" at Gethsemani. This staggered him and resulted in his offer to become novice master (letter of Dom James to Dom Gabriel, October 18, 1955, TMC).
4. Dom Pablo Maria, OCart.; see LETTER 18.
5. Vincent Oberhauser, CP; see LETTER 15, note 7.
6. Anselm Steinke; see LETTER 19.
7. Father Timothy; see letter of Dom James to Dom Gabriel (May 17, 1955, TMC).
8. Merton is not giving the whole picture here; yes, Moore advised him to try to

Since that time, since I have not been allowed to correspond with Dom Giabbani I have no idea what steps were taken by him, if the transitus was asked for, or what happened at all. Meanwhile, however, my Father Abbot permitted me to ask, by way of getting information, whether the Camaldolese of Frascati would consider receiving me *incognito* and keeping me as an unknown American priest, thus obviating the danger of causing a great scandal and disturbing souls. They replied in the affirmative,[9] but no steps were taken.

In the meantime, there is a faint possibility of my Superiors permitting me to live a more solitary life here at Gethsemani, and this is what they are discussing—namely whether I should live a more solitary life here, or go to the Camaldolese of Frascati. It would seem now my superiors wish me to discontinue my work as a writer.[10] In any case they wish me to stop writing for the time being, if not permanently. There are still several small manuscripts to be published. I had not directly asked to be relieved of this work, since it seemed to me that as long as I am here it does not make much difference whether I wrote or not. If I went to Camaldoli, I would assume Dom Giabbani would wish me to continue writing. At Frascati, according to the terms of the question I put to them, it would be understood that I was to enter incognito and not as a writer at all.

In my own opinion, if I were to live a somewhat more solitary life here and still continue writing, it would solve the problem from every point of view—understanding of course that the writing would be in small quantity, with a striving for better quality, and more time devoted to prayer and meditation. For the present, I am indeed frankly delighted to have a vacation from writing, and am sure that it will be for the best.

At the beginning of September, having been for long in doubt as to the result of my suggestion to Dom Giabbani, I wrote directly to Father Larraona[11] of the S[acred] Congregation [for Religious] asking if he knew of any developments on this transitus, whether Fr Giabbani had applied for one, and so on. I also presented the whole problem to him, and asked that, if he felt that I should visit and see the Camaldolese life, permission might be granted to do so. This was because the directors mentioned above felt that that problem could be settled only by my visiting and seeing the Ca-

---

obtain a *transitus*, but he had already asked Giabbani to try to obtain one.

9. See Merton's letter of September 5, 1955 (SCH, 91–92), to Dom Maurizio Levy-Duplatt, novice master at Frascati, thanking him for his invitation to come there for a trial of the hermit life. The thought that he could have done this incognito is of course preposterous.

10. A manifest misstatement, which indicates his periodic discomfort concerning the imbalance in his life between his writing and his time for prayer in solitude.

11. Letter 30; its date is in fact August 24.

maldolese life firsthand. However, Your Excellency has written and given a confirmation of things I had heard indirectly to the effect that probably little would be gained by transferring to Camaldoli of Arezzo, and I am fully willing to accept your wise decision in this matter. In the meantime, I am waiting to hear the decision of my Superiors which will hardly be revolutionary. I would be very surprised if they counselled a transfer to Camaldoli of Frascati. Whatever they permit, I will do, trusting in their judgement.

It seems to me, as I meditate and pray over this problem that has come to a head after so many years, that Our Lord has willed me to go through this as a purification and that the time has at last come for a more or less definitive settlement. It may be that He is asking of me the complete sacrifice of all hope of a more simple and monastic and contemplative life—more silence and solitude. Your Excellency is aware that no community is perfect, and that Gethsemani has its faults as well as any other monastery: particularly the lack of silence, due to the presence of so many machines constantly in operation.[12] It may be that God is asking of me the acceptance of a milieu characterized by many features which seem to me to be eminently undesirable. But these features are precisely those of an American milieu,[13] features which grate on my European sensibilities. If it is true that a missionary must sacrifice his homeland and hereditary outlook to settle in a new land and adopt the viewpoint of those among whom he has settled, how much more true is it, perhaps, that God asks of me the full acceptance of the American religious outlook, even though it may seem in many ways superficial and silly—especially since I am after all half American by blood and American by nationalization.

I am glad for this trial, and I thank God for it, although I regret having been a source of trouble for my Superiors. I would have been less than God wanted me to be if I had not at least made this attempt to verify the attraction He has given me. Yet I know too that I have erred in my way of going about it, that I have been at fault in my way of presenting the problem to my Superiors, have perhaps insisted too much on my own viewpoint. All these things have shown me how far I am from being a holy soul and I thank God for the light they have given me. I foresee that whatever may be the solution in the external forum, I shall interiorly find myself traveling by a new way, a much more solitary way, much more detached from ways and means of leading the spiritual life and of seeking God. Above all, my eyes are much more open to the perspectives of eternity, where the perfection I seek can

---

12. It is an exaggeration to say "constantly," but there is no doubt that Merton found the noise of machines irritating in the extreme, especially by contrast with the bucolic character of Gethsemani when he first went there.

13. This comes out very strongly in his letters about moving to a place in Latin America.

be truly found, but I am also more aware of the value of time, in which by self-renunciation and obedience I can merit[14] to be with God in eternity. Finally and above all, this has all brought me face to face with the great and consoling Mystery of the Church. I have perhaps been able at times to experience, in some small way, the disappointments and sorrows of those who have had to renounce works they esteemed to be great, at the bidding of the Church. I have realized, too, that the "Worker-Priests"[15] are not the only ones who can become attached to a single point of view to the extent of rebelling interiorly against the views of authority. If there is any merit in all this that I go through, and if I can merit anything for others by it, I deeply desire that whatever suffering and sacrifice I may have to sustain may be of value to the worker priests and all others who have had so much difficulty in reconciling themselves with the decisions of their superiors.

It should be a source of shame to me, to think that I have so little to complain of compared with those who, like yourself, charged with enormous responsibilities, have so much work to do for the Church and so little time for peace and silence and prayer when I, after all, am living in a contemplative monastery, have many hours a day in choir and other hours in which to pray and meditate and read, even though those hours may necessarily be disturbed by distractions and events which, one would think,[16] would be absent from the monastery.

Your Excellency was so kind and patient as to write me a long letter, and so I have presumed you would not be unwilling to read a long one in return. It has been a grace and privilege for me to open my heart to you, such as it is, with its poverty and its limitations. May I at least earn[17] your blessing and your prayers, that God may deign to overlook my sins and make me, someday, become something of what people believe me to be. It is not an exaggerated humility, but plain truth, which prompts me to assure your Excellency that I am a very poor piece of work, a miserable person without virtue and not a very good religious but one totally unworthy of the respect which is sometimes paid to him. I pray for your Excellency each day at Mass, and again thank you for all your kindness.

Your devoted servant and son in Christ,
f. m. Louis Merton

14. A theological misstatement. Christians believe they are saved by the work of Christ, not by their own merits.

15. A movement with its origins in France during World War II, closed down by the Vatican some years later because of its innovative and non-hierarchical character.

16. A sideways swipe at Dom James.

17. Cf. note 14; a blessing is granted, not earned.

LETTER 34 / *Merton to Sortais; typewritten, in French; original, if extant, in the Trappist Generalate[1] in Rome; a copy at the Thomas Merton Center. Translated by an unknown translator, and published in* The School of Charity, *92–93.*

[Gethsemani,
Trappist, Ky.]
October 18, 1955

[My very dear and Most Reverend Father,][2]

I thank you for your good letter from Citeaux.[3] I had to wait for Dom James' return and the result of the election at Genesee[4] before answering you, for everything holds together, and before arriving at the final solution of the problem I had to know everything.

First of all, I am now quite convinced that God does not want me to be a Camaldolese. Your advice, along with the advice of the Most Reverend Father Larraona [of the Sacred Congregation of Religious] and even of Monsignor Montini [later Pope Paul VI], give me the most complete assurance that it would be most imprudent for me to leave Gethsemani, or at least the Order, and that there would not be much to gain. So I am quite sure I know God's will on this point, and I accept it willingly with the most complete peace and without regrets. This gives me the opportunity to sacrifice an appeal, a dream, an ideal, to embrace God's will in faith. Forgive me for worrying you, perhaps out of a lack of faith: but I could not tell in conscience before the solution of the question, that it had received its answer—at least the answer that would have had the power of convincing me from the subjective point of view. Now, it is over, and I promise you I will not worry you any more with this business.

Does God want me to be a Cistercian hermit? You advise me not to seek a life of total solitude. But you have told Dom James that I could be allowed to make the trial of the solitary life here. I thought at first that God wanted this trial of me, and I was going to ask to do it, knowing that Dom

1. The international headquarters of the Trappist order in Rome.
2. Words in brackets, and the signature, are not in the published version.
3. The original monastery of the Cistercian tradition, founded in 1098 by St. Robert of Molesme and others; sometimes spelled Cîteaux.
4. A monastery founded by Gethsemani, near Rochester in upstate New York.

James would probably give me permission. Now, at the same time, one of our officers has been elected Abbot of the Genesee [Walter Helmstetter], which is very inconvenient for Dom James, since if I were to leave for the woods,[5] he will have to replace two of his Father Masters[6] at one time. So I thought I must, before God, leave myself entirely[7] in the hands of Dom James, and *he* has decided to give me the office of Father Master of the Choir Novices[8] to replace Father Walter (the new Abbot of the foundation[9]). You see how poor we are in personnel when it is I, the *only one* that Dom James can entrust with the novices without having to seek a dispensation.[10]

Perhaps you will say that Dom James is quite imprudent to make this choice. To protect him, and to protect the house and the novices, I have made a vow (it is only the third private vow that I have made!)[11] not to say anything to the novices that would diminish their respect for the Cistercian cenobitic life and orientate them towards something else. If I happen to violate this promise, I will have to notify the Father Abbot. I will try to do all that is possible to give them a truly Cistercian life, cenobitical and liturgical. Pray for me. Above all pray that I don't set them a bad example.

---

5. Here Merton refers to Dom James' idea that he might become the forest warden of the abbey, with his "hermitage" being the forest warden's fire tower. Mott, *Seven Mountains*, 286–87, gives a full account of this.

6. Master of Novices and Master of Scholastics.

7. A passage in the French original is missing from this point in the published translation in *The School of Charity*; it reads as follows: "at the disposal of my Father Abbot in this moment of need in the house, more so because I believe that I ought to challenge a little my attraction to solitude, which can only be a matter of my own will. So I put myself completely" [as the letter continues, "in the hands of Dom James . . ."].

8. That is, the novices preparing for the priesthood, not the lay brothers. Merton here is being disingenuous, because although it is true that appointment to the office of novice master was the responsibility of the abbot, it was Merton himself who had made it clear to Dom James that he was ready to take on this office when, if Dom James' intuition is correct (see Letter 33, note 3), Merton was frightened by the readiness of Dom James and the abbot general to permit him to be a hermit "one hundred percent."

9. New monasteries founded from Gethsemani were called foundations.

10. It was a requirement of the Trappist order that the novice master be a priest thirty-five years of age or older, with ten years' experience in the order. Merton met these qualifications, being forty years of age with fourteen years' experience in the order. Dom James had considered another priest, Father Romanus, who was only thirty-one and had been in the order for seven and a half years; but in order to appoint him as novice master, he would have had to ask the abbot general for a dispensation (letter of Dom James to Dom Gabriel Sortais, October 18, 1955, TMC).

11. The other two were his vow not to accept election as an abbot and to keep seeking the chance to live in solitude, i.e., to be a hermit.

So I will have the opportunity to make a second novitiate myself, and to re-immerse myself completely in the true spirit of my vocation. If, after that, the appeal to solitude persists, and if Dom James will allow it, maybe I will ask, after three years, permission to live in the woods.[12] Dom James wants me to be Novice Master for three years to allow a young priest[13] to be trained for this job.

There only remains for me to assure you of my regrets for having afflicted you with my problems, to ask you for your paternal blessing and your advice for my new job. I assure you of all my filial devotion and my entire loyalty in the Lord. Maybe I am not the best of your sons, but I love you all the same as well as those who are holier than I.

[Signed] F. M. Louis

---

12. He doesn't mean here to take up the office of forest warden, but simply to live the life of a hermit.

13. Father Romanus; see note 10.

Letter 35 / Fox to Montini, typewritten, in English; original in the Merton Dossier in the Montini Archive in the Milan Archdiocesan Archives.

[The Most Reverend Giovanni Battista Montini
Archbishop of Milan]
October 20, 1955

Your Excellency:

We have just returned from our General Chapter in Europe. Please pardon the delay in answering your beautiful letter of August 20.

Father Louis has replied already to your letter to him.[1] You certainly wrote him a most powerful and moving epistle, because he has been a changed man ever since he received it.

While I was still in Europe he wrote to tell me of it, and that his whole point of view has now changed. He sees that a great part of his striving for a change of orders has been self-will principally, as I suspected all along.

In your letter to me, Your Excellency, you mentioned that he should not be given any particular distracting duties, nor encouraged in writing books. Really, Your Excellency, I have been trying to curtail his writings, both books and letters to individuals, but always he has the most ingenious excuses to keep on writing and, at the same time, to nourish dreams of hermitages and being all alone in prayer. This "dualism" has kept me suspicious of projects in the spiritual order.

However, he says now he is completely at peace; in fact, he never had so much peace before. But I would like to narrate an incident which throws great light on Father's character . . .

Our present Master of Novices[2] has been elected the abbot of one of our foundations,[3] whose abbot died this summer. That leaves the position of novice master vacant at Gethsemani.

The day after I returned from Europe, I was telling Father Louis about the election. Then he wrote me a note, and the next day came in to see me in his impetuous and impulsive way, wanting to know my decision—in regard

---

1. Letter 33.
2. Dom Walter Helmstetter; see Letter 34, note 5.
3. Abbey of the Genesee, Piffard, New York.

to his taking on the charge of novice master, Your Excellency! He wanted to be completely abandoned, but yet he was willing to accept the office.

Our good Most Reverend General had told me that if Father wanted to be a hermit here at Gethsemani, he would give permission, provided he became a real hermit one hundred percent. Not just half a hermit. When I told Father this, it was evident that he began to be afraid of his proposal to be a hermit. Measuring his courage, or lack of it, he was very happy to be able to offer this alternative to being alone in the woods.

I believe he will make an excellent Master of Novices, so I am going to appoint him to that position.

The day after I told him of our decision, he admitted that he always had [had] scruples in regard to his pressure to change orders, that it was all his own will. And now with this new change, of being master of novices, he has felt for the first time really a part of the community of Gethsemani and has given up completely all desires to change orders.[4]

So we recommend good Father Louis and all our novices, and all our community, to your fervent prayers, Your Excellency. We know that Jesus must love you, because He has sent you so many crosses.

Be assured that you are always in the prayers and sacrifices of all the monks of Gethsemani,

All for Jesus—thru Mary—with a smile,

fr. M. James, O.C.S.O.
Abbot

Il Reverendissimo Giovanni B. Montini
Arcivescovo di Milano

---

4. Given up all desires to change orders, true—but Merton continued to consider other possibilities for his monastic life *outside* Gethsemani, notably in Latin America.

LETTER 36 / *Merton to Giabbani; typewritten in French, trans. DG; original at Camaldoli.*

There is another copy of this letter in the file at the Thomas Merton Center, typed on another typewriter. There is no difference in the text (except for the correcting of the typographical errors in the earlier copy); but in this second, unsigned, copy, after the first four paragraphs, emphasis is only given to the two Latin phrases, and not to the other words and phrases to which Merton has given italic emphasis in the first and signed copy, and which I have reproduced in this version.

jhs

Gethsemani
Trappist
Ky.
March 24, 1956

Right Reverend and dear Father:

Once again I have obtained permission to write a word to you because Dom Claude tells me that things are a little mixed up with the two versions of *Silence in Heaven*. That's unfortunate, but even so there is a good solution, the one we have decided on with my New York publisher, and which I suggest to you also.

Here is what has happened, in a nutshell.

I had written a little book for Dom Claude, *Silence in Heaven*. Now for the book of photographs, he only needed a brief text, and for that he took the first chapter: *In Silentio* ["In the silence"]. Fine. But he sold the whole book to Arthaud.[1] And it's at that particular moment that things became complicated. The complications have been as serious in America as for you. But here's what my New York publisher has done—after having, like yourself, rejected the entire book with the photographs. He ceded to Arthaud and their associates in America the rights to the first chapter, *In Silentio*. He took this chapter out of his edition (now entitled *The Silent Life*). I wrote *a new chapter* for him. So now we have two complete books—*Silence in Heaven*, published by Arthaud and the publishing houses in England, America, and

---

1. A French publisher.

so on, which are working with Arthaud, and then *The Silent Life*, which will be published in France and here by other publishers. You already have the greater part of this second book. It remains only to send you some chapters on the Benedictines, the Carthusians and the Cistercians, and then the new opening chapter. I will do this as soon as I receive your news. So you will have the *rights for Italy*, after the signing of a contract with my agent; and I don't think anyone can bother you [about this]. For the *In Silentio* chapter, perhaps the Italian publisher will let you publish it in your journal.

You must know, Right Reverend Father, that I do not have the least control whatever over the *In Silentio* text, because Dom Claude has sold *all the rights* to Arthaud, while assuring me that Arthaud promised to leave you the freedom to publish it in Italy. I had made the mistake of more or less implicitly leaving to Dom Claude the rights to this text for all countries. I don't even know who is publishing *Silence in Heaven* in Italy.

So there it is, Right Reverend Father. I now have the pleasure of speaking to you a little once again. Our project of last year has completely failed, as you know. Counselled by *Monsignor Montini* and by the Most Reverend Father *Larraona*, I have *let go* of the hope of [receiving] a *transitus to Camaldoli*, and I remain entirely in the hands and at the *disposal* of my good *superiors*. Moreover, they[2] have made me *master of novices at Gethsemani*, as of last October. So I am *definitively* ensconced here, I think. *Fiat voluntas Dei* ["May the will of God be done"]. Clearly I would have really preferred to be able to hope for a solitary life, but if God does not permit it, I have nothing to say. I am therefore seeking interior solitude in a heart abandoned [to God]. I try to be completely simple and sincere, and to leave entirely aside my preferences and my desires. Pray that I do not create any illusions, that I may sacrifice everything and give myself totally to God in union with the obedience of his Son, Jesus, *factus obediens usque ad mortem* ["made obedient unto death"].[3] I continue to pray for you and for all the hermits and monks of Camaldoli, and although I am unworthy of so beautiful a calling, I ask you to regard me as spiritually a hermit, as a secret and hidden Camaldolese, a Camaldolese in the eyes of God alone.[4]

I wish for you all the graces of the resurrection of Christ the King, and the joys of holy Easter. Bless me, Right Reverend and dear Father. I remain humbly devoted to you in Our Lord.

[Signed] f M Louis

2. I.e., Dom James.

3. Cf. Phil 2:8, referring to Jesus, who "became obedient to the point of death."

4. Cf. his comment in LETTER 12: "Although I am not able to become a real solitary, I continue to become one in my heart."

APPENDICES

Appendix 1

Brief descriptions of the Camaldolese houses of Montecorona, Fonte Avellana, Montegiove, and San Gregorio al Celio; sent with the letter of January 24, 1954, from Giabbani to Merton; trans. LDSF. The author is unknown, but Camaldolese authorship is suggested by the use of the word "ours" in the description of San Gregorio.

The Hermits of Monte Corona

Monte Corona is in Umbria, on a mountaintop just south of Umbértide, and very close to the E45 autoroute.

When Paul Giustiniani[1] came to the Holy Hermitage of Camaldoli in 1510, it was in decline, and so from that time, Giustiniani began to think about reform. This came soon, with the aid of Pope Leo X. In fact, this pope in 1520 approved the *Regula vitae eremiticae* [A rule of hermit life] drawn up by Giustiniani, and containing the text of the new Constitutions for the reform he had conceived.

On September 15, 1520, Giustiniani left Camaldoli and founded his first hermitage, that of Montecucco in Le Marche. He set up other foundations as well; he died in 1528, at the hermitage of Soratte, near Rome.

At first, this reform was called the Society of the Hermits of St. Romuald. Giustiniani's thought was not to make a complete break with Camaldoli, but simply to enjoy a certain autonomy for the realization of his project, while remaining under the authority of the Prior General of Camaldoli. But circumstances soon brought about a clean break with the motherhouse; and so in 1526, the new hermit community held its first General Chapter in the hermit village of Massaccio, and the society assumed the name of the Congregation of the Camaldolese Hermits of Monte Corona, as they were called from then on.

This name shows the close relationship with the Tuscan hermits, a relationship that the Coronesi have not relinquished, in spite of the many struggles between the two congregations. And with good reason, for the Coronesi are sons of Camaldoli, although, if you will forgive me this image, prodigal sons who have left their mother's house to live on their own, when

---

1. Merton wrote a preface to Jean Leclercq's book on Giustiniani: *Alone with God*, xiii–xxvii.

it was possible to popularize the hermit life while remaining in the one flock which had the Prior General of Camaldoli as its shepherd. But Giustiniani had such an aversion to the cenobitic element—together with the eremitical element, an essential element in the Camaldolese structure—that he tried to undertake his journey without a horse—the cenobitic one—or by eliminating from the Camaldolese coat of arms one of its two doves, the one that represented the cenobitic lifestyle. In this way the Coronesi became a purely eremitical congregation.

Giustiniani's program went ahead in earnest, and moved very quickly; the reform had great success. After the death of the blessed one [Giustiniani], the foundations multiplied. The reform crossed the border of Italy and arrived in Poland in 1604, in Austria in 1628, and in Hungary in 1705. By the mid-1700s, thirty hermit villages had been founded. However, after 1794, a period of tribulation began for the Coronesi, as was the case for all monastic communities. They were persecuted in Poland, Hungary, and in Italy, where between 1797 and 1810, all the hermit villages were suppressed. Again between 1873 and 1885 [under the Italian government] there was a time of closure of the hermit villages.

At the moment,[2] the Coronesi have a hermit village in Spain, in the diocese of Burgos, two in Poland (although I don't know how they are faring after recent political events [the Communist takeover], and five in Italy (Naples, Nola, Frascati, Garda, and Rua).

In spite of the strong affirmation [they have received], the Coronesi have long felt the desire to reunite with the motherhouse [of Camaldoli]. In 1540 an initial reunion took place, but it only lasted two years. In 1634, Urban VIII ordered all the [Camaldolese] hermits to reunite. But again they stayed united only for a very few years. In 1651, Innocent X once again imposed a reunion, mandating punishment for anyone who breached it; but there were so many disagreements that in the end, Clement IX in 1667 decreed that each congregation should govern itself. Once again a reunion was attempted, but in a letter of 1672, Clement IX prohibited any further discussion of reunion. Despite this, negotiations were recommenced in 1695 to conclude a union; but the talks were shipwrecked before reaching land. Later centuries did not lack other attempts, but all failed.

It is interesting to take note of this repeated aspiration to form a single family; but it is likewise interesting to note how every good-willed attempt bumped into obstacles. And what kind of obstacles? The spirit of independence and the fear of the cenobium on the part of the Coronesi. But the

---

2. This was written, or at least sent to Merton, in 1954.

difference between the two congregations is just that: without this difference the Coronesi would have no real reason for separate existence.

And so to be more consistent with themselves, they shouldn't any longer call themselves a congregation of Camaldolese hermits, but simply "the Hermits of Monte Corona," because the idea of Camaldoli evokes the double identity: monastery and hermit village together.

The Hermit Village of Fonte Avellana

Fonte Avellana is in Le Marche, a few kilometers northwest of Sassoferrato. The headquarters of the Associazione Thomas Merton Italia is now located there.

Strictly speaking, it shouldn't be called a hermit village, because it is a real monastery. But because in former times it had separate cells, and is in a solitary and secluded location in the mountains, with no near neighbors (the closest are about seven kilometers away), it continues to keep its old name. Its geographical position is described by Dante Alighieri in his *Paradiso* (Canto 21.105).[3]

Fonte Avellana is a true place of holiness, made holy by the many saints and blessed who have lived there. Of these we know twelve, but there are many others not so recognized but bearing the title of Venerable. Among all of them, St. Peter Damian stands out.

The story of this place of ascetic practice may be divided into three periods:

(a) 1000–1325: the golden age. During this time Fonte Avellana was a true hermit village such as Camaldoli.

(b) 1325–1569: from being a hermit village, Fonte Avellana became an abbey,[4] against the stated wish of St. Peter Damian, who in one of his writings had threatened the worst kind of punishment to whomever converted the hermit village into an abbey. And the punishment arrived, because in 1325 began the decay of Avellana, which continued throughout this period.

(c) 1569 to the present. With the edict of Pope Pius V (December 10, 1569), Fonte Avellana became a Camaldolese abbey, that is, with this edict the Congregation of Avellana was canonically united with Camaldoli.

This union turned out to the advantage of Avellana, which had another time of flourishing, but only for a short time, because beginning in 1642, the monastery became continuously subject to taxation from the Holy See,

---

3. For the relevant passage from the *Paradiso*, see the following page.
4. The only Camaldolese house ever to have this designation.

which materially reduced the patrimony of the monastery. The contribution required by the Holy See in 1795 in payment of the six thousand *lire* imposed on it by the Treaty of Tolentino surpassed the ability of the monastery to pay, and forced it for economic reasons to reduce its membership. Then came the Napoleonic suppression of 1810, which forced the monks into exile; and again in 1866 came another suppression, this time by the Italian government, which plundered the monastery and expelled all the monks.

Thirty years later the monks returned, but the monastery did not recover, and continued to languish until in 1935, with the union of the hermits and cenobites of Camaldoli, a genuine monastic family was reorganized. A seminary came first, then a scholasticate in philosophy and theology, and finally a novitiate, a pattern that continues to the present time.

The buildings have undergone many renovations, but the church, dating back to the twelfth century, has remained intact. There is one part of the monastery that dates from the fourteenth century, another from the fifteenth, and another from the eighteenth. The scenery is unattractive, but quaint.

Now let us examine the passage from the Paradiso *referred to in the above description of Fonte Avellana. Earlier in Canto 21, Dante, encouraged by his muse and guide, Beatrice, asks why in the place he finds himself with her "the sweet symphony of Paradise falls silent" (line 59). A voice replies that "the most enlightened soul in heaven" (line 91) could not answer his question. Dante then asks the speaker who he is.*

The speaker then identifies himself as Peter Damian, also known, he says, as Peter the Sinner (lines 121–22). The translators note (524) that Dante has here mistakenly conflated the identity of two ascetics—Peter Damian, who died in 1072, and Peter the Sinner, who died almost fifty years later. The writer of the description of Fonte Avellana has slightly misquoted the reference in the Paradiso: it is actually found in lines 106–11. "That cloister" (line 118) is of course Fonte Avellana.

[Peter Damian speaks.]

"Between Italy's two shores
and not far distant from your homeland,
crags rise so high that thunder rolls below them.

They form a ridge called Càtria.
A consecrated monastery stands below,

once dedicated wholly to God's worship."

Thus a third time he began,
addressing me, and then went on:
"There I became so constant serving God,

my simple fare seasoned with olive oil alone,
that I readily endured the heat and frost,
content in contemplation.

That cloister which used to yield abundant harvest
to these heavens now is barren,
but soon its barrenness must be revealed.

In that place I was known as Peter Damian,
but Peter the Sinner in the House
of Our Lady on the Adriatic shore."[5]

The Hermit Village of Montegiove

Montegiove is in Umbria, halfway between Orvieto and Perugia. It is currently a dependent house of Fonte Avellana.

This hermit village was founded in 1609 and completed in 1627. In 1797, because of abuse from the civil power, it was abandoned. The hermits returned in 1815, and stayed until 1863, when because of the law of suppression [of the Italian government], they moved to a nearby locality called the Prelato. After 1870 they were readmitted to the hermit village as custodians, and in 1900, by agreement with the municipality of Fano, became lessees of the property. But the hermit village had by then lost, or almost lost, its character as a sacred place, and had become a destination for noisy field trips. For this reason, in 1902, the superiors decided to close it.

Until this time, the village had always been inhabited by the hermits of Monte Corona. In 1925, the village, by this time in wretched condition, was acquired by the hermits of Camaldoli and reopened as a community for monks, who are still there. And so in that year it became a Camaldolese hermit village.

Montegiove is located at a height of 220 meters above sea level, and is in an enchanting location. It rises above a hill, from which can be seen the valley of the river Metauro, most of the city of Fano, and part of the Adriatic Sea from Pesaro to Ancona.

5. Dante Alighieri, *Paradiso*, 21.106–23 (Hollander and Hollander, 513–14).

The village was built on a very harmonious plan: the church is in the center, flanked by two rows of cells, nine in all. It possesses a beautiful guesthouse, a fine little wood of pines and oaks, and a very large cloister, quite sufficient for the hermits to walk in. The climate is good.

The Monastery of San Gregorio al Celio

San Gregorio al Celio (sometimes San Gregorio Magno) is a church and monastery in the city and province of Rome, where it rejoices in the elegant address of Piazza di San Gregorio, 1.

This monastery was originally called St. Andrew's *in Clivo Scauri*[6] and was the home of Gregory the Great. The missionaries he sent[7] to evangelize England left from here. From the beginning, it was inhabited by Benedictine monks; around the year 750, some more monks came from the east, and in 950 more Benedictine monks arrived, until in 1573 the Camaldolese took it over, and are still there.

The glory of this notable monastery began to decline in splendor in 1798, because of the political turmoil that followed the French revolution. In 1810 came the suppression ordered by Napoleon I; and in 1870 came the Italian [government's] suppression, which expelled the monks of St. Gregory's and confiscated all its wealth. The monastery no longer belonged to the Camaldolese, but to the state; the monks were granted only the minor role of serving in the house of the pastor of the parish. During the Fascist regime, the monastery was used as a Fascist High School for the Social Assistance of Girls. When the regime fell in 1943, the school was closed, but

---

6. Referring to its site along the principal access road that ran up the ancient slope [Latin *clivus*] that rose from the valley between the Palatine and Caelian hills of the city.

7. In the year 597, led by the monk Augustine, who became the first archbishop of Canterbury. In the interests of ecumenical understanding, I would add that when they arrived they found an already active Christian community, dating back at least to the third century, in its Celtic form. As time went on, however, tension developed between the two traditions, exacerbated by their celebrating Easter at different times. The competition was resolved in favor of the Roman tradition at the Synod of Whitby, in 664, when Oswy or Oswiu, king of Northumbria, much impressed when told that it was Peter (read: Rome) who held the keys of the kingdom of heaven (cf. Matt 16:19), decided for the Roman tradition, on the grounds that he did not want to take a chance of not being admitted to heaven by its doorkeeper. This makes it all the more gracious and irenic that the Camaldolese community invited St. Augustine of Canterbury's 103rd successor, Archbishop Rowan Williams, to give the keynote address on the occasion of its millennial anniversary.

the monastery remained empty. It was under these circumstances that the Camaldolese Fathers thought again of entering into possession of the house.

They began arrangements with the municipality of Rome, which at that time was the official owner. This process was very involved, until the City Council, on July 21, 1953, decided to let go of the whole monastery, or rather to return it to the Camaldolese, who were, however, required to pay an annual rental set by law; but they hope to be freed from this obligation.

However, the main thing was obtained; the monastery is ours in practical terms, and in fact large areas have been renovated. One part is reserved for the monks, including the Procurator [of the Order] to the Holy See, another for monks and students who have been authorized to attend the Atenei in Rome; they currently attend the Benedictine college of San Anselmo on the Aventine.

The other part of the monastery, the larger part, is devoted to guests, young leaders of Catholic organizations who by the necessities of their studies or their work must live in Rome for long periods. During their time of residence in the Gregorian guesthouse, they receive instruction and good preparation for the apostolate waiting for them when they return to their dioceses. These young folk are completely separate from the monastic commuity, because their organization is independent, and pays its own bills.[8]

---

8. There is another Anglican connection with San Gregorio in the person of its current prior, Peter Hughes, who hosted Archbishop Williams on his millennial visit there in 2012, together with Pope Benedict XVI. Peter Hughes is an Anglican priest, an identity he asserts that he has taken with him into the Roman Catholic Church, describing himself as "an Anglican who is now in full communion with Peter" (Kerr, "Convert Priest," para. 1). George Guiver, CR, superior of the Community of the Resurrection at Mirfield, West Yorkshire, a religious community in the Church of England, tells the story: "When they elected him as Prior he had to be received into the Roman Catholic Church and re-ordained, but was given permission to invite a large number of Anglican priests to lay hands on him with the Bishop, and to make a declaration afterwards that he still regarded himself as an Anglican priest" ("Behind the Scenes in Rome," 10). I met Father Hughes when I visited Camaldoli in 2008; he had been living in the *eremo* there since 2000. He told me that he had resolved his status as an Anglican with the Camaldolese community at that time by a recitation in common of the Apostles' Creed. The CNA article (Kerr, "Convert Priest") refers to this as his having been "received into the Catholic Church," but in fact the official reception took place at the time of his ordination as a Roman Catholic priest. Before that, he simply regarded himself as an Anglican in communion with his Camaldolese brothers. Thomas Matus describes the Camaldolese view of such situations as follows: "... monasteries live more by custom than by canon; if a community regards a permanent guest as one of its members, that is what counts in monastic terms" (NAA, 48). Of course when he was elected prior of San Gregorio, he needed to be authorized to function publicly in the Roman Catholic Church, and so was ordained in that church.

Appendix 2

A certificate issued in the name of Camaldolese Prior General Anselmo Giabbani, dated March 13, 1955, and certifying the authenticity of the relics of St. Romuald and St. Peter Damian that he sent to Merton; typewritten in Latin; trans. DEW. The original (see LETTER 6) *is at the Thomas Merton Center, as are the relics themselves.*

D.NUS ANSELMUS GIABBANI
MONACHORUM EREMITARUM CAMALDULENSIUM O.S.B.
PRIOR GENERALIS ET ABBAS

Universis et singulis has litteras perlegentibus fidem facimus atque testamur nos dono dedisse perticulas ex ossibus S. Romualdi Abb. Camaldulensium Patris et S. Petri Damiani E.C.D. ex O.N. canonice recognitas et approbatas, quas in theca argentea bene clausa, crystallo munita, funicolo serico coloris rubri colligata et sigillo muneris nostri signata reverenter collocavimus. In quorum fidem has litteras testimoniales a nostro Vicario subscriptas et nostro sigillo munitas dedimus.

Ex nostro Archicenobio Fontis Boni. Die 13 Martii 1955.

[Signed] Albertinus Bertozzi Infer. Archic. Fontis Boni.

LORD[9] ANSELM GIABBANI
Prior General and Abbot
Of the Camaldolese Hermit Monks
Order of Saint Benedict

To all and singular who carefully read this letter, we give assurance and we testify that by this gift have been given particles of the bones of Saint Romuald, abbot, father of the Camaldolese, and of Saint Peter Damian, E.C.D.,[10] of our Order, [a matter] canonically reviewed[11] and approved.

9. The Latin term is *Dominus* ("Lord"), the abbreviation for which, "Dom," has been the traditional title of professed monks in the Benedictine tradition but has largely fallen out of use in recent decades.

10. *Episcopus, confessor, doctor:* "bishop, confessor and doctor" [of the Church].

11. The Latin original here is *recognitas*—"you [singular] review." The translator believes that this is probably a typographical error, the intended form probably being *recognitatas* ("reviewed"), a parallel to *approbatas* ("approved").

[The relics] we have reverently placed well-sealed in a silver case, secured by a crystal, bound by a cord of red color and sealed with the seal of our office. In assurance of which we have given this testimonial letter signed by our Vicar and secured by our seal.

From our Archcenobium[12] of Fontebona[13]
March 13, 1955
[Signed] Albertino Bertozzi, Vicar
Archcenobium of Fontebona

---

12. I.e., the original monastery of the Camaldolese congregation.

13. From the Latin *Fons Bonus*, "good source," another name for the hamlet and monastery of Camaldoli, so named for the ample supply and high quality of the nearby water sources. This feature of the locale has been memorialized in a monumental fountain constructed in 1431, which faces the entrance to the monastery from across the road.

3

The Greater *acedia:* What the Letters Tell Us

The letters tell us the story of a man profoundly affected by *acedia*. He is anxious, restless and self-doubting, experiencing great swings of mood between encouragement and discouragement. He presents himself as engaged in a life-and-death struggle to fulfill his monastic vocation in the deepest possible way. The difference between him and his "superiors," a highly charged word in these letters, is not just a difference of opinion, but a difference over discernment of the will of God. For Merton, the shine was off Gethsemani, a place he had lauded on his first encounter as "the only real city in America."[1] Sometimes the reader gets the sense that Merton feels that anywhere else would be better than Gethsemani. But he doesn't want to go just anywhere: he wants to transfer to a contemplative order that would give him more exterior solitude. He could of course have packed his bags at any time and left Gethsemani; but without a *transitus,* a Vatican-authorized transfer from one religious community to another, this would have meant relinquishing his place in the monastic realm—indeed, relinquishing his identity as a monk, and this he would not do.

CAMALDOLESE SELF-UNDERSTANDING

In order to understand the letters, it is important to understand how the Camaldolese themselves regard their ancient form of monastic life, something

---

1. Merton, *Secular Journal,* 167.

that Merton, it has to be said, did not always seem to comprehend. Camaldoli is more than a thousand years old. The *eremo* and the *cenobio* have been there since the beginning, two houses for one community. The *stabilitas* of the Camaldolese, their commitment to God in monastic life, is held in common, even when lived in the two different sacred spaces with slightly different observances in each. Whether a profession for an individual monk is held at the *eremo* or the *cenobio*, the vow is the same, one vow for all, to life in *il Sacro Eremo e l'Archicenobio di Camaldoli* (the Holy Hermitage and the Archcenobium of Camaldoli). As Thomas Matus says, "The cenobio serves the eremo, yes, but the cenobio is ennobled by this service, and the monks therein are sanctified by this evangelical/monastic relationship with their brothers in the eremo."[2] Among these services are the formation of novices, the care of ailing or elderly monks, and the reception of guests, although there always have been, and are today, guests at the *eremo*. All the monks of Camaldoli, whether resident in the *eremo* or the *cenobio*, are quite simply Camaldolese monastics. They see their life together as a blend of structure and spiritual practice that integrates, in various ways, the solitude of the hermitage, the fellowship of the monastery, and the witness of whatever outreach the community chooses, within the grounding spirit of Christian contemplation.

Merton, as the letters show, was eager to join the Camaldolese at the *eremo*, and because he had already made a full monastic novitiate at Gethsemani, Dom Anselmo Giabbani was willing to accept him there without a further novitiate. However, Merton was, objectively, idealistic and unrealistic in the sharp separation he made between the *eremo* and the *cenobio*, a separation that the Camaldolese themselves do not make. In the opinion of Thomas Matus, Dom James (LETTER 23), Archbishop Montini (LETTER 27), Dom Anselmo (LETTER 31), and Cardinal Larraona (LETTER 32) were all correct in their intuition that a transfer for Merton should not be approved, both for his own good and that of the *eremo*. It is important to keep this in mind in a reading of the letters, especially Merton's.[3]

2. E-mail message to author, September 3, 2014. As Thomas Matus later writes, "Camaldoli itself (eremo and cenobio) is the only bipartite community the Camaldolese Constitutions recognize. All other Camaldolese communities are either hermitage or cenobium. This is a matter of structure, not of monastic vocation. The vocation is one and in this vocation every monastic must offer his/her response to the call to what we currently call 'the threefold good': community, solitude, and gospel witness; likewise, every community will have its special expression of these three. It is a question of *balance*, for both the community and the individual monastic" (e-mail message to author, October 1, 2014).

3. For many of the perspectives in this section, I am grateful to Thomas Matus, who made his vows as a monk at New Camaldoli Hermitage in Big Sur, California,

THE NARRATIVE

1952

It was out of this dissatisfaction and in the hope of receiving a *transitus* that Merton wrote to Anselmo Giabbani, prior of Camaldoli, on September 11, 1952 (LETTER 1, no longer extant), asking about the possibility of such a transfer. He also wrote to Dom Jean-Baptiste Porion, in Rome, prior general of the Carthusians, at the same time. Porion's reply, which reached him before Giabbani's, was encouraging:

> If you really decided to change [orders], without doubt it's to Camaldoli at Arezzo that is indicated, and this would not at all break your connection with the old monastic lineage. One of our Fathers, after having obtained a *transitus*, is there right now as a recluse, and, it would seem, very happy with this absolute solitude. If you think it's a good idea, I am quite ready to talk about the idea of a Carthusian *transitus*. (September 19, 1952, TMC)

This was music to Merton's ears, of course, not only in its recommendation of Camaldoli but also in Porion's willingness, failing a move to Camaldoli or even as an alternative to Camaldoli, to facilitate a transfer for Merton to the Carthusians, even if, as he records in his journal entry of October 10, Porion's strongest recommendation was "to stay where I am and abandon myself completely into the hands of God" (SFS, 19). A week after receiving Porion's letter, he records a conversation with his friend, Chicago psychiatrist Philip Law:

> ... he agreed that I ought to go somewhere else. Said he [had] thought of it for a long time. Rather than go to the Carthusians, he thought I should start something new—a "really contemplative order." I explained the Camaldolese set up and he said that sounded fine. (SFS, 17, September 25, 1952)

On October 10, he received Giabbani's reply (LETTER 2, also no longer extant), which told him that he could come to Camaldoli and enter the *eremo*:

> Very simply, said I could come if I wished and start right out as a hermit. . . . Somehow it seems to me that this may be it, after all. And yet—I cannot do anything right at the moment. Reverend Father would do *anything* to prevent me from moving one step

---

more than fifty years ago. After many years at Camaldoli itself, he has now returned to the New Camaldoli community.

further in the affair.... What am I certain of? If it were merely a question of satisfying my own desires and aspirations, I would leave for Camaldoli in ten minutes. (SFS, 19–20)

He follows this with a very moving and sincere expression of the ongoing struggle within himself between what the will of God for him might be, and what his own will (or self-will) might be:

> Yet it is *not* merely a question of satisfying my own desires. On the contrary: there is one thing holding me at Gethsemani. And that is the Cross. Some mystery of the Wisdom of God has taught me that perhaps, after all, Gethsemani is where I belong because I do *not* fit in and because here my ideals are practically all frustrated. (SFS, 20)

It was a struggle that would persist, in one form or another, until the time of his entry into the hermitage, when he would acknowledge in a fuller way that Gethemani was indeed where he belonged.

On Christmas Day, he writes again to Giabbani, in French (he had written his first letter in Italian), telling him that his letter had "brought [him] joy and peace" (LETTER 3). He offers an idealized commentary on Camaldoli, which he has never visited, and contrasts it with Gethsemani, where he lives, he says, as "a cenobite subjected to the demands of a timetable full of movement and activity which is more or less external."[4] At Camaldoli, by contrast,

> a truly contemplative life is lived ... totally consecrated by God, without the "monastic vanity" which suffocates souls in the cenobitic life, in which one must submit oneself, at whatever cost, to a kind of liturgical autocracy which, I admit, suits the majority of monks very well, but which cuts off the spiritual breath of those souls whom God calls to simplicity and solitude.

He doesn't explain what "monastic vanity" is; perhaps he is reacting against the great pride in his community that he regularly heard expressed by Dom James. His comment about the suffocation of souls denigrates Camaldoli as well as Gethsemani, something of which he is unconscious. His own calling to "the true solitude," he tells Giabbani, "is becoming stronger and stronger." He is living, he says, in "*misery* and *poverty*," "worn out by the intense activism of the life of a writer"—something his superiors are certainly not forcing him to undertake. Overwork, he says, has made him sick. He acknowledges that his superiors have made concessions to him, referring to St. Anne's, the

---

4. Burton-Christie notes Merton's "deep-seated tendency to idealize" ("Place-Making as Contemplative Practice," 362).

old tool shed that Dom James had put at his disposal,[5] as "a little hermitage in the woods." But it's not enough:

> If I need solitude, it's because I need to *be nothing*, to disappear, to be completely obscure and forgotten—*tamquam purgamenta huius mundi* [1 Cor 4:13: "as the scum of the earth" (NEB); "like the rubbish of this world" (NRSV)]. I am fearfully ashamed of the stupid public image which is attached to the name of Thomas Merton!

This statement, quite apart from his difficulties at Gethsemani, testifies to the self-negating, self-critical, and indeed self-indulgent and self-dramatizing streak that at this time was characteristic of Merton and that I have noted elsewhere.[6] *Pathetic* is not too strong a word for the tone of his letter, nor is *pleading*. Then four days later, in his journal, he says this:

> ... the question of solitude is closer to a solution. Christmas morning, after my three Masses,[7] I felt sure Jesus wanted me to press forward and really ask for solitude. . . . Meanwhile Dr. Law came down and I saw him. He said don't wait three years: go *now*. (SFS, 27)

1953

In LETTER 4, no longer extant, Giabbani replied, asking for Merton's views about the possibility of the establishment of a Camaldolese foundation in the United States. Merton replies to this letter in LETTER 5 (May 4, 1953). I record here my conviction, borne out by Giabbani's letter of August 24, 1955, to Archbishop Montini (LETTER 31), that Giabbani, at some point after his initial welcoming letter to Merton, concluded that having Merton at Camaldoli was not a good idea, and prescinded from any real intention to proceed on Merton's behalf in the obtaining of a *transitus*. However, he never says that to Merton, his longer-term motivation in continuing the correspondence, I conjecture, being to have Merton inform him about the practical realities of a possible American foundation from Camaldoli.

LETTER 5 is the first letter to be written during the long gap in Merton's journal, and in it Merton responds at great length to Giabbani's concerns about this American foundation. This foundation, if it came to pass, would

---

5. Shannon, *Silent Lamp*, 153–55.
6. Grayston, *Development of a Spiritual Theologian*, 81–84, 106–8.
7. See LETTER 3, note 11.

offer him a chance to live as a hermit-in-community, which he deemed, as he says in Letter 3, a safer option than living an independent eremitical life. He discusses the question of revenue, suggesting that income could be earned by the work of a retreat house. Or perhaps the Camaldolese could work in parishes, a suggestion from which he almost immediately retreats. Begging (a curious word) for money would have to be done "with great discretion"—perhaps "one or two very big benefactors" could be found. He counsels against a "too rapid expansion," meaning that potential vocations should be considered with "extreme care." Trappists such as himself, however, could be admitted to the *eremo* without a novitiate, given that they have already had initiation into the cenobium, a position that Giabbani confirms in Letter 8.[8] Apparently Giabbani has asked him about writing a book about Camaldoli, presumably for use in promoting the foundation. He demurs about writing a book but offers to do a short booklet. He says that he has already mentioned Giabbani's hopes to Clare Boothe Luce, newly appointed American ambassador to Italy, although he cautions Giabbani against expecting too much from her, inasmuch as "Catholics in public life in the U.S. are always under attack from the Protestant majority, accused of being interested in using their political power to further Catholic aims . . . [and so her involvement] would have to be prudent and unofficial."

This reflects a vanished world. I acknowledge that there was some reality of this at the time, although I believe Merton exaggerates here; certainly this phenomenon has faded almost entirely since the election in 1960 of John F. Kennedy to the presidency.

Letter 6, no longer extant, was a covering letter sent by Giabbani along wih the photos of Camaldoli that Merton had requested in Letter 5, and a book about St. Romuald. He would have received this letter in September or October 1953; he mentions it in a letter of October 9 (TMC) to Dom James: "I got a letter from Camaldoli when you were away but still haven't had time to write them . . ." He did reply in Letter 7. Meanwhile, concerned about Merton's attraction to Camaldoli, Dom James, while he was in Europe to attend the general chapter of the Trappists, visited Camaldoli, specifically to ask Giabbani to discourage Merton's initiative; he also

---

8. The novices under Merton received a thorough initiation into the monastic tradition; Merton in fact thought of himself as experiencing a second novitiate through his work with the novices. For what he gave the novices, see the six volumes edited by Patrick F. O'Connell: IMT 1, *Cassian and the Fathers* (2005); IMT 2, *Pre-Benedictine Monasticism* (2006); IMT 3, *An Introduction to Christian Mysticism* (2008); IMT 4, *The Rule of Saint Benedict* (2009); IMT 5, *Monastic Observances* (2010); and IMT 6, *The Life of the Vows* (2012).

visited Frascati, another Camaldolese house to which Merton had written.[9] While Dom James was in Europe, Merton wrote to him: "My visit with you this Sunday morning is by letter, and I hope I am visiting you at Camaldoli. And as I ask you how you like Camaldoli, I hear you reply that you are not impressed by anything much except the scenery. It seems to you to be a rambling and inefficient sort of place" (September 20, 1953, TMC). Five days earlier, Merton had written a letter to him containing this mischievous comment about Camaldoli:

> One day in the menology a few weeks ago we heard it read that some monk of the [Cistercian] Order in Italy was transferred by command of the Holy Father in order to take charge of the place [Camaldoli].... I can think of no better way for me to make the Cistercian menology than by being transferred to Camaldoli at the orders of the Holy Father. (September 15, 1953, TMC)

The menology was the calendar of saints and notables of the order, and Merton is saying that he would like to think that at some future time his name will be included in it in virtue of the pope having commanded him to go to Camaldoli and take over, which would have been an unchallengeable end run around the authority of Dom James as abbot. It had happened once before: why not again? (LETTER 12, note 8, gives the background to this.)

In LETTER 7, written November 6, Merton tells Giabbani that Dom James was "really captivated" by Camaldoli's "enchanting solitary ambiance. But for all that, he is not encouraging me to become a Camaldolese. I'm not expecting anything at all from him, because he is convinced that God in his goodness wants me here. *Fiat* ["May it be," or "Let it be," or, more colloquially, "That's it"]." Writing on November 26 (TMC) to Dom Gabriel, Dom James reports on his visits:

> Father Louis is quite interested in the Camaldolese Order. In fact, that is one reason I visited them in Italy, to know them first-hand, both Frascati and Camaldoli. I met the Prior General, Dom Anselmo Giabbani.... Dom Anselmo is very anxious to make a foundation in America, I know, and he urges Father Louis to write something about them in America, but if I were to speak confidentially, ... Dom Anselmo is interested more in the cenobitic side of the Camaldolese than he is in the eremitic. But of course to gain the attention of people, he would hold up the eremitic.

---

9. For Dom Anselmo's recollection of Dom James' visit; see NAA, 102–3.

One reason for the visits? The main reason, I would guess. Of course, these ancient monastic houses also have their own historic and architectural interest, and a solid place in the general history of Western monasticism. Given Camaldolese self-understanding, however, it is possible that Dom James misread Dom Anselmo's apparent preference for the cenobium.

Earlier in the year, Dom James had authorized Merton to use St. Anne's for solitude and prayer. In this letter, Merton tells Giabbani that Dom James, although opposed to a transfer, has given him "a sort of hermitage dedicated to St Anne.... There I am able to pray and to meditate a little under the gaze of God and to sound something of the depths of his infinite mercy." In spite of his ongoing complaints of not being understood by Dom James, he was genuinely grateful that he had been granted access to St. Anne's, about which he regularly waxed rhapsodic in this and later letters. I note also that at the end of this letter, Merton states to Giabbani his conviction that America "only needs your *eremo*—or that especially"—no reference there to the monks of the Camaldolese cenobium. Later he commends himself to Giabbani's prayers "and those of your hermits," again revealing a one-sided view of Camaldoli by not also asking for the prayers of Camaldoli's monks as well, a note that he continues to strike in later letters (cf. LETTER 9).

In LETTER 7, we also read about the preface that Merton has written for Jean Leclercq's book on Camaldolese hermit Paul Giustiniani, in which, as he tells Giabbani, he talks about "Camaldoli and the eremitical ideal"[10]: "He seems in fact to equate the martyr and the hermit, both tested in their different furnaces of tribulation, even quoting one theologian, Anselm Stolz, as granting 'to the hermit a high, even the highest place among all Christian vocations.'"[11] He tells how Giustiniani became a novice at Camaldoli in 1510 "at a time when the eremitical fervor had lost some of its ancient heat." Accordingly, he left Camaldoli and founded an eremitical congregation of his own, the Hermits of Monte Corona (see Appendix 1). He does make the interesting point that Giustiniani "bears the same relation to Camaldoli as the Abbé de Rancé does to the Order of Citeaux."[12] In general, however, the preface is an overheated piece of special pleading, which cannot have been of any particular interest beyond the narrowest of monastic confines, even if it was later published in *Disputed Questions*, a book intended for Merton's general reading public.

---

10. Leclercq, *Alone with God*; Merton's preface, xiii–xxvii.

11. Merton, "A Renaissance Hermit, Blessed Paul Giustiniani," in *Disputed Questions*, 166.

12. Ibid., 168.

1954

Early in 1954, he receives LETTER 8, written January 24, a brief letter from Giabbani couched in what one discerns as somewhat cooler tones than those he used in his first letter to Merton, in which he had invited Merton to come to Camaldoli, although he does address Merton as "Dearest Father Louis." With this letter he sent the descriptions of the Camaldolese houses that Merton had requested; these are included, after the letters, as Appendix 1. He tells Merton that the new Constitutions of Camaldoli will allow for "the passage of professed monks without a further novitiate to our Camaldolese *eremo*"—something Merton would have read with great satisfaction. On February 7 (TMC), Merton writes to Dom James about Camaldoli:

> It is the feast of St Romuald. I have been praying that the Camaldolese may have many vocations and foundations and spread the true ideal of St Romuald throughout the world. It is needed. As for myself, I still have the same desire for solitude, but my desires are to be directed more and more to the things precisely willed by God ...

One wonders about Dom James' feelings when he read this. I imagine him asking Merton, "And are you praying for the same things for the Trappists?" This is not Merton at his most sensitive or loyal. On the other hand, it does demonstrate, for the most part, how freely Merton shared his hopes and feelings with Dom James. A few months later, Dom James writes to Dom Gabriel:

> Good Father Louis seems more settled as the days go by. Although I know that he hopes ... that some day he may be able to live as a hermit on the grounds of Gethsemani and still remain a member of the community. But as far as I am concerned, he will have to obtain the permission of the General Chapter for any move like that. It might give [a] bad example for some less pure[ly] intentioned souls, some just trying to escape community life for a life of greater ease. (June 12, 1954, TMC)

Dom James followed up on this in the fall of 1964, when he approached the Chapter with the request that Father Louis be authorized to become a hermit, a request that the Chapter must have been expecting and to which it must have acceded.

Merton did not reply to Giabbani's January letter until December 20. In LETTER 9, he assures Giabbani that he has not forgotten him or Camaldoli. No, he says, "I often think of you and of Camaldoli, and my heart often travels to your solitary and silent refuge hidden in the heart of the

Appennines." (Violins in the background here.) He tells Giabbani about a book he is working on, *Silence in Heaven*, not published until 1956, which will include material on Camaldoli. He also invites Giabbani to America, something that would permit Merton "to give you all my ideas in person." In the event, Giabbani didn't make this American trip until 1957, and then without telling Merton that he was coming and without visiting Gethsemani. Merton ends the letter by assuring Giabbani that he prays every day for him "and for [his] hermits and recluses," and with concluding sentiments of a distinctly eschatological tone:

> ... I leave you at one with the Lord who is soon going to come to live among us where we live in exile, far from our heavenly homeland. . . . I pray every day at Holy Mass for you and for your hermits and recluses. Do not forget me, and ask the good Lord to listen intently to the deepest desire of my heart. . . . *Fiat voluntas Patris* ["May the will of the Father be done"].

This theme of exile runs all through Merton's writings (cf. SSM 350, 352), and most commentators relate this to his lifelong search for "home," the home that he didn't have in the changing circumstances of his childhood. He was still talking about "home" when he went to Asia in 1968. There were, in fact, times when he did feel at home, particularly in his first years at Gethsemani under the paternal care of Dom Frederic Dunne. "Home" and "exile" for Merton are best understood, it seems to me, not in terms of distinct periods but rather as spiritual currents or senses that coexist in him all the time, with one or the other dominating at any particular moment.

1955

In a letter from Merton to Dom James, undated but written sometime between November 29, 1954, and January 22, 1955 (to judge by its placement in the TMC files), Merton switches gears: "If I were to make some concrete proposal it would be this one: (a) Since the Camaldolese are out of the question (don't you think so?) and since there is no chance of my getting permission to live as a 'Cistercian hermit,' the obvious thing seems to be to look to the Carthusians." His rationale is perverse. He suggests going to the Carthusians because he believes it is unlikely that any Carthusian superior would accept him, and because there are so many things that he would have to give up and so many difficulties to overcome to enable him to lead the austere Carthusian life, that if he *were* accepted and *could* meet the demands of Carthusian life, this could then be taken as a sign of God's will. Is God's will discerned, in other words, by the choice of the least likely possibility? And so he asks for permission to write both to the charterhouse at Parkminster, in the UK, and to Dom Porion, in Rome, and concludes, "I abide completely by your decision. May God guide you, and may He sanctify me by loving submission."

Dom James' answer was no, as we would expect. But why did Merton think that Camaldoli was "out of the question"? He had not heard from Giabbani since the previous January, nor had he written him until December 20 (LETTER 9), a letter in which, although he refers to "the deepest desire" of his heart, he makes no reference to his coming to Camaldoli. However, in LETTER 10, written on January 10, 1955, on the feast of St. Paul the [first] Hermit, as Merton is careful to note, he wonders whether "the moment has arrived to restart the efforts of two years ago." It seems therefore more likely that his comment about Camaldoli in the letter to Dom James was written before rather than after January 10.

In LETTER 11 (January 24), Giabbani replies promptly to Merton's two letters of December 20 and January 10. But before considering that letter, this narrative demands the inclusion of one of the great gems of the Merton archive—Merton's letter of January 22 to Jesus, "sent" via his local representative, Dom James. I give it here in its entirety.

> January 22, 1955
>
> TO JESUS—through the person of Reverend Father.
>
> My Dearest Jesus:
>
> I was going to write you a note listing all the reasons why I want to live a solitary life. This would be a waste of time, Jesus. You, Who give me whatever good desires I have, know well enough what happens to those desires when they get moving inside me. You alone know. You alone know where grace leaves off and nature comes in. I do not know. Others can only guess. You know.
>
> You are not divided against yourself—although I am and most humans are. If You give me a good desire and it seems to be contradicted exteriorly by You in one who represents you, I must see that it is not really contradicted but fulfilled. The one who represents You may be wrong. But You are not wrong. He may contradict You but you cannot contradict Yourself. Why do I try to think of reasons why he should listen to my desires? He doesn't have to listen to anyone but You. Tell him what You want, Jesus, and then let him tell me, and then I will do it. Then, Jesus, I worried a lot for fear that I had lost his confidence. What has that got to do with it? Then again: when I start trying to

explain why I am not completely happy here, I begin to get sorry for myself. What is the good of that, Jesus? And I start wanting to change things that I can never change. Jesus: do I really need to have people pay attention to what I think or what I desire? Does it matter that much to me, even in the order of nature? It should not. How much more so supernaturally. If I want obscurity, why don't I just be obscure? Because I am a writer, and I suppose it is very hard for a writer to just sit back and let his thoughts remain hidden.

Jesus: do I really want to live in solitude? Yes. I do. You know that I do. You know that I will never desire anything else. You also know whether or not I am yet able to live in solitude. It is true, I think, that the solitude of another solitary order might help me a great deal to calm down and get organized. But You alone know whether or not that is an illusion. It is not for me to judge. But it seems to me very probable. So what?

In short, Jesus, here is what I really want to do for You, to prove my love. I do not love You nearly enough, and therefore, in order to begin to love You better I want to give you *my obedience* rather than give You anything else that is less fundamental. I believe that if I give You obedience, You will not fail to give me solitude.

Jesus, I submit completely. Amen.
Please bless me, Jesus.
f. m. Louis

(I have said earlier that sometimes when I read Merton's letters I can hear the violins playing in the background. Here, of course, what I hear is the old spiritual: "Nobody knows the trouble I've seen; nobody knows but Jesus.") To do it complete justice, this letter would require commentary of Talmudic proportions. Here I must content myself and the reader with only a few of the many thoughts that the letter evokes. First, even in spite of the beseeching, even anguished tone of the letter, there has to be a smitch of humor, if not mischief, if not chutzpah, in Merton going in one fell swoop over the head of Dom James, to say nothing of the father immediate, the abbot general, the Congregation for Religious, and the pope. Merton essentially instructs Jesus to tell Dom James what he, Jesus, wants for Merton, this being understood by Merton as permission to be a solitary. Dom James could have replied, of course, that he was already doing what Jesus was telling him in telling Merton that the time was not ripe for him to be a solitary. Merton ties himself in knots as he tries to reconcile his convictions that (*a*) Jesus has given him the desire to be a solitary; (*b*) this is being stymied by his official representative, the abbot; (*c*) but Jesus cannot contradict himself; and (*d*) somehow, therefore, this means that the will of Jesus is being fulfilled, one presumes by Merton's submission. Why, he wonders, does he try to convince Dom James about this when there are no determining reasons why Dom James should agree with him? Jesus alone knows "where grace leaves off and nature comes in.... Others [read: Dom James] can only guess. You know."

He struggles with the question of hiddenness, or obscurity (cf. LETTER 3 and LETTER 5), asking himself why he doesn't just "be obscure." The reason: "Because I am a writer, and I suppose it is very hard for a writer to just sit back and let his thoughts remain hidden." Indeed, heaven forfend that anything should inhibit his writing—because after all, he is a *writer*! In a moment of exasperation, he even asks, "So what?" (I trust that by this he meant "So what now?" Otherwise, it sounds disrespectful.) Finally, he focuses on love. He wants to love Jesus, whom he doesn't love "nearly enough." So he will offer his obedience (via Jesus' representative, who just isn't getting it) as the sign of his love. Then comes the tacit contract: "I believe that if I give you obedience, You will not fail to give me solitude." Is it a deal, Jesus? Solitude for obedience? Can I count on you? Not surprisingly, there is no evidence that Dom James made a written reply to this letter; but if he had, there is no doubt that he would have said that he was doing what Jesus wanted him to do to the best of his ability to discern it, and this did *not* include authorizing Merton to go to Camaldoli (or anywhere else) with his blessing.

In Merton's brief letter to Giabbani of January 10, 1955 (LETTER 10), he had updated Giabbani on one of his writing projects that included material on Camaldoli, an ongoing subject of discussion in the letters, and asked him for a relic of Camaldoli's founder, St. Romuald. Replying in LETTER 11, Giabbani offered to send him a relic of St. Peter Damian as well as one of St. Romuald, and assured Merton that the American foundation was still a live option, "if you and another well-known American will help" (probably Clare Boothe Luce, mentioned in LETTER 5). Interestingly, and probably in response to Merton's eremitical interests, he also characterizes this foundation as a "hermit community" rather than a bipartite community, a hermitage with a cenobium close by, as at the motherhouse of Camaldoli. This letter also bears the first mention in the correspondence of Giovanni Battista Montini, archbishop of Milan, a longtime friend of Camaldoli, to whom Giabbani has shown Merton's letters, and who has shown himself, Giabbani says, "very interested in your solitary vocation."

Between Merton's letters of January 10 (LETTER 10) and February 9 (LETTER 12), Merton turned forty, on January 31. Because he was not keeping a journal, we have no comment from him about this milestone, unlike the comment we do have from him ten years later about his fiftieth birthday, when he rejoices that he woke up on that day in his own hermitage (DWL,

200). Following Jung, I would posit that Merton's arrival at this birthday, as with many birthdays in round numbers, was a contributing factor to what we see in the correspondence of 1955, which reached its most intense outpouring in May of that year. The five letters that Merton wrote to Giabbani in that one month exhibit a now-or-never sensibility strongly suggestive of a consciousness of his having reached midlife, a moment that typically carries with it a confrontation with one's own mortality, a felt need to assess where one has been and where one is going, an intensification of the sense of the shortness of life and the perceived increase in the speed of the passage of time.

In LETTER 12 (February 9), Merton echoes Giabbani's reference to the "hermit community," asserting that this ought to be the focus of Camaldoli's work in the United States: "what we need is hermits, men engulfed in the poverty and silence of God himself." He also asserts that the presence of the Camaldolese "would not in any way hinder the growth of the Cistercians," which at that time was substantial, with Gethsemani sending out new foundations frequently. He mentions his joy at being able to sing the community mass on the feast of St. Romuald; expresses his satisfaction at knowing that Archbishop Montini was interested in his vocation; and chides himself for writing so long a letter in support of a vocation to silence. One does sense a certain ego-inflation when he credits in advance the relics he is awaiting to "help [him] mightily in [his] crossing of the Red Sea in order to seek God in the wilderness." A new Moses? Merton is a great man, but if this had been in any way conscious, he would have been aiming too high. Evagrius doesn't list ego-inflation in his paradigm; but it is not that far from pride.[13]

Giabbani's next letter to Merton (LETTER 13) is dated April 10. But in the weeks before its arrival, Merton's situation is the subject of three letters from Dom James to Dom Gabriel. Here is what he says in a letter of March 16 (TMC):

> [Father Louis] is not as cheerful and spontaneous as he used to be.... He seems to be one who resents any restraint or control. He claims that he feels this great urge to be more [of] a hermit. Although this sounds very high and idealistic, I doubt very much the purity of his intentions. I am almost convinced that what is moving him in this direction is not to have silence and solitude in which to pray to God and be more united to Him, but really to have silence and solitude to write books and to read books with greater freedom.... It seems that his urge for a change, which he tries to see as coming from God, comes rather

---

13. For Evagrius on pride, see his *Praktikos*, 20.

from his own self, seeking to find a means of escaping from the very arrangements God wishes him to comply with and accept.

In the second of these letters, written March 28 (TMC), Dom James refers to a letter from Dom Gabriel to Merton, reporting to Dom Gabriel that Merton

> said that your letter had brought him much peace of soul, especially to have been told by his higher superiors that he was in the right place, and just to keep on going. Although, way down deep, his innate restlessness and gyrovaguing[14] spirit still lives on. But he likes very much that you told him that he was neither a Trappist, nor a Carthusian, nor a Camaldolese, but . . . just Father Louis. So he said, "I guess my vocation is to have no vocation, living within a Trappist monastery." I said to him, "Your vocation is to have no solution, and keep on going."

And in the third letter (April 2, 1955, TMC), Dom James expresses to Dom Gabriel his larger intuitions about Merton:

> Father Louis knows that his troubles do not come from his Trappist surroundings in general, and Gethsemani in particular. He knows, because he practically admitted it to me, that his problems are all inside himself. But as neurotics usually do, they blame everybody and everything else for their interior sufferings. His problem is that he would like to be without any restraint or discipline over him, so that he could always do what he wished. But if he were in such a position where would his spiritual life be?

This last letter in particular evokes chapter 12 of Evagrius' *Praktikos*, on *acedia*. We may take it that Merton was in the existential space it describes when he received Giabbani's letter of April 10. It did tell him that Giabbani had sent him the relics he had requested (see LETTER 20), as well as some photos of Camaldoli, but it also chided him for his idealization of the hermit life: "Perhaps—forgive me for this—you are a bit too enthusiastic about the hermit lifestyle because you don't have the experience of living as a hermit"—and then backs off from this chiding: "but I would like to be mistaken; and in any case, it is necessary always to start with enthusiasm." This letter was followed by Giabbani's "fine letter from Stapehill," sent sometime in April or May (LETTER 14), and no longer extant (see LETTER 22).

---

14. The gyrovagues were monks without an abbot, who wandered from one monastery to another. St. Benedict speaks very negatively of them in chapter 1 of his *Rule*.

On April 25, Merton pulls out all the stops, with letters to Thomas Verner Moore (LETTER 15), Archbishop Montini (LETTER 16) and Anselmo Giabbani (LETTER 17, no longer extant). Dom James was away, and Merton took advantage of the youth and inexperience of the prior, Anselm Steinke, who was in charge of the monastery in the abbot's absence. Steinke gave him permission to write to Moore, permission that it is unlikely Dom James would have granted. Merton is in this letter disingenuous when he says that the prior is "directing me more or less in this same matter." As we shall see, this will prove to be less rather than more. In fact, after citing the support he had received in his vocational searchings from the abbey's Father Bellarmine and Passionist Father Vincent Oberhauser, and telling Moore that his confessor does not seem to understand or appreciate his views, he contradicts himself, stating flatly, "I have no real director here."[15]

He tells Moore about Dom James' opposition; rebukes himself for too easily letting himself be "put off" by that opposition; asserts that he has no doubt about his vocation in the "internal forum," whatever Dom James may say in the "external forum"; describes his contacts with Dom Porion, with Camaldoli and with Frascati; reveals the suppression by Dom Louis, the father immediate, of Dom James' concessions in regard to solitude; shares with Moore his making of a vow at communion "to leave and go to the solitary life," something he now wonders about; mentions that his "French doctor" friend will pay his way to Italy; and ends by asking Moore four questions. Does Moore think that it is really the will of God for Merton to leave the Cistercians to seek a solitary life in some other order? If so, how should he urge his claims (to unresponsive superiors)? What about his vow? And finally, is there any way he can engage support from "the other end" (i.e., through Archbishop Montini or via the Congregation for Religious through Father Larraona)? He says that he will value Moore's response to all these questions and . . . the text of the letter ends there. Moore's response (LETTER 18) we will consider after our reading of the second extant letter from April 25, that to Archbishop Montini (LETTER 16), a shorter version of what he said in the letter to Moore. He tells Montini that he has had a vocation to solitude for ten years; that his superiors continue to block it; and that Camaldoli is ready to receive him if Gethsemani will let him go. Then he asks Montini for what he wants: "A strong word of approval or encouragement from someone like your Excellency," which he could use to overcome Dom James' opposition, if not to persuade him of the validity of Merton's calling to solitude. And then this curious comment: that he believes the only real reason why Dom James is refusing him is that "he does

---

15. Cf. LETTER 24, note 1.

not want to be criticized and blamed," a slam that in my view Dom James did not deserve.¹⁶ The letter ends with a complimentary closing that reads as if it comes from the seventeenth century: Merton assures Montini of his "deepest esteem and grateful veneration," begs his blessing, kisses his hand, and remains his "most devoted servant."

Moore's reply (LETTER 18), written April 29, must have arrived before May 3, since Anselm Steinke refers to it in his letter of that date to Giabbani (LETTER 19); and because it arrived while Steinke was still in charge, he passed it on to Merton. Moore begins by insisting that he makes "*no claim whatever to being supernaturally illuminated*" (italics his). Given this disclaimer, he then tells Merton that, in his view, his persistent desire for solitude may be a particular grace from God. He also finds it significant that Camaldoli is willing to accept Merton on trial: Merton's going there would be more than personal, but would also have significance for the United States. He describes his own passages from the Paulists to the Benedictines to the Carthusians, assures Merton that it is well within the Benedictine tradition for a monk to want to "go forth from the ranks of the brethren to the single-handed combat of the desert,"¹⁷ and tells him, "You will not be false to Cistercian life when you answer God's call to the wilderness." He suggests that Merton ask Giabbani to ask Montini how to effect the *transitus*, and ends with the assurance of his prayers, and this comment, certainly one that Merton would have welcomed: "You have not suffered in vain."

Very soon after the receipt of Moore's letter, Prior Anselm Steinke, at Merton's request, wrote to Giabbani (LETTER 19, summarized rather than quoted in full). This was an attempt, of course, to enlist the support of a "superior" in his quest, a minor one, to be sure, but in the authority structure of the Trappist order, no less a superior for all that. His youth and naïveté are manifest in the letter, which at some level was written against his will, because he knew it could cause "a lot of suffering and anguish to our Reverend Father Dom James Fox." Then why *did* he write it? "To assist a brother . . . in the discernment of the will of God regarding his vocation." He acknowledges his youth and incapacity, and tells Giabbani that he is a former student of Merton's, whom he regards as "a true poet and a man of genius." He also says, very frankly—and it is questionable how happy Merton would have been to read this—that he sees Merton as someone who "lacks a way of limiting his interests. He gets enthusiastic about very many things, . . . [and] needs more prudence, maturity and mental discipline." Even so, on

---

16. Cf. Dom James' assertion to Montini in LETTER 23: "I am in no way afraid of taking the entire responsibility for this decision on myself."

17. Benedict, *Rule*, 47.

The Greater *acedia*: What the Letters Tell Us 187

the grounds of Merton's persistent sense of call, he supports his desire for the opportunity to test his "eremitical spirit." Then he says that if Merton does go to Camaldoli, it should be on condition that if things don't work out there, he return to Cistercian life, at Gethsemani or in another Cistercian house. "I think," he says, "that such a stipulation is opportune, given his tendency towards instability, which one day could be his ruin, if some superior doesn't guide him." He questions Moore's support for a testing of Merton's vocation, given that Moore "doesn't know the conditions of life here at Gethsemani nor does he know our Father Louis personally." He also expresses the hope that if Merton goes to Camaldoli, he would not go before the current class of scholastics, for whom Merton was responsible, had finished its program of formation. The end of the letter may also seem to be contradictory (he is writing the letter *against* his will; yet in the depths of his soul he feels that he is "acting in God's holy will"), but it is clearly deeply felt. Merton enclosed this letter with his own letter of May 3 to Giabbani.

The relics Merton had requested from Giabbani in LETTER 10 duly arrived, accompanied by a certificate of authenticity dated March 13 (see Appendix 2); Merton's gratitude in his reply of May 3 (LETTER 20) was palpable: "St Romuald and St Peter Damian are here, not only to console me but to put themselves seriously to work and to [help me] come to a decision about my vocation. A thousand thanks—it's magnificent." In the same letter he attributes to the presence of the relics the spontaneous offer of his doctor friend to pay for his travel to Camaldoli. Early in the letter Merton strikes a note of *kairos*:

> So, my Right Reverend Father, the decisive moment has arrived. It seems that this is really the moment willed by God for my *transitus* to Camaldoli. The indications are clear. I mustn't miss the moment. The opportunity may not come again for a long time. I have just received a letter from a Carthusian father, the first American Carthusian,[18] who tells me that I need to follow my vocation as a solitary, that it is necessary to obtain the *transitus*, and that it must be obtained by *your* Procurator General,[19] and not by ours. Then, he says, if the *transitus* arrives from Rome, sent by Monsignor Montini or by some other person well regarded at the Holy See, and if our Father Abbot is asked to make a favorable response, perhaps things will move ahead well.

There is a noticeable decline of certainty in this single paragraph, from "the decisive moment has arrived" to "perhaps things will move ahead well." The

18. Thomas Verner Moore; see LETTER 18.
19. The official representative of an order to the Vatican.

decline is more obvious still as the letter crashes with this comment: "But doubtless there is no hope for this *transitus*. Dom James is opposed to it." But by the end of the letter his confidence has returned: "I know for certain that this project is going to go ahead." He asks Giabbani, formally, to take steps to obtain the *transitus*, asserting that God is indeed calling him to solitude, and that he wants to offer himself "to help create an eremitical foundation in the United States, and to open for others the road to the holy desert." He states flatly that his work at Gethsemani is finished, and attributes to "his superiors" (read: Dom James) reasons for keeping him there "which are doubtless sincere, but which are motivated by impulses and considerations on human and natural levels"—an accusation that Dom James when he returns throws back at him, telling him that he is being ruled by a "natural" rather than a "supernatural" spirit, as Merton notes in his letter of May 17 to Giabbani (LETTER 24). He then writes at great length about his situation and makes the following points: that he has had a strong pull to the solitary life for many years; that the five spiritual directors whom he has consulted all support his desire to test this vocation;[20] that he is no longer needed at Gethsemani (he was Master of Scholastics, an important position, and within months would be Master of Novices); that his presence tends to upset the community; that he has made a vow "to move forward to a more solitary and contemplative life," a vow that has given him a lot of peace and that he wants to act upon; and that he could help Camaldoli make its American foundation. He ends this passionate outpouring by expressing the utterly unrealistic hope that in the following month he could be at Camaldoli to celebrate the Solemnity of St. Romuald and the feast of St. Benedict with the monks and hermits there.

This letter of May 3 exists in the file in three variants, in the first of which, variant (a), we find a fascinating postscript. In understanding Merton's reason for including it, we need to remember that at this time in Trappist history, an abbot would read all the mail coming into and going out of the monastery except for letters marked *res conscientiae* ("conscience matter"); this practice ceased in the sixties. This letter, however, was mailed with the prior's permission in the abbot's absence, and this accounts for Merton's inclusion of this postscript:

> Dom James will be back in a few days. If you write me, don't say anything about this matter, even in Italian. But if you want to tell me that you have taken steps to obtain the *transitus*, tell me something like "We have planted the roses at the hermitage."

---

20. In LETTER 21, May 6, he says "more than five."

And if you have obtained the *transitus*, tell me that "The roses are *in bloom* at the hermitage."

Here is Merton the trickster at work. His action in writing this long and anxious letter very critical of Dom James' opposition to his hopes, in taking advantage in the abbot's absence of the young prior (whose letter was ambivalent and full of qualifications, but did end up by saying that he thought Merton should have a chance to test his eremitical vocation), and in seeking to conceal his actions from Dom James offers a glimpse of Merton at one of the least attractive moments of his monastic career. It points ahead to his statement in LETTER 22 that if he came to Camaldoli, he could use a make-believe excuse "to take a trip without anyone knowing the reason for it"—although he quickly retreats from this possibility, saying that he doesn't like "these evasions." His trickster archetype is acting up again.[21]

His anxiety continues to show itself in his next letter, written May 6 (LETTER 21), in which he asks Giabbani if he has received his "important letter" of May 3 (LETTER 20), as well as the prior's letter (LETTER 19), and in which he again expatiates at length on the dynamics of an American Camaldolese foundation (or why not two, one in the East and one in the West?). Four days later, May 10, he writes again (LETTER 22), thanking Giabbani for his "fine letter from Stapehill" (LETTER 14, no longer extant). In that letter Giabbani must have encouraged him in his project, given him some advice for which Merton thanks him, and promised him another letter, which this letter implies will be the letter containing the *transitus*. He goes on to make a statement equal in firmness to his *kairos* statement in the letter of May 3: ". . . on April 25 a decision was made. I want as quickly as possible to let you know what is happening . . ." This is curious, because nothing notable is on record as having happened during the previous few days. I note the passive voice ("a decision was made"), when he means that he himself made a decision to go for broke on April 25, the day he wrote to Moore, Montini, and Giabbani. He simply restates what he has said in the letter of May 3, relying heavily on the letter he received from Thomas Verner Moore, and justifying his actions undertaken in the abbot's absence, citing the support he has received from "more than four" spiritual directors, indeed, five. He would have preferred, he says,

> to follow the regular procedures. But the circumstances render this morally impossible. Dom James doesn't look at these things directly. If I should run it by him, he will close his eyes and say, "It's not the will of God." You said in your letter that one cannot

21. On Merton as archetypal trickster, see Belcastro, "Praying the Questions," 135–40.

tell what the will of God is without a careful self-examination. But this is precisely what Dom James is doing. You can tell him about the problem. But he is occupied by the foundations, by administration, etc., etc. (which is fine: I don't criticize him for that); but while the telephone rings five or six times, and while he is answering those calls, he is "thinking" about the question; and after a few minutes he says "It's not the will of God."

Again referring to the advice he has received (or solicited) to make a trial of his vocation in a "solitary order," he says that he wants to do this on the grounds of being advised "by a real man of God." Probably, to judge from his substantial account in this letter of his contact with Moore, it is Moore who is in his eyes the "real man of God." This implicitly sets up a contrast with Dom James, and infers that Dom James is not "a real man of God," at least to the same degree; if so, it is one of the cruelest comments he makes about Dom James. Apart from these very specific critiques, stated and implied, of Dom James' approach to Merton's petitioning, there is very little new in this letter of May 10; Merton was simply keeping the heat on himself and Giabbani.

Dom James returned to Gethsemani May 15; and, once again in his presence, Merton, to his credit, immediately abandoned the plan of concealment evidenced by his postscript about the roses in LETTER 20. Here is what Dom James, in a letter of May 17 (TMC), told Dom Gabriel about what Merton had been doing:

> Father Louis, on my return, came in the very next day for a long conversation, and he told me also that he had written a letter to Dom Anselmo Giabbani, asking him to negotiate a transitus to the Camaldolese. I told Father that at least he could have waited until my return to the monastery before he could do that, because in order for a transitus to become effective it must have the permission of the superior "a quo."[22] He excused himself by saying that [he knew that] I would not approve his writing, but I said he could have waited for me to say "no" and then go ahead.

This last sentence is curious. I take it to mean that Dom James is saying that if Merton had waited to tell him what he wanted to do, and had then gone ahead and written to Giabbani, it would be clear that he was doing it

---

22. Regarding this phrase, Father Elias Dietz, presently abbot of Gethsemani, writes, "When a monk transfers from one community (or institute) to another, formal consent is needed from the superiors of the respective communities: the abbot he is leaving (*a quo*, literally, 'from whom') and the abbot he is going to (*ad quem*, literally, 'to whom')." E-mail message to author, July 7, 2014.

The Greater *acedia*: What the Letters Tell Us

with the abbot's permission, but without his blessing. Merton also told him (as he told Giabbani in LETTER 24) that he had the support of five different priests whom he characterized as directors: Father Ford, a Jesuit, and, interestingly, a friend of Father Raymond Flanagan, a particular nemesis of Merton in the abbey; Father Vincent Oberhauser, the Louisville Passionist; "Dr. Moore" (as Dom James names him in a distancing manner); Father Timothy, Merton's confessor, whom he had taken on when it became clear that his previous confessor, Father Andrew, was opposed to Merton's plans; and Father Anselm, the prior.

> I asked Father Louis' permission to speak to Father Prior on that point, because personally I did not believe that Father Prior was [his] director. Father Louis gave me his permission and I asked Father Anselm. He was very much disturbed that Father Louis was calling him one of his directors. He absolutely denied it and went to see Father Louis about it.

The recollection of Father Anselm (Joseph Steinke) is more direct: "When he asked me what Merton had been doing in his absence, and I told him, Dom James threw a fit."[23] It is clear that Merton, for the strengthening of his case, was making a serious misstatement in claiming that Father Anselm was his spiritual director, as he had claimed in his letters of May 3 and May 10 to Giabbani. In fact, it may be questioned whether any of the five, with the possible exception of his confessor, were spiritual directors to Merton in the usual sense of the term, that is, mutually committed to an ongoing spiritual-direction relationship. Father Ford, Father Moore, Father Oberhauser, and Father Anselm might more accurately be described as consultants rather than spiritual directors. Merton does in fact use the term "consult" in this context in LETTER 24.

Dom James, in this long conversation with Merton, decided to float the idea of Merton's being responsible for the abbey's projected fire tower, something that would give him more solitude. Merton liked the idea, as Dom James then told Dom Gabriel in the same letter:

> Why could we not let Father Louis spend some time each day on duty in this little fire tower, say from dinner to supper time, . . . and the family brothers could take care of the rest of the time? . . . We had a very calm and cordial conversation about all this, and he seems perfectly at peace now, with this hope.

In his reply of May 28 (TMC), Dom Gabriel is less sanguine than Dom James about Merton and the fire tower. He says that he thinks that Merton

---

23. Personal conversation, September 15, 2009.

is simply humoring Dom James while waiting for the decision from Rome that he is hoping to obtain with the support of Giabbani. He also cannot accept that the fire tower job is work "in the Cistercian sense." He hunches that Merton will just take his typewriter up the tower and carry on writing. He wonders whether Merton should not stop writing and publishing for, say, five years; or perhaps Dom James should send him to a quiet little monastery, such as Mepkin in South Carolina.

After his conversation with Merton on May 16, Dom James wrote to Montini (LETTER 23) about Merton. He doesn't explicitly ask Montini to discourage Merton's attempts at a transfer, but it is clear that he wants Montini to know his views before he replies to Merton's letter of April 25 (which he didn't do until August). He first lists his own reasons for his refusal to release him: he is resisting "God's Sovereign Will," the scholastics would be scandalized, his readers would be scandalized to realize how restless he had been while writing panegyrics on life at Gethsemani, and his influence as a writer would be destroyed. He speaks both frankly and charitably about Merton, highlighting his many outstanding capacities. He characterizes Merton's relations in himself: dynamic, extraverted, brilliant, complex. He mentions that he has given St. Anne's, the tool shed, to Merton, "principally that he might be able to pray and to be alone with God"—and then adds, regretfully, "He uses most of that time for typewriting his manuscripts." He shares with Montini his own attraction to the Carthusians, which has persisted in him not just for ten years, as with Merton, but for twenty. (It's not known whether at this time he had told this to Merton.) Then he turns to Merton's relations with others. He says that Merton does not realize or appreciate that he is "a public figure of tremendous importance." He encloses with this letter to Montini the greater part of a letter to Merton from Chicago Passionist theologian Father Barnabas Ahern, in which Ahern echoes some of Dom James' reasoning and strongly disagrees with Merton's hope to leave Gethsemani.[24] Ahern offers five reasons why this would not be a good idea: it would encourage religious who are "itching" for change for change's sake; it would cut vocations to Trappist life; it would reduce Merton's cultural influence; it would shake the faith of certain religious in their own stability; and it would raise suspicions about the real meaning or value of contemplation. Ahern ends with this severe and critical statement: "If you change you shall tear from your written works the seal of Him who never changes. . . . I do not think that under any condition you can leave Gethsemani, any more than a Bishop can leave his diocese; you are wedded to it until death—for better or worse."

24. Dom James does not provide a date in his letter for Father Ahern's letter.

The Greater *acedia*: What the Letters Tell Us   193

This is a very bold, even presumptuous statement, and, if carried to its logical extreme, would prohibit any kind of inter-monastic transfer, for which in fact there were legitimate and accepted procedures. I am not aware that Merton replied to this letter—given its absolutist tone, there would have been no point. One can only guess at his response: the possibilities range from discouragement, irritation, and resentment to anger, or perhaps the self-blaming to which he was prone. Dom James, having given Montini this long and severe letter, then carries on:

> Father Louis thinks that I do not give his case sufficient consideration. Just this very day we have talked for over an hour and a quarter together, and it is not the first time. I did tell him . . . [that] at the present moment it seemed to me there was more of nature than of grace, more of self-seeking than of seeking God. Your Excellency, before God I say to you, and I am ready to meet this decision at the Last Judgment, that I cannot see the finger of God in Father Louis' desire to change. I am in no way afraid of taking the entire responsibility for this decision on myself. I do not fear any criticism in any way.

Reading this, my empathy and respect for Dom James increases exponentially. I interpret his comment about Merton's believing that he does not "give his case sufficient consideration" simply to mean, from Merton's point of view, that he is not agreeing with Merton. Had he agreed with Merton, then Merton, conversely, would have been ready to grant that he had indeed given his case sufficient consideration. Dom James has endured his own Carthusian attraction for twice as long as Merton; he has thought of a number of ways to give Merton more solitude at Gethsemani; and he accepts full responsibility as abbot for the decision to keep Merton at Gethsemani—for his own well-being. If these exchanges were placed before a representative sampling of Cistercian abbots today, my hunch is that they would be in some awe at the patience and thoughtfulness that Dom James demonstrates in his dealings with a highly volatile and moody monk, afflicted, as I am convinced, with a classic case of *acedia*.

In his letter of May 17 to Giabbani (LETTER 24), Merton gave his side of the story, Dom James' side of which we have just considered:

> Dom James came back on Sunday. I laid everything in front of him, both in writing and conversation. He was very hurt to think that I had asked for a *transitus* without consulting him. But I *had* [italics mine] consulted him in January and I came to the conclusion then that nothing could be worked out with him. Even so, I think that the fact of my having asked for a *transitus*

> produced a helpful reaction, because for the first time we really considered the issue in detail, and for the first time Dom James gave me his reasons why I should remain at Gethsemani.

For the first time, really? Had Merton not been listening? He had told Dom James about Camaldoli the day after his return, May 16. Later in the letter he says that Dom James "expressed his unhappiness that Father Prior had permitted [him] to write to a Carthusian and to consult a Jesuit." Dom James, insisting on his abbatial authority, told him that (as Merton relates it) the advice and support he had received from such "spiritual directors" was worthless; that the abbot was the only one "who could make a decision which would really be God's decision." In his letter of May 17 to Dom Gabriel, Dom James made the same point: "I told Father [Louis] that at least he could have waited until my return to the monastery . . . because in order for a transitus to become effective it must have the permission of the superior 'a quo.'"[25]

Without the permission of the sending abbot and the receiving abbot, in other words, the monk may not transfer and remain in good standing. It is hard for those of us not within the monastic milieu to accept that the decision of any superior can be *ipso facto* understood and accepted as God's decision; but Dom James was working well within the Benedictine-Cistercian understanding of the abbot's role as described in the Rule of St. Benedict, an understanding that Merton had accepted when he became a Trappist. Of course I am speaking here of the typical understanding of abbatial authority in the pre-Vatican II Roman Catholic Church, rather than the understanding that comes from the early monastic writers, and that came again to the fore during and after Vatican II, not least because of Merton's own researches.

Merton's vulnerability shows up strongly toward the end of this letter. He uses the word "beg" three times. He begs Giabbani to let him come to Camaldoli and make trial of the solitary life; he begs him not to leave him at the mercy of Dom James, who, he believes, knows him but does not understand him; and, very curiously, he begs Giabbani to "guarantee" to him the possibility of consulting a spiritual director "three or four times a year—by means of a sealed letter." He asks this, he says, not only because of Dom James, but "especially because of his secretary, who is more autocratic than any superior whatsoever, who sticks his nose into everything, and even gives orders to Father Prior during Dom James' absence." The reference to Dom James and his secretary suggests that Merton expects to be at Gethsemani for some time; but if so, why would he need a guarantee from Giabbani in

25. See note 24.

regard to sealed letters? Finally, he signs himself the "most devoted... and perhaps the most miserable" of Giabbani's spiritual sons.

LETTER 25, from Giabbani to Merton, the writing of which we can calculate as occurring between May 17 and May 28, is no longer extant. It would have been instructive to know what Giabbani had to say about Merton's pleadings in his letters of May 3, 6, 10, and perhaps 17. Merton's letter of May 28 (LETTER 26) expands on Dom James' response. Dom James had in the first months of his abbatial tenure set before Merton the possibility of finding a resolution through which he would remain at Gethsemani, "so as not to have recourse to the *transitus*," and had now spoken of this again. But Merton, his heart still set on the dream of Camaldoli, asks him "to leave the final judgment... in the hands of the Sacred Congregation [for Religious]," to which he had not yet written himself, but which he had asked Giabbani to approach on his behalf—"and doubtless Monsignor Montini would be able to shed some light on it." In a remarkable shift in tone, Merton thanks God for having given him "Superiors with much good will and a truly supernatural spirit," and says that he is sorry that he has made them suffer: "but even so I believe God has called me here for a spiritual formation which will prepare me for a more solitary life." He encloses with this letter a copy of a letter he had written to Clare Boothe Luce, the potential benefactor of Camaldoli in America of whom he had earlier spoken to Giabbani (LETTER 5, note 12).

Between May 28 and August 20—three months—there is a gap in the correspondence: no word from Giabbani, and no word from Montini, although Merton continued to write to other correspondents, and to Dom James, about his vocation. Then Montini, ironically on retreat at a former Camaldolese house (Gussago, near Brescia), writes (LETTER 27) to Merton on August 20, ten years to the day before Merton's official entry into the hermitage at Gethsemani. The letter consists of eight handwritten pages and is highly pastoral and empathetic, although his extended praise for the tranquillity and serenity of the location might well have been painful for Merton to read:

> ... the natural surroundings of this ancient place of prayer and of silence are tranquil and serene. The bare hills bear upon their sides the ancient hermitage, and in front of them stretches in placid immensity the beautiful Paduan plain, overlooking a vision of the world, where human life hums with the modern intensity of its traffic, of its fatigue, of its ambitions; and from here one contemplates in silence, with a higher abandon that appears to discover in the open spaces and the heights a wisdom

> capable of judging, ... and of feeling oneself the closer to God the further one is from human beings and their affairs.

He goes on, without mentioning Dom James' letter (LETTER 23), to support his reasoning. Merton's departure would be a terrible shock to too many souls. His literary "fecundity ... no longer belongs to [him] alone; it belongs to souls; it belongs to the Church." He advises Merton to trust his abbot and a *single* spiritual director, and to recognize that

> perfection does not consists in the circumstances which favor it, but rather in the charity of the soul seeking it; and that the search at a given moment does not turn on the modification of the external conditions of spiritual feeling and orientation. ... All this tells you that—unless a better counsel should prevail—it seems to me that your place of sanctification is the one where you now are.

The same day, he writes briefly to Dom James (LETTER 28), informing him that he has written to Merton to this effect, and encouraging Dom James "to favor his desire for silence and solitude," and "not to oblige him [to take part in] excessively absorbing relations with the community." Though not himself a monastic, he offers here a beautiful example of monastic *discretio*, or discernment, a virtue proper to monks and a safeguard against illusion. I note Montini's balanced and compassionate suggestion that Dom James "favor" Merton and not "oblige" him to take part in those community activities that would cause him particular stress. The next day he writes to Giabbani (LETTER 29), on the same subject, together with a comment that if Merton did go to Camaldoli, he would bring his restlessness with him, and thereby offer no benefit to Camaldoli.

Montini's letter to Merton is the last one in the file at Camaldoli; and so my initial assumption was that Merton, on receiving it, would have abandoned his hopes of a transfer. However, on August 24, clearly from internal evidence not having received Montini's letter, Merton writes (LETTER 30) to Cardinal Larraona, Secretary of the Congregation for Religious, with whom he had made a good personal connection when he visited Gethsemani on August 23–24, 1952 (SFS 10–11). He sets out the chronology of his attempts to transfer to Camaldoli, asserting that Dom James, whom he regards as "unfair and unreasonable," wants to keep him at Gethsemani "at any cost," comments that stand in strong contrast to the gratitude for his superiors that he had expressed in LETTER 26. He mentions that Jean Leclercq has encouraged him to consider Frascati, a Camaldolese house "more solitary and more austere" than Camaldoli itself, and that he has received a letter from

Frascati inviting him to come there. Because he does not know whether Giabbani has acted on his request for a *transitus* with the Sacred Congregation, he asks Larraona, conditionally, to consider this letter such a request. Since Frascati is ready to receive him completely incognito, and as his leaving of Gethsemani would be unadvertised, is he not right, he asks, "in standing up for the call of God against the material and opportunistic interests of the Father Abbot?" And because Dom James has forbidden him to write again to Giabbani, he encloses a one-page letter to Giabbani in his letter to Larraona, asking him to forward it—an evasive if not *entirely* disobedient act (he didn't mail the letter *directly* to Giabbani).

Having slagged Dom James, he makes a feeble attempt to speak well of Gethsemani itself, and then in the same paragraph offers a volley of criticism:

> ... I am not speaking to you about Gethsemani. It's a good monastery, which exercises a very large influence for the good of souls.... However, we are undergoing a worrying evolution. Among us there is a spirit which is more and more superficial, external, technological, noisy, commercial.... I am not criticizing this monastery, but it makes me heartsick to think that I am being refused the satisfaction of a genuine desire for solitary life in order for my person to be used as a "façade" for this house where I live somewhat as an outsider who simply doesn't belong.

If he was not criticizing Gethsemani, then what are we to call this statement of complaint? Finally, in a significant postscript, he says that he knows "that the Sacred Congregation will give me the Church's answer and God's answer."

When Larraona's response came (LETTER 32, handwritten, September 26), it restated what Montini (whose letter by now Merton had received) had said: stay where you are, and wait a few years. In a warm, pastoral, almost chatty letter that includes a number of digressions and Spanish proverbs, he praises Merton's "thirst and hunger for solitude," acknowledges that he can't see into Merton's soul, and asks him, even so, to take seriously "the not unimportant repercussions that [his leaving Gethsemani] would have on the Trappist order and on Gethsemani [itself]." It would not be advisable in any case, he tells Merton, for him to go to Camaldoli, "because there are many question marks about the direction of that congregation," and adds that if Merton went there, he would be exposed to "painful disappointments" about its spiritual state. He makes comments, of a kind familiar to us, about how Merton's leaving Gethsemani would "cause disconcerting reactions on the part of many good and sincere souls." He doesn't definitively say that Merton should stay at Gethsemani, but that is the clear drift of the letter. That takes us back to Merton's journal entry for August 23, 1952, in which he describes Larraona's visit to Gethsemani and says that in listening to Larraona, he had come to "the realization that Christ was speaking, that [in him] the Church was making known God's thoughts and His will to us" (SFS 11). In LETTER 30, to Larraona, he had restated this point. He knew, he said, that the Congregation would give him "the Church's answer and God's answer." And so it did: stay where you are, and wait a few years.

The same day that Merton wrote to Larraona, August 24, Giabbani wrote to Montini (LETTER 31). He tells Montini that he had come to Milan on June 24 to give him letters from Merton and from his "spiritual directors." He had earlier spoken about Merton with the consultant for Camaldoli from the Sacred Congregation for Religious, Archbishop Lazzaro da Arbonne; and they had agreed to work together to forestall Merton's coming to Italy, either to Camaldoli or Frascati. This confirms in writing what Giabbani's letters to Merton have come to suggest: namely, that his interest in the correspondence by this time chiefly concerned the possibility of an American Camaldolese foundation, and that he had by this time withdrawn his support for Merton's coming to Camaldoli, a request to which he had at first responded very sympathetically. He now floats the idea that when the foundation is made, Dom James could be asked to second Merton to the project "for a period of time," and then gives very moving expression to his own journey: "Your Excellency knows my torment and the daily struggle I've had since I was sixteen years old"—he had entered Camaldoli at sixteen, in 1924, and so was speaking of a struggle of thirty years. He also laments that "the authority we have always looked up to with so much trust was not able to give us [the Camaldolese] clear direction, nor has yet corrected the rules that the same authority has recognized as wrong after approving them." My conjecture is that this is a reference to the Congregation for Religious, which was then in the process of assessing a new set of Constitutions for Camaldoli, statutes that would, I assume, correct whatever were the unhelpful rules to which Camaldoli had previously been subject.

In LETTER 33, written October 1, Merton writes again to Montini, whose reply of August 24 he has now received. "It is quite probable," he says, "that yours is really the final solution"—stay where you are, seek interior solitude. His situation is being discussed by his superiors in Europe (at the annual Trappist General Chapter, at which Dom James and Dom Gabriel were conferring), and he was waiting for their decision. He says that "there is a faint possibility of my Superiors permitting me to live a more solitary life here at Gethsemani"—not so faint, as he was about to discover on Dom James' return. He tells Montini that he has written to Larraona, whose reply

The Greater *acedia*: What the Letters Tell Us

he has not yet received. Then, having once again described his disaffection for how noisy and busy Gethsemani has become, he links it with its "American" ambiance:

> ... these features are precisely those of an American milieu, features which grate on my European sensibilities. If it is true that a missionary must sacrifice his homeland and hereditary outlook to settle in a new land and adopt the viewpoint of those among whom he has settled, how much more true is it, perhaps, that God asks of me the full acceptance of the American religious outlook, even though it may seem in many ways superficial and silly—especially since I am after all half American by blood and American by nationalization.

Poor miserable Thomas Merton! Constrained by a life decision freely made in 1941, a decision freely confirmed with life vows in 1947, including the vow of stability, and celebrated in many of his books as the work of God, an American citizen since 1951, he now presents himself as, essentially, a sophisticated European in exile in a community of unsophisticated Americans—"a duck in a chicken coop" (SJ, 95),[26] or, as St. Peter Damian said about St. Romuald in a difficult monastic setting, "a cedar of Lebanon in a briar-patch,"[27] a fate from which Merton had hoped Camaldoli could have rescued him.[28] He then adds two theological misstatements to this cry of cultural angst, expressing the hope that "by self-renunciation and obedience [he] can *merit* to be with God in eternity," and the related hope that he can *earn* Montini's blessing (italics mine), both statements being contradictions of the Christian understanding that human beings are saved by the grace of God and not by their own merits, and that blessings, of course, are freely given, not earned. The Roman Catholic Church, through Vatican II, moved away from this kind of language; however, it is a matter of regret to many that language of this tonality, of meriting and earning, has been reintroduced to Roman Catholic practice in the Roman Missal III.

The next two letters, 34 and 35, can only be understood with the aid of an account of what happened when Dom James returned to Gethsemani from Europe. He had discussed Merton's options with Dom Louis, the father immediate, and Dom Gabriel Sortais, the abbot general, and they had

---

26. Suggesting that he is not only out of place but also "cooped up," confined, at Gethsemani.

27. Matus, *Mystery of Romuald*, 62.

28. He was still thinking about this in 1960: "I must examine the superficiality of my European prejudices. There is a great deal wrong with my instinctive tendency to think in a French way about America" (September 29, SFS, 53).

come to the conclusion that if Merton were to be a hermit, he could be one at Gethsemani, but would need to be a hermit "one hundred percent right away" (letter of Dom James to Dom Gabriel, October 18, TMC). Here is what Dom James has to say about this: "When I returned home, he came rushing in ... in his characteristically impetuous impulsive manner. He told me he was ready to do anything now. He was completely reformed and disillusioned." I interpret this last word literally: by the letters from Montini and Larraona, Merton had been relieved of his illusions about the possibility of a move to Camaldoli, not that he was abandoning his consistent hope for a solitary vocation. Dom James continues,

> So I told him your opinion, that he should try the hermitage life one hundred percent right away. . . . He displayed some enthusiasm . . . , but I thought I could detect that he was completely taken by surprise at such a sudden proposal. . . . During the same interview I was telling Father Louis of the developments at Our Lady of the Genesee, and how they had [elected as abbot] good Father Walter, our present Master of Choir Novices. . . . Lo and behold, the next day I received a note from Father Louis . . . suggesting that he would be willing to be Father Master if I approved. The note seemed to breathe a great spirit of self-sacrifice of his most precious hermit project, but on reflection, I concluded that the sudden proposal of being a hermit one hundred percent immediately had unnerved him, and that he was . . . looking for an honorable way out of the hermitage dream, but without compromising all the protestations for a life of silence and solitude that he has been serving up to us all . . .

"[T]hat he has been serving up to us all"—to Dom James, Dom Louis, Dom Gabriel, Giabbani, Montini, Larraona, and his "spiritual directors"—serving them up (the "up" carries the feeling tone) a dish that became more and more unpalatable as the years passed without Merton offering a change of menu!

Merton's note to Dom James has been preserved (Thursday, October 13, 1955, TMC). He begins with a brief bow in the direction of the decision that would permit him to be a hermit, but then quickly addresses the possibility of his being novice master:

> . . . I realize that you are in rather a tough spot, so . . . I'd like to go on record as saying that I wonder also if Jesus wants me to make the sacrifice of this opportunity, for the time being, in order to help you fill the gap caused by the election at Genesee. . . . I am not asking for it but I am not refusing it. I make the fact known because at the back of my mind I feel that Jesus wants me to be perfectly at your disposition. If I can try solitude now, so much

the better. If later—OK. In either case I am indifferent and in perfect peace.

Dom James accepted the offer, and appointed him with the proviso already mentioned: "there is just one condition . . . : I would not want you to be teaching the novices to become Camaldolese or hermits." Merton accepted the condition, an acceptance that in LETTER 34, to Dom Gabriel, he refers to as a vow. Shortly after, he embarked on his ten-year-long stint as novice master, a substantial, indeed, magnificent contribution to the life of the community.[29] In his correspondence of the time, however, Merton obscures the fact that he had volunteered, or perhaps better, made himself available, or put himself forward for the position. Disingenuously, he writes to Dom Gabriel on October 18 saying that "*he* [Dom James, italics Merton's] has decided to give me the office of Father Master of the Choir Novices." To Jean Leclercq, on December 3, he writes, "It happens that I am now master of novices!" And to Anselmo Giabbani, in LETTER 36, he says "they" have made him master of novices. Indeed Dom James did make the decision, which was his alone to make; *and* he was assisted in his making of that decision by Merton's active readiness, neither insisting nor refusing.

In LETTER 34, to Dom Gabriel, Merton refers to Dom Walter's election at Genesee and then shares his thoughts on the subject. Curiously, the phrases I have bolded here (my translation) have been omitted from the published version of the letter (SCH, 92–93), the text of which I am using in the collection:

> So I thought I must, before God, leave myself entirely in the hands of Dom James, **in this moment of need in the house, more so because I believe that I ought to challenge a little my attraction to solitude, which can only be a matter of my own will,** and *he* has decided to give me the office of Father Master of the Choir Novices to replace Father Walter. . . . You see how poor we are in personnel when it is I, the *only one* that Dom James can entrust with the novices without having to seek a dispensation.

The bolded words point to Merton's ongoing struggle around the issue of the will of God, both with Dom James and in himself, a struggle that we discuss in chapter 4. His comment that he is the only one whom Dom James can entrust with the novices, however, ignores Dom James' earlier thought about who might undertake the office. The other possibility for the position was Father Romanus, who would have been academically suitable but who did not meet the order's requirements for being a novice master (i.e., that he be thirty-five

---

29. See note 8, above.

years of age with ten years' experience in the order). His appointment would have required Dom James to ask for a dispensation, whereas Merton's did not. I smile at the satisfaction implicit in Merton's italicizing of his comment that he is the "*only one*" to whom the position could be entrusted. Merton was a Four on the Enneagram,[30] with a strong tendency to see himself as special, to be recognized as special, and, probably unconsciously more than consciously, to want special treatment. His appointment, in response to his putting himself forward for it, fitted this temperamental need exactly. Merton tells Dom Gabriel about this major shift in his life and in his attitude to his vocation. He says that he is "completely convinced that God does not want [him] to be a Camaldolese," that he is very sure that he is in possession of the will of God in this regard, and that he is in "utter peace and with no regrets." The various responses to his proposals—from Dom James, from Montini, from Larraona, from Dom Porion, from Father Ahern, and others, and the lack of action on his behalf from Dom Giabbani—have given him an opportunity for the sacrifice of his long-held dream, which he names as such in his note to Dom James. He says that after three years as novice master, if his attraction to solitude persists, he would perhaps ask for permission "to live in the woods." In the event, he served ten years as novice master, a task that he thoroughly enjoyed and that channeled at least some of his energies away from his obsession with his own solitude.

There is another account of Merton's appointment in Dom James' letter of October 20 to Archbishop Montini (LETTER 35), a reply to Montini's letter of August 20 (LETTER 28). He thanks Montini for his reply, and for his letter to Merton. He describes Merton as a changed man and provides Montini with the circumstances of Merton's appointment as novice master, beginning with his shock at the immediate possibility of being a hermit "one hundred percent." He also tells Montini about Merton's "admission" that the attempt to become a hermit was "all his own will"—Dom James' own conviction from the beginning of the struggle. He says that he believes that Merton will make an excellent novice master, and so it proved.

1956

The last letter in the sequence, LETTER 36, is Merton's final letter to Giabbani; the correspondence had begun with a letter to Giabbani, and it ends with one. The occasion for writing, for which he had Dom James' permission, was a necessary clarification of publishing details relating to Merton's

---

30 Some synonyms for the Four: ego-romantic, ego-melancholic, overdramatizer. Zuercher, *Merton: An Enneagram Profile*, 5.

book *Silence in Heaven*, which was to be published in French and Italian translations. Thus on March 24, 1956, having discussed the translations, he summarizes the saga of the previous three and a half years in a passage marked by his most substantial use of italics in any of the correspondence, and by notes of equivocation and self-dramatization:

> Our project of last year has completely failed, as you know. Counselled by *Monsignor Montini* and by the Most Reverend Father *Larraona*, I have *let go* of the hope of [receiving] a *transitus to Camaldoli*. . . . So I am *definitively* ensconced here, I think. *Fiat voluntas Dei* ["May the will of God be done"].

He asks Giabbani to pray that he may "sacrifice everything" and give himself totally to God, as did Jesus, made obedient to death.[31] He ends by assuring Giabbani of his prayers for him and for all the monks and hermits of Camaldoli; and although he describes himself as unworthy of a calling as beautiful as theirs, he asks Giabbani, with undeniable melodrama, to regard him, if not canonically or officially, then "as spiritually a hermit, as a secret and hidden Camaldolese, a Camaldolese in the eyes of God alone." I find myself wincing a little at this last sentence; once again I hear the violins. Merton is trying to have his cake and eat it too. He is not living as an actual hermit but is asking to be considered a kind of honorary hermit. He was letting go, he says—and he was not letting go. The dream of Camaldoli, only a dream after all, would, he implies, remain in his heart forever—or as a source, when recalled, of chagrin, as we will see in chapter 5.[32]

---

31. Cf. Phil 2:8.

32. Just as this book was going to the publisher, I learned from Albert Romkema, in Toronto, after the Thomas Merton Center the leading collector of Mertoniana (merton-artifacts.com), that he had purchased a booklet called *The Camaldolese Way*, with a soft cover, dated 1957, written in English, and published in Italy by Morcelliana of Brescia. Its text is similar to that of *The Silent Life*, but with textual variations and twelve images. My assumption is that this was one of the results of Merton's earlier correspondence with Giabbani about publishing material about Camaldoli: see on this LETTERS 5, 10, 12, 16, and 36. Romkema's copy contained an undated correspondence card from Giabbani, inscribed as follows: "Many thanks for your attention [sic]. / With God's blessings / +fr Anselm [sic] Giabbani / S. Gregorio al Celio, Roma." Given the impersonal character of the inscription, it seems likely that this was not sent to Merton, but to someone else in the United States who had asked Giabbani for information about Camaldoli. My thanks to Albert Romkema for bringing these items to my attention.

4

Acedia and the Will of God

ACEDIA IN THE LETTERS

As paradigms or checklists through which to identify evidence of *acedia* in the letters, I will be using two main sources: the ur-source, Evagrius, chapter 12 of *The Praktikos*,[1] and the last source explored in chapter 1, Merton's lectures to the novices. As Bamberger and others recommend, I will continue to use the word *acedia* as the basic term, because, as a Latin word, it can carry all the meanings suggested by its English near-synonyms, from among which I have, as earlier mentioned, excluded *sloth*, with its contemporary connotation of laziness. The English word that comes closest to what Evagrius is talking about, it seems to me, is *restlessness*, a term favored by Solomon. Indeed, Merton's heart was not at rest for most of the time during these years. There is indeed, he would have believed, a Sabbath rest for the people of God into which we are invited to enter (cf. Heb 4:9–10); but this was not his experience during these years, except for some very brief and specific moments. It is impossible to deny that the letters give evidence of ongoing restlessness.

Of the eleven characteristics of *acedia* Evagrius mentions, two in particular, it is clear, do not apply to Merton at all. Far from having hatred for manual labor, he entered into the work parties in the monastery, often shared with the novices, with considerable vigor, even enjoyment, as this comment from a September 26, 1954 note (TMC) to Dom James suggests:

---

1. The full text of chapter 12 of *The Praktikos* is in chapter 1 of this book.

> Yesterday, extra work, cutting corn in the middle bottom. . . . It was good. That side of Trappist life is very good. All of it is good, but the cornfield side is good for *me*. It would be the aspect of life I would miss most if I became a Carthusian or a Camaldolese. Hence, perhaps the real solution is to be a hermit in America, on your own, and work for a living.[2]

Nor was he afflicted with recollections of dear ones and his former way of life. All his immediate family had died; only two aunts in New Zealand remained. As for his former life as a budding New York intellectual, there was no emotional pull there. In fact, he says in various places in the SSM, in effect, that New York is one of the capitals of Hell, although when he went there in 1964 to visit D. T. Suzuki, he discovered that this was far from the case. He had left his former life behind definitively, to become a monk; about that there was no question. The real question was, as David Belcastro frames it, "If a monk, what kind of monk?" Belcastro's riff on this is illuminating:

> While he is never able to say exactly who he is or what kind of monk or hermit he might be, he was none-the-less aware of how living the question moved him in the direction of becoming more authentically human, free and alive in relation to and for the sake of the world in which he lived.[3]

All through his struggles revealed in the letters, with Dom James and other superiors, and with himself, there is never any suggestion that he should, would, even could abandon his monastic commitment. This makes it all the more appropriate that we should use Evagrius' checklist for *acedia*, written specifically for monks and hermits.

Other features mentioned by Evagrius that likewise do not seem to apply to Merton are the sense that time drags, or that of hatred for life itself, or the quick taking of offense, or the sense that life (like the Egyptian desert) stretches out into a featureless horizon. However, in regard to the Evagrian category of distractions, I would conjecture that this is where his highly ambivalent relation to his writing comes in. His statements about this, especially in the crucial year of 1955, come from the far realms of fantasy. On August 11, in a letter to Jean Leclercq, he says, "I have stopped writing,

---

2. A contemporary example of this form of eremitical life: Charles Brandt, Roman Catholic priest, bookbinder, ecologist; at one time a member of the Hermits of St. John the Baptist, a small eremitical *laura* founded in Merville, British Columbia, by Jacques Winandy, friend and correspondent of Thomas Merton, whose work inspired both of them to embrace the hermit life. See Holloway and Jones, "Father Charles Brandt."

3. Belcastro, "Praying the Questions," 128. Note the internal reference to Rilke: "living the question."

and that is a big relief."[4] In a letter of August 15 to Dom James (TMC), he says that he has received a letter from Dom Gabriel in reply to the one he had written him in which he told him that he was "no longer writing." On August 24, in a postscript at the end of LETTER 30, to Larraona, he says, "If I stay here [Gethsemani], I will write nothing more." Again writing to Jean Leclercq on December 3, he says, "I shall cease to be a writer at least as long as I am in charge of the novices," a period during which, again according to Patricia Burton's *Vade Mecum*, he published thirteen books; and in another letter to Leclercq, written February 6, 1956, he grandly says, "I have abandoned all writing now."[5] Then, in a letter of September 14, 1956 (TMC) to Gregory Zilboorg, he says, "I am stopping all writing, including the writing of a journal, of occasional poems, etc. Until further notice, I cease to be a writer." "Further notice" appears, according to Patricia Burton, to have lasted all of five months, until January 1957, when he published *The Silent Life*, and in March, *The Strange Islands*. Finally, in his journal for May 21, 1960, he reflects at some length on this tension, nuancing the absolute character of some of his previous statements:

> I wonder if the time has come for me *to cease writing for publication*. Not to stop writing altogether. On the contrary to write what I really need to write myself, not what the readers of some magazine would or what "my readers" expect.... To write more poetry perhaps... Not to stop publishing altogether—obviously there are several books waiting to be printed. But do they need to be printed? Or printed *now*? ... To put more feelings into this Journal which is not for publication. And in which I can therefore speak freely. (SFS, 392)

This is not to derogate from the indisputable fact that Merton was indeed a very creative writer, but simply to assert that his ambivalence toward his writerly vocation was often in tension with his understanding of his hoped-for eremitical vocation. If one of the tasks of the demon of *acedia* is to lead his subject into confusion, these instances provide ample evidence of its success.

Hatred of the place, another Evagrian category, is well represented in the letters. Gethsemani, the *paradisus claustralis* of his early years there, became at times a place of real distaste for him:

> I am beginning to face some facts about myself ... something very deep and very fundamental in myself. A fault that has been basic for the last twelve years—all my life. Continual,

---

4. Merton and Leclerq, *Survival or Prophecy?*, 67.
5. Ibid., 72, 74.

uninterrupted resentment. I resent and even hate Gethsemani. I fight against the place constantly.[6]

Gethsemani, he says, is a place of "racket and moral pressure" (LETTER 22). In LETTER 30, to Larraona, he expands on this, beginning with a classic Mertonism—a statement that he is not going to explain something, followed immediately by his explanation:

> ... I am not speaking to you about Gethsemani. It's a good monastery, which exercises a very large influence for the good of souls.... At Gethsemani, however, we are undergoing a worrying evolution. Among us there is a spirit which is more and more superficial, external, technological, noisy, commercial.... I am not criticizing this monastery....

... and so on. The noise, of course, comes from the tractors, jackhammers, and air compressors that Dom James has brought in to build the factories and work the land in the interest of Gethsemani paying for itself, which it had not been doing before his election in 1948. In LETTER 33, to Montini, Merton speaks of an environment that is noisy and distracting because of "the presence of so many machines constantly in operation." Merton is exaggerating when he says "constantly," but that is how it seemed to him in contrast with the bucolic character of Gethsemani when he first went there.

Cassian picks up on Evagrius' identification of the temptation to "desire other sites where he can ... make a real success of himself" by his more concrete reference to the tendency of the *acedia*-afflicted monk to make "a great deal of far-off and distant monasteries, describing such places as more suited to progress and more conducive to salvation, and also depicting the fellowship of the brothers there as pleasant and of an utterly spiritual cast."[7] There is no question that this was happening for Merton. If not the charterhouse, then Camaldoli; and if not Camaldoli, then Frascati. Merton, given his contempt for "success" in its contemporary meaning,[8] would never have accepted the thought that he wanted to go to Camaldoli to "make a real success of himself." He would of course have said, as he did say, that he wanted to go there in response to God's undoubted call to him to be a solitary. But the rhapsodic and inflated way in which in the letters he describes Camaldoli, which he has never seen, to Giabbani, who lives there, is all the evidence we need of his vulnerability to this dimension of the disease (a term, incidentally, that Merton himself favors).

---

6. Letter to Dom James, April 4, 1954, TMC.
7. Cassian, *Institutes*, 219.
8. See on this Merton, *Love and Living*, 11–13.

We turn now to Merton's own teaching to the novices about *acedia*. My suggestion here is that the reader return to what chapter 1 says about this teaching. Here I will simply list those aspects of *acedia* that he mentions and that show up in the letters: the fascination with distant monasteries, the inability to get along with oneself, and the tendency to instability. Instability here we may take as referring not to emotional instability, although there is some of that. Rather, its root reference is to the vow of stability made at profession, that is, the vow to remain in the monastery of one's profession unless sent elsewhere by legitimate authority. Merton's hold on this vow, or perhaps its hold on him during the time of the letters, is shaky at best. There is also the broad statement from Merton about *acedia*, which includes a reference to "the best minds" and the "intellectual elite," categories in which we can legitimately place Merton himself:

> *Acedia* is in fact one of the great spiritual diseases of our time. In a sense it is a disease of the best minds. The intellectual elite is faced with despair because it sees the utter hollowness of the world that man has made for himself and sees no hope for an improvement.... *Acedia* is the disease which afflicts the whole world, especially the unbelieving world. (IMT 1, 185)

We will encounter more reference to this dimension of *acedia* when we consider Merton's desire to move to Latin America. Here I will only note that Merton has enlarged the reach of *acedia* from the monastic to the global. *Acedia*, then, afflicts us all; and when we read what Kathleen Norris says about *acedia* as restless boredom, frantic escapism, and commitment phobia, we can find support for Merton's vision of *acedia*'s reach. Here I will only link it to the highly elitist comment he makes in LETTER 33, to Montini, in which he bemoans how his "European sensibilities" are misunderstood and frustrated at Gethsemani.

Do we then see the ancient demon of *acedia* at work in the Merton whom we meet in the Camaldoli Correspondence? Do we see it trying to take up residency in the life of Thomas Merton between 1952 and 1955? I submit that, yes, we do.

DOM JAMES AND THE WILL OF GOD

One of the major themes that runs through the letters is that of the will of God.[9] Merton and Dom James sparred with each other over this con-

---

9. For Merton's understanding of God, see Raab, "Insights from the Inter-Contemplative Dialogue," 90–105. For Merton's thoughts on the will of God as presented

cept—Merton saying that he was convinced that the will of God for him was solitude, the life of a solitary, and Dom James saying that, although that might be so, it did not necessarily entail Merton's leaving Gethsemani. It is a subject with many dimensions, a very elusive if not slippery one. The reader may wonder at times whether "the will of God" is indeed a theological or spiritual category, or, as sometimes it seems, simply a rhetorical device by means of which one can one-up one's opponent. A fuller discussion of the topic would include the objective will of God, whatever that might be discerned to be, as well as Dom James' perception or intuition of the will of God, and Merton's, with both of them accepting what the *Rule of St. Benedict* says about the role of the abbot in discerning and declaring the will of God to his monks. It further includes the *authority* to declare the will of God, or to make a decision that can be accepted as the will of God, an authority that Merton granted to the Congregation for Religious (cf. LETTER 30). There is also Merton's relationship with Dom James as monk and abbot in an order with a strong historical emphasis on penance; and finally, and not least important, there is their personal relationship to one another as, in both a monastic and personal sense, father and son. To the postmodern mind, the thought of granting to any human being the authority to represent Christ beyond any challenge, or even to speak so in the name of God, is countercultural, if not abhorrent. It raises the possibility of abuse by abbots who might make decisions more in their own interests than in the interests of their charges, or even make decisions to thwart or punish particular monks whom they dislike. I hope it will be clear that I do not in any way attribute such abuses to Dom James, in spite of Merton's fairly frequent readiness to attribute to him some less than fair or honest motivations.

For Merton and Dom James, this is essentially a monastic question. Both Merton and Dom James are working within the same monastic framework of discernment. Merton's lectures to the novices, for example, testify to his classic, monastic understanding of the will of God. He relates his discernment of this, again, to Evagrius:

> ... for Evagrius the ascent to *gnosis* is not just a matter of seeking one's own spiritual purity. *It is a response to the will of God* for the restoration of the cosmos to its primitive state. God wills that all should come to the knowledge of the truth, that is, of Himself. (IMT 3, 101)

---

to the novices, see IMT 2, 100–101, 129, 206–7, 302; IMT 3, 101, 126; IMT 4, xxiii, xliv, 83, 101, 113, 132, 178; IMT 5, 43. For Merton's later thoughts on the will of God, see *New Seeds of Contemplation*, 18–20. Cf. also chapter 3, note 8.

This last sentence is a partial quotation of 1 Tim 2:4—in the KJV, "[God] will have all men to be saved, and to come unto the knowledge of the truth"; in the NRSV, "[God] desires everyone to be saved and to come to the knowledge of the truth." The word *knowledge* in this text is *epignosis* in the Greek, meaning the *process* of coming to a salvific or transformational knowing. This is a personal and spiritual knowing, not a propositional or informational knowing. For the monk, the ascent to this salvific knowledge is a lifelong process, a continuing search for ways in which he may participate in "the restoration of the cosmos to its primitive state," a *conversio/conversatio morum*, or as Merton often says in other contexts, the recovery of paradise. In seeking to know and respond to the will of God, the monk is not simply attempting to make a good decision in a particular instance, but to co-participate with all those who have heard the call to *gnosis* as a call to *epignosis*[10] and to *anakephalaiosis*, the summing up or integration, cosmically, of all things in Christ,[11] a comment very close to the ascetical view of Evagrius. Here is one of Merton's comments on the will of God to the novices:

> The "will of God" is [not] a blind force plunging through our lives like a cosmic steamroller and demanding to be accepted willy-nilly. On the contrary, we are able to *understand* the hidden purposes of the creative wisdom and the divine mercy of God, and can cooperate with Him as sons with a loving Father. (IMT 3, 126)

Some years later, Merton sets out a very similar statement in his journal:

> Strange thing, that expression, "the Will of God"—meaning not just "a virtuous act" or "something that would be good to do"—but an act springing from the intimate depths of my own life and my own providential destiny—an act which is new and mysterious and contradicts everything that has so far been planned and arranged. A new departure, in a life that seemingly admits no new departures. Of this I can say nothing. I can only let myself be led. (June 18, 1959, SFS, 295)

When he wrote this, he was living through the time of the lesser *acedia*, as demonstrated in his attempts to go to Latin America. But if it is a valid statement about the will of God, who is eternal, and whose will is therefore also eternal, it is just as relevant to any other crisis as to the Camaldoli crisis. I read it as a statement of submission, a recognition that the will of God

---

10. Rom 15:14; 1 Cor 8:10.
11. Col 1:17; Eph 1:10.

can and sometimes must be done in circumstances not of the individual's choosing, and that therefore the individual should be ready to look for the will of God in events or decisions that may contradict his own preferences, indeed his own will, as well as in those that accord with his own will.

In another reflection, written at the time of his correspondence with his friend Archbishop Paul Philippe about the reopening of the request for exclaustration refused by Cardinals Valeri and Larraona, he frames the question very sharply, reflecting once again (September 11, 1960) on what it means to speak of the will of God.

> My life must have meaning. This meaning springs from a creative and intelligent harmony between my will and the will of God—a clarification by right action. But what is right action? What is the will of God? ... I can no longer accept the superficial verbalism ... which evades reality by simply saying the will of the Superior is the will of God and the will of God is the will of the Superior. I do not mean that the will of the Superior does not, or cannot, indicate where God's will may be for me—but the will of the Superior simply defines and points out the way in which I am to try to act intelligently and spiritually, and thus clarify the meaning of my own life ("giving glory to God"). Simply to go ahead blindly, muttering "the will of God, the will of God" clarifies nothing. . . . The sanctification of falsity by the magic will of the Superior. . . . Precisely this is the greatest lie, for the will of the Superior is not supposed to have any power but the power of Christ's humility and of His love. (TTW, 46–47)

Merton wanted co-discernment rather than the very limited view of monastic obedience which automatically equated the superior's will with God's, and vice versa. He resists what he calls a "magic" view of obedience (the word *obedience* itself comes from a Latin root simply meaning "to hear," rather than "to obey" in a literal sense). There were times when Merton and Dom James were not hearing each other, and other times when they were. Basic to their difficulty in agreeing with each other, or even understanding each other, was what I will call the size of their worlds. Dom James lived in a small, monastic world, of which Gethsemani was the center. His perspectives were circumscribed by his Cistercian identity, which was regularly and conservatively reinforced by his annual attendance at the General Chapter of Cistercian abbots, always in Europe. He was not an intellectual, and to my knowledge had no cultural interests outside the Cistercian tradition. Merton, contrariwise, lived in a very large world, a world without a boundary such as the Cistercian boundary within which Dom James operated. Gethsemani for Merton, as well as being the place of his monastic stability, was a base for his activity as a public intellectual, rather than the kind of life-center it was for Dom James. Thinking of the Platonic-Augustinian description of God, known to Merton, as a reality whose center is everywhere and whose circumference is nowhere (SSM, 225), we can say that if Merton's center, even if up for discussion, was not everywhere, certainly his circumference, his cultural boundary, was nowhere, or at least was undefined: he was interested in almost everything. What Merton and Dom James shared, and shared very deeply, was their commitment to the monastic vocation; but as events demonstrated, this was a commitment that could be interpreted in very different ways.

Also basic to knowing and responding to the will of God in monastic understanding is the spiritual contract between the abbot and his monks. Here is Patrick O'Connell's summation, from his lectures to the novices, of Merton's view of this relationship.

> Merton stresses that for Benedict the abbot's role is not merely to oversee the monastery, or to enforce obedience to the *Rule*, but to act in the place of Christ, to lead the monastic community as Christ led and formed and instructed the band of the apostles. . . . This happens not automatically but through the faith of both abbot and community, who trust that the Holy Spirit will act through the abbot despite inevitable human weaknesses. The abbot has a responsibility both to the monks under his care and to God, to make the will of God for the community known and lived by both teaching and example, using discretion and discernment to deal with different types of monks in ways most appropriate to each. (IMT 4, xxiii)

Dom James, it is clear, took this last responsibility seriously. He encouraged John Eudes Bamberger, for example, to pursue his psychiatric studies, and another monk, Chrysogonus Waddell, to spend time in Europe exploring the monastic musical tradition. However, it can be argued that he dealt with Merton as with no other of his monks, responding both to the exercise of Merton's gifts and to Merton's tendencies to exaggeration, hyper-enthusiasm, impulsiveness, and, as Merton himself admitted, willfulness, or self-will. Patrick O'Connell again:

> . . . [Merton] points out that often there is no immediately clear indication what God wills or does not will in some particular situation, and humility entails a willingness to remain in "the provisional," without attempting to manipulate uncertainties to become certainties. (IMT 4, xliv)

Acedia and the Will of God

This acknowledgment of "the provisional" can be seen as a willingness on the part of both abbot and monk in the larger Benedictine tradition to submit any decision to the final judgment of God. All such decisions, then, have an eschatological dimension. As the ecumenical monastic Community of Taizé, in France, phrases it, *"Tout est provisoire en vue de l'eschaton"*—"everything is provisional until the *eschaton*/the day of judgment." Decisions must be made in order for life to proceed, and somebody has to make those decisions; but *all* decisions are provisional if, as both Dom James and Merton believed, their final assessment will not come until the arrival of the *eschaton*. An eschatological understanding, however, does not, cannot simply mean waiting to make a decision until the day of judgment, as a purely future-oriented eschatology would mandate ("Thy kingdom *come*"). It also carries with it a reference to the present moment, to a realized eschatology ("Thine *is* the kingdom"). This goes some way toward explaining both the seriousness and complexity of monastic decision-making, as well as, in Merton's approach, the desire for an immediate solution that shows up so strongly in the letters.

It is an interesting exercise to read through the letters looking for references to the will of God. "In the end," says Merton, "it is always necessary to abide not in our own desires, but in the Holy Will of God" (Letter 9). "[B]efore anything, I must seek the will of God" (Letter 12). In Letter 21, writing to Dom Anselmo, Merton makes two interesting distinctions: ". . . I believed it was the will of God for me to test my vocation to the solitary life. I did not say that it was absolutely the will of God for me to be a solitary." So for Merton, first, it was the will of God that he be allowed to test his vocation to the solitary life—at another and in his view more contemplative monastery; and second, he distinguished between the will of God, of which he was certain, and the *absolute* will of God, on which he was not prepared to be definitive.

In Letter 23, writing to Montini, Dom James expands on how he works with what he understands to be God's will:

> In all this matter, we keep before us that the question is, what is God's Will? Not what is Father Louis' Will or what is my will, or anybody else's will. . . . I myself had terrific inclinations and attractions and urgings to leave Gethsemani for the Carthusians. . . . And yet I know that it is not God's Will for me to follow those urges. . . . It becomes more and more clear to me

> that what God wants is the immolation of my desires and wills to His spoken Will, no matter how I feel about it.

This word to Montini, filtered through Ricoeur's hermeneutic of suspicion, may suggest that Dom James believes that if he had not been given the opportunity to test his vocations with the Carthusians, neither should Merton. The reference to immolation may also suggest that Dom James is again filtering his sense of God's will through the historic emphasis on penance that came to the Trappists through de Rancé, who focused his Cistercian reform around that concept, one that without being rejected has, since the time we are exploring, slipped from a primary place in Cistercian emphasis to a secondary or even tertiary place. In the eucharistic spirituality of the time, it was understood that at the time of the consecration in the mass, Jesus "immolated" himself as a sacrifice in a mystical representation of his sacrifice on the cross, an "immolation" that monks (and other Christians, for that matter) were expected to emulate in their life decisions. What the "spoken Will" refers to I have no idea, unless it refers to certain scriptures that Dom James may be thinking of but does not cite. He carries on thus:

> Your Excellency, before God I say to you, and I am ready to meet this decision at the Last Judgment, that I cannot see the finger of God in Father Louis' desire to change. I am in no way afraid of taking the entire responsibility for this decision on myself. I do not fear any criticism in any way.

Here Dom James is speaking squarely out of the eschatological dimension of the Benedictine tradition in which the Cistercians, as a Benedictine reform, located their lineage. Here is what St. Benedict says, in chapter 2 of the *Rule*:

> The abbot should always remember that he will be held accountable on Judgment Day for his teaching and the obedience of his charges. The abbot must be led to understand that any lack of good in his monks will be held as his fault. However he shall be held innocent . . . if he has done all within his power to overcome the corruptness and disobedience of his monks.

This is a very sobering admonition, and one that Dom James took very much to heart. Three weeks earlier, also writing to Montini (LETTER 16), Merton had given his very different take on this point:

> . . . I am sure that if our Father Abbot here did not have to take the whole responsibility for the decision [about Merton leaving Gethsemani] on himself, and if there were chances of someone in a high position [he means Montini himself] viewing my case with positive favor, he would much more easily assent to my

leaving for Camaldoli. I believe the only reason why he really refuses is that he does not want to be criticized and blamed.

Merton is seriously misreading Dom James here, as indicated by what Dom James later says to Montini, just quoted. Dom James, acting in congruence with the abbot's responsibility as described in the *Rule*, is entirely prepared to take the whole responsibility for the decision on himself. Nor is this mistaken reason "the only reason why [Dom James] really refuses" to authorize Merton's departure. In LETTER 23 he gives a number of other reasons: Merton's departure would cause great scandal, both in the Roman Catholic community and among his non-Catholic readership; it would shake the vocations of many other religious; and it would devalue the meaning of contemplation. A further reason, which he doesn't mention in this letter but does mention in many other contexts, is that it would be an unnecessary response to a need that could be perfectly well met at Gethsemani. An overarching reason, which he does not express in so many words but which in his letters to Dom Gabriel as well as Archbishop Montini he unmistakably manifests, is that such a change would not be good for Merton himself. It would encourage him in his restlessness (which brings us back to *acedia*), which could end up with him making change after change, like the gyrovagues, the wandering monks whom St. Benedict criticizes. Merton adverts to this when he tells Dom Anselmo (in LETTER 24) that Dom James "supposes" that once away from Gethsemani, he would "walk about the entire world living it up," as Merton says Dom James has said to prior Anselm Steinke.

The issue is finally resolved for Merton, in terms of the will of God, when he receives the letters from Montini (LETTER 27) and Larraona (LETTER 32). Writing to Dom Gabriel (LETTER 34) he frames his peaceful acceptance of their "counsels" in these words:

> ... I am now quite convinced that God does not want me to be a Camaldolese. Your advice, together with the counsels of the Most Reverend Father Larraona ... and of Monsignor Montini ... give me the most complete assurance that it would be very imprudent of me to leave Gethsemani, or at least the Order, and that there would not be much to gain. So I am sure that I know God's will on this point, and I accept it willingly with the most complete peace and without regrets.

He has received, definitively, "the Church's answer and God's answer" (LETTER 30). He has fought the good fight, and in terms of his own will, his self-will, as Dom James sometimes named it, has "lost," although to "lose" in such a struggle is, paradoxically, to "win" in terms of the will of God, not that winning and losing are the most appropriate categories for the resolution of issues of monastic discernment. As regards self-will, Dom James, in a letter of October 18, 1955 (TMC) to Dom Gabriel, says that Merton has admitted "that since January he had been doing so much pushing to get into the Camaldolese or a hermitage that all the time he had great scruples that it was his own will." In another letter to Dom Gabriel (November 29, 1955, TMC), Dom James recounts Merton's response to the permission to be a hermit "one hundred percent" that he and Dom James were ready to grant. He quotes Merton:

> I felt very upset interiorly: some little voice was saying to me, "So you obtained your own will at last." And that completely upset me, because I knew then that all the time it was just my own will, and I did not have peace. Now that I have given up the whole thing, really, I never had so much peace in all my life.

But as we know, Merton at this point retreated from the possibility of being a full-time hermit, and in the spirit of monastic obedience made himself available to Dom James to be novice master. "And so," says Dom James in the same letter, "just letting God's grace take its course, we see how much was self-will and how little was really divine."

Yet as I have said, this is not a win/lose situation. On the basis of his own understanding, Merton cannot "lose" if he peacefully accepts the will of God for him as declared by those in high positions (LETTER 16 and LETTER 30) in the Church, those who in the ecclesial culture of the day were granted the authority to speak for God. Their decisions were not beyond challenge (as we will see in chapter 6), but they were authoritative.

In November 1955, just after Merton began his term as novice master, he wrote a kind of study paper for the novices titled "Your Will and Your Vocation." The focus in that paper is not on the discernment of the will of God, but rather on the need for the novices to exercise their own wills in the interests of their monastic vocations. He defines the will for them as "the principle of autonomous spiritual acts, acts that are 'mine' because they proceed from the deepest and most intimate center of my own personal and spiritual being."[12] He insists that although the monks are bound by their vows to obedience to their superiors, "[they] do not simply let the superior will everything for [them]. . . . [They] are free agents, conforming [their] will to that of the superior. He makes known his will, and [they], in turn, *will* to put it into effect."[13] Having read in the letters about his struggle with

---

12. Merton, "Your Will and Your Vocation," 5.
13. Ibid., 6.

Dom James over the will of God, something that certainly engaged Merton's own will, or, as he once admitted, his self-will, it is instructive to read what he gave to the novices on the subject of will. There is no sense of crisis in the paper, and no suggestion of what Merton and Dom James had been through together in the months preceding his appointment. The focus of the paper is on the cultivation and strengthening by the novices of their own wills rather than the discernment of God's will; and it is noteworthy that the question of discernment or co-discernment between monk and abbot occupies very little space in the article.

Finally, Merton and Dom James as father and son. Merton had had a very warm father-son relationship with his first abbot, Dom Frederic Dunne, and there is no reason to think that he was not ready and willing to work within this same familial paradigm in his relationship with Dom Frederic's successor. Of course, no issue arose during Dom Frederic's time that challenged their relationship in the way that Merton's attempts to leave Gethemani challenged Dom James. Born in 1896, Dom James was nineteen years older than Merton, and had been at Gethsemani for fourteen years before Merton's arrival there; so he was very much his senior both in years and in monastic experience. I prescind here, prudently, I believe, from a full-scale Freudian riff on this relationship. But it does have many resonances with what Freud says about contests of will between fathers and sons. Many of Merton's comments, in these letters and elsewhere, are unfair, sometimes insulting, sometimes very angry indeed. We still have to read about the lesser *acedia*, Merton's attempt to go to Latin America; and when that was happening, once again the father-son tension flared up between Merton and Dom James. However, I will simply refer here, by way of resolution, to the very beautiful letter that Merton wrote from India, on October 20, 1968, to Dom James, whom he addresses as "Father James," and in which he acknowledges the "warm and gracious letter" he has received from him:[14] "Be sure that I have never changed in my respect for you as abbot and affection as Father; our different views certainly did not affect our deep agreement on the real point of life and of our vocation." I find it deeply moving that they now lie peacefully side by side, abbot and monk, longtime sparring partners, father and son, in the monastic cemetery at Gethsemani.

---

14. For the full text of Dom James' letter, see Fox, "The Spiritual Son," in Hart, *Thomas Merton, Monk,* 153–54. The letter is held in the archives of the Thomas Merton Center.

5

The End of the Dream of Camaldoli

CONTRA-INDICATIONS

Even before Merton's dream of going to Camaldoli faded into the light of common day with the letters from Archbishop Montini and Monsignor Larraona, there were contra-indications showing up, even in Merton's own thinking. Thus in a letter of April 27, 1955, just two days after his salvo of letters to Montini, Moore, and Giabbani, he asks Jean Leclercq whether or not it is true "that they do not truly live a contemplative life at Camaldoli, that 'silence is poorly observed,' that the Prior entirely disposes of the hermits' vocations, that he can send them back to the cenobium against their will . . .?"[1] Then in a letter of June 3, 1955 (TMC), he writes to Dom Maurizio Levy-Duplatt at Frascati, a Camaldolese house of hermits only, with no cenobium. Frascati was his backup plan if things didn't work out with Camaldoli—except when it seemed preferable to Camaldoli! He tells Dom Maurizio that "the wisdom of going to Camaldoli itself has been called into question, especially by Dom Leclercq." The word "especially" suggests that others beside Jean Leclercq had raised questions about Camaldoli, although there is no evidence of who they might have been, other than his superiors, nor any evidence of Leclercq's doing this in their published letters, *Survival or Prophecy?* He asks Dom Maurizio whether, if the *transitus*, which he hopes is in process, were to be granted, he would consider it advisable for him to accept it and go to Camaldoli—and this is after saying that his

---

1. Merton and Leclercq, *Survival or Prophecy?*, 60–61.

The End of the Dream of Camaldoli

plan would be to leave Gethsemani secretly—but with permission—travel to Italy, and enter, not Frascati, but one of the other *eremi* of the Monte Corona congregation—under an assumed name. The virtue of this, he says, would be that "it would not create the noise and comment that a publicly known admission to Camaldoli would cause." Camaldoli, Frascati, not Frascati: "Hell is murky," says Lady Macbeth (V.i.41), and so are Merton's hopes and plans in June 1955. A letter of July 6, 1955 (TMC) to Naomi Burton confirms this:

> Naomi, things are in rather a turmoil between me and the Superiors of the Order. What happened was (this in confidence) that I proposed I change Orders and go to this Camaldoli joint which I love so dearly, and they all hit the ceiling, nor have they come down as yet. . . . It may just happen by some kind of miracle that out of the blue will drop a permission to change over to Camaldoli, but it seems unlikely.

The same image had appeared in a letter of June 13, 1955 (TMC) from Dom James to Dom Gabriel: "[Merton] is still hoping that some decision may come out of the sky somewhere and give him a *transitus*."

August 11 he writes to Jean Leclercq. He has heard from Frascati: they have told him that he could make a trial there of the solitary life, incognito. "I could remain with them without being a writer, in true obscurity and solitude."[2] Without being a writer? Why not say without eating, breathing, and sleeping? Merton is losing touch with himself here. His lament about his writing in the SSM (410–13) makes it clear that monk or not, he *is* a writer, cursed/blessed with a writerly shadow, a double, who rides his shoulders "like the old man of the sea" (410). As he says in his preface to *A Thomas Merton Reader*, "It is possible to doubt whether I have become a monk (a doubt I have to live with), but it is not possible to doubt that I am a writer . . ."[3]

Four days later he receives a letter from Dom Gabriel (August 15, TMC), who tells him that he, Dom Louis, *and* Dom James are all of one mind about the unsuitability of the fire tower position, even though it was Dom James' suggestion originally. In a letter of the same day to Dom James, Merton therefore asks, "Don't you think it would be wiser [than his trying to live as a hermit at Gethsemani, given the opposition from the "anti-hermits" in the community] if . . . I just went secretly to Frascati and tried the thing out?" And then, knowing Dom James was soon to leave for Europe, comes this wheedling request (also August 15, TMC):

2. Merton and Leclercq, *Survival or Prophecy?*, 66.
3. Merton, *Thomas Merton Reader*, 17.

> Gee, Reverend Father: can't I just slip out with you as you go to the General Chapter and go over to Italy and enter Frascati incognito at least for the length of time you are to be over there? No one would be surprised at you taking a companion, it has been done before. N.B. I am *not* just asking for a trip.

Then came the letter from Montini (LETTER 27) and the letter from Larraona (LETTER 30); and the dream of Camaldoli died. *Roma locuta est: causa finita* ("Rome has spoken; case closed").

DIFFICULTIES AT CAMALDOLI

But had the *transitus* come through, and had Merton gone to Camaldoli, what would he have found there? In a letter of June 8, 1955, to Jean Leclercq (TMC), later forwarded to Merton, Dom Maurizio had given his frank opinion of Camaldoli's situation at that time:

> I have never gone personally to visit Camaldoli, but I know that those who have gone there have found neither the solitude nor the silence that they were looking for, nor even peace, because there are different currents of thought there which are colliding with each other. It is difficult to foresee what the future result of all this will be. The current atmosphere is certainly tense and difficult.

Archbishop Montini offers a comparable opinion in his letter of August 20, 1955 (LETTER 27):

> I am favorably inclined to the Camaldolese monks and follow with interest the efforts they are making to give back to their religious family a consistency which time, adversity, [and] the diversity of internal opinions have caused them to lose. They are outlining more sharply their spiritual features, their constitutions, their function in the Church of God, the numbers [they need]. The effort is a noble one but it is not finished.

The key phrase here is, as we shall see, "diversity of internal opinions," or, as Dom Maurizio says, "different currents of thought . . . colliding." Both the archbishop and Dom Maurizio see Camaldoli as *in medias res*, not at a good moment for any foreigner, let alone Thomas Merton, to enter. A month later came Larraona's letter (LETTER 32, September 26, 1955), confirming their opinion:

> ... I believe that right now it would not be advisable [for you] to go to Camaldoli, because there are many question marks about the direction of that congregation—a direction which will be serenely but seriously studied shortly—and because, also, irrespective of what transpires, the internal conditions [at Camaldoli] could expose you to painful disappointments.

Internal conditions . . . painful disappointments . . . question marks about the direction of the congregation: not a good idea, not a good time. Given the situation at Camaldoli, both Montini and Larraona encourage Merton to stay at Gethsemani and seek interior solitude in the well-functioning monastery that they believe Gethsemani to be and that indeed it was.

A fuller picture of what was happening at Camaldoli is offered by Thomas Matus, himself a Camaldolese monk, in two books: *The Mystery of Romuald and the Five Brothers: Stories from the Benedictines and Camaldolese*, and *Nazarena: An American Anchoress*. Matus, now in California, lived at Camaldoli and in Rome, for many years, during which time he received from Dom Anselmo Giabbani,[4] his first mentor in the order, a personal account of the struggles to which Giabbani refers in LETTER 31, and to which Merton's other correspondents are referring obliquely. (Matus uses the Italian form of address, Don Anselmo, which I will use when quoting him, rather than the monastic form that Merton uses, Dom Anselmo.)

Don Anselmo, then, was born in 1908, and formally entered the Camaldolese order in 1924, at sixteen, the minimum canonical age for simple profession, having entered a year earlier to do his novitiate. In 1945, aged thirty-seven, he became procurator general for the order in Rome, an office he held until 1951. In 1946, while procurator general, he met Sister Nazarena and became her spiritual director and confessor, a ministry he carried on until her death in 1990. In 1951, having finished his term as procurator general, he was elected prior general, an office he held for two six-year terms, until 1963. So he was just into his first term as prior general when he received Merton's first letter in 1952. From 1963 to 1969 he acted as first assistant to the new prior general, Don Aliprando Catani, who had previously been his first assistant. The general chapter in 1963 had in fact confirmed Dom Anselmo for a third mandate; but since Camaldoli was under the supervision of an apostolic visitor, Archbishop Lazzaro da Arbonne, OFM-Cap, a consultant for the Sacred Congregation of Religious, the Holy See canceled the election, perhaps on the grounds that it was not unanimous,

---

4. On Don Anselmo, Matus comments, "For the kind of monastic life I have been living as a Camaldolese Benedictine, I owe more to don [*sic*: not capitalized] Anselmo than to anyone else on earth" (*Mystery of Romuald*, 10).

and prevailed on Don Aliprando—a monk, according to Matus, of exquisite humility—to accept a six-year term in Giabbani's stead. In 1969 Giabbani became prior of San Gregorio and once again procurator general, offices he held until 1987. He retired at San Gregorio and Camaldoli, and died in 2004, at the venerable age of ninety-six.[5]

Thomas Matus continues his account of the reforming ministry of Don Anselmo, at Camaldoli and in Rome, on behalf of the order:

> Don Anselmo's twelve years (1951–63) as abbot general[6] ... were a time of struggle, if not war, within the Camaldolese Order. The conflict was for the most part one of ideas: the progressive ideas of a far-seeing, almost prophetic abbot (don Anselmo foresaw the effects of an Ecumenical Council in the Catholic Church even before John XXIII summoned the bishops to Rome) and the ideas of a few monks whose false sense of certitude made them incapable of reading either the history of our Order or the signs of the times. By 1967, a year after the council ended,[7] everyone realized that the *aggiornamento* don Anselmo had been talking about for the past fifteen years had now become the official program of renewal for the entire Church.[8]

Matus says that Anselmo (he refers to him by his first name), a "blend of peasant gruffness and Renaissance refinement,"[9] was very much a reformer. The issue was essentially one of spiritual formation. Should Camaldolese novices have the very narrow preparation for monastic life that Anselmo and his contemporaries had had, or should they have a broadly textured program of the kind that Merton as novice master at Gethsemani between 1955 and 1965 offered to his novices? Don Anselmo was dealing with a cohort of the Camaldolese who misconstrued his intentions, fearing that his openness to the larger humanistic tradition would contradict or undermine the Camaldolese traditions that they valued.

The reference to Anselmo as a man of "Renaissance refinement" and his program as one of monastic humanism points to his formational orientation. As did Merton at Gethsemani, he believed that if the order were to

---

5. Thomas Matus, e-mail message to author, July 26, 2014. Regarding Archbishop da Arbonne, see also LETTER 31.

6. I.e., prior general, the title he uses in his letters to Merton. The prior general of Camaldoli, as the head of an order, has the rank of abbot. See Appendix 1, where he uses both titles.

7. The Council ended on December 8, 1965.

8. Matus, *Mystery of Romuald*, 10.

9. Ibid., 16.

survive and thrive in a fast-changing world, present and future generations of Camaldolese would need not only a deep rooting in monastic tradition, but would also need an orientation to the culture in which they were living. It was a classic situation. If most people, as has been said, experience change as loss rather than as gain, Anselmo, a cultured and far-seeing man, was faced with resistance from those for whom security and change were oppositional realities.

Anselmo had become prior general of Camaldoli in 1951, the year before Merton wrote him for the first time. Midway through his first six-year term, he tackled the revision of the *Constitutions and Declarations* of the order; they were revised in 1954 and confirmed by the Vatican in 1957. A particular motivation for the accomplishment of this task was the prospect of the American foundation, New Camaldoli, about which he had questioned Merton. Immediately following the Second Vatican Council, the Camaldolese organized a revision committee, with representatives elected from all their communities (including New Camaldoli). These post-conciliar Constitutions were promulgated at the extraordinary general chapter in 1968 and confirmed *ad experimentum*.[10]

In 1957, having just been reelected for another six-year term, Anselmo traveled to the United States, without contacting Merton, and returned to a polarized community without having decided on the location of the new monastery. He then sent two monks of Camaldoli, Don Aliprando and Father Augustine Modotti, a former Jesuit who, having lived many years in Australia, spoke fluent English, to find land for the new Camaldolese house. The two encountered difficulties, and differences arose between them; Anselmo, judging that Father Modotti had overstepped his mandate and shown disobedience, recalled him and had him expelled from the order. But what Matus calls the "imbroglio" in the United States gave the Vatican occasion to launch an investigation of the Order of Camaldoli and its superior. Anselmo "found himself the object of grave accusations, public and anonymous, on the part of a few monks of Camaldoli" (NAA, 123)—members of the cohort that had also opposed his attempts at *aggiornamento*. The report of the investigation, concluded in 1961, described New Camaldoli, in particular, as flourishing and enthusiastic; but the accusations were still considered serious enough to warrant the removal of Anselmo from his office. This was resolved by Anselmo, the prior general, and Aliprando, the assistant general, exchanging offices in 1963. "Aliprando's gentle mien," Matus comments, "would eventually defuse the explosive situation, and within

---

10. That is, for a limited period of experimentation (Thomas Matus, e-mail message to author, September 2, 2014).

another three years nearly everyone at Camaldoli would be saying, 'Don Anselmo was right after all'" (NAA, 69). Another three years from 1963 takes us to 1966, by which time Vatican II had completed its sessions. With John XXIII and Vatican II, Anselmo was vindicated, but only after years of painful controversy.

If Merton had come to Camaldoli in 1955, he would have found himself in a severely divided community. Given their similar views on monastic formation, he and Anselmo would have most likely found themselves allied. He might, however, have found himself at odds, as we shall see shortly, with another prior general of the order, Benedetto Calati, although this is debatable. But Merton was looking for solitude and silence, even simple peace and quiet; intra-monastic conflict was the furthest thing from what he wanted. It is understandable, of course, why Anselmo, in writing to Merton, would not have revealed the divisions in the community. There is no indication of the dividedness of Camaldoli in any of his extant letters (LETTERS 8, 11, and 13), nor is it likely that Anselmo would have adverted to any divisions in the letters no longer extant (LETTERS 2, 4, 6, 14, and 25). Here is the account Matus gives of a conversation he had with Anselmo about the prospect of Merton's coming to Camaldoli (Anselmo is speaking):

> During the 1950s Merton wrote to me saying he wanted to become a Camaldolese hermit at whatever cost. So his abbot from the Trappist monastery in Kentucky came[11] to plead with me not to accept him. But I said, "What do you mean, telling me not to take him?" Then the abbot general of the Trappists came, and I said to him, "Excuse me, do you have the right to tell me what to do? You think Merton is wrong to ask to become a Camaldolese hermit, and you may or may not be mistaken. But when he writes to me, how can you stop me from answering him?" In the end their will prevailed over his, and poor Merton wrote me saying, "If I cannot come to Camaldoli, you must bring Camaldoli to America." And so we went to California—this was when we founded New Camaldoli. (NAA, 102–3)

There are some interesting differences between Anselmo's recollections and what the letters tell us. Was it a case of "their will" prevailing over Merton's? It is true that neither Dom James nor Dom Gabriel favored Merton's moving to Camaldoli. But this is not the whole story. From LETTER 31 we learn that by 1955, Anselmo himself had concluded that it would not have been good either for Merton or Camaldoli for him to have moved there, something, to my knowledge, that Merton never learned. Beyond this, what was decisive

---

11. In the fall of 1953.

for Merton, with what at this remove seems an exaggerated trust in, even a veneration for, hierarchical authority (as evidenced in LETTER 16), were the letters from Montini and Larraona (LETTERS 27 and 32). Thinking also of the differences between Merton and Dom James over the will of God, I would prefer to say that Merton would have understood what Montini and Larraona said as giving him clarity in regard to the will of God, rather than his superiors' will "prevailing" over his will; that is, that in the decision of the Congregation for Religious, confirmed by so eminent an ecclesiastic as Montini, the will of God had become clear for him. As regards the American foundation, which these words of Don Anselmo suggest was Merton's idea, we know from his letters to Merton that it was his own; or perhaps this is simply a time-reference. As for Merton mentioning the American foundation only after learning that he would not be going to Camaldoli himself, Merton in fact mentions it as early as LETTER 3, written at the end of 1952. But there is no reference to the American foundation in LETTER 36, the only letter Merton wrote to Anselmo after it was clear that he would not be coming to Camaldoli.

MERTON'S DREAM

A fascinating perspective on Merton and Camaldoli comes from some notes (TMC) he made on his dreams during the monastery's annual retreat in January 1956, two months before he wrote the last letter to Giabbani (LETTER 36). Here is the first and longest of these dreams:

> I drive away from the house where I used to live in Douglaston, in a fancy Jeep, which is very easy to drive, but the road is rough. We (two novices and myself) get out and enter a big, dark room which reminds me of rooms in two abandoned hotels I knew of, one in France and one in Havana ([the] latter I discovered was not abandoned but used as a brothel). In this room, a few pieces of furniture, big flag-stone floor. I sit down and pick up a newspaper, which I find contains an article put out by the Camaldolese, about me. It is full of falsehoods (which may yet in a strange way become true). I read "The Author of *The Sign of Jonas* will soon enter the solitude he has so long desired— T. M. is coming to Camaldoli!" (The C's [Camaldolese] had in fact spread this rumor in Rome last year.)
>
> I put it aside to read later.... But when I turn back to the newspaper I hunt and hunt through it but cannot find the article, which I have not yet read. Suddenly a man enters in a grey-brown lounge suit—I recognize him as "The General of the

Camaldolese" (however, it is not Dom Giabbani.) He is portly, clean-shaven, has small eyes, perhaps something of a phony, but in this situation, I realize, I can trust him. Babbling Italian, I kneel to kiss his ring, but he has none. I don't mind. He says reassuringly, "Come, I will show you your future home." I leave the companions who had come with me, and pass through a door. We are now in a pleasantly ramshackle Italian monastery, dirty, old, in a valley full of trees. I like the feel of the place.

We enter a room. The "chapter of the hermits" is assembled, in plain secular clothes—they have come down from a hermitage somewhere in the mountains to pass on my case. They welcome me. There is something English about them. They smile, and I feel that they are not very intelligent people, are overawed and will accept me willingly.

They all begin to pray aloud and during the prayers, one of them says to me, behind his hand, but officially though: "Is it your firm intention to enter the Camaldolese *eremo* of Tre Fontane near Rome?"

I am startled: "Tre Fontane is a Trappist monastery!" But no. We are there. I look around. Nothing Trappist about it. The valley is very quiet. No machines, big trees. I will be really quiet here. Tentatively I ask the General about Camaldoli in the mountains. No, he evades the issue, but I understand that this is my only chance. I am ready to take it.

Going around the back of the building, I see some smoke seeping through a window. I am disturbed, but investigate and am reassured: the place is not on fire. I wake with the renewed conviction that I will one day enter the Camaldolese of Monte Corona and that I belong with them.

The dream, he says in these notes, is typical of a whole series of Camaldolese and Carthusian dreams that he has had. To anyone with a knowledge of dream interpretation and of Merton's life, many of the references in this dream seem clear enough. "The road is rough"—as indeed Merton's struggle to reach Camaldoli has been. Vestiges of his background: the "English" character of the hermits, his visit in 1933 to Tre Fontane (SSM, 114, 263). "No machines"—one of his major gripes about Gethemani was the noise of tractors and jackhammers. His conviction upon waking that he will one day enter the congregation of Monte Corona. If a dream holds up a mirror to the soul, then this dream suggests that psychically he has not finished with Camaldoli, or perhaps better, with what it represents. I would be glad to see someone with expertise both in dream interpretation and in Merton's writings give us a full exposition of what the dream suggests about Merton's state of soul, four months after what he will later call Larraona's "NO," and two months before he will write his last letter to Giabbani—and so sign off, at least formally, on the project that has taken up so much of his energy and prayer during the previous three years.

BENEDETTO CALATI

Rilke's famous comment about living and loving the questions in preference to the answers illuminates Merton's response to a review[12] of a collection of essays of which one of the authors was Dom Benedetto Calati.[13] Born in 1914, he joined the Order of Camaldoli some years after Giabbani. In 1951 he was elected procurator general and prior of San Gregorio, offices he held until 1969. In that year he started teaching at Sant' Anselmo, the international Benedictine university in Rome, holding the chair of Medieval Monastic Spirituality there. During thirty years of teaching, he formed close friendships with many luminaries in the political and intellectual life of Rome, becoming, as was Merton, a public intellectual, with a left-leaning political orientation. Elected prior general in 1969, he served until 1987, dying in the year 2000. Thomas Matus describes him as "a brilliant scholar, a great homilist, and the perfect guide for the Camaldolese during the postconciliar period."[14] In the view of many, he was the most important Camaldolese monk of the twentieth century.

In his contribution to the collection, "The Theory of Monasticism in the Literature of the Last Thirty Years," Calati surveys the writings of French, Spanish, and Italian authors, and from America, Merton only. He discusses the nature of the monastic life, characterizing it as in different ways eschatological, angelic, prophetic, apostolic, and evangelical, as well as an opportunity for martyrdom and for the recovery of paradise, all themes of monastic life that we also find in Merton. He also includes a section on eremitism, in which he objects to the search for new formulas (something that, as we know, much engaged Merton) "on the grounds that the surviving forms of semi-eremitical life . . . are sufficient."[15] His conference concludes with his reflections on work appropriate and inappropriate for monks, on contemplation and action, and on the work of Thomas Merton. The reviewer, writing during Vatican II, concludes that the

---

12. Peifer, Review of *Problemi e orientamenti*, 137–65.
13. Vagaggini et al., *Problemi e orientamenti*.
14. I.e., 1966 and later; e-mail message to author, July 27, 2014.
15. Peifer, Review of *Problemi e orientamenti*, 161.

conclusion to which Calati's views logically lead is that nothing new should be attempted. Apparently he is quite satisfied with the present status of monasticism and sees no need for any changes. . . . This attitude is precisely the thing that closes the doors upon any possibility of progress. . . . This is the very antithesis to Pope John's challenge to renew the Church in every aspect of her life. Should monasteries leave their windows tightly closed, when those of the Vatican Palace have been flung wide open to let in the fresh air?[16]

As we will see shortly, the reviewer and Merton are very much on the same wavelength in regard to this *status quo* point of view.

Apparently there had been a controversy in Italy a few years previous about Merton's value as a spiritual writer. Calati admits that the warm welcome with which Merton's works had been received was an indication of the continuing appeal of monasticism and of Merton's enthusiasm and writing ability. "He then proceeds to denounce his 'discontinuity of thought' and his estheticism, and to suspect him of a naturalism akin to that of Thoreau,"[17] complaining that Merton never brought together his thoughts about monasticism into "a coherent monastic theory."[18] Any careful student of Merton's writings will of course recognize both that this is so, and to be fair, that it was something that Merton in his unsystematic way never even tried to do. The reviewer here takes Merton's part:

> There may be different opinions about the value of Merton's spiritual writings, but I think that a reviewer ought to do him the justice of taking his books for what they were meant to be. *The Sign of Jonas* was never intended to be a treatise on contemplation or a synthesis of monastic theology: it is a diary. . . . Calati's basic error in this discussion is his failure to identify *genera litteraria* [literary categories].[19]

It was to Calati's critique that Merton was responding in a journal entry of January 31, 1964—his forty-ninth birthday, I note, and therefore also (a

---

16. Ibid., 158. This last comment is a reference to a memorable incident in which Pope John XXIII, when asked what he meant by *aggiornamento* ("updating"), said nothing, but simply walked to a nearby window and opened it.

17. Ibid., 159. On Merton and Thoreau, see Albert, "Lights Across the Ridge," 271–317. There is no reference in this article to Calati's critique. The references to Thoreau to which Calati was referring are in *The Sign of Jonas*, 306–7, the journal entries for December 6 and 8, 1950.

18. Peifer, Review of *Problemi e orientamenti*, 159.

19. Ibid., 159–60.

The End of the Dream of Camaldoli

point he himself makes) his entry into his year of jubilee: "I begin my jubilee year, not exactly clear what I am doing, for everything is always beginning again" (DWL, 68).[20]

> The new *Monastic Studies* is out. . . . A long review takes in that Italian collection of monastic conferences in which Dom [Benedetto] Calati discusses me as—precisely what? As utterly out of his world. And of course he is right. I do not belong to his monastic world at all, am not part of it—the world where the status quo is just all right. On the other hand I do not rebel against it either, I am just not concerned with it. And thus from many points of view I am "not a monk." In general that is all right with me, since I need only to be concerned with loyalty to my own graces and my own task in life, not with being recognized by "them" in "their" categories. (DWL, 68)

Responding to Merton's journal entry, David Belcastro reflects on Merton's sense of his monastic vocation:

> Abandoning easily prescribed definitions of what a monk is, Merton takes a different path; one less certain but more promising, one guided not by an established theology of answers but by one led by Wisdom into deeper and more complicated questions. There is a line in *Opening the Bible* where Merton says that religious thought does not move from question to answer but rather from question to question, with each new question opening a larger field of vision for understanding oneself in relation to God and the world.[21]

Merton's comment here recalls the classic image from Kabbala, in which the practitioner, being given a box (read: question), opens the box and takes out of it a box larger than the first, a process that continues through an infinite series of boxes. It also recalls another Jewish spiritual practice, the *haver* method of Torah discussion, in which two *haverim*, two partners in discussion, keep their discussion going with no expectation that it need ever end, since the object/subject of discussion, God and the divine word in scripture, is infinite. Indeed, if one partner cannot think of a response, the other partner is supposed to give him (in this chiefly male enterprise) something to say so that the conversation can continue. Merton was never able to say *finally* what a monk or a hermit is; but he was "none-the-less aware of how living the question moved him in the direction of becoming

---

20. Cf. Lev 25 and the Jubilee page on my website: donaldgrayston.ca/?page_id=32.
21. Belcastro, "Praying the Questions," 127–28.

more authentically human, free and alive in relation to and for the sake of the world in which he lived."[22]

Calati's critique of Merton rippled out into the monastic world of Europe, at least in its French and German quarters. Other monastics, however, came to Merton's defense. Here he waggishly thanks his fellow monk of Gethsemani, Chrysogonus Waddell, for his support: "The FBI informs me that you have sprung to my defense against the wicked Calati, in the monastic problems class. I am very grateful and sorry you did not have a more worthy and defensible cause. But it's good to feel oneself a monastic problem..." (SCH, 193).

He also received strong support from his friend Jean Leclercq. In two letters reprinted both in *The School of Charity* and in *Survival or Prophecy?* he thanks Leclerq for coming to his defense—first in this letter of May 11, 1965 (the letter of November 18, 1966, offers similar comments):

> ... I want to thank you for your generous defense in the German article. It is gradually dawning on me that there must have been more discussion and criticism of me than I had imagined.... In many respects my life and work are certainly very equivocal. If anyone wants to measure me by "normal" standards, it will be easy to find that I fail to meet the requirements.... I am certainly a *Geheimnis* [mystery] even to myself.... Thus in the end I must do what everyone else does and fall back on the mercy of God.... Certainly if I tried to please everyone, I would fail Him, and if I am to please Him I must inevitably displease a lot of very earnest and well-meaning people.... The inner contradictions of the Dom Calati people are in any case rather amusing. *They* are the hermits and monks who have precipitated themselves with open arms toward the world. They blame me because I have refused to do this and have instead tried to get back into the desert. Yet the *real* source of their objection and anger is that, after all, the world is listening to me rather than to them.... And I don't think that I am entirely in contradiction with myself because I have consistently held that a monk can speak *from the desert*, since there is no other place from which he has a better claim to be heard.[23]

In a footnote to this letter in *Survival or Prophecy?* editor Patrick Hart comments, "Dom Benedetto Calati ... had criticized the writings of Merton, especially those on the solitary life. Leclercq ... rose to Merton's defense...."

22. Ibid., 128.

23. SCH, 279–80, and Merton and Leclercq, *Survival or Prophecy?*, 125–26; for the letter of November 18, 1966, see SCH, 321, and *Survival or Prophecy?*, 143.

Calati later had a change of heart, due no doubt to Leclercq's intervention on Merton's behalf."[24]

Indeed he did have a change of heart. In an article in *Vita Monastica* in 1978, written for the tenth anniversary of Merton's death, Calati called Merton "a gift of God for the monks of our time."[25] I take as a summary of his change of heart the abstract of his article, provided in English in the journal:

> Although the author's initial opinion of "Merton the contemplative" was highly critical, the latter's obvious sincerity and depth of human experience led one to expect an evolution and clarification of his concept of the monastic ideal. In fact, some of Merton's last writings, often concerned with social questions, evidenced a profound evolution in the thought of the zealous convert who perhaps at first did not clearly distinguish between the type of romantic and naturalistic estheticism exemplified in Thoreau's *Walden*, and the authentic monastic ascesis of the Fathers, with its perennial vitality and its prophetic thrust. The later Merton was perfectly consistent with the sincerity and mystical *élan* of his younger years, while evolving toward a broader vision both of the monastic-contemplative ideal and of the "signs of the times."[26]

He ends by saying, "I thank the Lord for the gift he made to the Church in giving us Thomas Merton."[27]

His original objection had been to what he saw as Merton's equating of Thoreau and St. John of the Cross as apparently equal masters of asceticism. Here is what Merton had said about that in *The Sign of Jonas*: "Compare the basic asceticism in *Walden* with that of Saint John of the Cross—agreement

---

24. Merton and Leclercq, *Survival or Prophecy?*, 126.

25. Calati, "Thomas Merton: un dono di Dio per i monaci del nostro tempo."

26. Ibid., 16. Thomas Matus, OSBCam, is the author of this abstract (e-mail message to author, October 2, 2014). On the "signs of the times," see Matt 16:3.

27. Calati, "Thomas Merton," 16. Thomas Matus writes, "I had conversations with Don Benedetto in which I questioned his initial assessment of Merton's thought. Benedetto knew little English, and so he read Merton in the Italian translations of his earlier writings. Merton was writing many other things by then, in which he pulled away from his overzealous Catholic convert persona, but these reached Italy only after the death of Merton. Hence, having discovered the 'later Merton,' Don Benedetto publicly changed his earlier evaluation" (e-mail message to author, October 1, 2014). In regard to what was available to him in Italian, Patricia Burton's listing (*More Than Silence*, 194–95) shows that all of Merton's major works up to the time of his 1978 article had been published in Italy. These connections suggest that a substantial project of research, by someone who knows Italian, remains to be undertaken on the relation between Merton and Calati.

on the fundamental idea, not of course on the means or technique, except to some extent. Ascesis of solitude. Simplification of life. The separation of reality from illusion" (December 8, 1950, SJ, 306–7). This comment was recorded relatively early in Merton's time at Gethsemani. His later emphasis on the spirituality of the desert appears to have reassured Calati that Merton's monastic understanding had stabilized, had come closer to the tradition, that he had moved beyond the "romantic and naturalist estheticism" of Thoreau. Arguably, without moving away from his commitment to transmitting the monastic wisdom of the ancient writers, Merton also came closer to Thoreau's "estheticism" in his later years, by his ever-deepening embrace of the natural world, than he was when he wrote the journal entries that Calati objected to. A comment in "Day of a Stranger" demonstrates that in 1965 Merton was still remembering (and still resisting) Calati's critique:

> I am accused of living in the woods like Thoreau instead of living in the desert like St. John the Baptist. All I can answer is that I am not living "like anybody." Or "unlike anybody." We all live somehow or other, and that's that. It is a compelling necessity for me to be free to embrace the necessity of my own nature.[28]

There is no reference to "Day of a Stranger" in the later Calati article. One wonders if Calati would have maintained his revised view of Merton if he had read it, not simply because of the reference to Thoreau but because of the picture it gives of an eremitical life deeply committed to an ecological perspective. Interestingly, however, Calati in this later article also applauds Merton's emphasis on nonviolence.[29] The "wicked Calati," so named in Merton's slapdash way, yet a sobriquet undeserved in the view of Thomas Matus, had come around.

---

28. Merton, "Day of a Stranger," 215.

29. Calati, "Thomas Merton," 16. Two versions of Merton's work on faith and violence/nonviolence appeared in Italy before Calati wrote this article: *Faith and Violence* (1965), a collection of essays and freedom songs; and *Faith, Resistance, Protest* (1969), with the same text as *Faith and Violence: Christian Teaching and Christian Practice*, published in the United States in 1968. In the article, Calati mentions both books (10). Thomas Matus believes that Merton misunderstood Calati's reference to him being "out of his world" (DWL, 68) as referring to the monastic world, whereas, in Matus's view, he was referring to "the emphatic anti-world rhetoric of the early Merton." He further points out that although Merton knew Italian, there is no evidence that he read Calati; and he finds it a matter of regret that phrases such as "the wicked Calati" or the "Calati people" (examples of Merton's frequent use of slang) derogate from a man whom he and others in the order much admire (personal email, October 1, 2014).

LAST REFERENCES TO CAMALDOLI

After Merton's last letter to Giabbani in 1956, references to Camaldoli in his journals are infrequent. In his entry in SFS for February 15, 1958, in a time when he is contemplating a move to Latin America, he has an epiphany, a kind of gestalt moment about his American identity, which concludes with a bleak comment on Camaldoli, which, through no fault of its own, is in Europe and not in America:

> Suddenly saw, this afternoon, the meaning of my *American* destiny—one of those moments when many unrelated pieces of one's life and thought fall into place in a great unity towards which one has been growing.
>
> My destiny is indeed to be an American—not just an American of the U.S. We are only the fringe of the True America.... Never so keenly felt the impermanence of what is now regarded as American because it is *North* American—or the elements of stability and permanence which are in *South* America. Deeper roots, Indian roots. The Spanish, Portuguese, Negro roots also. The shallow English roots are not deep enough. The tree will fall.
>
> To be an American of the Andes—containing in myself also Kentucky and New York....
>
> My own vocation—it would have been dreadful to have returned to Europe, to Italy, to Camaldoli. It would have been fatal. (SFS, 168)

And so is Camaldoli dismissed, and Italy and all Europe with it. This European-American dialectic appears earlier in LETTER 33, Merton to Montini. Here there is a further development, however, a shift from America-understood-as-the-United-States to "the Americas," a geographical, cultural, and spiritual—indeed poetic—reality beyond the technocratic, frantic, shallow culture of the United States, as Merton saw it. It was a shift from the American cultural reality, represented at one level by Dom James and his business orientation, to a "True America" (false self, true self?) with its spiritual center relocated to an idealized South America. As with Camaldoli, this was a place to which he had never been, something that once again did not prevent him from offering a romantic and rhapsodic description. When he says *North* America, it is simply, of course, to set up a contrast with *South* America. Nothing he says suggests, however, if I may make a Canadian point here, that when he says North America he was giving any thought to Canada, that "kinder, gentler America," to quote George H. W. Bush entirely out of context. Given his fluency in French, I find it curious that he never showed any interest in Québec, nor qualified his dislike for

"North America" with a recognition of the "Latin" character of one-third of Canada.³⁰ Then in his journal entry for July 28, 1959, a year and a half later, when he was focused on the possibility of a move to Latin America, he offers this sober (and sobering) retrospective on his attempt to go to Camaldoli:

> Got together and read the correspondence that took place in 1955, 4 years ago, about my proposal to go to Camaldoli. It is a frightening and disheartening mess (one most important letter, that of Tom V. Moore is missing [LETTER 18]).
>
> What could have been very simple was turned into a sickeningly complicated and futile jamboree, partly through my own fault and partly through the stubborn and adroit politics of my superiors.
>
> In the end it was settled by Larraona with a NO—and with advice to wait a few years.
>
> I have waited a few years and now am in danger of doing the same thing and making the same mistakes over again. I start out boldly with an attack and make a bold bid for something perfectly legitimate—but when I do I am opposed then I defeat myself by *suggesting* compromise—in order not to displease anyone—and finally end up with nothing.
>
> 1. In May 1955 I thought I had applied for a *transitus*, through the Camaldolese. (copy of this letter missing also.) [Perhaps mentioned in LETTER 17, not extant, although he makes a formal request in LETTER 20.] I suppose the request was presented to the Congregation—but how and with what effect I never learned.³¹
>
> 2. After that a letter of Dom Leclercq³² *discouraged* the idea of Camaldoli and I practically gave it up, making a grab instead for Frascati. Permission to go there was asked and refused.
>
> 3. I think my superiors, after the General Chapter of 1955, were ready to let me be a hermit here, but I realized this would never work. The novitiate was the final compromise—something of a change, some silence, and a face saver.
>
> Today, be *careful*. (SFS, 311)

---

30. Cf. his comment on Latin Catholicism in the SSM: "One needs the atmosphere of French or Spanish or Italian Catholicism before there is any possibility of a complete and total experience of all the natural and sensible joys that overflow from the Sacramental life" (279).

31. To my knowledge, it was not.

32. Perhaps his letter of May 26, not extant: see Merton and Leclercq, *Survival or Prophecy?*, 63.

Indeed he was "in danger of doing the same thing and making the same mistakes over again." There is some advance in self-knowledge here, but not enough to balance the strength of his eremitical hopes. Wanting to move to Latin America, he once again excites himself and gives himself false hopes with his letters to bishops and others, once again making an end run around Dom James by asking Dom Gregorio Lemercier of Cuernavaca to arrange for his bishop to make an appeal to the Congregation on Merton's behalf. And Merton's "I think" in point (3) obscures the documented readiness of his superiors to let him be a hermit at Gethsemani.[33] His being appointed Master of Novices was a face-saver, yes, but as the record shows, much more. It was a sincere if temporary sacrifice of his efforts to find a way of living out his solitary vocation either at Gethsemani or elsewhere, as Dom James recognized, and as Merton himself stated in his note to Dom James putting himself forward for appointment to the office (October 13, TMC). It was also a vote of confidence in him, based in part on Merton's excellent exercise of the office of Master of Scholastics, a confidence fully justified by Merton's ten-year, strongly committed, and very effective exercise of the office.

With this long passage, substantial journal references to Camaldoli come to an end. Merton had devoted much of his time and prayer to the project for three years and more. It took him a further four years to come to the reflective position represented by this long journal entry of July 28, 1959; but that passage also reveals that the restlessness that had fueled the attempt to realize the Camaldoli dream was still active in him, and about to express itself in the lesser *acedia*—his push to move to an idealized Latin America.

---

33. See on this the section in chapter 3 prefatory to the discussion of LETTERS 34 and 35.

6

After the Dream

THE LESSER *ACEDIA*: LATIN AMERICA

So Thomas Merton would not be going to Camaldoli. What then? He was still not happy personally at Gethsemani, although he very much enjoyed his work as novice master. His desire for solitude, as he then conceived it, was as strong as ever. God, he believed, was calling him from within the divine solitude, to enter deeply into God's own solitude.

Then, in 1957, a young Nicaraguan novice came to Gethsemani: Ernesto Cardenal. With his arrival, Merton embarked on a two-track adventure in regard to Latin America. He soon found himself, fluent as he was in Spanish, on the cusp of developing a rich set of relationships with many of the leading literary figures of Latin America, and on the cusp of a second major attempt to leave Gethsemani. In both those concerns, Cardenal was central.

For health reasons, Cardenal left Gethsemani in 1959; but he and Merton kept in touch. He was ordained in 1965, and in the same year founded a lay monastery, Our Lady of Solentiname, destroyed in 1977 by the forces of Nicaragua's dictator of the time, Anastasio Somoza. Cardenal then became chaplain to the Sandinista National Liberation Front (FSLN), which overthrew Somoza in 1979. Appointed minister of culture in the new government, he campaigned for "a revolution without vengeance,"[1] continuing as minister until 1987. He left the FSLN in 1994, in protest against the

---

1. en.wikipedia.org/wiki/Ernesto_Cardenal; see note 2.

authoritarian direction it had taken under Daniel Ortega, while continuing on the political left. He is regarded today as the most important poet in Latin America.[2]

Soon after his ordination in 1965, Cardenal established his community on the island of Mancarrón, the largest of the thirty-six islands of the Solentiname archipelago in Lake Nicaragua—a small community of the kind he and Merton had been discussing. He also acted as parish priest on the island. The Solentiname community nurtured political consciousness and artistic practice, seeing both of these as integral to a holistic spirituality. After its destruction by Somoza, the community as such was not refounded, but in recent years the local people have revived the artistic tradition in which Cardenal encouraged them: primitivist paintings in oil and acrylic of the rainforest with its prolific numbers of egrets and herons.

In her introduction to the early letters exchanged between Merton and Cardenal, Christine Bochen gives this summary of their relationship and its ramifications:

> . . . conversations with Cardenal roused [Merton's] passion for Latin American literature and culture. He read voraciously and peppered Cardenal with questions. He began to feel a deep affinity for the people of Latin America and to experience a sense of solidarity with them in their struggle for freedom. Merton began corresponding with friends of Cardenal's in Nicaragua, and before too long he was in contact with writers throughout Central and South America. Just as surely as the novice master initiated the novice into the mysterious world of the monastery, the novice drew the master into a world which both novice and master thought they had left behind when they came to Gethsemani. Merton was very much at home in that world and he felt a deep kinship with its people, particularly its writers. . . .[3]

A full and illuminating account of these literary relationships may be found in the award-winning *Thomas Merton and Latin America: A Consonance of Voices*, by Malgorzata Poks.

Merton's fascination with Latin America, however, began long before he met Cardenal, with his trip to Cuba in 1940. He was twenty-five, newly graduated from Columbia, a very new Roman Catholic and a naïve *norteamericano* when he undertook his pilgrimage to the shrine of Our Lady of Cobre, near Santiago de Cuba, a pilgrimage that he admitted was of a medieval

---

2. For Merton's letters to Cardenal, see CFT, 110–63; Bochen, "Time of Transition," 162–200; Bochen, "Cardenal, Ernesto," in Shannon et al., *Thomas Merton Encyclopedia*.

3. Bochen, "Time of Transition," 164–65.

or Chaucerian kind, "nine-tenths vacation and one-tenth pilgrimage" (SSM, 279). His naïveté shows up in his Cuban diaries, particularly in their lack of any reference whatever to the brutal dictatorship under which Cubans were suffering at the time of his visit. What appealed particularly to Merton was what he idealized as the Catholic character of Cuban society:

> Every step I took opened up a new world of joys, . . . but on the plane of innocence, and under the direction of grace. There was a partial natural explanation for this. I was learning [what] could not be completely learned except in a culture that is at least outwardly Catholic. One needs the atmosphere of French or Spanish or Italian Catholicism before there is any possibility of a complete and total experience of all the natural and sensible joys that overflow from the Sacramental life. (SSM, 279)

There is no record, to my knowledge, of the chagrin with which any German, Dutch, Czech, Polish, or indeed Chinese Catholic reader may have read these words; but once again they point to Merton's tendency to employ hyperbole and projection in describing his enthusiasms.

It was in Merton's journal entry for February 15, 1958, that he had recorded the moment of epiphany when he realized that his destiny was to be a citizen, not simply of the United States, which he saw as "only the fringe of the True America," but of America in its entirety, North and South, "an American of the Andes—containing in myself also Kentucky and New York" (SFS, 168). There is a triple dynamic here. On the one hand he criticizes, even derogates, the United States; then he idealizes Latin America; and finally, circling back to scoop up Kentucky and New York, he comes to a place of integration: "This, then, is what seems to me so important about America—and the great function of my vocation in it: to know America in its totality, to be a complete American, a man of the whole hemisphere, of the whole New World."[4]

As Malgorzata Poks says, "Ever a man of reconciliation, he was attempting to reconcile in himself first America's, then the world's contradictions."[5] In so doing, he was called upon to accept—and did accept—his role as "*maestro* and spiritual guide for South American intellectuals," both to offer an act of reparation for North American neglect of the culture and spirituality of Latin America and to "help the whole hemispheric America become

---

4. Merton, *"Honorable Reader"*, 37.

5. Poks, *Thomas Merton and Latin America*, 42. Merton often used the similar phrase "unite in myself" to express this perspective. Classic examples of this are in *Conjectures*, 21 and 144.

'a great living unity.'"[6] He wanted to see nothing less than the birthing of an eschatological community in Latin America, which he saw as the "relatively uncorrupted part of humanity."[7]

Merton's plans and projects for a move to Latin America included fantasies, invitations, personal initiatives, and, most substantially, the possibility of an authorized leave of absence enabling him to go to Cuernavaca, near Mexico City, and to the experimental Benedictine community there. Fantasies, then, to begin: Venezuela first. "Perhaps the best country for us to start in. More our speed. Better chance of a good beginning. Transportation no difficulty. . . . Near Caracas or near Valencia or near Maracay. Or in the mountains overlooking the lake of Valencia" (SFS, 113). (He must have been making ample use of an atlas.) Or why not Brazil? An abbot in São Paulo wrote Frater Bede at Gethsemani, asking him to encourage Merton to make a foundation (SFS, 213). Merton makes it clear there that if he goes to Latin America it would not be to set up a Trappist foundation on the model of Gethsemani, but something much simpler, and discounts the suggestion. Then Ecuador, as evidenced by this journal entry of July 30, 1957:

> The hope of a monastery in Ecuador.
> Can such a hope be realized by anything except prayer?
> Is it a hope or a temptation? . . .
> St. Mariana of Jesus, you who prayed in Quito and loved God there and are venerated still and have power there still: give power to your prayers now and beg for a monastery near Quito or perhaps Riobamba under Chimborazo, a monastery in one of the large valleys. We would not need so many tractors. But there would be some tractors. . . . (SFS, 103)

Ah, cries the old poet, "Chimborazo, Cotopaxi, they had stolen my soul away!"[8] And so indeed was Merton's soul "stolen away," fascinated by the visions of new monastic possibilities that Chimborazo and the other names evoked.

But given Merton's feelings about the tractors of Gethsemani, his calm reference to tractors is risible in the extreme. Are South American tractors perhaps quieter than North American tractors? On Christmas Eve, he once again goes deep into fantasy:

---

6. Ibid., 67. The internal quotation is from a letter of Merton to Cardenal, CFT, 141.

7. Poks, *Thomas Merton and Latin America*, 31.

8. Walter James Redfern Turner (1889–1946), "Romance," line 7.

> If I could ask for anything I liked . . . , then I would put it this way—that I would ask for the grace . . . to be perfectly consonant with God's Will and that if it were His will, that I become a saint by making a monastic foundation in Ecuador and that the community there would be a very happy and simple one that would do much good in that country and everywhere else too . . . in short that there I might fulfill all that God has destined for me, and find myself completely in Him, and bring him many holy souls, and make that monastery a great spiritual force in Latin America. (SFS, 148)

Here he contradicts his frequent statements to the effect that he doesn't want to start a "foundation," even something that could be called a "monastery," but wants something simple, poor, and primal, preferably in an indigenous context. "Holy souls"—yes, they spoke that way in those days, and we can grant him that; but in talking about making such a monastery into "a great spiritual force in Latin America" he has again moved away from a project simple, happy, and poor toward inflation and grandiosity.

The first mention of Colombia occurs in his journal entry of August 29, 1957, as part of a list that also includes references to Nicaragua, Ecuador, Venezuela, and Paraguay—this latter sensibly ruled out because of the mosquitoes (SFS, 113–14). "There would be a wonderful place near Medellin in Antioquia or in the Cauca Valley. Not too high for work. High enough for cool weather and coffee, etc. Bogota too high? Or Tunja?" (SFS, 113). As in so many of his journal entries of the time, he is dazzling himself with a profusion of proper names, as Milton taught us to do in *Paradise Lost*. These are the words of the poet as well as the would-be solitary. Later Merton mentions an offer of property near Medellín that Dom James has received but decided not to take (SFS, 128). Then comes "a wonderful letter" from a Monseñor Ricaurte in Bogotá, who has spoken "to the Bishop of Tunja who was already to get out the necessary documents and start things moving" (SFS, 159). One possibility would be an abandoned Dominican house with no running water—indeed, "no water at all. That is the catch" (SFS, 159). A second possibility: the church and convent of Moniquira, a place of pilgrimage with many seventeenth-century paintings (SFS, 159–60); one trusts that that one did have water.

He has now (January 1958) become convinced that Dom James does intend to make a South American foundation and concludes that his prime contribution to this possibility is, as novice master, "to form the South American postulants as [God] brings them here" (SFS, 160). There had been two Colombian novices, Fr. Crisanto, who had a breakdown and had to leave (SFS, 177–79), and Fr. Pedro, who, as Merton writes, was about to leave because of his inability to sleep in a cold climate:

> There goes our second Colombian, then—and perhaps with him the hope of the Colombian foundation. But Rev. Fr. prefers, he says, to make a South American foundation with North Americans. And everywhere I see the horror from which there is no escape—the monotony of good, empty headed, generous, rather dizzy American monks who are not horrified by commercialism, who accept Franco, who are utterly dumb and impervious to all the sources of real corruption capable of ending their monasticism in one generation. And I, with my resentments, my weakness, am full of the same corruption only in a slightly more subtle form. (SFS, 183–84)

Merton had up to this point been willing to contemplate the launching of a "foundation" from Gethsemani in South America, rather than a simpler monastic establishment, a *laura*; but this angry and self-critical response to Dom James' preference for American monks in a new foundation makes it clear that Merton was thinking of any such foundation as being composed of him as spiritual father and his South American novices as founding brethren. The reference to Franco, someone far away from Latin America, is a curious one. I take it that Merton was simply using his name to characterize the political naïveté of the monks of Gethsemani; Franco, after all, albeit a cruel dictator, presented himself as a devout Catholic.

The possibility of Merton's going to Nicaragua was somewhat more likely than any of these much slighter possibilities, Cardenal being his prime connection. Here is Cardenal's memory of his first conversation with Merton after arriving at Gethsemani in 1957:

> . . . he informed me that the Abbot wanted to make a Trappist foundation in Latin America. It would be with Merton, who had thought first about the Virgin Islands, then Colombia or Ecuador, a place in the Andes, with the indigenous people. I talked to him about Nicaragua and Nicaragua began to be another alternative, in addition to Mexico. Later he changed his mind: it wasn't practical to establish a Trappist foundation there, but rather a contemplative life more free and more simple without the rigid anachronism of the old orders, without habit, rules, bureaucratic structures, a group small and poor. . . .[9]

---

9. Bochen, "Time of Transition," 164.

Merton changed his mind when he realized that Dom James planned to staff any projected Latin American foundation with North American monks, not the Latin American novices whom Merton was actively cultivating—although most of them left Gethsemani, Cardenal included. A simpler, *laura*-type community, in Nicaragua, in cooperation with Cardenal, held much more appeal. I note that in his descriptions of a number of the locations he had considered, Merton mentions the crops that he and his imagined brothers would cultivate: coffee in one Colombian location, corn and *frijoles* in another, sugar cane and oranges in a third. To these he now adds lemons and papayas in Nicaragua. There is a touch here of what is sometimes called visualization, a chiefly therapeutic exercise through which one visualizes one's desired future; here it is fantasy's first cousin. But for Merton, they were evocations of the fruit of the Spirit, all growing in a next-thing-to-being-promised land.

Merton's last letter to Cardenal is dated July 21, 1968, not long before he leaves for Asia. He tells Cardenal where he is going, or expects to go, or wants to go: Japan, Thailand, Nepal, Burma, Indonesia—the list is almost as long as the list of his Latin American possibilities. Father Flavian, the new abbot, and Merton have put together a plan for him, on his way to Asia, to explore locations in northern California for a hermit colony; Father Flavian himself, in fact, a hermit before his election as abbot, returned to the hermit life when his term as abbot ended. "But I also wonder about Nicaragua: I am too well known there also [as well as in California]. But in any case, if I do not go further into Asia I think I will spend a few weeks at least with you, if God grants it. But I make no firm promise" (CFT, 162). Too well known in Nicaragua? Yes, after all the years of interchange with Nicaraguan writers: yet wasn't this interchange what he had wanted to happen if/when he moved to Latin America? "Further into Asia"—the phrase would make an excellent title for the novel that yet remains to be written about Merton's Asian journey, which could include not only his actual journey but also the journeys he had projected for the months after December 1968. "A few weeks with you"—something less than the time he had mentioned to Cardenal in 1966. And finally, "if God grants it": as Merton had said earlier to Cardenal, both of them must do "everything that is required, leaving all the rest to divine Providence"—which, if we understand Providence the way Merton and Cardenal did, God did not grant. Another beautiful dream. Merton also took a number of personal initiatives, writing to three bishops (of Reno, Nevada, San Juan, Puerto Rico, and Bluefields, Nicaragua). All the bishops replied with varying degrees of encouragement, but Dom James became aware of the correspondence and put an end to it.

CUERNAVACA

One initiative did continue, however, the *pièce de résistance* of the whole Latin American project—Merton's attempt to go to Dom Gregorio Lemercier's Monastery of the Resurrection at Cuernavaca; and indeed he did encounter resistance, not of course unexpected, from Dom James and, eventually, from the Congregation for Religious. The first reference to Dom Gregorio is in a letter of August 22, 1955, to Dom Damasus Winzen, at Elmira, New York: "Yes, I . . . admire his little monastery at Cuernavaca" (SCH, 91). Then, in his journal of July 30, 1957, he writes as follows: "To visit first Dom Gregorio at Cuernavaca and learn from him how to make a small, simple monastery as unlike Gethsemani as possible" (SFS, 103). This doesn't indicate that Merton knew or had corresponded with Dom Gregorio; most probably he had simply read about his experimental and "primitive" Benedictine community and was intrigued. His first letter to Merton, held in the Thomas Merton Center archives, was written on August 28, 1957, in response to a letter (also in the TMC archives) from Merton, dated August 7, a week after the journal reference. Then, on May 6, 1959, almost two years later, Dom Gregorio, with no notice, appears at Gethsemani:

> Without wasting time, he came directly to the point—that if I was not fully satisfied here I should leave and start out on my own. . . . His suggestion—that I get an exclaustration [permission to be absent from one's monastery for a period of time], with the help of the bishop of Cuernavaca, move to Cuernavaca, live for a while as a hermit under the auspices of the Monasterio de la Resurrecion until I got oriented.
> It was quite a mouthful all at once, but it seemed to me absolutely necessary to take it and do what I could to digest it. He left this morning with the agreement that he would approach his bishop and then let me know and I would write to the Congregation [for Religious, in Rome].
> The opposition here, of course, will be formidable, and I hate the idea of starting all that again. . . . This time, it is not of my doing—but God's work entirely! (SFS, 277-78)

Merton was impulsive and, it might even be said, easily led, when his interlocutors told him things that accorded with his own *a priori* view of Providence and that he wanted to hear. *The Seven Storey Mountain* abounds in such moments. Essentially he lacked confidence in his own promptings, which, as we have seen, continued to fluctuate, apparently believing that they were not as reliable as what others would say to him at moments of high discernment. It might seem that this does not apply to the firmness with which he approached Dom James, especially in the time of his attempt to go to Camaldoli; but once the decision about Camaldoli was made *for him* by the Congregation for Religious, he accepted it wholeheartedly and was ready to see his own leadings as expressions of self-will. So when Dom Gregorio tells him it is time to leave Gethsemani—not a new thought for Merton—he immediately deems it "God's work entirely," because it comes not from himself but from another person, someone he respects.

In a long reflection in his journal, he continues to pick at the scabs of his confusion. He talks about how his leaving would be interpreted, or misinterpreted; but he knows that there is nothing he can do about that. He says that there is something inexplicable that draws him away from Gethsemani but not *toward* any place in particular:

> ... always the old story of "something missing." What? Is it something essential?
> Won't there always be "something missing"?
> Yet always that urge to "go forth," to leave, to take off for a strange land and start another life....
> It was that kind of desire that brought me here. (SFS, 285)

Here he is in full *non finis quaerendi* mode; I can hear Evagrius muttering "*Acedia!*" to himself. But Merton is coming closer to himself with the insight that it was the same kind of desire for a new start he was then experiencing that had brought him to Gethsemani in the first place. At this point he gets a note from Dom Gregorio, who is *not* having second thoughts about Merton's coming to Cuernavaca, telling him that all is well at the Monastery of the Resurrection and that he hopes to see him again before September (May 30, 1959, TMC).

On June 30, he mentions that he has received another letter (no longer extant) from Dom Gregorio, "cryptic, but asserting firmly that in a case like this the decision is not to be left simply to the abbot" (SFS, 299). Then on July 16, another visit from Dom Gregorio; in the presence of this minister of Providence, confusion dissipates:

> Within a few minutes everything was clear. He will present my case to Rome himself, when he goes in September. Was a great help in my various doubts and misgivings, showing clearly that it is not "disobedience" or "obstinancy" [*sic*] to present the matter directly to Rome. (SFS, 305)

He records in his journal how grateful he is to Dom Gregorio: "His charity is one of the most striking and comforting things about the whole business because it is obvious that it is beyond all possible engineering of mine and that it is a gift of God" (SFS, 307). Yes, it is a gift of God because it is *someone else's* initiative, not Merton's, *and* an initiative that accords with Merton's hopes, another testimony to his view of Providence. Later (August 22, SFS, 320) he will say something very similar—that he can't do anything on his own initiative. He ends by saying that he has little doubt that the indult will be granted, and then offers this reversal of so many of the things he has been saying about the monastery: "My view of Gethsemani is suddenly back to normal. . . . And I *do* love the monastery" (SFS, 307).

Volatile as Merton's ideas about the location of his prospective *laura* were, a factor that does unite and indeed transcend them all is his deep feeling about indigenous peoples, strongly stated in his comments about the "True America" and reiterated in a passage from his journal entry of August 18. In it he stands apart for a moment from the plans and projects that fill most of the pages of his journal in these weeks, and touches into his deepest motivations, offering himself and us a moment of respite from his tensions and confusions. It represents the longed-for counterpart of his distaste for what he sees the United States becoming: technological and technocratic, shallow and bureaucratic, and alienated from the natural world:

> What I need—as far as I can interpret the desire in my heart, is to make a journey to a primitive place, among primitive people, and there die. It is at the same time a going out and a "return." A going to somewhere where I have never been or thought of going—a going in which I am led by God, a journey in which I go out from everything I now have. And I feel that unless I do this my spiritual life is at an end. (SFS, 318)

In this strongly felt passage, he is applying to himself what he will write in his 1964 essay "From Pilgrimage to Crusade." This is the kind of pilgrimage in which Abraham goes he knows not where at the call of God (Heb 11:8); or in which St. Columba goes into exile from his beloved Ireland, landing by the action of the waves, also understood as a channel of the Providence of God, on the island of Iona; or in which St. Brendan launches out on his fabled voyage. This is Merton as pilgrim—*monastic* pilgrim:

> . . . the object of [monastic] pilgrimage is to take the monk to his peculiar and appointed place on the face of the earth, a place not determined by nature, race and society, but by the free choice of God. Here he was to live, praise God, and finally die. His body would then be buried in this spot, and would there await the resurrection. The pilgrimage of the . . . monk was not then just endless and aimless wandering for its own sake. It was a journey

to a mysterious, unknown, but divinely appointed place, which was to be the place of the monk's ultimate meeting with God.[10]

Both statements testify to the depth of Merton's desire to know himself held lovingly and providentially in the hands of God, his decisions determined by Providence and not by his own self-will: to return, in fact, to paradise. He wants to find the "source of indefectible life," "the mountain where the ancient fathers were in direct communication with heaven," "paradise itself, with its sacred tree of life."[11] Wherever he goes, he wants to know that he is going to the "divinely appointed place," "the place of [his] ultimate meeting with God"—and nothing less.

We return now to the narrative, as Merton did. On August 30, 1959, he notes that Dom Gregorio will come to Gethsemani on the 5th or 6th of September:

> The best thing is to be content that it [the application for exclaustration] needs no excuse and be patient with the things Rev. Father will say about it, because it will really make him angry. He leaves Thursday for the General Chapter and will think the whole thing was plotted in his absence. (SFS, 324–25)

When Merton speaks of presenting "the matter directly to Rome" (SFS, 305), he is remembering what he did in regard to Camaldoli, with what results we know. Dom James is Merton's monastic superior, to whom in the Benedictine tradition he has pledged obedience and fidelity; but it has to be said that he is having a kind of monastic affair in the authority that he is granting Dom Gregorio over his decisions. Dom Gregorio, when he goes to Rome with his bishop, will hand Merton's letter directly to Larraona.

On September 23 (TMC) he writes to Dom James, finally revealing to him what is taking place. He says that everyone he consults supports his right to seek a leave of absence in order to undertake a trial of some kind of solitary or alternative-monastic life. Once again he fudges, however, when he says that given Dom James' opposition, he "may perhaps feel obliged to ask some help from higher superiors"—something he has already done two weeks earlier via a letter to Larraona in Rome (WF 205–7). He has told Dom James some of the truth, but not the whole truth. He now tells Dom James that faithful to his promise after the failure of his attempt to go to Camaldoli

---

10. Merton, "From Pilgrimage to Crusade," 96. The reference to "wandering" points to the Russian model of pilgrimage, that of the *strannik*, or "wanderer"—not one that appealed to Merton, although he does say in the same essay that "man instinctively regards himself as a wanderer and wayfarer" (91).

11. Ibid., 91.

he is not attempting to leave the order, a matter of intense pride for Dom James, but desires only a leave of absence.

October 6 Merton receives a letter, dated October 1 (TMC), from Dom Gregorio. He tells Merton that things are going well. He has seen Larraona twice, and quotes him as saying that although Larraona expects opposition to Merton's request from Merton's superiors, this would not change his favorable opinion. Then, on November 15, "[a] complete bombshell":

> Today . . . Father Abbot announced by surprise and without explanation that he is going to Rome tomorrow for an important conference. A complete bombshell—and I have no doubt that one of the main reasons for the trip is my petition to the Congregation. For a while I was secretly angry. It is not going to be easy just sitting here powerless to do anything while he has full power to completely wreck everything by fair means or foul. (SFS, 343)

Merton's intuition was correct. Dom James (I note that he refers to him here as "Father Abbot," a much more formal address than Merton's usual form, "Rev. Father," or even "Dom James") had received a letter from the abbot general expressing his consternation that the indult, a copy of which he has seen, has authorized a three-year leave of absence from Gethsemani for Merton.

Here then is what Dom Gabriel in this letter of November 8 (TMC) says about this to Dom James. The letter he partially transcribes is the response of the Congregation[12] to Merton's request for an indult, and is addressed formally to the pope—at the time, John XXIII—although in the normal course of events he would not be expected to deal with it. It too is dated November 8, and signed by Archbishop Larraona:

> . . . Dom Déodat, our Procurator General, sent me the document from the S[acred] Congregation the essential elements of which I here transcribe for you.
>
> "Father Thomas Merton, of the Order of Cistercians Reformed, humbly throwing himself at the feet of Your Holiness, requests an indult of exclaustration, for the reasons stated . . ."

Then comes the ruling of the Congregation:

> *Vigore facultatum a SSmo Domino Nostro concessarum, S. Congregatio Negotiis Religiosorum Sodalium praeposita, attentis expositis, P. Abb. Gen. benigne indulget ut, veris existentibus*

---

12. Now called the Congregation for Institutes of Consecrated Life and Societies of Apostolic Life.

> *narratis, pro suo arbitrio et conscientia, oratori concedat petitam facultatem exclaustrationis non ultra triennium....*

> (By the power of the faculties granted by our Most Holy Lord [i.e., the Pope] the circumstances having been examined by the Father Abbot General, and the pertinent truths having been stated, the Congregation for Religious kindly allows, and, for the sake of [i.e., on the basis of] his own judgment and conscience, grants to the petitioner the faculty requested of living outside the cloister for not more than three years....)

Dom Gabriel continues, and the plot thickens:

> I don't need to tell you how stupefied I was when I learned about this. Dom Déodat was no less flabbergasted than I, for we knew NOTHING about this request of Father Merton. You can see, moreover, that in the text, a significant part of which is a form printed in advance, the words *audito voto* ["the request having been heard"] which appear in the pre-printed part and are generally followed by the name of the Procurator General, have been scratched out by the same hand that has written, at the end, *attentis expositis* ["having been considered"]. Not even for a single instant is there any possibility that I should sign this indult, and so bring it into force, even if it is to me that the Sacred Congregation assigns this duty. On the other hand, I can't hold on to an indult like this without sending it back to the S[acred] Congregation and giving them the reasons for my position. This is where I need your support.

The indult says that the application has been examined by the abbot general; but Dom Gabriel's letter makes it clear that this is not the case. He goes on to wonder what channel Merton "borrowed" in order to obtain the indult. Very likely, he thinks, he had the support of a bishop: and yes, he did, the bishop of Cuernavaca, enlisted in the cause by Dom Gregorio. He stresses how important it is that the indult not reach Merton. For the *sake of his soul* (italics Dom Gabriel's) his leaving of Gethsemani must be prevented, to say nothing of the sake of the many persons he has influenced. He asks Dom James to come to Rome as soon as he can, but to say nothing about his trip to Merton before he comes. He also asks Dom James to see to it that during his absence no mail coming in should reach Merton, nor should any mail from Merton be sent out, including items marked conscience matter. Finally, he asks Dom James to bring with him any letters that show disrespect to Merton's superiors or to the hierarchy of the Church itself, to which he will add similar letters already in his possession to show to Larraona to persuade him to cancel the indult.

Merton's suspicions about Dom James' trip were well founded, and certainly, given the large amount of mail he received every day, he would have noticed that his mail had been cut off. On November 18 he writes to Cardenal about his suspicions. He also tells Jean Leclercq that he has applied for the indult, and about Dom James having been summoned to Rome. He tells Leclerq that there must be some reason besides his application for Dom James to go to Rome; but in this he is mistaken—the application and the intention of Dom Gabriel to forestall it is the only reason. Leclercq replies that given how seriously applications for an indult are taken in Rome, Merton can count on the decision being one of the "surest indications of the will of God,"[13] a viewpoint that matches Merton's. A day later he records a Zen moment during this tense time: "I have a koan to work on: 'Who is this who wants to go to Mexico?'" (SFS, 346).

December 16, the letter he has been waiting for from Larraona arrives. In fact, it is signed both by Larraona, as secretary to the Congregation, and by his superior, Cardinal Valerio Valeri, prefect of the Congregation, and is dated December 7:

> It was a large envelope—had come by surface mail. Too large an envelope. I took it back to the novitiate and read it on my knees before the Bl[essed] Sacrament—and it said "No."
>
> It was a long, personal detailed letter, in fact a very fine letter signed by the Cardinal Prefect and countersigned by Card. Larraona. Two cardinals. What could be more definitive and more official—what could be more final? (SFS, 358)

His departure, they said, would upset too many people. What they asked him to do was to stay in the monastery where God had put him, and where he would find interior solitude. In what was perhaps the "most unkindest cut of all" (*Julius Caesar*, III.ii.187), they quoted back to him his own words from *No Man Is an Island*:

> Our Father in Heaven has called us each one to the place in which He can best satisfy His infinite desire to do us good. His inscrutable choice of the office or the state of life or particular function to which we are called is not to be judged by the intrinsic merit of those offices or states, but only by the hidden love of God. My vocation is the one I love, not because I think it is the best vocation in the Church, but because it is the one God

---

13. Merton and Leclercq, *Survival or Prophecy?*, 88.

has willed for me. (NMI, 138, also in the letter of December 7, TMC)

They counseled him to concentrate on interior solitude, and not to concern himself with the exterior contexts of that solitude. "Develop solitude in yourself, not the solitude of grottoes or woods[14] where one can still live in oneself and for oneself; but the genuine solitude which one enters by leaving oneself in order to give oneself to the One who desires to fill us" (December 7, TMC). Merton responds in his journal entry of the same day:

> I felt no anger or resistance. The letter was too obvious. It could only be accepted. And this first reaction was one of relief that at last the problem had been settled....
>
> A kind of anesthesia. Certainly surprised myself by not getting at all upset and feeling the slightest disappointment. Rather, felt only joy and emptiness and liberty. Funny....
>
> The letter is obviously an indication of God's Will and I accept it fully. So then what? Nothing. Trees, hills, rain.... A mountain lifted off my shoulders—a Mexican mountain I myself had chosen. (SFS, 358–59)

By "a kind of anesthesia," I take him to mean numbness. Of course he had to write Dom Gregorio, which he does the same day. He recounts the substance of the cardinals' letter and tells him that he would like to stay in touch. Then he speaks personally and directly:

> As for me, I am just letting myself be. I accept, I consent. This is for me the will of God. I believe that God Himself will intervene either to arrange things exteriorly or to give me in my heart the solitude I seek. I am experiencing a great deal of peace, an emptiness, a truly wonderful silence, and an enormous amount of freedom. I am perfectly at peace, in union with the Christ of God and very near our heavenly Father. (WF, 214)

The next day, December 17, he writes two letters to Dom James. In the first letter he repeats his conviction that God's will has been discerned and that he accepts it without hesitation. "I only took the steps I did," he says, "in order to find out what the Congregation thought, and hence what was the will of God" (WF, 215). He will take no steps to leave the order, will carry on as novice master if Dom James wants him to, and again raises the prospect of his living as a hermit in the woods. It is a peaceful and submissive letter.

---

14. Cf. the cancellation in 1951 by the father immediate of Dom James' permission to Merton to spend time in the woods; and Calati's discomfort about the influence of Thoreau on Merton, chapter 5, notes 17 and 18.

Then comes the second letter, in a strikingly different tone (did Thomas Merton have an evil twin?). He tells Dom James that he resists his view that any monastic subject can appeal to higher superiors only through the abbot, not directly. He does recognize Dom James' right to refuse a leave of absence, and then offers some biting criticism:

> Are you not so intent on your own views, in this matter, that you are willing to stifle the Holy Ghost in a soul? Can you say with certainty that you have not stifled Him in souls before, in the question of vocation particularly? Do you not have an inordinate tendency to interfere in the workings of conscience and to suppress by violence those desires and ideals which run counter to your policies? I appeal to the right, granted and assured by the Father Visitor, to consult directly outside the monastery by letter, without interference, so that this problem of mine can be settled. (WF, 216)

Can be settled? But had he not earlier that very day, writing in his journal, said that he was relieved that the problem *had been settled*? Yes, he had; but this was a conviction that did not hold. Within twelve hours he had moved from total acceptance and peace to bitterness and a renewed readiness to leave Gethsemani. More than a year later, he is still stewing about the decision of the Congregation as influenced by the abbot general and Dom James:

> I should love my abbot, my order, my community. But really I doubt if I do, I doubt if I *can* love them spontaneously. I am too obsessed by the unfairness, the injustice that was done me in Rome by the abbot, and above all embittered and frustrated by the fact that he was able to do this with a good conscience subjectively, thinking himself perfectly right....
>
> Such are my thoughts. They are "uncharitable." Yet I cannot not have them.
>
> And he is kind to me, very considerate in many ways. That makes it worse.... But all the time I cannot help feeling he is so for business reasons. I cannot forget the letter he wrote to Montini [LETTER 35], and that someone saw. Incredible! (TTW, 158–59)

He accepts the decision of the Congregation—"the Church's answer and God's answer" (LETTER 30)—*and* he resents the role played in that decision by Dom James; he gives no indication that he ever learned that the Congregation's original response had been a positive one. This was not going to be his last slam aimed at Dom James, however. He was about to launch into what William Shannon calls "the year of the Cold War letters";[15] and in confronting the potential horror of global nuclear war, his personal struggles, though not forgotten, assumed a lower profile.

And as it happened, the monastery at Cuernavaca to which he had hoped to go was closed some years later after a debacle related to Dom Gregorio's decision that all the monks of his monastery should undergo psychoanalysis. Then on July 27, 1968, nine years after the Congregation's refusal of the indult, came further news of Dom Gregorio:

> Bro. Benedict showed me a newspaper photo of Dom Gregorio Lemercier—just married! So that's that. All the old Cardinals in Rome will be nodding wisely: they knew all along what this psychoanalysis would lead to!
>
> For Dom G. personally—I can't judge. But it is a shame for monasticism. Whatever way you look at it, it does mean *giving up* a monastic experiment. Maybe he'll go on to something else. As for me, I'm interested in the *monastic* life and its values. In doing something with it, not just abandoning it. (OSM, 147)

The three years' leave for which Merton had applied would have expired in 1962, which was some years before the Cuernavaca monastery closed. And of course there is no way of knowing what Merton's role and influence would have been during those three years, or whether, having lived three years away from Gethsemani, he would ever have returned. Dom James, of course, if he heard about Dom Gregorio's marriage, would have been "nodding wisely" along with the cardinals in Rome.

Once again we come to the issue of *acedia*. The same symptoms of the presence of the noonday demon that appeared in relation to Camaldoli are clearly present in Merton's multifaceted attempt to move to Latin America. Once again restlessness is key. Merton's changes of mind within a twenty-four-hour period or within a day or two or within a week give evidence of an unsettled mind and an unquiet heart. This is not to say that this was his situation at all times; there were some beautiful times to which his journals testify when he did know the joy of faith in God, and the peace that passes all understanding.

Another major temptation in Evagrius and Cassian: the lure of distant monasteries, whether actual, as Camaldoli or Cuernavaca, or projected, as with the many options that he considered in Colombia—with or without

---

15. Shannon, *Silent Lamp*, 209–24.

water! I find it especially significant that what he identified to the novices as "a disease of the best minds" never struck him as something that might apply to himself. What might he have said about these grandiose words of his to Cardinal Valeri, had they been presented to him as the words of someone else?

> What I wanted . . . was to help him [Dom Gregorio] in forming a small group, more or less solitary, under his direction and with a limited apostolic outreach: that is to say, with the possibility of certain limited contacts with intellectuals in Mexico City who are somewhat communistic in outlook, but who would have accepted me with much goodwill as a person who could understand them. (WF, 217)

Canadian humorist Stephen Leacock once told a story about a knight who mounted his horse and rode off in all directions. He wasn't thinking of Thomas Merton, but he might as well have been. I smile at the word "limited," repeated for emphasis. Certainly there would have been more intellectuals in Mexico City and Cuernavaca than there would have been in Reno, Nevada, San Juan, Puerto Rico, or Bluefields, Nicaragua; and fortunately, the Mexican intellectuals were only *somewhat* communistic in outlook. Given the general American view of Communism at the time, even this qualifier would have set off very loud alarm bells in the minds of many of his monastic confreres. I make no comment on his statement that he could have come among them as someone who could understand them. This is not, of course, to derogate from the seriousness with which Merton took his "apostolate" to intellectuals, as Kathleen Deignan has laid out for us in her article "Cosmopolitan: Thomas Merton's Urbane Spirituality," a very helpful follow-up to David Belcastro's article on Merton as the last of the "urban hermits."[16] In that article she picks up on Belcastro's linking of Merton with Clement of Alexandria, as perhaps the first Christian public intellectual. She also directs us to Merton's important letter to John XXIII of November 1958, written while he was hoping to go to Latin America. In that letter he speaks of his "sympathy for the honest aspirations of so many intellectuals everywhere in the world and the terrible problems they have to face" (HGL, 482). He has had the experience, he says, of how his reaching out to intellectuals has generated strong responses from many artists and writers who have become his friends without his having to leave the cloister. As he says to Pope John, ". . . I have exercised an apostolate—small and limited though it be—within a circle of intellectuals from other parts of the world; and it has been quite

---

16. Deignan, "Cosmopolitan," 15–21, and Belcastro, "Praying the Questions."

simply an apostolate of friendship" (HGL, 482). It was an apostolate that he continued to exercise for the rest of his life, from Gethsemani.

My only remaining question is whether or not I have erred in naming his Latin American project as the lesser *acedia* as compared to the Camaldoli project. In both instances he poured into them time, energy, and prayer; and in both instances he involved a number of people at all levels of his hierarchical church and order in his often convoluted enterprise. I can distinguish them geographically, at least: it was more of a push for a monk from Kentucky to tackle the possibility of entering one of the historic holy places of Europe than it was to aim at setting up from scratch a simple form of monastic life in a developing country. In any case, the noonday demon could congratulate itself that in these two notable instances it had complicated the life of the outstanding Christian spiritual writer of his century and the lives of his monastic superiors.

7

Solitude and Love

Merton wrote to Camaldoli in 1952 because he was concerned about the lack of solitude (from his perspective) at Gethsemani. The letters of that extended correspondence provide a useful benchmark from which to assess how his mind changed about solitude in the years following. When he wrote to Camaldoli he was very restless, afflicted, as I have conjectured, by the active work of the demon of *acedia*. Later, his ideas about solitude moved forward, backward, and sideways in his consciousness and concern until during the hermitage years love and solitude came together in one integrated dynamic, distinguishable but inseparable. In the event, he came through these years not only into possession of his own hermitage at Gethsemani[1] but to a spiritual place in which he saw, indeed, knew love as the dominant and unifying dynamic of his solitude. I am trusting the reader to integrate into the following account of this spiritual journey the two major attempts by Merton, already explored, to move either to Camaldoli or to Latin America in search of solitude as he then conceived it.

---

1. Cf. "Solitary Life in the Shadow of a Cistercian Monastery," 3-8. Its original was published in French as "La Vie Solitaire à l'ombre d'un monastère cistercien." The phrase *à l'ombre du monastère* ("in the shadow of the monastery") had in fact been used in a letter from Dom Louis, the father immediate, to Dom James, at the peak of the Camaldoli crisis. If a hermitage could be arranged at Gethsemani *à l'ombre du monastère*, he said, "it would keep Father Louis in the Order and would permit him to take his place among his brothers..." (June 5, 1955, TMC). It was a phrase that Merton picked up soon after and used in LETTER 30, when he referred to "the theoretical possibility of letting a Cistercian live as a hermit in the shadow of his abbey" (August 24, 1955).

THE HERMIT QUESTION

"The hermit question": this is a phrase he uses in a letter of September 28, 1964, to Jean Leclercq: "I have at least a faint hope that we might actually attempt to face the hermit question here. This is very confidential. But I am glad to say that in a recent conversation Father Abbot showed himself very open and understanding on this subject."[2] Less than a year later, Merton had been relieved of his responsibility as Master of Novices and had been authorized to live as a hermit in a cinder block cottage on the grounds of the abbey. As we have seen in his attempts to make an authorized move to Camaldoli or to Cuernavaca, he had been struggling for years to find the right setting for a truly eremitical life, the life of a hermit. The solution, when it came to pass, was simple in the extreme: he could be a hermit on the grounds of the very abbey to which he had pledged his stability when he made his final vows as a Cistercian monk in 1947. Eventually, he would bloom where he had been planted—a cliché, I grant, but one justified, I would suggest, by Merton's instruction to Dom Giabbani in LETTER 20, that if he obtained the *transitus* that Merton had asked for, he should tell him that "The roses are *in bloom* at the hermitage." When in 1955 he had been offered the possibility of living as a hermit "one hundred percent," he knew he was not ready, and declined the offer. "Ripeness is all," as Edgar says in *King Lear* (V.ii.11), and Merton knew that the time was *not* ripe, that he was not ready to go into the desert full-time. His ten years as novice master, however—the period of his life in which as never before he came intimately into contact with what he refers to as the solitudes of others—did prepare him for the hermitage; and when the offer came again, in the summer of 1965, he *was* ready.

The cinder block retreat center, as it was first called, later to become Merton's hermitage, was built in November 1960. Merton had for some years been corresponding with Protestant pastors and theologians, and the idea that they should come to Gethsemani for ecumenical conversations was a very natural one; the little building was built to facilitate this. Almost immediately, Merton was given permission to spend "intervals" there; and over the next five years this expanded to include permission to sleep there from time to time. On December 10, 1960, with the building only a month old but already christened by Merton as St. Mary of Carmel, he records his satisfaction at being able to use it:

> Totally new perspectives on solitude. Afternoons at St. Mary of Carmel. It is true, places and situations are not supposed to

---

2. Merton and Leclercq, *Survival or Prophecy?*, 117.

> matter. This one makes a tremendous difference. Real silence. Real solitude. Peace.... The valley in front. The tall, separated pines to the west ... elm and oak to the southwest, when [sic] a shoulder of hill hides the abbey. And a great dance of sky overhead. And a fire murmuring in the fireplace. Silent.... (TTW, 73).

Later that month, he writes again of the hermitage, even more intensely. To trees and perspectives he adds the moon and the stars:

> ... St. Mary of Carmel (after Vespers) this is tremendous: with the tall pines, the silence, the moon and stars above the pines as dark falls, the patterns of shadow, the vast valley and hills everything speaks of a more mature and more complete solitude.... There is frankly a house, demanding not attachment but responsibility.... the sense of a journey ended,[3] of wandering at an end. *The first time in my life* I ever really felt I had come home and that my waiting and looking were ended. (TTW, 79–80)

These are the words of a romantic (another term for the Four on the Enneagram), and yes—he is "in love" with the little house, in the sense that to be "in love" means to envisage a shared future. They are also the words of an artist. As an artist, Merton was affected by the aesthetic of the place. As someone who had had a fractured childhood, he was touched by the possibility that he had "come home"—words with enormous emotional potency. Douglas Christie speaks of Merton's "lifelong search for home,"[4] and while granting that his relation to the hermitage was a deep one, cautions us against reading what he says here as final, a caution that can apply to many of Merton's statements that testify to his desire for resolution, for homecoming:[5]

> There is a sense of finality to this statement that is perhaps deceptive. Merton was to live eight more years, and his "waiting and looking" continued unabated. Still, one can sense something in him beginning to settle, integrate, heal; he is truly beginning to feel at home—perhaps for "the first time" in his life.[6]

In his beautiful article, full of feeling for Merton, "Place-Making as Contemplative Practice," from which this quotation comes, Christie expands on this caution:

---

3. A phrase he has used before: cf. SSM, 4.
4. Christie, "Place-Making," 359.
5. Cf. his telling Dom James in 1948 that his Carthusian temptations had "ceased to be a problem" (ES, 262).
6. Christie, "Place-Making," 366.

> It is no wonder that this metaphor [to feel at home] should surface so strongly within the discourse of spiritual longing. Nor is it easy to imagine once such awareness becomes real, how one could ever lose hold of it. And yet it happens. The old restlessness returns. The wounds inflicted by all the losses one has endured turn out to be still tender. The sense of exile resurfaces with renewed force, and the search for home recommences.[7]

And so it was that Merton, grateful as he was for the hermitage, but by early 1968 recognizing that it no longer provided him with the exterior solitude that he desired, went on his journey to Asia; and on the plane on the way there, he says, "I am going home, to the home where I have never been in this body . . ."[8] Again Douglas Christie comments: "What a strange idea: going home to a place where one has never been—at least in the body. And yet this is how Merton framed his journey to Asia: as a homecoming to an as-yet-unknown place."[9] No, not known in the body, but known in mind, heart, and spirit; in the reading he had been doing, in his correspondence with Asian men of spirit, and in his meeting with Asian religious figures at Gethsemani, Thich Nhat Hanh being the best-known of these (LTL, 72, 76).

Merton formally began his solitary life at Gethsemani, his life as a hermit, on August 20, 1965, the feast of St. Bernard, the archetypal cenobitic Cistercian, ten years to the day after Archbishop Montini had handwritten him his decisive letter (LETTER 27). His journal records something of the meaning of this life-shift for him. He was reading Hebrews 11, a chapter that lists a number of biblical figures who had lived "by faith" and had looked forward to the fulfillment, even if not in their own time, of God's promises:

> Entering upon the new way, I think especially of this: that from part of the promise and fulfillment for which others have suffered and hoped: and in turn I will suffer and prepare the way for others. In leaving immediate contact with people and society I enter into this other close-knit society of witnesses. I am very aware of their presence. (DWL, 282)

He is pointing here to the communion of saints as he has experienced it. In "Day of a Stranger," written three months before his formal entry into the hermitage, but having already eaten, studied, written, and slept there, he has already testified to the reality of this:

---

7. Ibid., 368.
8. Merton, *Asian Journal*, 5.
9. Christie, "Place-Making," 370.

> There is a mental ecology [here], a living balance of spirits in this corner of the woods. There is room here for many other songs besides those of birds. Of Vallejo, for instance. Or Rilke, or René Char, Montale, Zukofsky. . . . Or the dry, disconcerting voice of Nicanor Parra, the poet of the sneeze. Here also is Chuang Tzu whose climate is perhaps most the climate of this silent corner of woods. . . . Here is the deep vegetation of that more ancient forest in which the angry birds, Isaias [Isaiah] and Jeremias [Jeremiah], sing. Here should be, and are, feminine voices from Angela of Foligno to Flannery O'Connor . . . and, more personally and warmly still, Raissa Maritain.[10]

He was now in an official, recognized sense a hermit. The "hermit question" had been resolved on the physical level, and the inner search could continue.

SOLITARY AND WRITER

From the time he began to feel drawn to solitude to the very end of his life, the consistent thread in his writing is that of the living of the contemplative life through prayer, meditation, and silence. In contemplation, one simply is. For Merton it means, at perhaps its most challenging depth, a willingness not only to be lonely, but to unite his loneliness with the loneliness of God:

> Man's loneliness is, in fact, the loneliness of God. That is why it is such a great thing for a man to discover his solitude and learn to live in it. For there he finds that he and God are one:[11] that God is alone as he himself is alone. That God wills to be alone in him.[12]

This is not so far from what George Bernard Shaw puts into the mouth of Joan of Arc—Saint Joan—at a moment of crisis for her:

> France is alone; and God is alone; and what is my loneliness before the loneliness of my country and my God? I see now that the loneliness of God is His strength; . . . my loneliness shall be my strength too; it is better to be alone with God: His friendship will not fail me, nor His counsel, nor His love.[13]

---

10. Merton, "Day of a Stranger," 216.
11. The Christic experience: cf. John 10:30.
12. Merton, "Notes for a Philosophy of Solitude," 74.
13. Shaw, *Saint Joan*, 119.

Under very different circumstances, this was to be very much a part of Merton's experience in the hermitage, particularly after the end of his relationship with Margie (LTL, 319).

Another voice: Robert Kull spent a year in solitude on a little island in the coastal wilderness of Chilean Patagonia. His book, *Solitude: Seeking Wisdom in Extremes*, tells the story of that year, which he undertook as research for a doctoral dissertation on the experience of solitude for an extended time. Here is a summary statement of his experience:

> We each have a social identity, a persona held in place by our interactions with other people. In solitude, without others to mirror this persona, it begins to lose solidity and dissolve. The process can be terrifying, and one powerful aspect of solitude is that there are few easy escapes from such difficult experiences.... In solitude I experience a full range of emotions, from feeling painfully isolated to feeling joyfully woven into my physical surroundings and into my fabric of personal relationships.... I'm more fluid and profoundly part of the flowing whole.[14]

This very much accords with Merton's experience. In the monastery, he was a monk. In the world of letters, he was a public intellectual. In the hermitage, he is nobody in particular; he can let his persona go. Kull's last sentence evokes Merton's approval of Chuang Tzu's description of the "man of Tao" (and now, of course, Merton would want to include the woman of Tao): one in whom the "Tao acts without impediment."[15] The Tao, in other words the ultimate reality of the cosmos, flows through him or her, without the impediments of regret, anxiety, confusion, or fear. As Kull says, such a person becomes "profoundly part of the flowing whole." Given that Kull self-identifies as a nonreligious person, it is interesting to read this further comment about the breadth of his experience, which again accords, from outside the Christian thought-world, with Merton's view of solitude:

> ... to be fully human, we need relationship not only with other people but with the nonhuman world, with our own inner depths—and with Something Greater. For me, that nonmaterial Presence is mysterious and sacred. It can be experienced, but not defined.[16]

---

14. Kull, *Solitude*, 211.
15. Merton, *Way of Chuang Tzu*, 25.
16. Kull, *Solitude*, x.

"Something Greater": this is close to Wordsworth's idea in lines 94–96 of "Tintern Abbey" (incidentally, a former Cistercian monastery, now a ruin). The "Something Greater" for Wordsworth is a

> ... presence that disturbs me with the joy
> Of elevated thoughts; a sense sublime
> Of something far more deeply interfused ...

Kull's statement as a whole lays out the breadth of the agenda of the solitary, all of which Merton acknowledges: relationship with others, with the rest of creation, with his own soul, and with that Something Greater, the reality that Kull sensed on his island, that disturbing "presence" that Christians call God. Merton is living out his solitary vocation in the context of a Christian worldview, but what Kull says makes it clear that Merton is also undertaking something fundamentally human.

It is therefore no contradiction to say that the life of solitude is one with a profoundly social dimension. Arguably, Merton's intense desire for solitude was balanced by the intensity and breadth of his concern for the social and political health of the planet. The implications of global social and political dysfunction made the expression of his prophetic impulse a spiritual necessity, a spiritual response to human need. As Merton says, "My solitude belongs to society and to God" (TTW, 74). The intentional solitary life is thus an advance toward, a confrontation with "poverty and the void, . . . the empirical self"[17] on behalf of the human race—or, better, in this ecological time, on behalf of the entire wounded creation (cf. Evagrius' concept of the *gnosis* through which the divided creation is returned to its primal unity). "It is in deep solitude," as Merton says of himself, "that I find the gentleness with which I can truly love my brothers" (ES, 398). In this solitude, the solitary stands with Christ, the New Adam, in whose humanity, in principle, are to be found all people, through whom God has taken "to himself the solitude and dereliction of man: every man."[18] Douglas Christie again:

> ... for Merton, the life of the solitary has an inescapably social dimension. His mention [in "Rain and the Rhinoceros"] of the SAC planes flying overhead, the guns booming at Fort Knox, the electrical wires soon to be connected to his hermitage, is telling: he is part of a world in which militarism, technology and

---

17. Merton, "Rain and the Rhinoceros," 17.
18. Ibid., 18.

consumerism are central driving forces. He is part of that world, complicit in it.[19]

Contra his belief on entering Gethsemani that he had left "the world," Merton had come to a place of acknowledgment that as a human being he was unable to leave the world, that he was in the world and the world was in him. Similarly, as a solitary, he takes all his memories and understanding of these concerns with him into the hermitage, throws them into the purifying fire of solitude, the fire that dissolves all illusions and reconciles all contradictions, and receives them back from that fire purged and healed. And he acknowledges that solitude for him is not reclusion, much as he had been fascinated by the thought of the recluses at Camaldoli: speaking for himself, he says, "there is a return from solitude" (SJ, 261) to the larger world.

These affirmations granted, there were still illusions and contradictions to take us back to the ancient notion of the demons, emblematic of the struggle that is inescapable in solitude. It is true that on the one hand the ancient monks thought of the solitude of the desert as a kind of paradise; and there is something undeniably Edenic about Merton's hermitage. "But they also knew [the desert] as a place of the demonic, where the terrors lurking deep within us could be unleashed with a nearly uncontrollable power and fury," writes Christie.[20] Historian Peter Brown expands on this, suggesting, as Christie cites him,

> that the monk in the desert was, above all, a person grappling with his own personality. For the monks ... the demonic was "sensed as an extension of the self. A relationship with the demons involved something more intimate than attack from the outside. . . . The demonic stood not merely for all that was hostile *to* [the human person]; the demons summed up all that was anomalous and incomplete *in* [the human person]."[21]

The hermit as he entered solitude would bring all his anomalies and incompleteness with him, just as Merton recognized that when he entered Gethsemani he had brought "the world" with him. In the hermitage, he would attempt to live "in a silence which so reconciles the contradictions within us that, although they remain within us, they cease to be a problem."[22]

---

19. Christie, "Work of Loneliness," 25–26.

20. Ibid., 29.

21. Brown, *Making of Late Antiquity*, 89–90, cited in Christie, "Work of Loneliness," 33.

22. Merton, *Thoughts in Solitude*, 84.

Merton's 1960 article "Notes for a Philosophy of Solitude" William Shannon regards as "one of the best, most insightful articles Merton ever wrote. Reading it, one has to say: 'This man has been there.'"[23] In this article, Merton sets out his understanding of the responsibility for oneself that must be accepted and honored in solitude:

> One of the first essentials of the interior solitude of which I speak is that it is the actualization of a faith in which a man takes responsibility for his own inner life. He faces its full mystery, in the presence of the invisible God. And he takes upon himself the lonely, barely comprehensible, incommunicable task of working his way through the darkness of his own mystery until he discovers that his mystery and the mystery of God merge into one reality....[24]

... just as the loneliness of the hermit merges with the loneliness of God. As he works through the darkness of his own mystery in the context of a solitary commitment, he finds it necessary to face and accept his own absurdity. In authentic solitude, the solitary will face himself honestly as he was never able to do while "in society." He will seek to have the image of God in which he knows he was made renewed in him as he gives himself daily to the surrender of contemplative prayer. He will let go of the power of the ego, which sustains the false self, and permit the sometimes shy true self to emerge in the beauty that God intends for it, to come "to full maturity in emptiness and solitude."[25] In regard to this true self, George Kilcourse reflects on how the deer that Merton regularly encountered in the vicinity of the hermitage could in his journal and his poetry (especially in "Merlin and the Deer"[26]) represent this shy and true self[27]—deer of course being natural contemplatives. In a late journal entry, Merton describes an awe-inspiring encounter with four of these deer:

> The thing that struck me most—when you look at them directly and in movement, you see what the primitive cave painters saw.... The "deerness" that sums up everything and is sacred and marvelous. A contemplative intuition, yet this is perfectly ordinary, everyday seeing—what everybody ought to see all the time. The deer reveals to me something essential, not only in

23. Shannon, *Silent Lamp*, 159.
24. Merton, "Notes for a Philosophy of Solitude," 68.
25. Ibid., 84.
26. Merton, *Collected Poems*, 736–37.
27. Kilcourse, *Ace of Freedoms*, 76–87. See also Weis, "Merton's Fascination with Deer," 35.

> itself, but in myself.... Something profound. The face of that which is both in the deer and in myself. (DWL, 291)

Merton has captured a primal moment here, a moment of *participation mystique*. The millennia between the twentieth-century monk and the ancient cave painters collapse into the present moment. Any speciesism that might have separated him from these beautiful creatures vanishes. As he watches them, he and they have become one in God's universe. They remain wild, of course—which moves me to wonder: is the true self wild and the false self tame? Then in a remarkable set of images, Merton brings together a vision of the conscious and unconscious dimensions of the hermit's experience. Referring to the wild and overgrown area behind the hermitage, he writes about this in April 1965, not yet in full-time residence in St. Mary of Carmel:

> All this is the geographical unconscious of my hermitage. Out in front the "conscious mind," the ordered fields, the wide valley, the tame woods [the monastery!]. Behind, the "unconscious"— this lush tangle of life and death, full of danger, yet where beautiful beings move, the deer, and where there is a spring of sweet, pure water—buried! (DWL, 224; cf. DWL, 231)

It was his neighbor in the hills, Andy Boone, who had told him about this spring, and Merton was hoping to pump its water to the hermitage (DWL, 220). Alas, it turned out to be contaminated;[28] and after getting sick drinking from it, Merton thenceforward had to bring his drinking water up from the abbey. Behind the hermitage, in all its lushness, there is a tangle of life and death, his wild unconscious, full of untamed energy that Merton knows he must work through as he does the solitary work that the hermitage demands of him. He will do this in the spaciousness that his life in the hermitage makes possible for him, by bringing out of the unconscious into consciousness the wounds that need healing, the contradictions that need resolving, the illusions that need dissolving.

WHAT KIND OF HERMIT?

David Belcastro, in his article on Merton as urban hermit, suggests that Zilboorg would have been more help to Merton if he had accepted and explored, with Merton, the large questions of identity that Merton was struggling with, instead of attacking and criticizing him, and trying to colonize him as a patient. "His preoccupation with institutional definitions and psychological categories prevented him from hearing, and assisting Merton in

---

28. Mott, *Seven Mountains*, 408.

exploring how Merton was answering the question, 'If a monk, what kind of a monk?'"²⁹ That Merton knew he was a monk there is no doubt. But yes, what kind of a monk was he, in his own understanding and in ours, beyond his juridical status as a member in good standing of the Cistercian Order, monk #127 (his laundry number)? So it was with his identity as a hermit: if a hermit, what kind of hermit? There are some of a traditionalist mind who question whether Merton, with his many correspondents—and, in the last year of his life, all his travels, to say nothing of Margie—was a hermit at all. As Zilboorg or Calati did, they are, in my view, making a category error. What does he in fact say of himself as a hermit? He gives one clear answer in his circular letter of Easter 1967 (TMC): he is a writing hermit. He had years before resolved the false dichotomy between being a monk or a writer: he was a writer who was a monk and a monk who was a writer. If he was going to love God or anyone else, it would have to be out of the twofold reality of his life—monk and writer. As a hermit, this remains true: he is a hermit who is a writer, a writing hermit.

Merton had written to Cardinal Valeri in early 1960 about this in regard to how he saw his potential role in the little community at Cuernavaca: "I wanted to help [Dom Gregorio] in forming a small group . . . under his direction and with a limited apostolic outreach: that is to say, with the possibility of certain limited contacts with intellectuals in Mexico City . . ." (WF, 217). This may read as if Merton envisaged a cenobitic role for himself at Cuernavaca (which is close to Mexico City) rather than an eremitical one. Merton, however, would have contrasted the very small Cuernavaca community with the very large community that was Gethsemani in his time there, and would have seen it as a kind of *laura*, a small monastic community eremitical in spirit, with himself as "spiritual father."³⁰ In his sketch of what his life in Mexico would have been like, we encounter the hermit both as spiritual father and as public intellectual, fostering and enjoying "certain limited contacts with intellectuals in Mexico," although it is to shake the head in wondering what "limited" might have meant for Merton, the man of 2100 correspondents.

On March 26, 1964 (TMC), writing to the Carthusian Dom Porion, Merton further articulates his understanding of his vocation as a monastic hermit:

> As I reflect over the past and over God's grace in my life there are only two things that are more or less certain to me: that I have

---

29. Belcastro, "Praying the Questions," 129.

30. For what this meant to Merton, see his "Spiritual Father in the Desert Tradition," 282–305, part of a larger discussion of the hermit life.

been called to be at once a writer and a solitary *secundum quid*. The rest is confusion and uncertainty. At present however I do have a measure of solitude, more than I would have expected in the past, and it is the only thing that helps me to keep sane. I am grateful for this gift from God, with all the paradoxes that it entails and its peculiar interior difficulties, as well as its hidden and dry joys. I think that there is no solitude but a solitude *secundum quid*, lodged in paradox, and that one becomes a solitary in proportion as he can accept the paradox and the irony of his position.

But what does he mean here by *secundum quid*? This term comes from a Thomistic (originally Aristotelian) distinction between something said *without* qualification (*simpliciter*) and something said *with* qualification (*secundum quid*). We have already seen that he has qualified his use of the word *hermit*: he is a writing hermit and a public intellectual, not a hermit in some absolute sense. He is a writer *simpliciter*, then, and a solitary *secundum quid*, that is, a writer pure and simple and a solitary in a qualified sense; being the writer that he was, he *couldn't* be a solitary in an unqualified sense, a hermit pure and simple.[31] As he had written in his journal two years earlier, "obviously I am a writer . . . as well as a contemplative of sorts, and my solitude etc. is that of a writer and teacher, not of a pure hermit" (TTW, 264).

Writing to Dom James on July 28, 1966, and still emotionally involved with Margie, his "friend in Louisville" (letter of July 29, 1966 to Dom James, TMC), he resists Dom James' suggestion that, given the irregularity of the relationship, he should move back into the community, and says what it means for him to be a writing hermit:

> It is true that to some extent I need more normal contacts, but routine work in the community will not provide the kind of contacts that will help me. The kind of contacts that will help me will, I think, be occasional visits or talks with people who do unusual creative work, or are in some way interesting and exceptional people, or come from foreign countries, etc. This will provide challenge and stimulation and perhaps occasions for interesting work.

Evagrius, I surmise, would take a dim view of this statement and regard it as unmistakable evidence of *acedia*. I am also compelled to notice that everything Merton says about the contacts he wants to have also applies to himself: he does unusual and creative work; he is interesting and exceptional; he even comes from a foreign country. It also fairly describes the contacts

---

31. Douglas E. Williams, e-mail message to author, June 17, 2014.

he had already had with visitors and correspondents when he lived in the monastery, and which he wanted to maintain. He wants to stay in the hermitage as a writer and intellectual, and not subject himself to the "routine work in the community" to which he has already given twenty-four years of his life, and which he would, having re-found Eden in the hermitage, find frustrating. Whatever of ego we detect in his letter to Dom James, it is undeniable that he had outgrown the institutional life of the monastery, and was in the right place in the hermitage—which even so he had imperiled by his relationship with his "friend in Louisville," Margie. In the next section of this chapter we will cite Belden Lane's view that it was the hermitage itself that saved the hermit from himself during his time of *amour fou* in the spring and summer of 1966.

AMOUR FOU

The relationship of Merton and Margie encountered many impediments, to use a word used both by Shakespeare (Sonnet 116) and Chuang Tzu.[32] But the textual evidence suggests that their love, although not able finally to sustain a long-term being "in love," continued in spite of these impediments. Evagrius would not of course have seen their relationship as a marriage of true minds. He would very likely have identified it as caused by the presence of the demon of lust, *epithumia*, or as John Eudes Bamberger translates it in *The Praktikos*, "the demon of impurity."[33] Probably this was also Dom James' view, although he may also have simply regarded the relationship as a particularly troublesome example of Merton's volatility. I find it more helpful to think of the relationship as testimony, not to a visitation of the demon of lust, but of a more primal spirit—Eros, the divinity of connectedness, a reality that includes the sexual dimension but is not limited to it.[34] This mischievous divinity had paid a number of brief visits to Merton before he met Margie;[35] and Belden Lane affectionately calls Merton-after-Margie "a crazy

---

32. See note 14.

33. Evagrius, *Praktikos*, 17.

34. Cf. Whitehead and Whitehead, *Holy Eros*. See also Weis, "Merton's Fascination with Deer," in which she extrapolates from Merton's fascination with deer to assert that the mystery of his relationship with them points, in terms of his relationship with Margie, not to *agape*, but to "*eros*, that equally mysterious and valued love between human beings" (42).

35. At first glance, Merton and Margie's connection seems to have come out of nowhere. But a careful reader of the Merton corpus will notice a number of foreshadowings pointing to the possibility that Eros was planning a major visit. Two articles in *The Merton Seasonal* provide background to these foreshadowings: Lauridsen,

old fool."[36] This fits, because he (we can say "he" of Eros—we can only say "it" of the demon of *epithumia*) bestows upon those he visits a kind of divine craziness. Merton and Margie, in the vernacular, were indeed crazy about each other, swimming together in the sea of what the French call *amour fou*, "crazy love." After a number of preliminary visits from Eros, the scene was set; his heart was ready.

Volume 6 of Merton's journals tells the story: from March 31, 1966, when they met in St. Joseph's Hospital in Louisville after Merton's back operation, she being his nurse, to August 20, 1968, when he burns her letters. Before becoming a nurse, she had for a time belonged to a religious community, and had read some of Merton's books; so she knew who he was, and the connection was immediate. There was a significant age difference between them, but it is often part of the craziness of erotic love that any such potential impediment will be dismissed as irrelevant. More to the point, I would conjecture that in a developmental sense they were peers, or near-peers. First, for any woman to enter an intimate relationship with Thomas Merton, she would have had to be a woman of considerable ego-strength. Second, it could also be argued that Merton's psychosexual development had been to some extent arrested at the point at which he entered Gethsemani, put on hold until Eros paid his preliminary visits. Merton was not quite twenty-seven when he entered; Margie (born in October 1941) was twenty-four when they met; the instantaneous and profound character of their connection suggests that developmentally they were well matched. Sometimes it is conjectured that Merton—older, better educated, and a priest—somehow took advantage of his young sweetheart. I find this unconvincing: Merton's journal records that she was as active as he was in moving the relationship forward. The year of their meeting, 1966, was one of the peak years for Roman Catholic priests to leave the active priesthood: it would not have been unreasonable for her to wonder whether Merton, in such a time, might not be among them. She was as crazy about him as he was about her; yet Belden Lane is able to characterize her as "a singular woman of deep intelligence,

---

"Merton and the Feminine," 3–5; and Thurston, "'I never had a sister,'" 4–8. Other adumbrations: the dream of Proverb (February 28, 1958, SFS, 175–76, 182); his August 30, 1959, meeting with Carolyn Quenon (SFS, 322–23); a week later, an encounter with Natasha Spender, wife of the poet, and her friend Margot Dennis, "a Naiad-like creature" (SFS, 326); on his fiftieth birthday, January 31 1965, his admission that one thing on his mind is sex (DWL, 198); the highly erotic passage in "Day of a Stranger," which he wrote in May 1965, about his marrying "the silence of the forest" (219); and his comment in the same essay about sleeping *alone* in the hermitage (222); finally his recollection of Ann Winser (June 26, 1965, DWL, 259).

36. Lane, "Merton's Hermitage," 141.

integrity and compassion"[37]—qualities that for Merton must have weighed on the other side of the scale from whatever were their scruples about their coexisting commitments. I am trusting that should he ever produce a revised version of the *Divine Comedy*, Dante would place Merton and Margie in the *Purgatorio*, and not the *Inferno*.

On April 19 he receives a letter from her (LTL, 41), a letter he had asked her to write (LTL, 122). This launches a series of letters, phone calls, and surreptitious meetings that continues for two months, in a romantic journey marked, as his journal reveals, by agony and ecstasy, certainty and ambivalence, in relatively equal proportion. Then on June 13, the gatehouse brother listens in on a conversation between them, and reports him to Dom James. Merton learns of this, and goes to see Dom James the next day. Dom James, thinking that Merton's life alone in the hermitage had made him vulnerable, or, better, had activated the vulnerability of which Dom James was well aware, suggests that he return to the community, but Merton resists this suggestion. Contact between them continues, but less frequently. He begins to mistrust her and to be critical of her. He reaches a low point, in my view, when on September 4 he imputes "seductiveness" to her (LTL, 124), and when on October 31 he says that "the whole thing was a mistake, a subtle and well-meant seduction to which I too easily and completely yielded" (LTL, 154). This is Merton as cad, essentially placing the entire responsibility for the relationship, the ambivalence it generated in him, and the trouble he got into with Dom James over it onto Margie, something patently unfair. This simply does not compute with what he had said about her undisguised and frank affection for him, to which he of his own free will had responded by asking her to write to him.

On September 8, Merton makes in the presence of Dom James a commitment of permanence in the hermit life—"to live in solitude for the rest of life in so far as my health may permit" (LTL, 129)—and then the next day phones Margie from Bardstown (LTL, 130). On October 31, he says in his journal that the affair is "clearly *over*" (LTL, 154)—but contacts continue. On June 21, 1967, he calls her again and discovers that she has broken up with her fiancé, who has been in Vietnam with the American forces (LTL, 253). Her fiancé! Complication and contradiction: *neither* of them had in fact been free to initiate a relationship in the first place. Margie was engaged (the engagement was later broken off), and, to continue the metaphor, Merton was already married to the monastery, and in forming a relationship with Merton, Margie was breaking her nursing code of ethics; but even these are the kinds of impediments to which those immersed in *amour*

---

37. Ibid., 149 n. 81.

fou typically pay no heed. She sends him a card at Christmas 1967 (OSM, 29)—and this is the last reference to her contacting him. March 31, 1968 comes, the second anniversary of their meeting; but he doesn't refer to it in his journal. Then on August 20, another anniversary: the third anniversary of his entry into the hermitage. A major life-shift is approaching—his journey to Asia. "Today, among other things, I burned M.'s letters. Incredible stupidity in 1966! I did not even glance at any one of them" (OSM, 157). So their shared story ends; but as he had said on February 6, 1967, "I can never again be the person that did not know or love her in a deep, mysterious way, because we gave ourselves to each other almost as if we were married" (LTL, 193). The classic ontological view of marriage supports this intuition. Even if a marriage ends in a public and societal sense through separation or divorce, the parties *will always have been married to each other*; and this was true, I believe, on their own level, as Merton suggests, of Margie and himself as well.

In his journal for March 30, 1958, Palm Sunday, eight years before he and Margie met, Merton had spoken painfully of love: "One reason I am so grateful for this morning's sermon [by Father John of the Cross, a monk to whom Merton was close] is that my worst and inmost sickness is the despair of ever being truly able to love, because I despair of ever being worthy of love" (SFS, 187). Summary statements by three careful readers of Merton tell us how far he came from this despair through his relationship with Margie, and how his "inmost sickness" was healed. Here, first, is Michael Mott's final assessment of what the relationship gave to Merton (regrettably, we have no way of knowing what it ultimately meant to Margie):

> He loved greatly and was greatly loved. He was overwhelmed by the experience and it changed him forever. While this brought a sense of humiliation no exercise of Rancé could have achieved, Thomas Merton never again talked of his inability to love or to be loved.[38]

Belden Lane also speaks of Merton loving and being loved (as does Mott, he means in an intimate sense) for the first time in his life:

> ... in meeting a woman with whom he shared so many interests, in learning to love and be loved for the first time in his life, and (most importantly) in giving up the relationship as something that ultimately would have destroyed them both, Merton

---

38. Mott, *Seven Mountains*, 348.

Solitude and Love

discovered a deepening rather than a denial of his vocation as a solitary.[39]

A threefold cord not being quickly broken, I add to these two assessments a word from Suzanne Zuercher: "Nothing before his relationship with Margie had convinced him that he was lovable. And nothing after their relationship began was needed to prove to him that he was lovable."[40]

Eros had done his work.

LOVE AND SOLITUDE

In her *Revelations of Divine Love*, Julian of Norwich, one of Merton's favorite mystical writers, asks what God's "meaning" is, and answers her own question by saying, "Love: love is [God's] meaning." I take this to indicate that she understood God's fundamental intention toward the creation to be one of love. She knew, as any reader of the New Testament knows, that "God is love" (1 John 4:9). So God's "meaning," love, came out of God's own being, which is love. God wants to share the divine love with the cosmos, and desires that we humans share in that love by loving God, one another, and the creation.

I begin this section of this chapter with these thoughts in case it may seem to the reader that in describing the love that Merton and Margie had for each other, I have neglected the love of God. Merton had a very strong sense of the love of God from the time Christian faith awakened for him in his mid-twenties. His early journals, notably those portions of the journals published as *The Sign of Jonas*, testify unmistakably to this, many of these testimonies being strongly affective: "I have only time for eternity, which is to say for love, love, love" (SJ, 124–25).[41] In his "Notes for a Philosophy of Solitude," however, his attempts to move to Camaldoli or Latin America having come to an end, there is by contrast a somewhat severe view of love, in its relation to solitude:

> [The solitary's] solitude is, for him, simply reality. He could not break away from [the will of God that he be a solitary] even if he wanted to. To be a prisoner of this love is to be free. . . . Hence the life of solitude is a life of love without consolation, a life that is fruitful . . . with the will of God; and all that has his will in it

---

39. Lane, "Merton's Hermitage," 139.
40. Zuercher, *Ground of Love and Truth*, 18.
41. Cf. Christie, "Rediscovering Love's World," 64–82.

is full of significance, even when it appears to make no sense at all.[42]

This is love as will, not as feeling. It commits the solitary to grit his teeth and live without affective consolation in union with the will of God as he perceives it. It is a paradoxical love: the prisoner is free, and his experience of solitude is "full of significance" even when it makes "no sense at all." It is a stern and bleak view of love, especially as compared with his views of love in his last years. Although expressed in the third person ("the solitary"), it seems to me another example of autobiography masked as general understanding. This is how he was feeling about solitude in 1960.

Merton, as we know, identified the false self with the *individual*—that is, the human being divided into a discrete or atomized unit, as it were, spiritually if not socially separated from the human community, and the true self with the *person*; in this terminology he was following Emmanuel Mounier and Jacques Maritain. In "Love and Solitude," then, Merton asks, "What is the person? Precisely, he is one in the unity which is love. He is undivided in himself because he is open to all. He is open to all because the one love that is the source of all, the form of all and the end of all is one in him and in all."[43] What Evagrius wanted to happen for all the monks and hermits is what Merton is describing here; he is also describing what Arasteh meant by final integration. The human being identified as a person, united in himself, as Merton so often says, has included and transcended the divisions caused by the fall. He has opened himself to "the one love that is the source of all," or, as Dante says in the last line of the *Divine Comedy*, "the love which moves the sun and the other stars," or, as Merton says in his journal entry for November 4, 1964, the love that "keeps us all together in being" (DWL, 162). This is love as both ontology and mystical union. He continues in the same vein:

> Love is not a problem, not an answer to a question. Love knows no question. It is the ground of all, and questions arise only insofar as we are divided, absent, estranged, alienated from that ground. . . . To recognize ourselves as grounded in our true ground, love, is to recognize that we cannot be without it.[44]

He has already said that it is love that keeps us all together in being: therefore we *are* being kept in being by love whether or not we know it, or think about it, or feel it. What Paul Tillich (whom Merton had read) says about

---

42. Merton, "Notes for a Philosophy of Solitude," 83.
43. Merton, "Love and Solitude," 17.
44. Ibid., 17–18.

God as the ground of being is echoed here with Merton calling love the ground of being: for God is love, and what he says here is very close to Julian's conviction as well as Tillich's.

His writing about love up to this point has a measured quality about it: but in "Love and Need: Is Love a Package or a Message?" he abandons the measured approach; the river of love overflows its banks. It was published in December 1966, and so must have been written when, although he was not seeing Margie, his experience with her was still very fresh for him. Here he describes his own experience:

> ... love takes you out of yourself. You lose control. You "fall." You get hurt. It upsets the ordinary routine of life. You become emotional, imaginative, vulnerable, foolish. You are no longer content to eat and sleep, make money and have fun. You now have to let yourself be carried away with this force that is stronger than reason and more imperious even than business.[45]

Indeed he was taken out of himself, if by this is meant that his ordinary eremitical and monastic routine was seriously disrupted. He did lose control, he did fall, he did get hurt (as did Margie). He did become emotional, vulnerable, and foolish (he had always been imaginative). He did yield to Eros, did let himself be carried away with this force that is stronger than reason, which is what his reasonable friends, notably John Eudes Bamberger and Jim Wygal, kept trying to tell him. How much reason was there in his apparent belief, especially in the early months with Margie, that he could maintain a relationship with her *and* live the life of a monastic hermit? Once again he is walking on two paths simultaneously, not a reasonable thing to do. If the possibility of the bilocation about which the medieval scholastics argued had been available to Merton, it is likely that he would have jumped at it. But it isn't available to him or to any of us, and so reason, for a time, had to be set aside. Pascal told us this centuries ago: "The heart has its reasons that the reason does not know." Thus, neither disrespecting reason nor being dominated by it, Merton, who always writes out of his own experience, rational or otherwise, offers these thoughts about love's meaning:

> Love is the revelation of our deepest personal meaning, value and identity. But this revelation remains impossible as long as we are the prisoner of our own egoism. I cannot find myself in myself, but only in another. My true meaning and worth are shown to me not in my estimate of myself, but in the eyes of the one who loves me; and that one must love me as I am, with

---

45. Merton, "Love and Need," 26.

> my faults and limitations.... What matters is this infinitely precious message which I can discover only in my love for another person. And this message, this secret, is not fully revealed to me unless at the same time I am able to see and understand the mysterious and unique worth of the one I love.[46]

Love can be willed, yes, and at difficult moments this is an important dimension of love; and it can also be understood as the ground of being. But beyond both of these, it is revelation. The worth of the lovers is *revealed*, each to the other; each one's "meaning, value and identity" is received as if *revealed truth*, an opening from the heart of existence to those who love. Even if anticipated or hoped for, when it comes, it is a surprise, a revelation.

The most substantial, indeed magisterial, reflection on the meanings of love for Merton is to be found in Douglas Christie's 1989 article "Rediscovering Love's World: Thomas Merton's Love Poems and the Language of Ecstasy." It is a review essay on Merton's *Eighteen Poems*, a synopsis of Merton's reflections on love as found in his journals, and a consideration of the dynamics of his relationship with Margie and of its effects on Merton and on his understanding of love. The poems, he says,

> present us with an opportunity for rethinking a central issue in spirituality, namely the experience of love.... The astonishing newness of this love [for Margie] and its undeniable power compelled Merton to rethink some of his most cherished assumptions about love and the meaning of the spiritual life.[47]

They can also be understood, from a longer perspective, "as the fruition of a life-long search to enter more deeply into the experience of love."[48] Merton now experienced love as a modality of healing and as a release from perfectionism, and became ready to acknowledge "the depth of his own need with greater honesty, and ... to perceive this need as integral to the experience of love."[49] He also experienced it as a way of recovering paradise, one of his longtime mystical themes, which turned from black-and-white into technicolor as the relationship developed.

Even at the end of their relationship, when Merton knew he was not likely to see her again, he states that in his exile, the paradise engendered by her touch remained a vivid and enduring reality: "the edge of this hot town /

---

46. Ibid., 35.
47. Christie, "Rediscovering Love's World," 65.
48. Ibid., 66.
49. Ibid., 75.

Is still the edge of Eden."⁵⁰ Here is Christie's moving summary statement of how love (how easily, I note, we ascribe a kind of personal agency to it: hence the Greek personification of the experience of love in the divine Eros) transformed Merton:

> He discovered that through an honest acknowledgement of his own brokenness, he could begin to reach out in love to another human being. He found that only by risking the chaos of abandoning control and becoming lost—emotionally, physically and spiritually, in an experience of human love—could he enter more deeply into love's world. His honesty regarding the depth of his need opened him to a shared experience of human love the likes of which he had never known. He came to see that obedience to the fire of love's intimate touch, painful as it was, helped to heal past wounds and enabled him to give new meaning to the powerful symbols of birth, creation and paradise. The use of these symbols reveals that, for Merton, the experience of love brought about nothing less than rebirth or re-creation.⁵¹

And, I would repeat, recovery of paradise. Merton after Margie was living in a qualitatively new world, "love's world," as Christie says. He could have taken as his own Miranda's words from *The Tempest*: "How beauteous mankind is! Oh, brave new world, that has such people in't!" (V.i.183–84).

In the mid-1950s, as we have seen, Merton tried very hard to move to Camaldoli's *eremo*. The difference between what that move would very likely have meant for him, if successful, and where he ended up—in his own hermitage at Gethsemani, an experience challenged to its foundations by his relationship with Margie—is astonishing. From what he says in the letters about hiddenness, poverty, and abnegation, to what he says about love during and after his time with Margie, represents a shift that is nothing short of tectonic in his understanding of both solitude and love.

It is a curious aspect of the letters that although in them Merton talks continually about solitude, he very seldom says what he means by the term. In Letters 3 and 12 he speaks about silence, also saying in Letter 12 that, in solitude, he wants to suffer in silence. In Letter 3 he also says that he wants relief from the active life, community life at Gethsemani, which

---

50. Merton, "A Long Call Is Made Out of Wheels," in Christie, "Rediscovering Love's World," 79.

51. Christie, "Rediscovering Love's World," 81–82.

together with the clearly excessive writing burden he has placed upon himself is exhausting him. In LETTER 5 he says he wants to lead "the hidden life," in ascetical understanding a way of uniting the monk with the life Jesus lived in Nazareth between his appearance in the temple at the age of twelve (Luke 2:41–52) and the beginning of his public ministry (Luke 3:21–23a). In LETTER 3 he had already spoken of his desire to be "nothing": "If I need solitude, it's because I need to *be nothing*, to disappear, to be completely obscure and forgotten—*tamquam purgamenta huius mundi* [like the rubbish of the world],[52] a self-loathing and self-lacerating comment. In LETTER 12 he says that he seeks "poverty" in solitude; and finally, in LETTER 33, he tells Archbishop Montini that he wants to live in solitude in order to give more time to prayer and meditation. Beyond these few references, the letters reveal little texture of what the solitude he was so earnestly seeking would have meant to him.

Once love finds him, however, in the spring of 1966, the meaning and content of solitude changes dramatically. Here is a journal entry from April 14, when it still seemed possible that the relationship could continue in some form or other:

> One thing has suddenly hit me—that nothing counts except love and that a solitude that is not simply the wide-openness of love and freedom is nothing. Love and solitude are the one ground of true maturity and freedom. Solitude that is just solitude and nothing else (i.e. *excludes* everything else but solitude) is worthless. True solitude embraces everything, for it is the fullness of love that rejects nothing and no one,[53] is open to All in All. (LTL, 40)

For anyone familiar with the New Testament, it is impossible to read this and not think of 1 Cor 13, Paul's paean to love: "if I have all faith, so as to remove mountains, but do not have love, I am nothing" (13:2). In fact Merton *equates* solitude and love: "True solitude . . . is the fullness of love . . ." One goes into solitude for love, and by love and in love one lives in solitude, the true solitude. His concluding phrase I take to mean that love/solitude is open to God in everything, open to the All in All things, to the Real in all that is Real, as the Sufis would say. True love and true solitude, then, cannot be in competition with each other. "Clearly this love is not a contradiction of my solitude but a mysterious part of it. It fits strangely and without conflict into my inner life of meditation and prayer . . ." (LTL, 59). By "this love," he does not mean anything abstract or philosophical, but the life-giving love

---

52. 1 Cor 4:13 (Vulgate and NRSV).
53. Cf. Merton, *Asian Journal*, 233.

that he and Margie are sharing. So on June 19, he addresses Margie directly in his "Midsummer Diary for M." as he expands on this conviction: "To be alone in a solitude that is with you, though without your bodily presence, is certainly a special kind of freedom: as though we were even free of time and space, and could be together at will in our love, in all its simplicity" (LTL, 319). I find it telling here that he speaks of being "without your bodily presence," rather than of her physical presence. The first term speaks much more directly than the second of the erotic character of his assertion. She was with him in his solitude, and always would be, even through and beyond his frettings, his criticisms, the end of the relationship and even his regrets. He also makes a link between freedom ("a special kind of freedom") and love, as does Anselmo Giabbani. Monastic education, says Giabbani, begins in the community, the cenobium,

> and fosters the monk's growth toward greater and greater freedom—freedom, that is, to follow the inner guidance of the Holy Spirit. This is the whole meaning of the passage from the Cenobio to the Eremo: not the search for solitude [as such], but the love of freedom. And the freedom to love.[54]

So even if Merton's concept of solitude was in itself relatively undeveloped at the time of the letters, and if he had gone then to Camaldoli, might he perhaps have come, with Giabbani as his mentor, to a place of freedom and love? So far from solitude being a path to abnegation, poverty, misery, and a view of oneself as rubbish, might he have come to know and live out solitude as one reality with freedom and love? This would only have happened, of course, if he had learned in some other way what he learned with Margie: that he was both lovable and capable of love.

One particular comment of Merton's about solitude and love very much needs to be carefully examined and understood before we conclude. On July 8, 1966, he speaks of a choice that he has made: tentatively, I conjecture, given that the relationship was still continuing, but one that grew into a solid and permanent position. "I am alone," he says, "and I love her, but the choice between her and solitude presented itself and I chose solitude" (LTL, 93). He loves her, and he chooses to live in solitude, to continue to live as a solitary. However, it must be understood that he was choosing not between love *as such* and solitude, but between *marriage* and solitude. Having chosen solitude, he continues to love her, and to experience her presence with him; but he has realized that for both their sakes, the freedom that is part of

---

54. Quoted in Matus, *Mystery of Romuald*, 21.

love required that she be set free to live her own life, to marry if she chooses to, and that he continue, in love and freedom, to live in the hermitage.

Belden Lane offers this thoughtful comment, first, about what the relationship meant for Merton in terms of love and solitude, and second, about the critical function of the hermitage in enabling him to persist in the decision he had tentatively made in July 1966:

> ... a deeper personal authenticity had been born in him through the solitude of the hermitage, making possible a new intimacy. A resolute honesty had started to emerge in the woods.... Hence, in meeting a woman with whom he shared so many interests, in learning to love and be loved for the first time in his life, and (most importantly) in giving up the relationship as something that ultimately would have destroyed them both, Merton discovered a deepening rather than a denial of his vocation as a solitary....
>
> Ultimately, it was the house that saved him. Giving himself to the cell,[55] Merton continued to practice the solitude out of which love had emerged and into which love had to return.[56]

Merton would have agreed. "Keeping to the woods was what saved me" (LTL, 260). These were the woods to which Dom James so long before had granted him access. The hermitage permitted him to live in the woods, to be close to birds and deer and snakes and pine trees, and to sun, moon, and stars. Both before and during the hermitage years, the woods were his "cell." The horarium he sketches out in "Day of a Stranger," repeated day after day, grounded him and eventually clarified for him that although his solitude could include, *had* to include, love and freedom, it could not include marriage.

I give a last word to one of Merton's favorite poets, Rilke: "Love consists of this: two solitudes that meet, protect and greet each other." Margie and Merton, two solitudes—not in the sense that they did not have relationships with other human beings, but in the sense that as Merton so often affirmed, every human being is solitary at the deepest level—met, greeted, indeed embraced, and then *protected* each other by parting and moving on with their own lives, changed forever by love. We place beside this the two solitudes that were and are Merton and God; these also embraced and protected each other. Does this mean that they were both changed forever by love? Does God change in this way? Does God need "protection" from us? The process theologians, moving our understanding of God beyond the changelessness

---

55. Cf. Evagrius, *Praktikos*, 28.
56. Lane, "Merton's Hermitage," 139–40.

mandated by Greek philosophy, would say so, and probably would be ready to affirm what Merton incandescently and memorably says of God in the concluding paragraph of "Hagia Sophia":

> A vagrant, a destitute wanderer with dusty feet, finds his way down a new road. A homeless God, lost in the night, without papers, without identification, without even a number, a frail expendable exile lies down in desolation under the sweet stars of the world and entrusts Himself to sleep.[57]

A new road? Yes, always, and also a very old road, the road of love. The spiritual journey sketched out in this book, which started with Merton's anxious, even obsessional attempt to move from Gethsemani to Camaldoli, had come to its completeness in a union of solitude and love.

And the sweet stars that shine even on God, on Merton and Margie, and on all of us? They too, like us, are moved by the "one love that is the source of all,"[58] by Dante's "love which moves the sun and the other stars."

---

57. Merton, "Hagia Sophia," in Merton, *Collected Poems*, 264.
58. Merton, "Love and Solitude," 17.

Bibliography

A NOTE ON READING MERTON

Thomas Merton is not always an easy writer to get into. His most famous book, *The Seven Storey Mountain*, which many people pick up first, is an uneven work. The story is a very engaging one, and Merton's combination of high style and slang keeps us reading in the narrative sections. But it also contains turgid chunks of semi-digested theology; and there are places where his satisfaction at having found a faith, a working religious tradition and a place in the world transmutes unattractively into rigidity, smugness and triumphalism. These were less noticeable when the book came out, in a time when Roman Catholicism appeared to be a fortress built on a rock of unchanging truth and practice (not that that had ever been the case, but that was the perception, particularly among people who were not Roman Catholics). But readers today are more aware, more critical and more individualistic; and too many potential friends of Merton have been put off by these features of the SSM.

Another problem is that the book is often referred to as his autobiography, when in fact it is only *the first installment* of an autobiographical series. He published it when he was thirty-three, and lived another two decades. Those years are presented in his journals, now available in seven volumes, and also available in summary in *The Intimate Merton*, edited by Patrick Hart and Jonathan Montaldo. So if you are a new reader of Merton, I would encourage you to read *The Intimate Merton* first. That will give you an outline of Merton's life and show you how much he grew over the years. After that, it will be safe to read the SSM.

Then, to fill out your basic acquaintance with the breadth of his writing and thought, read *Thomas Merton: Spiritual Master*, edited by

Lawrence S. Cunningham. That book provides a good general introduction to Merton, offers excerpts from his most important writings, and places them in context, both in terms of Merton's personal history and his ever-developing interests. And when you read Cunningham, don't miss "Day of a Stranger" (214–22; also available in *Thomas Merton: Selected Essays*, 232–39), a little masterpiece, in my view the most brilliant piece he ever wrote. For two very perceptive takes on Merton, I also commend the Lane and Sheldrake articles in the bibliography below.

Another brief volume, a very personal take on Merton that I can warmly recommend, is Ontario writer J. S. Porter's *Thomas Merton: Hermit at the Heart of Things*. Then after that, a more recent book, *Thomas Merton: Monk on the Edge*, the book of essays published in 2012 by Canadian scholars for the Thomas Merton Society of Canada, and available through the Society's office (merton.ca). Then, if you are still motivated, you can move on to the full seven volumes of the journals and the five volumes of the selected letters. Once you've read this much, or even half as much, you are well and truly launched on the good ship Thomas Merton! Happy sailing, happy reading.

Albert, John. "Lights Across the Ridge: Thomas Merton and Henry David Thoreau." *The Merton Annual* 1 (1988) 271–317.

Allchin, A. M. "The Importance of One Good Place." *Cistercian Studies* 14 (1979) 93–97.

Aquinas, Thomas, Saint. *Summa Theologica*. Translated by the Fathers of the English Dominican Province. New York: Benziger, 1947.

Arasteh, Reza. *Final Integration in the Adult Personality: A Measure for Health, Social Change, and Leadership*. Leiden: Brill, 1968.

Bamberger, John Eudes. "A Homily." *Continuum* 7 (1969) 226.

Basset, Bernard. *The Noonday Devil: Spiritual Support in Middle Age*. Garden City, NY: Doubleday, 1968.

Bear, Virginia. "A Woodshed Full of French Angels: Multilingual Merton." *The Merton Annual* 15 (2002) 136–54.

Belcastro, David. "Praying the Questions: Merton of Times Square, Last of the Urban Hermits." *The Merton Annual* 20 (2007) 123–50.

Belisle, Peter-Damian. *The Language of Silence: The Changing Face of Monastic Solitude*. London: Darton, Longman and Todd, 2003.

Benedict, Saint. *The Rule of Saint Benedict*. Translated by Anthony C. Meisel and M. L. del Mastro. Garden City, NY: Doubleday, 1975.

Bochen, Christine M. "A Time of Transition: A Selection of Letters from the Earliest Correspondence of Thomas Merton and Ernesto Cardenal." Translated by Robert Goizueta. *The Merton Annual* 8 (1995) 162–200.

Buchanan, William. "The Search for Brahmachari." *The Merton Seasonal* 19 (1994) 11–13.

Burton, Patricia A. *Merton Vade Mecum: A Quick-Reference Bibliographic Handbook*. 3rd ed. Louisville: The Thomas Merton Center, 2013.

———. *More Than Silence: A Bibliography of Thomas Merton*. With a special section on rare books by Albert Romkema. Lanham, MD: Scarecrow, 2008.

Burton-Christie [now Christie], Douglas E. "Place-Making as Contemplative Practice." *Anglican Theological Review* 91 (2009) 347–71.

———. "Rediscovering Love's World: Thomas Merton's Love Poems and the Language of Ecstasy." *Cross Currents* 39 (1989) 64–82.

———. *The Word in the Desert: Scripture and the Quest for Holiness in Early Christian Monasticism*. New York: Oxford University Press, 1993.

———. "The Work of Loneliness: Solitude, Emptiness and Compassion." *Anglican Theological Review* 88 (2006) 25–45.

Calati, Benedetto. "Thomas Merton: un dono di Dio per i monaci del nostro tempo." *Vita Monastica* 135 (1978) 9–16.

Carfagna, Rosemarie. *Contemplation and Midlife Crisis: Examples from Classical and Contemporary Spirituality*. Mahway, NJ: Paulist, 2008.

Cashen, Richard Anthony. *Solitude in the Thought of Thomas Merton*. Kalamazoo, MI: Cistercian, 1981.

Cassian, John. *The Institutes*. Translated by Boniface Ramsey. New York: Newman, 2000.

Chaucer, Geoffrey. *The Works of Geoffrey Chaucer*. Translated by F. N. Robinson. 2nd ed. Boston: Houghton Mifflin, 1957.

Colegate, Isabel. *A Pelican in the Wilderness: Hermits, Solitaries and Recluses*. London: HarperCollins, 2002.

Crider, Glenn. "Editor's Note." Preface to David Belcastro, "Praying the Questions: Merton of Times Square, Last of the Urban Hermits." *The Merton Annual* 20 (2007) 123–24.

Dante Alighieri. *Paradiso*. Translated by Robert Hollander and Jean Hollander. New York: Doubleday, 2007.

———. *Purgatorio*. Translated by Jean Hollander and Robert Hollander. New York: Doubleday, 2003.

Deignan, Kathleen. "Cosmopolitan: Thomas Merton's Urbane Spirituality." *The Merton Seasonal* 39 (2014) 15–21.

Evagrius, Ponticus. *The Praktikos and Chapters on Prayer*. Translated by John Eudes Bamberger. Trappist, KY: Cistercian, 1972.

Frigerio, Salvatore. *Camaldoli: Note storiche spirituali artistiche*. Verucchio, Italy: Pazzini, 2005.

Ghini, Emmanuela. *Oltre Ogni Limite: Nazarena monaca reclusa 1945–1990*. Casale Monferrato, Italy: Piemme, 1993.

Giabbani, Anselmo. *L'Eremo: Vita e spiritualità nel monastero camaldolese primitivo*. Brescia, Italy: Morcelliana, 1945.

Grayston, Donald. "'Monastic in His [Own] Way': Thomas Merton and Leonard Cohen." *The Merton Seasonal* 34 (2009) 3–9.

———. *Thomas Merton: The Development of a Spiritual Theologian*. New York: Mellen, 1985.

Guigo, 5th Prior of the Grande Chartreuse. *The Solitary Life: A Letter of Guigo*. Translated by Thomas Merton. Arlington, VT: Carthusian Booklets, 2006.

Guiver, George. "Behind the Scenes in Rome." *CR Review* 446 (2014) 9–11.

Harford, James. *Merton and Friends: A Joint Biography of Thomas Merton, Robert Lax and Edward Rice*. New York: Continuum, 2006.

Hart, Patrick, ed. *Thomas Merton, Monk: A Monastic Tribute*. 2nd ed. Kalamazoo, MI: Cistercian, 1983.

Henry, Gray, and Jonathan Montaldo, eds. *We Are Already One: Thomas Merton's Message of Hope*. Louisville: Fons Vitae, 2014.

Holloway, Julia Bolton, and David Jones. "Father Charles Brandt, Canadian Hermit and Ecologist." citydesert.wordpress.com/2013/03/29/father-charles-brandt-canadian-hermit-and-ecologist/.

Kerr, David. "Convert Priest Thrilled to Host Pope and Archbishop of Canterbury." Catholic News Agency, March 9, 2012. http://www.catholicnewsagency.com/news/convert-priest-thrilled-to-host-pope-and-archbishop-of-canterbury/.

Kilcourse, George. *Ace of Freedoms: Thomas Merton's Christ*. Notre Dame: University of Notre Dame Press, 1993.

Kull, Robert. *Solitude: Seeking Wisdom in Extremes; A Year Alone in the Patagonia Wilderness*. Novato, CA: New World, 2008.

Labrie, Ross, and Angus Stuart, eds. *Thomas Merton: Monk on the Edge*. North Vancouver, BC: Thomas Merton Society of Canada, 2012.

Lane, Belden C. "Merton's Hermitage: Bachelard, Domestic Space, and Spiritual Transformation." *Spiritus* 4 (2004) 123–50.

Lauridson, James R. "Merton and the Feminine: A Reflection." *The Merton Seasonal* 15.1 (1990) 3–5.

Leclerq, Jean. *Alone with God: The Eremitical Life, According to the Doctrine of the Blessed Paul Giustiniani*. Preface by Thomas Merton. New York: Farrar, Straus and Giroux, 1961.

———. *Seul avec Dieu: La vie érémetique, d'après la doctrine du Bienheureux Paul Giustiniani*. Preface by Thomas Merton. Paris: Plon, 1955.

Lovelace, Richard. *Dynamics of Spiritual Life: An Evangelical Theology of Renewal*. Downers Grove, IL: InterVarsity, 1979.

Matus, Thomas. *The Mystery of Romuald and the Five Brothers: Stories from the Benedictines and Camaldolese*. Trabuco Canyon, CA: Source Books/Hermitage Books, 1994.

———. *Nazarena: An American Anchoress*. New York: Paulist, 1998.

Merton, Thomas. "Action and Contemplation in Saint Bernard." *Collectanea* (January 1953) 26–31; (July 1953) 203–61; (April 1954) 105–21.

———. *The Asian Journal of Thomas Merton*. Edited by Naomi Burton et al.; Amiya Chakravarty, consulting ed. New York: New Directions, 1973.

———. *Bread in the Wilderness*. New York: New Directions, 1953.

———. *Cassian and the Fathers: Initiation into the Monastic Tradition 1*. Edited by Patrick F. O'Connell. Kalamazoo, MI: Cistercian, 2005.

——— *Cold War Letters*. Edited by Christine M. Bochen and William H. Shannon. Maryknoll, NY: Orbis, 2006.

———. *The Collected Poems of Thomas Merton*. New York: New Directions, 1977.

———. *Conjectures of a Guilty Bystander*. Garden City, NY: Doubleday, 1968.

———. *Contemplation in a World of Action*. Garden City, NY: Doubleday, 1973.

———. *The Courage for Truth: Letters to Writers*. Edited by Christine M. Bochen. San Diego: Harcourt Brace Jovanovich, 1993.

———. *Dancing in the Water of Life: Seeking Peace in the Hermitage*. Edited by Robert E. Daggy. San Francisco: HarperSanFrancisco, 1997.

———. "Day of a Stranger." In *Thomas Merton, Spiritual Master*, edited by Lawrence S. Cunningham, 214–22. New York: Paulist, 1992.

———. *Disputed Questions*. London: Hollis and Carter, 1961.

———. *Eighteen Poems*. Edited by James Laughlin. New York: New Directions, 1985.

———. *Entering the Silence: Becoming a Monk and Writer*. Edited by Jonathan Montaldo. San Francisco: HarperSanFrancisco, 1996.

———. "Final Integration: Toward a 'Monastic Therapy.'" In *Contemplation in a World of Action*, 219–31. Garden City, NY: Doubleday, 1973.

———. "From Pilgrimage to Crusade." In *Mystics and Zen Masters*, 91–112. New York: Dell, 1967.

———. *The Hidden Ground of Love: Letters on Religious Experience and Social Concerns*. Edited by William H. Shannon. New York: Farrar, Straus and Giroux, 1985.

———. *"Honorable Reader": Reflections on My Work*. Edited by Robert E. Daggy. New York: Crossroad, 1991.

———. *The Intimate Merton*. Edited by Patrick Hart and Jonathan Montaldo. San Francisco: HarperSanFrancisco, 1999.

———. *An Introduction to Christian Mysticism: Initiation into the Monastic Tradition 3*. Edited by Patrick F. O'Connell. Kalamazoo, MI: Cistercian, 2008.

———. *Learning to Love: Exploring Solitude and Freedom*. Edited by Christine M. Bochen. San Francisco: HarperSanFrancisco, 1997.

———. "A Life Free from Care." *Cistercian Studies* 3 (1970) 217–26.

———. *Love and Living*. Edited by Naomi Burton Stone and Patrick Hart. New York: Farrar, Straus and Giroux, 1979.

———. "Love and Need: Is Love a Package or a Message?" In *Love and Living*. Edited by Naomi Burton Stone and Patrick Hart, 25–37. New York: Farrar, Straus and Giroux, 1979.

———. "Love and Solitude." In *Love and Living*. Edited by Naomi Burton Stone and Patrick Hart, 15–24. New York: Farrar, Straus and Giroux, 1979.

———. *Monastic Observances: Initiation into the Monastic Tradition 5*. Edited by Patrick F. O'Connell. Kalamazoo, MI: Cistercian, 2010.

———. *Mystics and Zen Masters*. New York: New Directions, 1967.

———. "The Neurotic Personality in the Monastic Life." *The Merton Annual* 4 (1992) 3–19.

———. *New Seeds of Contemplation*. New York: New Directions, 1962.

———. *No Man Is an Island*. New York: Harcourt, Brace, 1955.

———. "Notes for a Philosophy of Solitude." In *Selected Essays*. Edited by Patrick F. O'Connell, 65–85. Maryknoll, NY: Orbis, 2013.

———. *Pre-Benedictine Monasticism: Initiation into the Monastic Tradition 2*. Edited by Patrick F. O'Connell. Kalamazoo, MI: Cistercian, 2006.

———. *The Other Side of the Mountain: The End of the Journey*. Edited by Patrick Hart. San Francisco: HarperSanFrancisco, 1998.

———. *Raids on the Unspeakable*. New York: New Directions, 1966.

———. "Rain and the Rhinoceros." In *Raids on the Unspeakable*, 9–23. New York: New Directions, 1966.

———. *The Rule of Saint Benedict: Initiation into the Monastic Tradition 4*. Edited by Patrick F. O'Connell. Kalamazoo, MI: Cistercian, 2009.

———. *The School of Charity: Letters on Religious Renewal and Spiritual Direction*. Edited by Patrick Hart. San Diego: Harcourt Brace Jovanovich, 1990.

———. *A Search for Solitude: Pursuing the Monk's True Life*. Edited by Lawrence S. Cunningham. San Francisco: HarperSanFrancisco, 1996.

———. *The Secular Journal of Thomas Merton*. Garden City, NY: Doubleday, 1969.

———. *Seeds of Contemplation*. Norfolk, CT: New Directions, 1949.

———. *The Seven Storey Mountain*. New York: Harcourt Brace, 1948.

———. *The Sign of Jonas*. Garden City, NY: Doubleday, 1953.

———. *Silence dans le ciel*. Edited by the Monks of La Pierre-Qui-Vire. Translated by Marie Tadié. Paris: Arthaud, 1955.

———. *Silence in Heaven: A Book of the Monastic Life*. New York: Studio, 1956.

———. *The Silent Life*. New York: Farrar, Straus and Giroux, 1957.

———. "Solitary Life in the Shadow of a Cistercian Monastery." *The Merton Seasonal* 37 (2012) 3–8.

———. "The Spiritual Father in the Desert Tradition." In *Contemplation in a World of Action*, 282–305. Garden City, NY: Doubleday, 1973.

———. *Thomas Merton on Peace*. Edited by Gordon C. Zahn. New York: McCall, 1971.

———. *A Thomas Merton Reader*. Edited by Thomas P. McDonnell. Expanded ed. Garden City, NY: Doubleday, 1989.

———. *Thomas Merton: Selected Essays*. Edited by Patrick F. O'Connell. Maryknoll, NY: Orbis, 2013.

———. *Thomas Merton, Spiritual Master*. Edited by Lawrence S. Cunningham. New York: Paulist, 1992.

———. *Thoughts in Solitude*. New York: Farrar, Straus and Cudahy, 1958.

———. *Turning Toward the World: The Pivotal Years*. Edited by Victor A. Kramer. San Francisco: HarperSanFrancisco, 1996.

———. "La Vie Solitaire à l'ombre d'un monastére cistercien." *La Lettre de Ligugé* 121 (1967) 30–36.

———. *A Vow of Conversation: Journals, 1964–1965*. Edited by Naomi Burton Stone. New York: Farrar, Straus and Giroux, 1988.

———. *The Way of Chuang Tzu*. New York: New Directions, 1965.

———. *Witness to Freedom: Letters in Times of Crisis*. Edited by William H. Shannon. San Diego: Harcourt Brace Jovanovich, 1994.

———. "Your Will and Your Vocation." *The Merton Seasonal* 34 (2009) 3–11.

Merton, Thomas, and Jean Leclercq. *Survival or Prophecy? The Letters of Thomas Merton and Jean Leclercq*. Edited by Patrick Hart. New York: Farrar, Straus and Giroux, 2002.

Mott, Michael. *The Seven Mountains of Thomas Merton*. Boston: Houghton Mifflin, 1984.

Neenan, Benedict. *Thomas Verner Moore: Psychiatrist, Educator, Monk*. New York: Paulist, 2000.

Norris, Kathleen. *Acedia and Me: A Marriage, Monks, and a Writer's Life*. New York: Riverhead, 2008.

Nouwen, Henri. *Pray to Live: Thomas Merton, Contemplative Critic*. Notre Dame: Fides, 1972.

O'Connell, Patrick F. "Merton's Earlier *Commedia*: Dante and *My Argument with the Gestapo*." *The Merton Journal* 21 (2014) 28–38.
Oury, Guy. *Dom Gabriel Sortais: An Amazing Abbot in Turbulent Times*. Translated by Brian Kerns. Kalamazoo, MI: Cistercian, 2006.
Palmer, Horatio R. "Yield Not to Temptation." Hymn 642 in *The Book of Common Praise*. Toronto: Oxford University Press and Anglican Church of Canada, 1938.
Peifer, Claude. Review of *Problemi e orientamenti di spiritualità monastica, biblica e liturgica*, by Cipriano Vagaggini et al. *Monastic Studies* 2 (1964) 137–65.
Poks, Malgorzata. *Thomas Merton and Latin America: A Consonance of Voices*. Katowice, Poland: Wyzsza Szkola Zarzadzania Marketingowego, 2007.
Porter, J. S. *Thomas Merton: Hermit at the Heart of Things*. Toronto: Novalis, 2008.
Raab, Joseph Quinn. "Insights from the Inter-Contemplative Dialogue: Merton's Three Meanings of 'God' and Religious Pluralism." *The Merton Annual* 23 (2010) 90–105.
Renzetti, Elizabeth. "Loneliness: The Trouble with Solitude." *The Globe and Mail*, November 23, 2013, F1, 4.
Rice, Edward. *The Man in the Sycamore Tree: The Good Times and Hard Life of Thomas Merton*. Garden City, NY: Doubleday, 1970.
Shannon, William H. "Reflections on 'Notes for a Philosophy of Solitude.'" *Cistercian Studies* 29 (1994) 83–99.
———. *Silent Lamp: The Thomas Merton Story*. New York: Crossroad, 1992.
Shannon, William H., et al., eds. *The Thomas Merton Encyclopedia*. Maryknoll, NY: Orbis, 2002.
Shaw, George Bernard. *Saint Joan*. London: Constable, 1924.
Solomon, Andrew. *The Noonday Demon: An Atlas of Depression*. New York: Scribner, 2001.
Thurston, Bonnie B. "'I never had a sister': Merton's Friendship with Women." *The Merton Seasonal* 17.1 (1992) 4–8.
Vagaggini, Cipriano, et al. *Problemi e orientamenti di spiritualità monastic, biblica e liturgica*. Rome: Edizioni Pauline, 1961.
Weis, Monica. "Merton's Fascination with Deer: A Graceful Symphony." *The Merton Journal* 15 (2008) 33–46.
Whitehead, James. D., and Evelyn Eaton Whitehead. *Holy Eros: Pathways to a Passionate God*. Maryknoll, NY: Orbis, 2009.
Williams, Rowan. "Monastic Virtues and Ecumenical Hopes." Address at "Monasticism and Ecumenism: A Conference," San Gregorio Magno al Celio, March 11, 2012. www.archbishopofcanterbury.org/articles.php/2385/monastic-virtues-and-ecumenical-hopes-at-san-gregorio-magno.
Zuercher, Suzanne. *The Ground of Love and Truth: Reflections on Thomas Merton's Relationship with the Woman Known as "M."* Chicago: In Extenso, 2014.
———. *Merton: An Enneagram Profile*. Notre Dame: Ave Maria, 1996.

PERSONAL COMMUNICATIONS

Bamberger, John Eudes, OCSO—personal emails, January 31, 2013, February 1, 2013, May 8, 2014.
Chang, Dave—personal email, July 11, 2014.
Conner, James, OCSO—personal emails, June 19, 2014, July 2, 2014, October 25, 2014.

Dietz, Elias, OCSO—personal emails, December 7, 2009, July 7, 2014, July 14, 2014, October 2, 2014, October 23, 2014.

Guiver, George, CR—personal email, August 3, 2014.

Matus, Thomas, OSBCam—personal interview, December 10, 2008; personal emails, November 24, 2009, June 11, 2014, July 26, 2014, July 27, 2014, September 2, 2014, September 3, 2014, September 4, 2014, October 1, 2014, October 2, 2014.

McCartney, Alfred, OCSO—personal email, November 21, 2009.

Mills, John—personal emails, May 28 and 30, 2014.

Mirhady, David—personal emails, June 8 and 9, 2014.

Mitchell, Joseph, CP—personal email, November 2, 2009.

Mivasair, David—personal email, July 1, 2014.

Steinke, Joseph—telephone interview, September 15, 2009.

Williams, Douglas Elliott—personal emails, April 27, 2014, June 17, 2014, July 8, 2014, September 30, 2014.

Index of Subjects and Names

abbots *a quo* and *ad quem*, 132n8, 190n22, 194
Abraham, 245
acedia, xii, xx, 7, 8, 10, ch. 1, *passim*, 44, 120n11, ch. 3, *passim*, ch. 4, *passim*, 252–54, 255
Ahern, Barnabas Mary, 124–25, 192, 202
Alberic, Frater, 60, 97, 98, 111n21
Allchin, A. M., 40n9
Ambrose, saint, 146
Ambrosians, 146
amour fou, 267–71
Ancona, 165
Andrew, Father, 98n3, 191
Angela of Foligno, saint, xvii
Anglicanism, 15, 25, 36, 166, 167
Anthony the Great, saint, 7
Anthony Mary Claret, saint, 148
Antioquia, 240
Appenine hills, 5, 84, 179
Aquarius, 36
Arasteh, Reza, 3, 50–53, 272
Aristotle, 266
Arthaud, publisher, 159, 160
Arezzo, 5, 70, 99, 136, 140, 152, 172
Asia, 242, 258
Augustine of Canterbury, saint, 166n7
Augustine of Hippo, saint, 3, 23, 36, 38, 212
axis mundi, 39

Bamberger, John Eudes, xix, 13, 13n3, 14, 22–23, 40, 43, 47, 49, 204, 212, 267, 273

Bardstown, 269
Basil the Great, saint, 13, 14
Basset, Bernard, 8n13
Bear, Virginia, 65
Beatrice, 164
Bede, Frater, 239
Belacqua, 20
Belcastro, David, xix, , 47, 48, 189n21, 205, 229, 253, 264, 265n29
Bellarmine, Father, 98n1, 185
Bellefontaine, abbey of, 64
Benedict, saint, 7, 17, 28, 75, 77, 106, 113, 128n3, 132n9, 184n14, 186n17, 188, 209, 214, 215
Benedict XVI, pope, 167n8
Benedictines, 63, 74n1, 75, 82, 84, 105, 128, 136, 160, 166, 167, 186, 213, 239, 246
Bennett, Tom, 38
Bernard, saint, 80, 82, 135, 258
Bertozzi, Albertino, 169
Bethlehem, 17
Bianchi, Girolamo, 81n13, 83n5
Biblical citations
  Gen 1:26, 5
  Psalm 70:1, 15
  Psalm 90:6/91:6, 7, 12
  Isa 2:4, xv
  Isa 58:7, xv
  Mic 6:8, xv
  Matt 4:1–11, 14
  Matt 5:16, 77n15
  Matt 20:12, 18
  Luke 2:41–52, 276
  Luke 3:21–23a, 276

Biblical citations *(continued)*
  John 3:1–12, 51n42
  John 3:7–8, 52
  John 4:16–18, 127n1
  John 10:30, 259n11
  Romans 15:14, 210n10
  1 Cor 4:13, 72n9, 174, 276n52
  1 Cor 8:10, 210n10
  1 Cor 9:22, 51n41
  1 Cor 12:10, 14
  Eph 1:10, 210n11
  Phil 2:8, 160n3
  Col 1:17, 210n11
  1 Thess 4:11–12, 31
  1 Tim 2:4, 210
  Heb 4:9–10, 204
  Heb 11, 258
  Heb 11:8, 245
  1 John 4:1, 14
  1 John 4:9, 271
Blake, William, 37, 38
Boccacio, Giovanni, 20
Bochen, Christine M., 237, 241n9
Boniface VIII, pope, 93n8
Boone, Andy, 264
Bradfer, Jérome, 83n5
Brahmachari, Mahanambrata, 38
Brandt, Charles, 205n2
Brazil, 239
Brendan, saint, 245
Brescia, 140, 195
Brokaw, Ann, 76n12
Brown, Peter, 262
Bruno, saint, 125
Burns, Flavian, 50, 242
Burton (Stone), Naomi, 47, 219
Burton, Patricia, 50n35, 85n7, 206, 231
Burton-Christie, Douglas E. *See* Christie, Douglas E.
Bush, George H. W., 234
Butler, Cuthbert, 105

Cagney, James, xi
Calati, Benedetto, 224, 227–33, 250n14, 265
Calcutta (Kolkata), 4
Camaldoli, the monastery, and the Camaldolese community, xv, 4, 5n11, 5–6, 43, 49, 55, 56–58, 68, 74, 79, 108, 122, 141, 144, 151, 170–71, 184, 185, 201, 205, 221, 222, 223, 234, 244, 255
Cambridge University, 38, 39, 65
Camus, Albert, 30
Canada, 234
Caracas, 239
Cardenal, Ernesto, 236, 239n6, 241, 242
Carmelites, 57, 58, 148n3
Carthusians, 4, 55–58, 69, 84, 91, 97, 98, 104, 105, 111, 122, 123, 128, 129, 140, 148, 160, 172, 179, 184, 186, 187, 192, 193, 205, 214, 225
Casentino, forest, 5, 76n8
Cassian, John, 17, 18, 23, 27, 44, 207, 253
Catalan, region and language, 35n5
Catani, Aliprando, 221, 222, 223, 224
Catholic Encyclopedia, 55
Catholic University of America, 63
Cauca Valley, 240
Chadral Rinpoche, 50, 52
Chang, Dave, xx, 25n39
Chaucer, Geoffrey, 21–22, 23
Chemin Thomas Merton, 37
Chimborazo, 239
Chronology of the letters, 60–61
Christ in the Desert Monastery, 75
Christie (Burton-Christie), Douglas E., xi–xiv, xix, 15n16, 173n4, 257, 258, 261–62, 271n41, 274
Chuang Tzu, 260, 267
Church of England, 25
Cistercians, 55, 57, 59, 81n15, 91, 160, 183, 192, 193, 211, 214
Citeaux, 154
City College of New York, 38
Claretians, 63, 147
Clement of Alexandria, 48, 253
Clement IX, pope, 162
Clotet, Giacomo, 148
Cobre, Shrine of Our Lady of, 238
Cohen, Leonard, 53
Collectanea, 80

Index of Subjects and Names

Colombia, 240, 241, 242
Columba, saint, 245
Columbia University, 38, 39, 66, 67
Communism, 253
Conner, James, xix
Constantine I, emperor, 107
Constantinople, 13, 17
Copenhagen, bishop of, 125–26
Corpus Christi Church, Manhattan, 36
Cotopaxi, 239
Crider, Glenn, 71
Crisanto, Frater, 241
Crislip, Andrew, 13n5
Cuba, 66, 238
Cuernavaca, 3, 8, 49, 58, 235, 239, 243–52, 253, 256, 265
Cunningham, Lawrence S., 18, 282

da Arbonne, Lazzaro, 145, 198, 221
Dalai Lama XIV, Tenzin Gyatso, 1, 50, 53
Daniélou, Jean, 49
Dante Alighieri, 20, 65, 163, 164, 165, 269, 272, 279
David, Venerable, 93n8, 176
de Gonzague le Pennuen, Louis, 58, 99n4, 112n24, 181, 185, 199, 200, 219, 250n14
de Hueck, Catherine, baroness, 39
Deignan, Kathleen, 253
Demons, 7–8, 14–16
Déodat, Dom, 247, 248
de Rancé, Armand-Jean, 56, 177, 214, 270
Desert Fathers and Mothers, 13
Dietz, Elias, xix, 93n8, 132n8, 190n22
Dominicans, 24, 240

Douglaston, 225
Downside Abbey, 104
Dunne, Frederic, 40, 179

Ecuador, 239, 240, 241
Edmund (Murphy), Father, 39
Egypt, 17
Elmira, New York, 243
encheiridion, 34

Enneagram, 33, 37, 202n30, 257
epithumia, 9, 267
eros, 267, 273, 275
Evagrius Ponticus, 10, 13, 13n4, 14, 17n21, 18, 19n25, 23, 24, 31, 41, 43, 183n13, 184, 204–6, 209, 244, 253, 261, 266, 267, 272, 278n55

fana and *baqa*, 52
Fano, 81, 165
Fascist regime, 166
Fielding, Larissa, 107
Finley, James, 11
Flushing, NY, 36
Following of Christ, The
Fonte Avellana, 62, 81, 161, 163
Fontebona, 5
Ford, Father, a Jesuit, 127n1, 128, 191
Ford, Barry, 127n1
Fort Augustus, 105
Fox, James, xvi, xvii, 6, 7, 9, 26–28, 43, 47–49, 56, 58, 59, 61, 62, 64, 69, 75, 78, 80, 92, 97, 98n2, 99, 100, 102, 103, 108, 109n7, 110, 111, 113, 114, 119–22, 127, 128, 130, 132, 137, 139, 140n1, 142, 143, 151, 154–57, 171, 174, 175, 176, 178, 181–86, 188–98, 200–202, 203n32, 204–9, 211–13, 215, 216, 217, 219, 224, 229, 235, 240–42, 244, 246, 247, 249, 251, 252, 255n1, 266, 267, 269, 278
Francis, pope, 63
Franco, Francisco, 241
Frascati, 99, 142, 147, 151, 152, 176, 185, 196, 197, 198, 218, 219, 220
Freud, Sigmund, 24
Friendship House, 39
Frigerio, Salvatore, 5n9

Gandhi, Mohandas, xvii
Genesee, 154, 155, 157n3, 200, 201
Germanus, 17
Ghini, Emmanuela, 77n13, 80n7, 107
Giabbani, Anselmo, 2, 6, 7, 8, 60–62, 64, 68, 69, 70, 73, 74, 76n10, 78, 79, 82, 84–87, 94, 101–5, 109, 114, 115, 118, 127, 131, 136, 139n1,

Giabbani, Anselmo, *(continued)* 140, 142, 145, 151, 153n16, 159, 168, 171–79, 182–87, 188, 189, 193, 195, 198, 200, 201, 203, 207, 213, 215, 218, 221–26, 227, 256, 277
Gilson, Etienne, 20n27, 38
Giroux, Robert, 41
Giustiniani, Paul, blessed, 79, 80, 161, 162, 177
God, will of, 208–17
Grayston, Donald, 46n20, 53n47, 174n6
Gregory the Great, saint, 19, 166
Guiver, George, 167n8
Gussago, Camaldoli di, 135, 139, 140, 195
Gyrovagues, 184n14

Harford, James, 54n49, 79n5
Hart, Patrick, 217n14, 231z, 281
Havana, 225
Hayes, Patrick Joseph, 105
Helena, empress, 107
Helmstetter, Walter, 155, 157, 201
Henry, Gray and Jonathan Montaldo, *We Are Already One*, 1n1, 53n48
Hollander, Robert, 20, 21
Hollander, Robert, and Jean Hollander, 165
Hopkins, Gerard Manley, 37, 38
Hughes, Peter, 167n8
Humanae Vitae, 63

Ignatius of Loyola, saint, xiii, 38
Imitation of Christ, The, 38
Immaculate Heart Hermitage. See New Camaldoli
Innocent X, pope, 162
Inquisition, 24
Iona, 245
Ireland, 245
Israelis and Palestinians, xiv

Jerome, saint, 7,
Jesus Christ, 14, 180–81, 214, 261
Jewish spiritual practice, 229
Joan of Arc, saint, 259

John Albert, brother, 228n17
John of the Cross, Father, 270
John of the Cross, saint, 38, 125, 147, 232
John the Baptist, saint, 232
John XXIII, pope, 63, 222, 228, 247, 253
Joyce, James, 37
Jubilee, 79, 80
Julian of Norwich, xvii, 10, 271, 273
Jung, C. G., 183

Kennedy, John F., 175
Kennett, Peggy Teresa Nancy (Houn Jiyu-Kennett), 25n39
Kilcourse, George, 263
Kull, Robert, 260, 261

Lane, Belden, 267, 268, 270–71, 278, 282
La Pierre-Qui-Vire, abbey, 84–87, 91, 115
Larraona y Segui, Arcadio Maria, 2, 9, 49, 61–66, 100, 109, 112, 113n27, 141, 147, 151, 154, 160, 171, 185, 196–98, 200, 202, 203, 206, 207, 211, 215, 220, 221, 225, 227, 234, 235, 246, 247, 249
Latin America, 4, 8, 17, 30, 43, 46, 49, 66, 152n13, 158n4, 208, 210, 216, 218, 233, 234, 235, 236, 239, 242, 252, 255, 271
Lauridson, James R., 267n35
Law, Philip, 99n5, 172, 174
Lawrence, D. H., 37
Lax, Robert, 38, 41
Leacock, Stephen, 253
Leclercq, Jean, 9, 57, 79, 80, 82, 99n4, 142, 161n1, 177, 196, 205, 206, 218, 219, 230, 231, 235, 249, 256
Lemercier, Gregorio, 49, 235, 243, 244, 246, 247, 248, 250, 265
Leo X, pope, 161
Les Editions Braun de Mulhouse, 91
Lévi-Strauss, Claude, xiii
Levy-Duplatt, Maurizio, 151n9, 218, 220
Lipsey, Roger, xvi

Index of Subjects and Names

logismoi, 14, 31
Lombardi, Riccardo, 48
Lombardy, 63
Long Island Railroad, 43
Lovelace, Richard, 52n43
Luce, Clare Boothe, 76, 89n4, 175, 182, 195
Luce, Henry R., 76n12
Lycée Ingres, Montauban, 37, 65
lype. See *tristitia*

Macy, Joanna, 54
Maldolus, 5
Mancarrón, 237
Mantua, 136
Maracay, 239
Marian year, 82
Mariana of Jesus, saint, 239
Marioni, photographer, 115
Maritain, Jacques, 118n2, 272
Maritain, Raïssa, xvii
Marseilles, 17
Massaccio, 161
Matus, Thomas, xx, 77n13, 94n2, 145n3, 146n4, 146n5, 146n6, 167n8, 171, 199n27, 221–24, 227, 231–33, 277n54
McCartney, Alfred, xix
Medellin, 240
melancholia. See Merton, depression
Melleray, 58
Mepkin, 192
Merton, John Paul, 36, 37
Merton, Owen, 35–38
Merton, Ruth, 35–37
Merton, Thomas
  Artist, 1
  Autobiographer, 28, 34
  Baptisms, 36, 38, 123n4
  Bishops, writes to, 242, 253
  Breakdowns, 43, 52
  Canonization, unlikeliness of, 41n12
  Depression, 22–23, 26, 30, 43
  Dreams, 225
  Environment, 2
  European sensibilities, 37, 48, 152, 199n28, 233
  Franciscans, 39
  Grandparents, 38
  Hermitage, 58, 132n6, 256, 257, 264
  Indult, request for, 247–49
  Languages, facility with, 64–67
  Louisville epiphany, 44
  Master of novices, 26, 44, 45, 50, 155, 158, 188, 200, 201, 202, 216, 235, 256
  Master of scholastics, 44, 45, 58, 71n7, 123, 188, 235
  Nuclear weapons, 2
  Orthography, 65
  Phases of his monastic life, 40
  Pilgrimage, 238, 245, 246
  Publications
    The Asian Journal of Thomas Merton, 4n7, 50n36, 50n37, 276n53; *Bread in the Wilderness,* 85; *Cold War Letters,* 50, 76n12; *Collected Poems,* 263n26; *Conjectures of a Guilty Bystander,* 34, 45n19, 66n12, 238n5; *Dancing in the Water of Life,* 32, 182–83, 229, 232, 258, 263–64, 268n35, 272; "Day of a Stranger," xvii, 35, 232, 259, 268n35, 278, 282; *Disputed Questions,* 43n16, 177; *Eighteen Poems,* 274–75; *Entering the Silence,* 56–57, 57, 58, 101n5; *Faith and Violence,* 232; "Final Integration: Towards a 'Monastic Therapy,'" 3n2, 4n4, 4n5, 52n44; "From Pilgrimage to Crusade," 246n10; "Hagia Sophia," 279"; *The Hidden Ground of Love,* 254; "Honorable Reader," 238n4; *The Intimate Merton,* 34, 281; *Introduction to the Monastic Tradition 1: Cassian and the Fathers,* 26, 175n8, 20; *Introduction to the Monastic Tradition 2: Pre-Benedictine Monasticism,* 175n8, 208n9; *Introduction to the Monastic Tradition 3: An Introduction to Christian; Mysticism,* 175n8, 208n9, 209, 210;

Publications *(continued)*
Introduction to the Monastic Tradition 4: The Rule of Saint Benedict, 175n8, 208n9, 212; *Introduction to the Monastic Tradition 5: Monastic Observances,* 175n8, 208n9; *Introduction to the Monastic Tradition 6: The Life of the Vows,* 175n8; *Learning to Love,* 258, 260, 269, 270, 277, 278; "A Life Free from Care," 41; "Love and Need: Is Love a Package or a Message?," 273; "Love and Solitude," 272n43, 279; *My Argument with the Gestapo,* 33; "The Neurotic Personality in the Monastic Life," 46; *New Seeds of Contemplation,* 4n8, 34, 46, 50, 208n9; *No Man is an Island,* 85n8, 101, 249, 250; "Notes for a Philosophy of Solitude," 259n12, 263, 271; *The Other Side of the Mountain,* 252, 270, 272–72; "Rain and the Rhinoceros," 262n17, 262n18; *The School of Charity,* 151n9, 201, 230, 231n23; *A Search for Solitude,* 9n16, 19, 45n19, 47n25, 66, 68, 71n6, 98n1, 99n5, 100n7, 141n2, 172–74, 196, 198, 206, 210, 233, 235, 238, 239, 240, 243–47, 249, 250, 268, 270; *The Secular Journal of Thomas Merton,* 39; *Seeds of Contemplation,* 46, 66n11; *The Seven Storey Mountain,* xvi, 1, 20n27, 32, 34, 36, 37, 38, 39, 41, 54, 55, 55–56, 65n4, 65n5, 66, 70n5, 72n10, 127n1, 132n4, 179, 212, 219, 227, 234n30, 238, 243; *The Sign of Jonas,* 34, 41, 42, 43, 56, 118, 225, 228n17, 229, 232, 262, 271; *Silence dans le ciel/Silence in Heaven,* 84n2, 86, 91, 117, 159, 203; *The Silent Life,* 76n9, 101n3, 159, 160, 203n32, 206; "Solitary Life in the Shadow of a Cistercian Monastery," 255n1; "The Spiritual Father in the Desert Tradition," 265n30; *The Strange Islands,* 206; *Thomas Merton on Peace,* 4n6; *A Thomas Merton Reader,* 219n17; *Thomas Merton: Selected Essays,* 33, 282; *Thomas Merton, Spiritual Master,* 281; *Thoughts in Solitude,* 262n22; *Turning Toward the World,* 46, 211, 251, 257, 261, 266; *A Vow of Conversation,* 34; *Witness to Freedom,* 47n26, 71n8, 250, 251, 253, 265; "Your Will and Your Vocation," 216n12, 216n13

Public intellectual, 2, 26
Racism, 2
Relics, 87, 89, 168, 184, 187
Return to the United States, 38
Solitude, 42, 52, 181, 197, 236, ch. 7, *passim*
Spiritual writer, 33, 34–35
transitus, 58, 103, 109, 110, 113, 114, 115, 119, 127–29, 132, 142, 143, 160, 170, 172, 174, 187, 188, 189, 195, 197, 218, 219, 256
trickster, 6, 189
Merville, British Columbia, 205n2
Mexico, 239, 241, 250, 253, 265
Midi-Pyrénées, 37
Milan, archdiocese of, 7, 90, 135
Milton, John, 240
Miraflores, 56, 63, 641,
Mirhady, David, xx, 13n2
missa sicca, 104
Mitchell, Joseph, 98n2
Mivasair, David, xx, 12
Modotti, Augustine, 223
Montaldo, Jonathan, 281
Monte Corona, congregation of, 62, 147, 165, 177, 219, 225, 227
Montecuoco, 161
Montgiove, 62, 161, 165
Montini, Giovanni Battista (Paul VI), 6, 7, 60, 61, 63–65, 90, 93, 99–101, 105, 110, 113, 115, 122, 135–38, 139, 140, 145, 150, 154, 157, 160, 171, 174, 182, 183, 185, 187, 189, 192, 193, 195–200,

Index of Subjects and Names

202, 203, 207, 208, 213, 214, 215, 218, 220, 225, 233, 258
Moore, Thomas Verner (Pablo Maria, Carthusian), 56, 60, 63, 97, 104, 108, 109, 111n21, 112n25, 119, 120n10, 127n1, 142, 150, 185–87, 189, 190, 218, 234
Mott, Michael, 46n23, 46n24, 47n27, 47n28, 71n6, 80n7, 111n17, 155n5, 264n28, 270
Mounier, Emmanuel, 272
Mount Savior Monastery, 75

Napoleon I, emperor, 136n2, 164, 166
Navarra, 63
Nazarena of Jesus, recluse, 63, 77n13, 83n6, 221
Nesmy, Claude Jean, 86, 87, 91, 159, 160
New Camaldoli, 63, 72, 73, 74, 104, 105, 110, 116, 145, 171n3, 174, 176, 182, 188, 223–25
New Clairvaux, abbey of, 64, 120n14
New York, 48, 205
New Zealand, 205
Nhat Hanh, Thich, 4, 52, 53, 258
Nicaragua, 236, 240, 241, 242
Nitria, 14
Norris, Kathleen, 7, 8n13, 10, 13, 14n7, 24–26, 30, 44, 208
Nouwen, Henri J. M., 42

Oakham School, 37, 65
Oberhauser, Vincent Mary, 98n2, 105, 127n1, 140, 150, 185, 191
O'Connell, Patrick F. xix, 26–29, 212
Ohlone College, 64
Ortega, Daniel, 237
Orvieto, 165
Oswy or Oswiu, king of Northumbria, 166n7
Oury, Guy, 9n18,

Pachomius, saint, 5
pacte autobiographique, xvi
Palmer, Horatio, 31n73, 32
Paraguay, 240
Paris, 48

Parra, Nicanor, xxvii
participation mystique, 264
Pascal, Blaise, 273
Patagonia, 260
Patrologia Latina, 76n11
Paul, saint, the first hermit, 180
Paul VI, pope. *See* Montini, Giovanni Battista
Paulists, 63, 104, 186
Pawsey, Humphrey, 68n2, 69n2, 111n21
Pearl Harbor, 40
Pedro, Frater, 241
Peifer, Claude, 227n12, 228n15, 228n18
Perpignan, 35
Perugia, 165
Pesaro, 165
Peter Damian, saint, 62, 65, 67, 76, 89, 93, 94, 109, 113, 163, 164, 168, 182, 187, 199
Peter the Sinner, 164
Philippe, Paul, 71, 211
Pius V, pope, 163
Pius X, pope, 81
Pius XII, pope, 122n1, 181
Plato, 14, 212
Poks, Malgorzata, 237, 238, 239n7
Poppi, 5
Porion, Jean-Baptiste, 68n2, 69n2, 172, 180, 185, 202, 265
Porter, J. S., 282
Prades, 35, 36
Prelato, 165
Psychoanalysis, 3
Pyrénées-Orientales, 35

Quakers, 36
Quenon, Carolyn, 268n35
Quito, 239

Raab, Joseph, 208n9
Ravenna, 5
Raymond [Flanagan], Father, 127n1, 191
Ricaurte, Monseñor, 240
Rice, Edward, 38, 39n7, 54, 79n5
Ricoeur, Paul, 214

Index of Subjects and Names

Rilke, Rainer Maria, 34, 205n3, 278
Riobamba, 239
Ripley Court, school, 37
Romanus, Father, 155n10, 201
Romkema, Albert, 203n32
Romuald, saint, 5, 62, 65, 67, 78, 87, 89, 92–94, 109, 113, 125, 140, 144, 161, 168, 175, 178, 182, 183, 187, 188, 199
Rouergue, 37
Roussillon, 35

Sacred Congregation for Religious, 2, 9, 49, 58, 63, 99, 128, 132n7, 141, 151, 154, 181, 195–98, 209, 222, 225, 234, 235, 244, 247, 248, 250, 251
San Gregorio al Celio, 5n10, 62, 161,166, 203n32, 227
San Salvatore di Settimo, 93n8
Sant' Anselmo, 167, 227
Sant' Antonio Monastery, 63, 77n13
São Paulo, 239
Sartre, Jean-Paul, 30
Sassoferrato, 163
Satan, 129n7
Scythia Minor, 17
secundum quid, 266
Septuagint, 12
Sext, office of, 30
Shakespeare, William, xiv, 219, 249, 256, 267, 275
Shannon, William H., 3n3, 41n13, 46n24, 52–53, 55, 85n7, 174n5, 252n15, 263
Shaw, George Bernard, 259
Sheldrake, Philip, 282
Shelley, Percy Bysshe, 41
Sky Farm, 97, 98, 128
Smith, Margie ("M"), 3, 9, 10, 23, 50, 260, 265, 266, 267–71, 273, 274–75, 276–77
Solentiname, Our Lady of, 236, 237
The Solitary Life: A Letter of Guigo, 67
Solomon, Andrew, 10, 22–24, 30, 44, 204
Somoza, Anastasio, 236, 3237
Soratte, 161

Sortais, Gabriel, 9n15, 9n18, 26n49, 48, 56, 61, 64, 80n7, 98n2, 100, 103, 111, 114n35, 125, 127n1, 129, 132, 154, 158, 176, 178, 183, 184, 190, 191, 198, 199–201, 215, 216, 219, 224, 247, 248, 249
Spender, Natasha, and Margot Dennis, 268n35
St. Anne's (the toolshed), 71, 111n15, 123, 177, 192
St. Anselm's Abbey, 63
St-Antonin, 37
Stapehill, abbey of, 61, 96, 118, 184, 189
St. Bonaventure College/University, Olean, NY, 38, 39
Steinke, Joseph (Anselm), xix, 7, 61, 64, 65, 71n7, 97, 107, 110, 111, 113, 115, 119, 127n1, 129, 130, 142, 150, 185, 186, 194
St. John's University, Collegeville, 47
St. Mary of Carmel. *See* Merton, hermitage
Stolz, Anselm, 177
Sufis, 3
Suzuki, D. T., 205

Taizé, Community of, 213
Tardini, Domenico, 63
Tauler, Johannes, 123n3
Teresa of Avila, saint, xvii, 125, 148
Thomas Aquinas, saint, 19, 21, 124n7, 266
Thomas Merton Center, Bellarmine University, 7, 59
Thomas Merton Society of Canada, 5n12, 282
Thoreau, Henry David, 228n17, 232, 250n14
Thurston, Bonnie B., 268n35
Tillich, Paul, 272
Timothy, Father, 127n1, 150n7
Tolentino, Treaty of, 164
Toulouse, 65
Trappists. *See* Cistercians
Tre Fontane, 226, 227
tristitia, 29
Tunja, 240

Turner, Walter James Redfern, 239n8

United States Foreign Service Institute, 65
Urban VIII, pope, 162

Vagaggini et al., 227n13
Valencia, 239
Valeri, Valerio, cardinal, 9, 211, 249, 265
Van Doren, Mark, 38
Vatican II, Council of, xv, 222, 223, 228
Venezuela, 239, 240
Vermont, 64, 97, 104, 119
Vietnam, 269
Villa Diane, 37
Virgil, 20
Virgin Islands, 241
Vita Monastica, 62, 85n7, 132n2, 132n3, 231

Waddell, Chrysogonus, 212, 230
Walsh, Dan, 38, 39

Weis, Monica, 267n4
Whitby, Synod of, 166
Whitehead, James D., and Evelyn Eaton Whitehead, 267n34
Wilber, Ken, 52
Williams, Douglas E., xx, 266n31
Williams, Rowan, archbishop, 166n7
Winandy, Jacques, 205n2
Winzen, Damasus, 243
Wordsworth, William, 261
worker-priests, 153
Writers and recipients of the letters, 62–64
Wygal, James, 49, 273

Yeats, W. B., xvi
"Yield not to temptation," hymn, 31

Zen, 1, 25, 249
Zilboorg, Gregory, 46–49, 206, 264, 265
Zion Episcopal Church, Douglaston, 36
Zuercher, Suzanne, 271

www.ingramcontent.com/pod-product-compliance
Lightning Source LLC
Chambersburg PA
CBHW021649230426
43668CB00008B/570